German Strategy and the Path to Verdun

Almost ninety years since its conclusion, the battle of Verdun is still little understood. *German Strategy and the Path to Verdun* is the first detailed English-language examination of this seminal battle to be based on research conducted in archives long thought lost. Material returned to Germany from the former Soviet Union has allowed for a reinterpretation of Erich von Falkenhayn's overall strategy for the war and of the development of German operational and tactical concepts to fit this new strategy of attrition. By taking a long view of the development of German military ideas from the end of the Franco-German War in 1871, *German Strategy and the Path to Verdun* also gives much-needed context to Falkenhayn's ideas and the course of one of the greatest battles of attrition the world has ever known.

ROBERT T. FOLEY is Lecturer in the Defence Studies Department, King's College London at the Joint Services Command and Staff College. He is the editor and translator of *Alfred von Schlieffen's Military Writings*, 2002.

Cambridge Military Histories

Edited by

HEW STRACHAN
Chichele Professor of the History of War, University of Oxford and Fellow at All Souls College, Oxford

GEOFFREY WAWRO
Professor of Strategic Studies, US Naval War College

The aim of this new series is to publish outstanding works of research on warfare throughout the ages and throughout the world. Books in the series will take a broad approach to military history, examining war in all its military, strategic, political and economic aspects. The series is intended to complement *Studies in the Social and Cultural History of Modern Warfare* by focusing on the 'hard' military history of armies, tactics, strategy, and warfare. Books in the series will consist mainly of single author works – academically vigorous and groundbreaking – which will be accessible to both academics and the interested general reader.

German Strategy and the Path to Verdun

Erich von Falkenhayn and the Development of Attrition, 1870–1916

Robert T. Foley

CAMBRIDGE UNIVERSITY PRESS
Cambridge, New York, Melbourne, Madrid, Cape Town, Singapore, São Paulo

Cambridge University Press
The Edinburgh Building, Cambridge CB2 8RU, UK

Published in the United States of America by Cambridge University Press, New York

www.cambridge.org
Information on this title: www.cambridge.org/9780521841931

First published 2005
Reprinted 2007
This digitally printed version 2007

A catalogue record for this publication is available from the British Library

Library of Congress Cataloguing in Publication data
Foley, Robert T.
German strategy and the path to Verdun: Erich von Falkenhayn and the development of attrition, 1870–1916 / Robert T. Foley.
p. cm. – (Cambridge military histories)
Includes bibliographical references and index.
ISBN 0 521 84193 3
1. Verdun, Battle of, Verdun, France, 1916. 2. Falkenhayn, Erich von, 1861–1922. 3. Attrition (Military science) I. Title. II. Series.
D545.V3F65 2004
940.4'013 – dc22 2004045708

ISBN 978-0-521-84193-1 hardback
ISBN 978-0-521-04436-3 paperback

Contents

Illustrations

Acknowledgments

While writing, I have become beholden to a great number of individuals for their encouragement and support. In the first rank must stand my family. Without them, researching and writing this study would never have been possible. Despite sometimes not understanding the work I had undertaken, they stood by me through what was often a difficult process. My special thanks go to my grandfather, Mr. Robert M. Stroker. I am also especially grateful to Dr. Helen McCartney, whose insightful comments and sharp eye helped to transform this work into its final form. Moreover, I could not have completed this project without her unflagging support and encouragement.

This study also owes much to my *Doktorvater*, Professor Brian Bond, who provided much assistance and many helpful comments from beginning to end. Further, Professors Michael Dockrill and Brian Holden Reid gave me a great deal of good advice and were good friends to me during my time at the Department of War Studies.

I am also grateful to Professors Hew Strachan and Richard Overy. They gave me much food for thought, and the final product has been greatly improved by their comments. Professor Dennis Showalter also offered excellent advice when the path forward was not so clear.

Good friends, among them James Beach, James F. Gentsch, Andrew Haughton, Joe Moretz, Jon Robb-Webb, Martin Samuels, Gary Sheffield, and Andrew Stewart, helped give shape to my ill-formed ideas over the occasional pint and read and commented on much of my work. My special thanks go to Dr. Annika Mombauer, who helped me develop my ideas, particularly about the pre-war era. My knowledge of Moltke the Younger and the Wilhelmine army benefited greatly from her thoughts. However, not only was she an excellent colleague, she was a good friend to me through some very difficult times. I thank them all for tirelessly listening to my ideas when they could have been engaged in more enjoyable pursuits.

I also owe a debt of gratitude to two who were instrumental in setting me on the path of military history. First, Dr. Elihu Rose of New York University, who offered great encouragement throughout my time at New

York University. Second, Bruce Gudmundsson, who has been a close friend and mentor since my Quantico days. He generously allowed me free run of his extensive library and archives, as well as providing me with a great source of encouragement, ideas, and hospitality when on my trips to Washington, DC.

Finally, I must thank the staffs of the various institutions which have assisted me. The inter-library loan staff at the King's College Humanities Library went to great lengths to secure me many obscure titles, without which this study would not have been possible. The staff of the Captured German Records collection at the US National Archives and the staff of the Bundesarchiv/Militärarchiv, Freiburg, were also extremely helpful during my research trips. Last, the University of London helped make my research possible by providing me with a grant from the Central Research Fund.

Ranks

Leutnant	2nd Lieutenant
Oberleutnant/Premierleutnant	1st Lieutenant/Lieutenant
Hauptmann/Rittmeister	Captain
Major	Major
Oberstleutnant	Lieutenant Colonel
Oberst	Colonel
Generalmajor	Brigadier General/Brigadier
Generalleutnant	Major General
General der Kavallerie	Lieutenant General
Generaloberst	General
Generalfeldmarschall	General of the Army/Field Marshal

Map. 1 The Western Front, 1914–16
Source: Colin Nicolson, *The Longman Companion to The First World War*. London, 2001

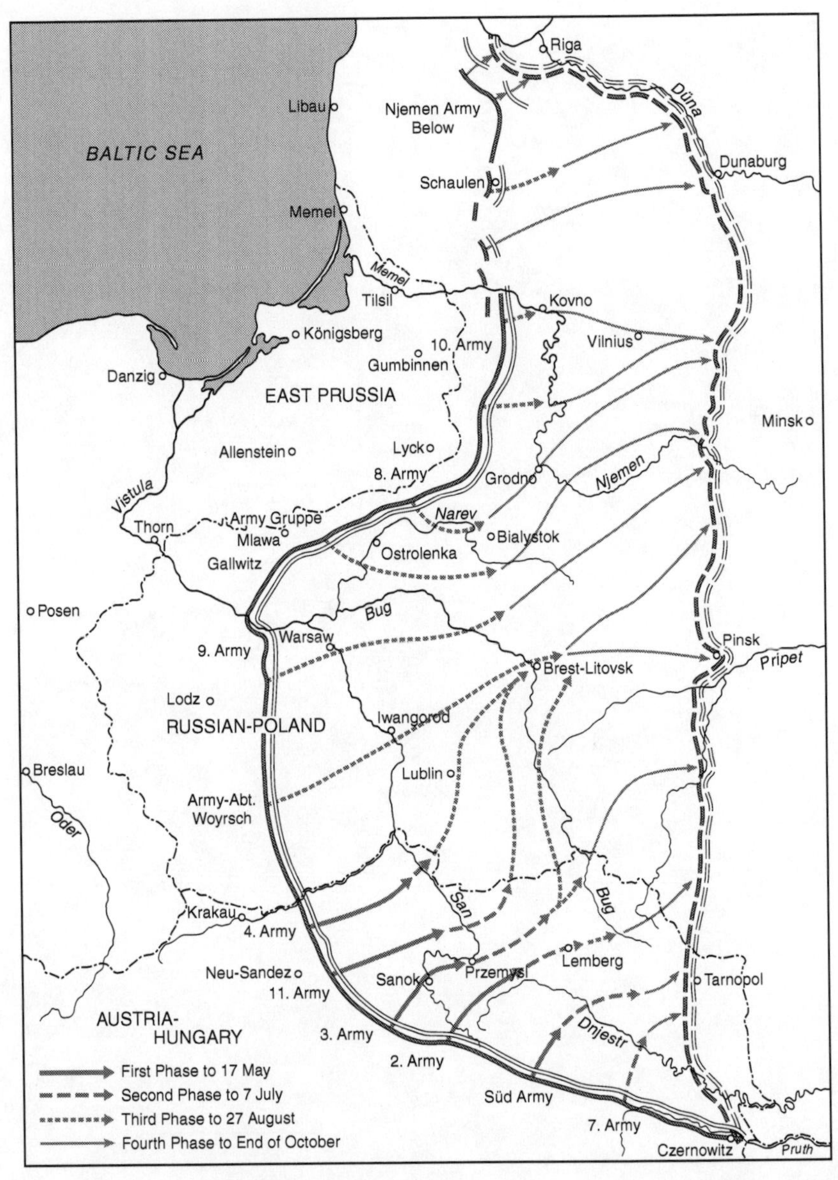

Map. 2 The Eastern Front, 1915
Source: Hans Dollinger (ed.) *Der Erste Weltkrieg*. Munich, 1965

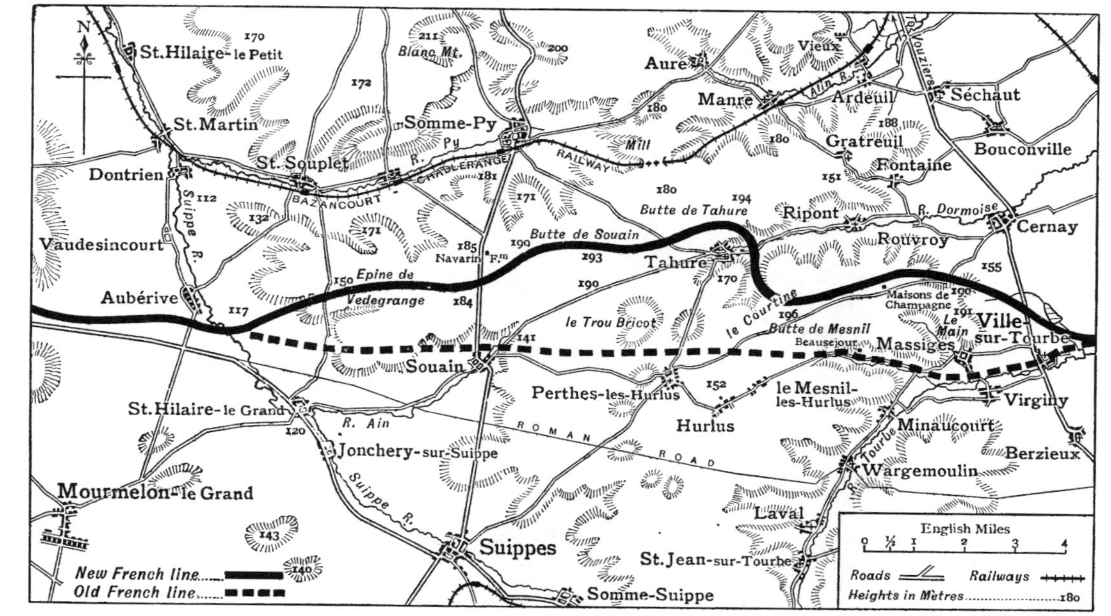

Map. 3 The *Herbstschlacht* in the Champagne, 1915

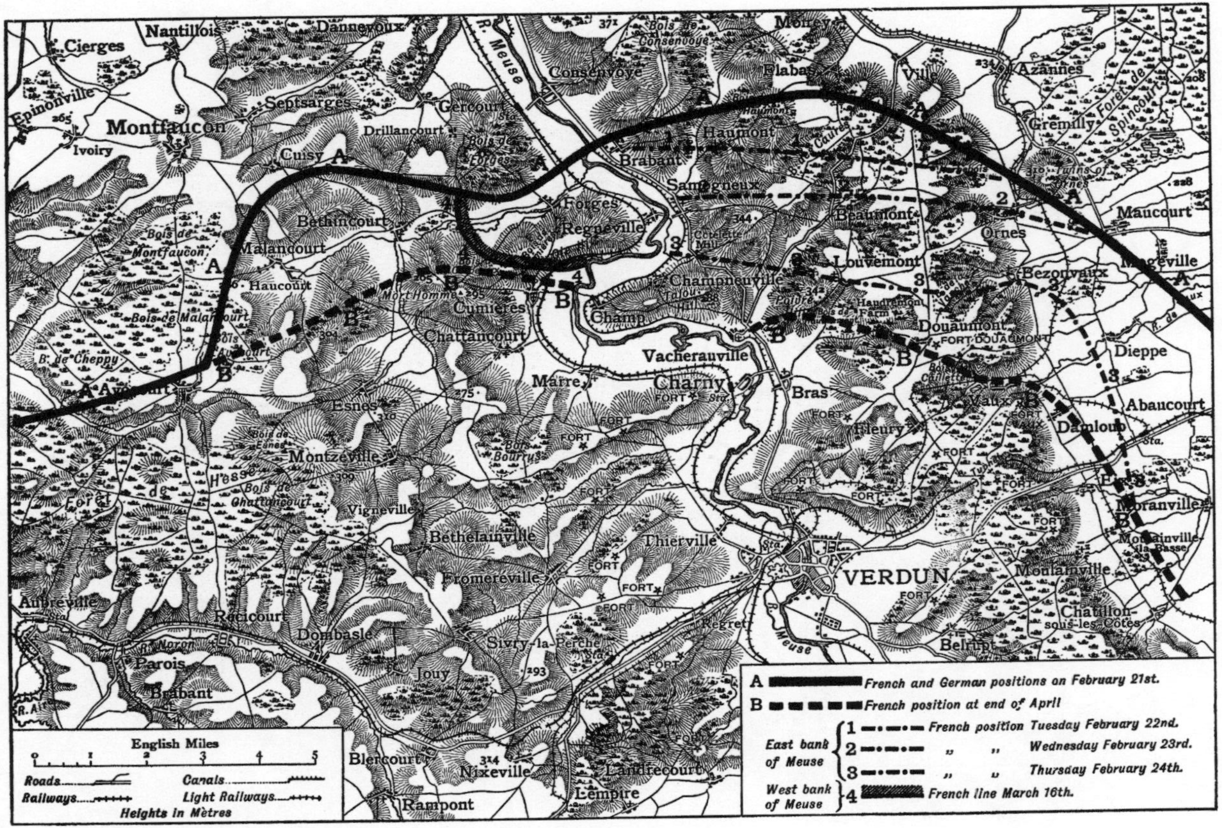

A French and German positions on February 21st.
B French position at end of April

East bank of Meuse
1 French position Tuesday February 22nd.
2 " " Wednesday February 23rd.
3 " " Thursday February 24th.

West bank of Meuse
4 French line March 16th.

English Miles
0 1 2 3 4 5
Roads Canals
Railways Light Railways
Heights in Mètres

Map. 4 The Battle of Verdun, 1916

Introduction

In a lecture to the Military Society in Berlin in 1888, Major August Keim of the *Kriegsakademie* (War Academy) gave his view of German military thinking near the close of the nineteenth century. To Keim, his army's approach to military education and thinking was one of intellectual openness that challenged past views of war. He spoke of how poorly commanded and thought out German maneuvers and war plans would appear to the generals of Prussia's past. Were Duke Ferdinand of Brunswick to inspect the German plan of operations for the Franco-German War, declared Major Keim, he would in all probability "find little satisfaction in a plan of campaign, according to the views of his time, so thoroughly unscientific and inadequate." If General Friedrich von Saldern, Frederick the Great's drillmaster, were to see the German maneuvers of 1888, he "would shake his head at the decay in tactics, over the complete lack of the finer comprehension of the true tactical art, which certainly [to von Saldern], consisted principally in permitting the genius for drill to shine in complex forms." Keim saw the negative impressions of past Prussian masters to be an indication of progress within the German army. To him, the orthodoxies of the day had constantly to be questioned in an effort to keep the German army ahead of its opponents, and the army should be kept free of all rigid tactical and strategic schemes. Finally, Keim said he hoped that "at the end of the next century" the German approach to preparing for war would be judged favorably.[1]

Toward the end of the "next" century, historian Martin Kitchen published an article examining German strategic thinking of the nineteenth century. Keim's hopes were to be dashed by Kitchen, who did not judge him and his colleagues favorably. Kitchen denied that the German army

[1] [August] Keim, "Kriegslehre und Kriegsführung. Vortrag, gehalten in der Militärischen Gesellschaft zu Berlin am 12 Dezember 1888," *Beiheft zum Militär-Wochenblatt* 1 (1889), pp. 1–2. Keim, a sometime journalist, later became one of Alfred von Waldersee's "pen hussars." After retiring from the army as a *Generalmajor*, he continued his political bent by becoming a leading member of the *Flottenverein* and later founding the nationalistic *Deutsche Wehrverein*.

possessed the very attribute of which Keim was so proud – intellectual openness. He wrote, "the development of German strategic thought is marked by a slow hardening of a subtle dialectical approach to military problems into a set of unchallenged axioms."[2] In Kitchen's view, from Carl von Clausewitz in the beginning of the nineteenth century to Alfred Graf von Schlieffen at the end of the century, the German approach to war had become more rigid and obsessed with purely military thinking, ignoring the changes in warfare that had occurred over the previous century. The German strategic thinkers, with Alfred von Schlieffen being Kitchen's prime example, believed that the uncertainties could be removed from war if only enough planning was put in before war's outbreak. "In pursuit of a perfect strategic plan," he wrote, "general staff officers pored over railway timetables, examined production figures of industry, undertook countless exercises and manoeuvres, and produced reams of memoranda."[3] The result was an "infallible key" to success – the so-called "Schlieffen Plan," a purely military solution to Germany's strategic situation. The Schlieffen Plan was based on principles that its author believed were constant, and thus provided Germany with a recipe for success. These principles, particularly encirclement and annihilation, in Kitchen's eyes, became the philosopher's stone of the German military, who permitted no questioning of their beliefs from within.

Martin Kitchen's view that the *Kaiserheer*, or Imperial German army, was actually dogmatic and doctrinaire, and not intellectually open as Keim believed, echoes much of the literature concerning the German army before World War I. Historians have constructed a picture of a German army that was obsessed with winning a future war rapidly by means of one or two great "decisive" battles, battles that would disarm the enemy and allow Germany to dictate whatever peace terms it liked.[4] In the process, so the argument goes, German military intellectuals either did not identify or even ignored both the tactical and strategic lessons of recent wars such as the Anglo-Boer War and the Russo-Japanese War. German soldiers did not recognize the power of modern weapons and did not foresee the tactical stalemate that such weapons might bring. Moreover, German soldiers did not predict the consequences of fighting enemies whose armies numbered millions and who could draw upon the

[2] Martin Kitchen, "The Traditions of German Strategic Thought," *International History Review* 1, 2 (April 1979), p. 163.

[3] Ibid., p. 170.

[4] For example, Gunther Rothenberg, "Moltke, Schlieffen and the Doctrine of Strategic Envelopment," in Peter Paret, *Makers of Modern Strategy from Machiavelli to the Nuclear Age* (Princeton: Princeton University Press, 1986), pp. 296–325; and Detlef Bald, "Zum Kriegsbild der militärischen Führung im Kaiserreich," in Jost Düffler and Karl Holl, eds., *Bereit zum Krieg: Kriegsmentalität im wilhelminischen Deutschland, 1890–1914* (Göttingen: Vandenhoeck & Rupprecht, 1986), pp. 146–159.

resources of global empires. The result, according to this interpretation, was a strategy dominated by the "short-war illusion."[5]

In painting this picture of the *Kaiserheer* most of historians have focused on the General Staff and its head, and the origins of Germany's failed strategy and battlefield doctrine are generally found in the teachings of Alfred von Schlieffen, Chief of the Prussian General Staff from 1891 to 1905 and author of the infamous plan which bears his name. Gerhard Ritter, in his classic study of the Schlieffen Plan, wrote of Schlieffen as a "pure technician" who ignored the political implications of his war plan and thus sowed the seeds of Germany's defeat.[6] Jehuda Wallach traced the origins of the "dogma of the battle of annihilation," which kept German soldiers blind to other approaches, back to Schlieffen.[7]

However, while there is some truth in the opinions of historians such as Ritter, Wallach, and Kitchen, the Imperial German army defies such easy answers. Recent historiography has begun to present a more nuanced view of military thought within the *Kaiserheer.*[8] Even Alfred von Schlieffen, who indeed at first glance seems to be the archetypal narrow-minded strategist, was more complex than portrayed by the above historians. As the German army archives were destroyed during World War II, post-war historians have had to rely heavily on the interpretation of Schlieffen's plans and ideas developed during the interwar period. Almost invariably, these interpreters of Schlieffen's ideas were German soldiers. These men were motivated less by the desire to present a historically accurate picture of Schlieffen and his strategic plans, than by an aspiration to deflect blame for the German army's defeat and to instruct German soldiers how to avoid a stalemate occurring in a future war.[9]

[5] The term was popularized by L. L. Farrar, Jr., *The Short-War Illusion: German Policy, Strategy and Domestic Affairs, August–December 1914* (Santa Barbara, CA: ABC-Clio, 1973).

[6] Gerhard Ritter, *The Schlieffen Plan: A Critique of a Myth* (London: Oswald Wolff, 1958).

[7] Jehuda L. Wallach, *The Dogma of the Battle of Annihilation: The Theories of Clausewitz and Schlieffen and their Impact on the German Conduct of Two World Wars* (Westport, CT: Greenwood Press, 1986).

[8] For example, see Dennis Showalter, "German Grand Strategy: A Contradiction in Terms?," *Militärgeschichtliche Mitteilungen* 2 (1990), pp. 65–102; Showalter, "From Deterrence to Doomsday Machine: The German Way of War, 1890–1914," *Journal of Military History* 64 (July 2000), pp. 679–710; Antulio J. Echevarria, *After Clausewitz: German Military Thinkers Before the Great War* (Lawrence: University Press of Kansas, 2000); Stig Förster, "Der deutsche Generalstab und die Illusion des kurzen Krieges, 1871–1914. Metakritik eines Mythos," *Militärgeschichtliche Mitteilungen* 54 (1995), pp. 61–95.

[9] Wilhelm Groener, an important officer in the General Staff during the war and Reichswehrminister after the war, was the most prominent member of this group. See his *Das Testament des Grafen Schlieffen* (Berlin: E. S. Mittler, 1927); and *Der Feldherr wider Willen: Operative Studien über den Weltkrieg* (Berlin: E. S. Mittler, 1931). Also a member of the "Schlieffen School" was Wolfgang Foerster, a writer for the Reichsarchiv. See his *Graf Schlieffen und der Weltkrieg* (Berlin: E. S. Mittler, 1921) and *Aus der Gedenkenwerkstatt des Deutschen Generalstabes* (Berlin: E. S. Mittler, 1931).

Moreover, Schlieffen was but one of many strategic thinkers in Wilhelmine Germany, and, at the time, perhaps one of the least known.[10] By focusing narrowly on the General Staff and their plans, these authors have neglected other important streams of thought within the German army. After 1871, the German military journals were awash in debates over strategy and tactics.[11] Indeed, as one perceptive historian has noted, the volume of German military literature that appeared from 1870 to 1914 is so great that "to wade through the flood of technical and theoretical literature that appeared after 1870 could easily consume the worst years of one's life."[12] However, it is precisely within this "flood" of literature that we find the debates which foreshadowed the changes in German strategy and tactics during World War I.

Thus, this study begins by examining this alternative stream of thought, most of which originated from the experience of the Germans in the Franco-German War of 1870/71. While most accounts have focused on the decisive nature of this war, a number of prescient Germans recognized the challenges offered by the French *Volkskrieg*, or people's war, of the second phase of the conflict to the traditional German approach to warfare described by the likes of Ritter and Wallach. However, this second phase of the war offered important lessons for discerning German observers such as Helmuth von Moltke the Elder and Colmar Freiherr von der Goltz. Far from focusing purely on the decisive nature of the Franco-German War, these observers reacted to what they saw as a fundamental shift in warfare and a true problem for German strategy. In doing so, these military intellectuals developed alternative ideas about warfare, ideas that did not rest on the assumption of a short war ended by decisive battles, but instead on how Germany could fight and win a long-drawn-out war that comprised numerous, indecisive encounters.

The alternative ideas of these military intellectuals were seconded by one of Wilhelmine Germany's most perceptive military commentators, Hans Delbrück. Delbrück, a professor of history at the Friedrich Wilhelm University in Berlin, further challenged the accepted military wisdom of the day with his concept of *Ermattungsstrategie*, or "strategy of attrition," which offered a different approach to the short-war model

[10] Indeed, Rudolph von Caemmerer, in his influential book, *Die Entwicklung der strategischen Wissenschaft im 19. Jahrhundert* (Berlin: Wilhelm Baensch, 1904), never mentions Schlieffen.

[11] Already by 1859, the Germans produced 50 percent of the military literature in Europe. Samuel P. Huntington, *The Soldier and the State* (London: Harvard University Press, 1994; originally published 1957), p. 48.

[12] Jay Luvaas, "European Military Thought and Doctrine, 1870–1914," in Michael Howard, ed., *The Theory and Practice of War* (London: Cassell, 1965), p. 71.

prevalent within the General Staff. While Delbrück's writings ostensibly dealt only with historical matters, his work continually questioned the intellectual foundations of the army's assumptions about warfare and coincided with the crisis in strategy brought about by the re-emergence of *Volkskrieg*. This link was clearly understood by Delbrück, who applied his historical ideas to contemporary events, and to the army, who were struggling to deal with the challenges offered by modern, increasingly industrial warfare.

The results of these challenges to the accepted view of how wars would be conducted was the tentative birth of a new paradigm of warfare. Instead of the traditional concept of a war won quickly by the means of one or two "decisive" battles that annihilated the enemy's armed forces, thereby forcing the enemy to accept any peace terms, there now arose a vision, a nightmare to most, of a protracted war. This new form of war, brought about by the engagement of the entire nation in a "people's war," would be decided less by clear-cut battlefield victories, than by long-drawn-out battles that slowly sapped the resources of each belligerent. Wars would not be ended by a peace dictated by a clear winner, as most in the Kaiserheer believed, but rather would result in a negotiated peace without obvious winners or losers. Wars of the future would not be won by following the traditional *Vernichtungsstrategie*, or "strategy of annihilation," but instead by following some form of "strategy of attrition."

Yet despite these serious challenges to the German army's assumptions about warfare, the German military leadership continued to adhere to an operational approach and a strategy that assumed a short war. However, this was due less to a firm belief in the continued validity of the short-war model than the recognition that, given the vast economic and manpower resources available to their enemies, Germany could only hope to win a war that was short. Alfred von Schlieffen and Helmuth von Moltke the Younger both wrestled with this difficulty during their tenures as Chief of the Prussian General Staff and both reached this conclusion. Rather than jettison their hope of a short war, their conviction that Germany could not win a long war led them to make all possible efforts to bring about a rapid conclusion to any future war. The result was a plan in which neither man had complete confidence and an attempt to increase the combat effectiveness of the army to the point where it could defeat its enemies even if out-numbered. Thus, both men were forced to continue to train the German army in an operational approach in which they no longer had complete faith.

Moreover, both Schlieffen and Moltke the Younger and their successor, Erich von Falkenhayn, were constrained by structural deficiencies within the government of the *Kaiserreich* and within the *Kaiserheer* itself, which militated against developing a new strategic approach. As Chiefs of the Great General Staff, both occupied one of the most important positions within the army. They were responsible for developing Germany's war plan, advising the government on military matters, and for the intellectual development of the brightest officers in the army, their subordinates in the General Staff. However, there were great limits on the extent of their authority. At the governmental level, there existed no body that coordinated the various branches of the Imperial government. Informal consultation took the place of permanent cooperation. As a result, foreign policy decisions were often taken without consultations with the military leadership, and the General Staff certainly drew up its war plans with only minimal consultation with the Reich's political leadership.[13] Without open communication between the civilian and military leaders of the *Kaiserreich*, no coherent national strategy could be formulated. Assuming that the military knew what they were doing and afraid of a confrontation with a Kaiser who was jealous of his rights as "Supreme Warlord," the political leadership of the Empire left the army alone. For their part, unable to communicate their fears about a future war, the planners within the General Staff focused on areas they could control (like doctrine).

To make matters worse, the authority of the Chief of the Great General Staff was also constrained within the army. Although the General Staff was responsible for formulating German war plans, and hence German strategy, they had no authority over the structure of the peacetime German army. This responsibility fell to the various Ministries of War that represented the constituent armies of the *Kaiserheer* (although the Prussian Ministry of War was by far the largest and most important). These ministries decided on questions of army expansion, unit structure, weapons procurement, and even mobilization.[14] While these ministries consulted with the General Staff, the institutions often disagreed on important questions, and the desires of Schlieffen and Moltke the Younger were more often than not rebuffed.[15] In addition to the Ministry of War, the General Staff also had to contend with two other institutions

[13] For a good examination of this discord during the July crisis that preceded the outbreak of World War I, see Annika Mombauer, *Helmuth von Moltke and the Origins of the First World War* (Cambridge: Cambridge University Press, 2001), pp. 182–226.

[14] See H. O. Meisner, *Der Kriegsminister 1814–1914* (Berlin: Hermann Reinshagen, 1940) and Ludwig Rüdt von Collenberg, "Die staatsrechtliche Stellung des preußischen Kriegsministers von 1867 bis 1914," *Wissen und Wehr* (1927), pp. 293–312.

[15] See Stig Förster, *Der Doppelte Militarismus: Die Deutsche Heeresrüstungspolitik zwischen Status-Quo-Sicherung und Aggression, 1890–1913* (Stuttgart: Franz Steiner, 1985). Cf. Michael Geyer, *Deutsche Rüstungspolitik, 1860–1980* (Frankfurt: Suhrkamp, 1984), pp. 83ff.

within the army: the Military Cabinet and the Commanding Generals of Germany's corps districts. The Kaiser's Military Cabinet controlled promotions and assignments, and consequently exercised great influence within the army.[16] The Commanding Generals of Germany's twenty-some peacetime army corps had considerable power within the army. These generally independent-minded men dictated the training that their troops would receive. Their ideas about warfare, often at odds with those of Schlieffen and Moltke the Younger, deeply influenced their subordinates.[17] Thus, even within the army, the role of the Chief of the General Staff was limited; he could influence, but not command. Indeed, the consequences of this command structure would cause great problems during World War I.

Once the plans for a short war devised by Schlieffen and Moltke the Younger failed at the battle of the Marne in September 1914, Imperial Germany at last found a strategic head willing to entertain the alternative ideas developed before the war. The new Chief of the General Staff, Erich von Falkenhayn, appreciated and accepted the changed nature of modern mass warfare. After recognizing that Germany could not win the war exclusively on the battlefield, Falkenhayn abandoned the traditional German strategic goals of achieving crushing battlefield success and instead attempted to convince the Reich's political leader, Chancellor Theobald von Bethmann Hollweg, that a negotiated peace would have to be sought with at least one of Germany's enemies. Like Moltke the Elder toward the end of his career, Falkenhayn believed that victory on the battlefield could, at best, be a step to the negotiating table.

However, due to the weaknesses in Germany's strategic decisionmaking structure and to the opposition to this new concept of warfare before the war, Falkenhayn was left to develop from scratch the methods by which it could be implemented. Thus, the bulk of this study concentrates on Falkenhayn's effort to come up with such methods and his struggle to implement them in the face of opposition from within his own government and army. In the process, it traces the development of Falkenhayn's strategic goals and the means by which he hoped to achieve these goals during his time as Chief of the General Staff, beginning with the first tentative steps in the Russian offensive in 1915 and culminating with the

16 Rudolf Schmidt-Bückeburg, *Das Militärkabinett der preußischen Könige und deutschen Kaiser* (Berlin: E. S. Mittler, 1933).

17 The role of the commanding generals within the intellectual life of the army has not been well examined. For an introduction, see Eric Dorn Brose, *The Kaiser's Army: The Politics of Military Technology in Germany during the Machine Age, 1870–1918* (Oxford: Oxford University Press, 2001).

ultimate expression of his version of the strategy of attrition – the battle of Verdun.

Falkenhayn's strategic and operational concepts have suffered the same fate as the alternative ideas of warfare examined in the first part of this study: at best they have been distorted, but mainly they have been overlooked. Indeed, this disregard of Falkenhayn's ideas has come about for the same reasons that the alternative concepts from before the war have traditionally been ignored. His ideas were given short shrift by German authors in the interwar period who were focused on attempting to prove the validity of their own strategic and operational ideas. One of the greatest culprits in this process was a source used extensively by this study, the German official history of World War I – *Der Weltkrieg 1914–1918: Die militärischen Operationen zu Lande.*[18] This fourteen-volume series is an excellent example of "traditional" military history. It provides perhaps the most detailed and the most authoritative narrative of Germany's land war.[19] However, as a source it is not without its problems. As Annika Mombauer has noted, its writers had a clear political purpose – to demonstrate the innocence of the wider German army in the defeat of 1918 by implicating certain individuals.[20]

Moreover, and perhaps more importantly for this study, the work was written largely by former General Staff officers and was intended to be a source from which Germany's soldiers could learn. As such, it is often prescriptive rather than purely descriptive, and it reflects the strategic ideas of its authors.[21]

This raises *Der Weltkrieg*'s most significant problem, at least for this study. As most of its researchers and writers were former General Staff

[18] Reichsarchiv, *Der Weltkrieg 1914–1918: Die militärischen Operationen zu Lande* (14 vols.) (Berlin: E. S. Mittler, 1925–56); and Reichsarchiv, *Der Weltkrieg 1914–1918: Kriegsrüstung und Kriegswirtschaft* (2 vols.) (Berlin: E. S. Mittler, 1930). Several other series came out in the interwar period under the auspices of the Reichsarchiv, but these were usually written by former officers not directly associated with the Reichsarchiv. These were the *Forschungen und Darstellungen aus dem Reichsarchiv* (7 vols.), the *Schlachten des Weltkrieges* (38 vols.), and the *Erinnerungsblätter deutscher Regimenter* (250 vols.). See Hans von Haeften, draft of a letter dated 20 August 1928, in Haeften Nachlass, BA/MA, N35/24; and Erich Murawski, "Die amtliche deutsche Kriegsgeschichtsschreibung über den Ersten Weltkrieg," *Wehr-Wissenschaftliche Rundschau* 9 (1959), pp. 513–531, 584–598.

[19] Prior and Wilson's assertion that *Der Weltkrieg* is flawed because it was "written entirely during the Nazi period" is patently false. Eight of the fourteen volumes were published before the Nazi seizure of power, and volume 9 was largely completed. Further, the files of the KGFA indicate that the Nazis had little influence over the writing of the remainder of the work. Robin Prior and Trevor Wilson, *Passchendaele: The Untold Story* (London: Yale University Press, 1996), p. 219.

[20] Mombauer, *Moltke*, p. 11.

[21] In this, the Reichsarchiv was following a long German tradition. See Arden Bucholz, *Moltke, Schlieffen and Prussian War Planning* (Providence, RI: Berg, 1991) for a discussion of the writing of history in the German army.

officers, many had very pronounced views on how the war should have been fought. The first seven volumes of *Der Weltkrieg* were written under the direction of Hans von Haeften.[22] During the war, Haeften had been one of the strongest supporters of Erich Ludendorff and his idea of *Vernichtungsstrategie*, or "strategy of annihilation." As such, he was one of Falkenhayn's most bitter opponents. Indeed, during the war, he had actively worked to have Falkenhayn removed and replaced with Ludendorff.[23] After the war, Haeften brought his wartime beliefs to the writing of the official history.[24] In addition to Haeften, who as editor of *Der Weltkrieg* had the most impact on the interpretations contained within the work, the President of the Reichsarchiv, Hermann Ritter Mertz von Quirnheim, was also a wartime opponent of Falkenhayn.[25] The result of this was a bias against Falkenhayn and his operational and strategic ideas throughout the official history.[26]

The Reichsarchiv was not alone in its criticism of Falkenhayn's strategy. As we have seen, the post-war period saw a renascence of Schlieffen studies, which attempted to demonstrate that if Germany had only followed the teachings of its former Chief of the General Staff (as these "teachings" were interpreted by a select number of Schlieffen's "disciples"), then the war would have ended in a German victory.[27] Those who had deviated from Schlieffen's ideas, such as Moltke the

22 Helmut Otto, "Der Bestand Kriegsgeschichtliche Forschungsanstalt des Heeres im Bundesarchiv-, Militärisches Zwischenarchiv Potsdam," *Militärgeschichtliche Mitteilungen* 51 (1992), p. 430.

23 See Ekkehart Guth, "Der Gegensatz zwischen dem Oberbefehlshaber Ost und dem Chef des Generalstabes des Feldheeres 1914/15: Die Rolle des Majors von Haeften im Spannungsfeld zwischen Hindenburg, Ludendorff und Falkenhayn," *Militärgeschichtliche Mitteilungen* 1 (1984), pp. 75–111.

24 For the most blatant example of this, see the transcript of a planning meeting for Band VIII of *Der Weltkrieg* in which Haeften said the volume should proceed from the assumption that Falkenhayn's strategy "had led us to catastrophe." "Protokoll über die Besprechung bei Herrn General von Haeften am 6. Dezember 1930," BA/MA, W10/51408.

25 Mertz had served from 1914 to 1916 as the first General Staff officer (Ia) of Kronprinz Rupprecht's 6th Army. Rupprecht and his staff played a key role in undermining Falkenhayn's position as Chief of the General Staff. Mertz brought these wartime grudges with him to his post-war position. See Mertz to Foerster, 4 January 1935, BA/MA, W10/51523. Mertz was succeeded as president by Haeften in 1931.

26 This bias was noticed by many former officers who commented on drafts of the Reichsarchiv's work. For example, see Eugen Ritter von Zoellner to Reichsarchiv, 10 June 1930, BA/MA, W10/51305; and Hermann von Kuhl to Reichsarchiv, 7 January 1934, BA/MA, W10/51523.

27 The beliefs of the "Schlieffen School" were conveyed in the memoirs of some of the war's key participants. For example, see Hermann von Kuhl, *Der deutsche Generalstab in Vorbereitung und Durchführung des Weltkrieges* (Berlin: E. S. Mittler, 1920); Max Bauer, *Der grosse Krieg in Feld und Heimat* (Tübingen: Osiander'sche Buchhandlung, 1921); and Max Hoffmann, *Die Aufzeichnungen des Generalmajors Max Hoffmann* (ed. Karl-Friedrich Nowak) (Berlin: E. S. Mittler, 1929).

Younger and Falkenhayn, were castigated, and any strategy other than *Vernichtungsstrategie* was considered a false path. Even more than the Reichsarchiv work, this literature was prescriptive in nature, as these authors tried to inculcate a new generation of German officers with the "proper" operational and strategic ideas, which would prevent a repeat of the indecisiveness of World War I.[28]

The post-war case for Falkenhayn's strategic and operational approach was not helped by the fact that he never developed a "school" of his own within the army which could rally to the defense of his ideas after the war. This was the result of several factors. First, he had not served long within the General Staff before taking up the strategic reins of Germany's war effort, and, crucially, the time he did serve was after Schlieffen had retired. Thus, unlike the proponents of *Vernichtungsstrategie* during the war, Falkenhayn did not have a network of trusted colleagues and subordinates with whom he had worked and shared experiences for years. Poor choice of personnel to staff the OHL when he took over from Moltke the Younger and his lack of interpersonal skills ensured that he did not build up an effective network during his time as Chief of the General Staff. As a result, Falkenhayn's approach to the conduct of the war did not find many defenders in interwar Germany.[29]

With such an authoritative work as *Der Weltkrieg* biased against Falkenhayn and his concept of the strategy of attrition, as well as the criticisms of his ideas that came from the "Schlieffen School," it is hardly surprising that a good deal of the secondary literature has continued along this path.[30] With the destruction of the German army archives during World War II, a re-examination of the traditional interpretation of Falkenhayn's wartime ideas has proved problematic, and, until recently, it has been thought that writing a thorough history of Germany's military operations during World War I would be impossible.[31] Research from primary sources about the German side of the war was restricted to those archives that had survived the destruction of zealous censors and

[28] This aim was freely admitted by Groener, who wrote of his works, "I do not write for history . . . I write for the future, because I fear that our hollow-heads will make improvements for the worse in the strategy of the next war, as happened in the world war." Groener to Gerold von Gleich, 16 May 1935, quoted in Wilhelm Groener, *Lebenserinnerungen* (ed. Friedrich Freiherr Hiller von Gaertringen) (Göttingen: Vandenhoeck & Ruprecht, 1957), p. 16.

[29] After the war, Falkenhayn tried to enlist some of his former subordinates in his battle to defend his reputation, but had little success. See BA/MA, Nachlass Gerhard Tappen, N56/2; Holger Afflerbach, *Falkenhayn: Politisches Denken und Handeln im Kaiserreich* (Munich: R. Oldenbourg, 1994), pp. 500–517.

[30] For example, see B. H. Liddell Hart, *Reputations: Ten Years After* (Boston: Little, Brown, and Co., 1928), pp. 43–69; Holger Herwig, *The First World War: Germany and Austria-Hungary, 1914–1918* (London: Arnold, 1997), pp. 195ff.

[31] For a recent example of this belief, see Prior and Wilson, *Passchendaele*, p. 219.

World War II.[32] These tended to be political or archives of the smaller states of Germany (Bavaria, Württemberg, etc.), which held little of value to those historians looking for the decisions taken by Germany's strategic leaders regarding battlefield operations.[33] The nature of these archives, along with the changing idea of military history, has meant that accounts of the German side of the war have focused primarily on the political realm, rather than on strategic ideas and battlefield operations.[34]

The loss of the bulk of the army's archive has indeed caused difficulties in the writing of a comprehensive account of Germany's conduct of the war. However, this study has been greatly aided by the files of the German army archive that have recently come to light after the collapse of Communism in Eastern Europe, which make possible a fresh examination of Germany's military operations during World War I.[35] In 1988, the Soviets returned to East Germany some 40 tons of documents that had been seized by the Red Army at the end of World War II and kept in secret archives in the Soviet Union. Included in the material returned were 3,000 Prussian and German army files thought destroyed in the Allied bombing raid on Potsdam in 1945. At the heart of this material are the files of the section of the Reichsarchiv responsible for the writing of the German official history of the war, the Kriegsgeschichtliches Forschungsanstalt des Heeres (Army Research Institute for Military History, or KGFA).[36]

32 For German efforts to destroy sensitive material, see Holger Herwig, "Clio Deceived: Patriotic Self-Censorship in Germany after the Great War," *International Security* 12, 2 (Fall 1987), pp. 262–301.

33 Much of the material relating to military operations during the war contained within the smaller archives was removed to the central army archives during the interwar period and, hence, was lost during World War II.

34 Falkenhayn's tenure as Chief of the General Staff has, indeed, been relatively well researched. See Karl-Heinz Janßen, *Der Kanzler und der General: Die Führungskrise um Bethmann Hollweg und Falkenhayn* (Göttingen: Musterschmidt, 1967); Heinz Kraft, *Staatsräson and Kriegsführung in kaiserlichen Deutschland 1914–1916: Der Gegensatz zwischen dem Generalstabschef von Falkenhayn und dem Oberbefehlshaber Ost im Rahmen des Bündniskrieges der Mittelmächte* (Frankfurt: Musterschmidt Verlag, 1980); and most recently Afflerbach, *Falkenhayn*. Each of these works is largely focused on Falkenhayn's political role, rather than his role in military operations.

35 Afflerbach made extensive use of these files in his biography, as did Annika Mombauer in her *Moltke and the Origins of the First World War*. Holger Herwig has also made limited use of them in his *The First World War*.

36 The material was originally returned to the East German authorities in December 1988. With the unification of Germany in 1989, the material became available to Western scholars. It was kept in Potsdam until 1993, when it was moved to the Bundesarchiv/Militärarchiv in Freiburg. See Uwe Löbel, "Neue Forschungsmöglichkeiten zur preussisch-deutschen Heeresgeschichte: Zur Rückgabe von Akten des Potsdamer Heeresarchiv durch die Sowjetunion," *Militärgeschichtliche Mitteilungen* 51 (1992), pp. 143–149; and Otto, "Der Bestand Kriegsgeschichtliche Forschungsanstalt des Heeres," pp. 429–441.

To accomplish their task, the KGFA collected, in addition to the records of the army's various units, copies of private diaries, and testimonies of important figures in the war, which were used to elaborate the official records. For instance, the KGFA obtained from Generaloberst Hans von Plessen, the commander of the Imperial Headquarters, a typescript copy of his personal diary kept throughout the conflict. This, and many other similar sources, can be found in the files now stored in the Bundesarchiv/Militärarchiv in Freiburg im Breisgau.[37]

Another important source contained within these files are the various papers generated by the writing of *Der Weltkrieg*. The KGFA had a set methodology to which its writers worked. First, sources relevant to the subject at hand would be collected together into a *Materialsammlung*, or "collection of materials." This collection would include extracts from documents such as orders, war diaries, and post-war testimonies. From this *Materialsammlung*, the writers would construct a *Forschungsarbeit*, which would be a rough narrative with long extracts from key documents. In the *Forschungsarbeiten*, analysis was kept to a minimum; priority was placed on reconstructing the course of events and actions of the various commands. When completed, these works were then circulated within the Reichsarchiv and sometimes to important participants for comments. Only after the writers were confident that all relevant sources had been examined did they proceed from the *Forschungsarbeit* to writing drafts for *Der Weltkrieg*; it was during this final stage that the writer's historical analysis was added.

Unfortunately few *Materialsammlungen* have survived. However, many *Forschungsarbeiten* have, and these have provided an important source for extracts from documents that were destroyed in April 1945. Additionally, the comments of the readers of these works often provide crucial testimony of individuals who played central roles in the war. Although these works cannot fully replace the original material lost during World War II, they go a long way toward giving researchers a more complete picture of the development of German operations during the war. While historians of Germany's war effort have had to rely mainly upon archives which provided information about the relationship of Germany's military and political leaders, the resurfacing of the KGFA material provides researchers with a source from which to examine the planning, decisions, and actions of Germany's military leadership.

With the advent of this new source material, Falkenhayn's decisions and operational ideas can be examined anew, without the bias of his

37 A copy of Plessen's diary is spread through a number of files in the archive. The period 18 August to 10 October 1914 is in BA/MA, W10/51063 and the period 14 October 1914 to 29 August 1916 is in BA/MA, W10/50656.

contemporaries, and the following study will put his strategy into the context it deserves. As this study demonstrates, the strategic and operational concepts developed by Falkenhayn must be seen as a continuation of the ideas developed before the outbreak of the war as an alternative to the "traditional" German approach to warfare. Although no German soldier relished it, the more perceptive were forced by necessity to embrace a new approach to warfare if they were to have any chance of success in the "people's war" that was World War I. The "strategy of annihilation" with its "decisive" battles and dictated peace had no place in the world of trench warfare, mass armies, and national mobilization. As unpalatable and as difficult as it was to professional soldiers from every belligerent nation, only those who applied some form of "strategy of attrition" stood any chance of victory.

By examining alternative theories of warfare from the pre-war period and by re-examining the operational and strategic ideas of Falkenhayn during the war, a more elaborate picture of the intellectual state of the German army from 1870 to 1916 emerges. German soldiers were hardly the close-minded automatons portrayed in much of the current literature. Indeed, before World War I, there existed within the *Kaiserheer*, as August Keim had desired, an intellectual openness and a lively questioning of accepted beliefs. This led to a clear alternative strategic and operational approach to warfare that was developed and articulated by Falkenhayn during the war.

1 The *Volkskrieg* in German military thought

In 1817, in an essay dedicated to his mentor Gerhard von Scharnhorst, Carl von Clausewitz described the radical change in warfare brought about by the French Revolution. He wrote:

> Now war stepped forth in all its raw violence . . . War was returned to the people, who to some extent had been separated from it by professional standing armies; war cast off its shackles and crossed the bounds of what had once seemed possible.[1]

Clausewitz discerned clearly the shift from professional, dynastic armies of the eighteenth century to the people's armies of the Revolutionary period. The Revolutionary and Napoleonic Wars showed to the world the terrible destructiveness that nations could inflict upon other nations when the passions of the people became involved. The architects of the peace which followed the victory over Napoleon were anxious to put the genie of nationalism and its concomitant people's army back into the bottle.[2] In this goal, the powers of reaction were largely victorious. Of the European powers, only Prussia retained short-term conscription, and even in Prussia this was not fully implemented.[3] Through most of Europe, armies were once again small and beholden not to the people but to their monarchs.

Thanks in large part to the efforts of the participants in the Congress of Vienna, the nineteenth century was one of relative peace in Europe. The

[1] Carl von Clausewitz, "On the Life and Character of Scharnhorst," in *Historical and Political Writings* (ed. and trans. Peter Paret and Daniel Moran) (Princeton: Princeton University Press, 1992), p. 102.

[2] Dennis Showalter, "The Retaming of Bellona: Prussia and the Institutionalization of the Napoleonic Legacy, 1815–1876," *Military Affairs* (April 1980), pp. 57–63.

[3] In 1824, the term of service in France was extended to eight years. The Habsburg Empire followed suit in 1845, while in Russia, peasant soldiers served fifteen-year terms. Prussia, on the other hand, retained the three-year term of service introduced during the Napoleonic period. See Heinz Stübig, "Die Wehrverfassung Preußens in der Reformzeit. Wehrpflicht im Spannungsfeld von Restauration und Revolution 1815–1860," in Roland G. Foerster, ed., *Die Wehrpflicht: Entstehung, Erscheinungsformen und politisch-militärische Wirkung* (Munich: Oldenbourg, 1994), pp. 39–53.

few wars that occurred remained local and did not engage the passions of the masses. European wars had once again become *Kabinettskriege* rather than *Volkskriege*. The armies of Europe, including Germany's, took this political situation to be the norm and created strategies to fit this system. The experience of the second phase of the Franco-German War, though, reawakened the European powers to the potency of a "nation in arms." The consequences of this shift were, however, not widely comprehended by soldiers who were focused on fighting and winning battles and campaigns rather than wars.

Indeed, the German Wars of Unification, with their great battles of annihilation, suggested to many that future wars would be fought and concluded in the same fashion. As recent historiography has clearly shown, many German military intellectuals formed their ideas based upon the assumption that future wars would be won quickly through one or a few great battles.[4] Alfred Graf von Schlieffen is probably the prime example of this school of thought, and this idea found its expression in his war plans, which called for Germany to defeat its enemies in what amounted to one great battle. However, there were a number of German military intellectuals who held opposing views, which have until recently been ignored by historians.[5]

The same experience that had led to the expectation (or illusion as it is often called) of a short war amongst German military intellectuals, also led to the foundation of another school of thought that at least questioned this comfortable assumption and ultimately provided German soldiers with alternative strategic ideas during World War I. While most German commentators on strategy before World War I looked to the Austro-Prussian War and the first half of the Franco-German War for their inspiration, some viewed the second half of the Franco-German War, with its *Volkskrieg*, as more important, and perhaps a better model

[4] See Jehuda Wallach, *The Dogma of the Battle of Annihilation: The Theories of Clausewitz and Schlieffen and their Impact on the German Conduct of Two World Wars* (Westport, CT: Greenwood Press, 1986); Gunther Rothenberg, "Moltke, Schlieffen, and the Doctrine of Strategic Envelopment," in Peter Paret, ed., *Makers of Modern Strategy* (Princeton: Princeton University Press, 1986), pp. 32–63; L. L. Farrar, *The Short War Illusion: German Policy, Strategy and Domestic Affairs August–December 1914* (Santa Barbara, CA: ABC-Clio, 1973).

[5] This topic has begun recently to be examined by Stig Förster. See his "Facing 'People's War': Moltke the Elder and Germany's Military Options after 1871," *Journal of Strategic Studies* 10, 2 (1987), pp. 209–230; Förster, "Der deutsche Generalstab und die Illusion des kurzen Krieges, 1871–1914. Metakritik eines Mythos," *Militärgeschichtliche Mitteilungen* 54 (1995), pp. 61–95; and Förster, "Helmuth von Moltke und das Problem des industrialisierten Volkskriegs im 19. Jahrhundert," in Roland G. Foerster, ed., *Generalfeldmarschall von Moltke: Bedeutung und Wirkung* (Munich: Oldenbourg, 1991), pp. 103–115.

of future war. These observers saw that the conditions would not always be right for a short war based on a strategy of annihilation (*Vernichtungsstrategie*), favored by most of the military. Instead, the campaigns against the hastily raised armies of the French Republic in the winter of 1870–71 pointed to a slow, drawn-out war, one without spectacular, decisive, battles.

The *Volkskrieg* in France, 1870–71

On the morning of 2 September 1870, General Emmanuel Felix de Wimpffen surrendered the Army of Châlons to the Germans at Sedan. For the loss of 9,000 men, the German army captured over 100,000 Frenchmen and the Emperor Napoleon III himself. With the Army of the Rhine trapped in the fortress of Metz, the majority of the Imperial French army had been rendered *hors de combat* within six weeks of mobilization. By conventional reckoning, the Franco-German War was over, won stunningly by the German forces.[6] The battles of this period, particularly Sedan and Metz, were viewed by the world as spectacular successes and entered German mythology as quintessential battles of annihilation.[7]

However, with the surrender of Napoleon III came also the collapse of the Imperial government, which was replaced by the radical Gouvernement de la défense nationale on 4 September. Quickly this new government decided to continue the war, despite its many handicaps. To the German peace offer (with its demand for Alsace-Lorraine), they replied: "There can be no answer to such insolent demands but a *guerre à outrance*."[8] Within the next several months, the French went about mobilizing their nation for war. In mid-September portions of the government evacuated the threatened Paris for the provinces, where the government was reconstituted. On 14 October, an order went out to the provinces threatened with German occupation: all bridges, railways, and telegraphs were to be destroyed before being allowed into enemy hands; similarly any material that might be useful to the invaders was to be evacuated to a safe area. A series of calls to arms culminated on 2 November when

[6] On the German difficulties toward finding peace see Eberhard Kolb, "Der schwierige Weg zum Frieden: Das Problem der Kriegsbeendigung 1870/71," *Historische Zeitschrift* 241 (1985), pp. 51–79.

[7] For an example of the position of these battles in German military thinking, see Alfred von Schlieffen, "Cannae Studies," in Robert T. Foley, ed., *Alfred von Schlieffen's Military Writings* (London: Frank Cass, 2002), pp. 208–218.

[8] Quoted in Michael Howard, *The Franco-Prussian War* (London: Rupert Hart-Davis, 1961), p. 222. Howard's work remains the standard English-language treatment of the war.

a *levée en masse* was declared: all able-bodied men aged 21 to 40 were drafted into service.[9]

The efforts of the Government of National Defense produced astounding results. After the investment of Paris, the French army in metropolitan France, including active elements, troops in depots, the National Guard, and the *franc-tireurs* numbered some 7,000 officers and 494,000 men.[10] By 5 February 1871, the French army had increased by more than 400,000 men to a strength of some 950, 200.[11] These men were equipped from existing stocks of weapons and supplemented by importing arms from abroad. Within the space of several months, the Government of National Defense under the direction of the minister of the interior, Leon Gambetta, had reconstituted a French army, quite literally raising new armies from the ground.

Despite the impressive appearance of these figures on paper, the newly formed French armies had serious shortcomings. First, they lacked trained officers. Relatively few Imperial officers survived the destruction of their army. Retired officers and those coming from Algeria could only go a short way to meeting this deficit. Training suffered accordingly, as did leadership in battle. Even the remnants of the Imperial Army who had survived its destruction at Sedan and Metz had only received a month or so of training. Additionally, the new French armies lacked the artillery required for modern war, which proved a severe handicap when fighting the professional, well-equipped German armies.[12]

By sheer numbers, though, the new French armies were able to cause the Germans considerable difficulties. Moltke was forced to dispatch large numbers of troops to hunt down the new French armies, as well as maintain the siege of Paris and the numerous sieges of other French garrisons to his rear. *Franc-tireurs* kept large numbers of German troops occupied

[9] French mobilization is covered in detail in numerous sources, including: Howard, *Franco-Prussian War*, pp. 233–256; and William Serman, "French Mobilization in 1870," in Stig Förster and Jörg Nagler, eds., *On the Road to Total War: The American Civil War and the German Wars of Unification, 1861–1841* (New York: Cambridge University Press, 1997), pp. 283–294.

[10] Archivrat Greiner, "Der Volkskrieg in der zweiten Hälfte des Krieges 1870/71," unpublished manuscript in BA/MA, W10/50203, p. 9. This manuscript is part of a larger work written in the 1920s to examine the prospects of a German *Volkskrieg*. The interwar period saw a renewed interest in improvised and militia armies on the part of the Reichswehr. For examples, see Hugo Freiherr von Freytag-Loringhoven, "Das preussische Volk in Waffen der Befreiungskriege," *Wissen und Wehr* (1924), pp. 30–36; and Hermann Balck, "1813. Ein Feldzug mit improvisierten Heeren," *Wissen und Wehr* Jg. (1932), pp. 505–522.

[11] Greiner, "Der Volkskrieg," p. 16.

[12] See Howard, *Franco-Prussian War*, pp. 299–317, 397–406.

guarding lines of communication.[13] German manpower was stretched to the limit.[14] The French had turned the tables on the Germans, who had won the first phase of the war in large degree due to their superior numbers. However, the German superiority in training and organization told against the French in the end. The improvised armies, though they bought some months, could not in the end prevent the fall of Paris and with it peace on German terms.

Moltke's response

Perhaps not surprisingly, it was the victor of Königgrätz and Sedan, the intellectual father of the *Kaiserheer*, who was disturbed most by the campaign against Gambetta's improvised armies. It was Moltke who was faced with formulating a strategy to defeat an amorphous foe shortly after his spectacular victories over the Imperial French army. It was Moltke who had to bear the strain of conducting operations against armies to the north, south, and to his rear, as well as supervise the siege of Paris. Moltke realized quite clearly the shift in warfare represented by the war's second phase and the consequences this had for future wars. While he labeled the Austro-Prussian War a *Kabinettskrieg* fought purely "for an ideal end – the establishment of power,"[15] he labeled the Franco-German War a *Volkskrieg*. After this war, he wrote:

> The days are gone by when, for dynastical ends, small armies of professional soldiers went to war to conquer a city, or a province, and then sought winter quarters or made peace. The wars of the present day call whole nations to arms . . . The entire financial resources of the State are appropriated to military purposes . . .[16]

Indeed, as early as 1867, Moltke had recognized the difficulties in waging a war against France. In a memorandum of that year, he wrote: "Even if the French were to lose a battle on their own territory, it would

[13] Some 110,000 men alone were used just to guard lines of communication from Germany. Ibid., pp. 277–278. For the French partisan campaign see, Georg Cardinal von Widdern, *Deutsch-französischer Krieg 1870–1871: Der Krieg an den rückwärtigen Verbindungen der deutschen Heere* (6 vols.) (Berlin: R. Eisenschmidt, 1893–99).

[14] Julius Verdy du Vernois, *Im Großen Hauptquartier 1870/71* (Berlin: E. S. Mittler, 1895), pp. 229–231. The German manpower problem has not been the subject of much detailed research. The best source remains, Gustav Lehmann, *Die Mobilmachung von 1870/71* (Berlin: E. S. Mittler, 1905).

[15] Helmuth Graf von Moltke, "Über den angeblichen Kriegsrat in den Kriegen König Wilhelms I.," reprinted in *The Franco-German War of 1870–71* (trans. Archibald Forbes) (London: Harper & Brothers, 1907), p. 417. Rudolf Stadelmann wrote that this document, written in 1880, could be considered Moltke's "Military-Political Testament." *Moltke und der Staat* (Krefeld: Scherpe, 1950), p. 173.

[16] Moltke, *Franco-German War*, p. 1.

never cause them to conclude peace; rather their patriotism would cause them to summon up all the strength of their resource-rich land."[17] Once war had broken out in 1870, however, his early victories led him to hope for a speedy conclusion to the war. By December, though, frustrated by Gambetta's armies, he began to despair of concluding peace quickly and began instead to make preparations for a long war which would take the German army into the south of France and break once and for all French powers of resistance, to "punish" and to "humiliate" the "haughty French nation."[18] In early December, his headquarters had begun planning for an increase in the German army of 100 reserve battalions.[19] He wrote to a friend on 18 December that he could not foresee how long such a campaign would last, and warned that "a whole people under arms should not be underestimated . . ."[20]

The continued resistance of the French after the battles of Sedan and Metz and the encirclement of Paris had led Moltke to decide that the only recourse was to fight to the end against the French people, to fight a "war of extermination" (*Exterminationskrieg*) which would settle once and for all the great Franco-German rivalry. In early January, Moltke expressed his frustration and outlined his thoughts to the Prussian Crown Prince Friedrich Wilhelm. He saw the impending fall of Paris not as the end of the war, but rather as an opportunity to free troops to take the war deep into the French provinces. Convinced that the French would not give up until completely crushed, Moltke declared: "We must fight this nation of liars to the very end! Then we can dictate whatever peace we like."[21] As Moltke now believed France would fight on until the last of its resources, the task of the German army became to destroy or neutralize these resources.[22]

17 Quoted in Stadelmann, *Moltke*, p. 260.

18 Moltke to Privy Councilor Scheller, 11 October 1870, in Helmuth Graf von Moltke, *Gesammelte Schriften und Denkwürdigkeiten*, Vol. V: *Briefe des General-Feldmarschalls Grafen Helmuth von Moltke* (Berlin: E. S. Mittler, 1892), p. 178. See also Stadelmann, *Moltke*, pp. 244–245.

19 Paul Bronsart von Schellendorf, *Geheimes Kriegstagebuch, 1870–1871* (ed. Peter Rassow) (Bonn: Athenäum, 1954), pp. 212–213. This increase met with opposition from the Minister of War, Albrecht von Roon, and created tension between his and Moltke's staffs. Bronsart, Moltke's chief of operations, joked it would be better for Germany if they traded Roon for Gambetta! See also Eberhard Kessel, *Moltke* (Stuttgart: K. F. Koehler, 1957), pp. 575–576.

20 Moltke to Privy Councilor Scheller, 18 December 1870, in Moltke, *Gesammelte Schriften* V, p. 179.

21 Quoted in Howard, *Franco-Prussian War*, pp. 436–437. See also Emperor Frederick III, *The War Diary of Emperor Frederick III, 1870–71* (trans. and ed. A. R. Allinson) (London: Stanley Paul, 1927), pp. 253, 257.

22 Thus, Moltke too bears some responsibility for the shift from *Kabinettskrieg* to *Volkskrieg*. This point is drawn clearly by Förster in "Facing 'People's War'," pp. 213–214.

Moltke's decision to conduct a "war of extermination" met with resistance from the German leadership. Bismarck, despite some nasty rhetoric, stayed firm on his course for a swift conclusion to the war. This divergence of views between Moltke and Bismarck played a role in the well-documented split between the two which required the intervention of King Wilhelm I to solve.[23] Bismarck was not alone, however, in his resistance to Moltke's views. Even the Minister of War, Albrecht von Roon, balked at the prospect of prolonging the conflict and the further manpower and economic demands that this course would necessitate. As early as 20 August, Roon was already complaining about the difficulty in finding replacements for fallen officers.[24] Later, in a comment to one of Moltke's letters, Roon wrote that he felt it best to return the Landwehr troops to Germany after the fall of Paris and that, "a strategy which leads us to the foot of the Pyrenees is a task for years if we are not to over-tax our strength."[25]

In the end, Bismarck's point of view prevailed. With the fall of Paris came the end of the Franco-German War, and with it, according to Moltke's biographer Rudolf Stadelmann, a great disappointment for Moltke, who had wanted "to direct the Franco-German War as a war of extermination because he had hoped to settle unilaterally a 100-year-old rivalry."[26] With France not definitively defeated, Moltke soon began to fear that a chance such as the Franco-German War would never come again. He believed that France would learn quickly the lessons of its defeat and reconstitute rapidly its armies. By ending the war before Moltke could achieve his expanded goals, the war had, in his eyes, made France stronger rather than weaker in the long run.[27]

Moltke, and Bismarck as well, reckoned that France would never accept the loss of its two provinces and would look for an opportunity to take them back. Therefore, while Bismarck concentrated on keeping France diplomatically isolated, Moltke planned for possible war. In his deployment plan of 1871, Moltke believed he could achieve another rapid

[23] See Gerhard Ritter, *The Sword and the Scepter*, Vol. I: *The Prussian Tradition 1740–1890* (trans. Heinz Norden) (Coral Gables, FL: University of Miami Press, 1969), pp. 219–223; Stadelmann, *Moltke*, pp. 212–250; Kessel, *Moltke*, pp. 581–592.

[24] Albrecht Graf von Roon, *Denkwürdigkeiten aus dem Leben des General-Feldmarschalls Kriegministers Grafen von Roon* (3 vols.) (Berlin: E. S. Mittler, 1892), III, p. 193.

[25] Helmuth von Moltke, *Militärische Werke*, Vol. I: *Militärische Korrespondenz* (Berlin: E. S. Mittler, 1897), p. 581. Though the Moltke–Bismarck tension has received much attention from historians, this tension between the Ministry of War and the General Staff has received almost none.

[26] Stadelmann, *Moltke*, p. 280.

[27] Stig Förster, "Militär und staatsbürgerliche Partizipation. Die allgemeine Wehrpflicht im Deutschen Kaiserreich 1871–1914," in Foerster, *Wehrpflicht*, pp. 61–62.

victory against France's army.[28] The French, however, had learned from their defeat, and Moltke watched with trepidation the rapid rebuilding of their army. The French quickly introduced effective conscription to bring their army up to the level of the German.[29] By 1873, Moltke considered it to be strong enough to fight another war.[30] By 1875, although he toyed with the idea of a preventive war, French military reforms made it clear that France would not be defeated again easily.[31]

The re-emergence of *Volkskrieg* after 1871 called into question Moltke's basic way of war. Following the teachings of Clausewitz, Moltke had always aimed to destroy completely his opponents' armies as a means of achieving a decisive victory and a peace on German terms. The evidence of the second phase of the Franco-German War suggested, however, that this goal might not be attainable in the future. The Wars of Unification had shown the world the worth of universal conscription on the Prussian model, creating whole "nations in arms."[32] Moltke realized that even if he could defeat his opponent's armies quickly, this did not mean the fight was over, as the war in France had shown. Additionally, he assumed that Germany would be forced to fight a two-front war – against either a France allied with Austria or a France allied with Russia.[33] Moltke feared that even if he could defeat one foe quickly, he would be forced to shift his armies to meet the other, preventing him from exploiting any battlefield victories he might achieve. Rudolf Stadelmann captured the

28 Helmuth von Moltke, "Aufmarsch gegen Frankreich-Rußland," 27 April 1871, reprinted in Ferdinand von Schmerfeld, ed. *Graf Moltke. Die Aufmarschpläne 1871–1890* (Berlin: E. S. Mittler, 1929), pp. 4–14.

29 France instituted general conscription in 1872. See Douglas Porch, *The March to the Marne: The French Army, 1871–1914* (Cambridge: Cambridge University Press, 1981), pp. 23–32. See also Gerd Krumeich, "Zur Entwicklung der 'nation armée' in Frankreich bis zum Ersten Weltkrieg," in Foerster, *Wehrpflicht*, pp. 133–145.

30 Ritter, *Sword and the Scepter* I, p. 227.

31 For the most recent analysis of the "War-in-Sight Crisis" of 1875 and for a survey of the historiography, see James Stone, "The War Scare of 1875 Revisited," *Militärgeschichtliche Mitteilungen* 53 (1994), 304–326. See also Walter Kloster, *Der deutsche Generalstab und der Präventivkriegs-Gedanke* (Stuttgart: Kohlhammer, 1932), pp. 6–19.

32 Following the spectacular successes of the Prussian army, Russia, as well as France, began a long period of reform under the guidance of Dmitrii Miliutin, introducing the Statute on Universal Military Service in 1874. Bruce Menning, *Bayonets Before Bullets: The Imperial Russian Army, 1861–1914* (Bloomington: Indiana University Press, 1992), pp. 21–23; and Forrest A. Miller, *Dmitrii Miliutin and the Reform Era in Russia* (Charlotte, NC: Vanderbilt University Press, 1968), pp. 196–200. Austria had instituted short-service conscription in 1868. Gunther Rothenberg, *The Army of Francis Joseph* (West Lafayette: Purdue University Press, 1976), pp. 80–81.

33 On this point, Moltke saw perhaps more clearly than Bismarck. He believed that Austria and Russia were locked in a long struggle over the Balkans, and that "the way to Constantinople goes through Berlin." Quoted in Hugo Zeitz, "Der Schirmer des geeinten Reiches," in Friedrich von Cochenhausen, ed., *Von Scharnhorst zu Schlieffen 1806–1906: Hundert Jahre preußisch-deutscher Generalstab* (Berlin: E. S. Mittler, 1933), p. 233.

tension in Moltke's thinking after 1871, "in Moltke's deployment plans from 1871 to 1890, two tendencies battle one another: the hope for a new Königgrätz and the fear of a new Loire campaign."[34]

By 1877, his deployment plans clearly reflected his pessimism. Fearing that Germany could not completely destroy the armies of its enemies, he wrote into his war plan that it would be the responsibility of the diplomats to conclude a peace, even if the peace had to be concluded on the condition of status quo ante bellum. He wrote:

> Through an immediate offensive . . . we would have a large decisive battle already by the third week.
>
> If it is a success for us, we will indeed seek to exploit it, but the pursuit cannot stretch to Paris. It must be left to diplomacy to determine whether or not we can bring about peace again from our side, even if it is only on the basis of the status quo ante.[35]

Moltke's deployment plan for 1879, when the prospect of a Franco-Russian agreement became even greater, was even more pessimistic.[36] By this date, Moltke reckoned that the French army could field at least 10,000 more troops and around 160 more artillery pieces than Germany. Further, the French had created an "almost hermetically sealed border . . . from Switzerland to Belgium."[37] Even if the German army could breach this line, Moltke feared that the army's supply lines would be extremely vulnerable to French forces in his rear. If that weren't enough, the newly fortified Paris would, in Moltke's view, be able to hold off almost any German siege. He concluded that in case of another Franco-German war, Germany "could no longer expect a rapid conclusion to the struggle."[38]

However, while Moltke no longer assumed that a future war could be won by means of a few great battles, this did not mean that he changed the German army's operational approach. Despite his strategic pessimism, the victor of Königgrätz and Sedan still believed that Germany needed an army well trained in the art of *Bewegungskrieg* (war of movement) and

[34] Stadelmann, *Moltke*, p. 325.

[35] Helmuth von Moltke, "Zweifrontenkrieg gegen Frankreich-Russland," 3 February 1877, reprinted in Schmerfeld, *Aufmarschpläne*, p. 66. This memorandum has more recently been reprinted in Stig Förster, *Moltke: Vom Kabinettskrieg zum Volkskrieg: Eine Werkauswahl* (Bonn: Bouvier Verlag, 1992), pp. 610–612.

[36] Moltke reckoned that Germany's anti-Russian diplomatic stance during the Russo-Turkish War made the prospects of a Franco-Russian alliance more likely. Schmerfeld, *Aufmarschpläne*, p. 77.

[37] Kaiser Wilhelm I to Bismarck, 2 October 1879, reprinted in Schmerfeld, *Aufmarschpläne*, p. 80.

[38] Helmuth von Moltke, "Zweifronten Krieg gegen Russland-Frankreich," April 1879, reprinted in Schmerfeld, *Aufmarschpläne*, p. 77. See also Förster, *Moltke*, pp. 613–617.

capable of fighting and winning battles of an even larger scale than those of the Wars of Unification. Victory in such battles might no longer allow Germany to dictate peace to a defenseless foe, but it would make the diplomat's task of negotiating a peace acceptable to both sides somewhat easier. Thus, Moltke continued to prepare the army to fight large-scale battles of annihilation, battles which would serve as stepping stones to the negotiating table.[39]

As the years progressed, Germany's strategic situation worsened. The new Reich's relations with the other Great Powers remained tense, despite Bismarck's complex system of alliances. On the military side, the French and Russian armies grew in size relative to a German army constrained in size by internal political pressures. As a result, Moltke's pessimism grew, and he increasingly feared that the next war might destroy the new Reich and perhaps even German culture. His view is perhaps best summed up by his oft-quoted final speech in the Reichstag on 14 May 1890:

> The age of *Kabinettskriege* is behind us – all we have now is *Volkskrieg*, and any prudent government will hesitate to bring about a war of this nature with all its incalculable consequences . . .
>
> If war should break out, this war which has now been hanging like a sword of Damocles over our heads for more than ten years, no one can estimate its duration or see when it will end. The greatest powers of Europe, which are armed as never before, will fight each other. None can be annihilated so completely in one or two campaigns that it would declare itself vanquished and be compelled to accept hard conditions for peace without any chance, even after a year's time, to renew the fight. Gentlemen, it might be a seven, or even a thirty years' war – but woe to him who sets Europe alight and first throws the match into the powder-barrel![40]

Although Moltke was pessimistic about a future war, he was still a professional soldier, and it was his duty to try to create a workable strategy. His war plans from 1872 until his retirement in 1890 reflect his attempt to solve the dilemma that the re-emergence of *Volkskrieg* forced upon him.

The historian Gerhard Ritter believed that Moltke's solution to this strategic dilemma was to shift his approach in keeping with the change in warfare. Ritter felt that Moltke intended to fight on the strategic defensive, though he would begin with a tactical offensive to weaken Germany's enemies. Ritter wrote:

[39] Indeed, his "Instructions for Large Unit Commanders" from 1869 remained in effect with only minor revisions throughout the remainder of Moltke's tenure as Chief of the General Staff and beyond. See Daniel J. Hughes, *Moltke on the Art of War: Selected Writings* (Novato, CA: Presidio, 1993), pp. 171–172.

[40] This oft-quoted passage can be found in Helmuth Graf von Moltke, *Ausgewählte Werke*, III (Berlin: E. S. Mittler, 1925), p. 345; Wallach, *Dogma*, p. 66; Förster, "Facing 'People's War'," pp. 223–224.

All that was left to Germany was the strategic defensive – a defensive, however, that would resemble that of Frederic the Great in the Seven Years War. It would have to be coupled with a tactical offensive of the greatest possible impact until the enemy was paralyzed and exhausted to the point where diplomacy would have a chance to bring about a satisfactory settlement.[41]

In short, Moltke's *Vernichtungsstrategie* of the *Kabinettskrieg* would give way to the *Ermattungsstrategie* of the *Volkskrieg.*

Ritter's interpretation is disputed by Stig Förster who believes that Moltke's realization of the difficulty in fighting the next war drove him to reject the prospect of war and to rely instead upon a system of deterrence. Förster shows that Moltke's calls for a preventive war became weaker and weaker as he became more and more convinced that even if Germany were to win the initial battles, the war would drag on and ultimately destroy the social order of Germany. Instead, according to Förster, Moltke decided that the only true course was to avoid war if possible. To this end, he relied increasingly upon the deterrent effect of a strong German army to keep Germany's enemies from beginning a war.[42]

Clearly, Moltke feared the next war and preferred to put it off if at all possible. However, it is difficult to reconcile Moltke's often bellicose statements with Förster's view. Moltke believed that a war with France would come sooner or later and that it was his task to find a way to fight such a war.[43] While Moltke would probably not have used the term *Ermattungsstrategie* to describe his strategy, he clearly felt a quick annihilating victory was beyond the strength of Germany. However, he still believed it was possible to achieve significant successes against his enemies, which would make easier the diplomats' task of negotiating peace. Thus, though Moltke increasingly emphasized the role of diplomacy in concluding a war, he believed that the army had an important role in creating the preconditions for peace (i.e., a greatly weakened enemy).[44]

However, there is one crucial question that Moltke did not address in his war plans or his theoretical writings after 1871 – what to do if the enemy did not come to the negotiating table after a portion of his army was defeated in the field. This was clearly one of Moltke's greatest fears, but the struggle to answer this difficult question was left to other

[41] Ritter, *Sword and the Scepter*, I, p. 230.

[42] Förster, "Facing People's War," p. 224.

[43] Detlef Bald, "Zum Kriegsbild der militärischen Führung im Kaiserreich," in Jost Dülffer and Karl Holl, eds., *Bereit zum Krieg: Kriegsmentalität im wilhelminischen Deutschland, 1890–1914* (Göttingen: Vandenhoeck & Ruprecht, 1986), pp. 146–160.

[44] See Dennis Showalter, "From Deterrence to Doomsday Machine: The German War of War, 1890–1914," *Journal of Military History* 64 (July 2000), pp. 681ff.

German military intellectuals thinking about the changing nature of war before 1914.

Colmar von der Goltz and the "nation in arms"

Moltke's unease with the rise of *Volkskrieg* after 1871 was reinforced by the research and writing of a member of his staff, Colmar Freiherr von der Goltz. Drawing on his work with the Military History Section of the General Staff,[45] Goltz published a study of Leon Gambetta's improvised armies in 1874.[46] The young staff officer was full of admiration for Gambetta's achievements. He believed that Gambetta showed the world what was possible under a motivated and patriotic leader. However, Goltz correctly pointed out the shortcomings in Gambetta's improvised armies – their lack of proper training and equipment.[47] However, his studies of Gambetta and the second phase of the Franco-German War led him to conclude that Germany needed to improve its armed forces to deal with what France had shown possible.

Goltz believed that, in order to win the next war, Germany must increase the potential of its army by institutionalizing many of the ideas tried by Gambetta in his improvised armies, and, in his study, he advocated a number of ways in which Germany could and should prepare itself for future war. He wrote that German officer training should be improved, specifically that the reserve and *Landwehr* officers should be given better training. A more professional reserve officer corps meant, to Goltz, that the German reserve units would fight more effectively and could be used in wider roles. Aware of German manpower shortages in 1870–71, Goltz also believed that Germany should apply conscription more rigorously. He believed that Germany must make use of every able-bodied man. To make this so, he controversially declared that Germany should reduce its active service from three to two years, a stance that brought down upon Goltz the wrath of the Kaiser and resulted in his

45 Goltz served on the *Kriegsgeschichtliche Abteilung* of the General Staff from 1872 to 1874 and helped prepare the official history of the war. His wartime experience on the staff of the 2nd Army made him ideally suited for the task of examining the campaign against Gambetta's armies. Hermann Teske, *Colmar Freiherr von der Goltz: Ein Kämpfer für den militärischen Fortschritt* (Göttingen: Musterschmidt, 1957), pp. 25–26.

46 Colmar Freiherr von der Goltz, "Leon Gambetta und die Loirearmee," *Preußische Jahrbücher* 34 (1874). This was expanded and published in book form several years later as *Leon Gambetta und seine Armeen* (Berlin: Schneider, 1877).

47 Most other accounts of Gambetta's armies were based on Goltz's analysis and stress the weakness of militia-type armies. For example, see Hauptmann von Roeßler, "Vergleich des Feldzuges 1809 am Tajo mit den Kämpfen 1870/71 an der Loire," *Beiheft zum Militär-Wochenblatt* (1888).

removal from the Great General Staff.[48] To help ease the way for extended conscription, Goltz also proposed that the youth of Germany be prepared by schools and youth organizations for military service. He aimed at instilling Germany's young men with the discipline and love of Fatherland necessary for army service. By preparing thoroughly in peacetime, Goltz hoped to avoid the improvised nature of Gambetta's armies, and hence make Germany capable of fighting a *Volkskrieg* more effectively than the French had in 1870/71.[49]

Having witnessed the destructive nature of an improvised *Volkskrieg* during 1870–71, Goltz made the desire to harness the energies of a people in arms in a constructive manner central to his recommendations. In a newly founded conservative Germany, this meant *controlling* the elemental, often radical democratic, forces of the *Volkskrieg*. Thus, by preparing a nation in arms in peacetime, Goltz hoped to keep such dangerous forces firmly under the direction of the responsible authorities and limit their revolutionary potential.[50]

Despite being censured by the Kaiser himself, Goltz continued throughout his long career to stress the necessity for a greater application of conscription and preparation for war, believing that Germany must be able to do better than the French had in 1870–71. In a series of books and articles published over the course of his career, he elaborated his views. In *Roßbach und Jena* (1883), Goltz used the Prussian defeat at Jena to show how an army apart from its nation was doomed to failure, a theme which he continued with *Jena bis Preußisch Eylau* (1907).[51] He recognized that Prussia had lost in 1806, in part, because its leaders were still

48 The two-year service requirement had long been a goal of German liberals, who saw it as a way to weaken the conservative nature of the army. As such, it was vehemently opposed by Germany's conservatives. Goltz's career was only saved by the intervention of Moltke. For the Kaiser's reaction to Goltz's call for a two-year service period see, Dennis Showalter, "Goltz and Bernhardi: The Institutionalization of Originality in the Imperial German Army," *Defense Analysis* 3, 4 (1987), p. 306.

49 Goltz, *Gambetta*, pp. 289–295; Teske, *Goltz*, pp. 29–30. On the ultimately ambiguous nature of pre-war German youth organizations, see Derek S. Linton, "Preparing German Youth for War," in Manfred F. Boemeke, Roger Chickering, and Stig Förster, eds. *Anticipating Total War: The German and American Experiences, 1871–1914* (Cambridge: Cambridge University Press, 1999), pp. 167–187.

50 The fear of an armed population had a long history within Prussia/Germany. During the Napoleonic Wars, this fear held back efforts to mobilize the Prussian people. See Geoffrey Best, *War and Society in Revolutionary Europe 1770–1870* (Stroud: Sutton Publishing, 1998), pp. 150–167. In Goltz's time, this fear prevented an arming of the East Prussian population requested by the Commanding General of the I Army Corps district to face a Russian invasion. Wilhelm Dieckmann, "Der Schlieffenplan," unpublished manuscript in BA/MA, W10/50220, pp. 34–42.

51 Colmar von der Goltz, *Roßbach und Jena* (Berlin: E. S. Mittler, 1883), revised as *Von Roßbach bis Jena und Auerstedt* (Berlin: E. S. Mittler, 1906); *Jena bis Pr. Eylau* (Berlin: E. S. Mittler, 1907).

Fig. 1 Colmar Freiherr von der Goltz

fighting a *Kabinettskrieg*, not the *Volkskrieg* of Napoleon and Revolutionary France.[52] He believed that Prussia had become too complacent after Frederick the Great's victories, and had ignored the changes in warfare brought on by the French Revolution. Quite clearly, "Rossbach" was meant by Goltz to read "Sedan" – a warning to his contemporaries not to be complacent in their own victories.[53]

Goltz's best-known and most influential book was *Das Volk in Waffen*, which was first published in 1883 and translated into English as *The Nation in Arms*.[54] Goltz stated early that his goal with this book was to "recall to strategy the attention which hitherto has been diverted almost exclusively to generalship in battle."[55] To Goltz, the period of modern war brought on by the French Revolution allowed the use of the "whole manhood of the nation."[56] He believed this change in warfare was shown clearly during the Franco-German War, writing: "The day of Cabinet wars is over. It is no longer the weakness of a single man, at the head of affairs, or of a dominant party, that is decisive, but only *the exhaustion of the belligerent nations*."[57] Goltz's message was the same as in his earlier works: only by thoroughly preparing its population in peacetime could Germany hope to win the next war. Goltz believed that there was no better place to start than with the nation's youth, and in *The Nation in Arms* he once again advocated the training of German youth.[58]

Throughout *The Nation in Arms*, Goltz looked back to the experience in the second phase of the Franco-German War – the *Volkskrieg* – for his inspirations. He maintained that a future war would pit nation against nation, and wrote:

> It is, indeed, conceivable that, in order to impose one's will by force upon an obstinate people, led by a great man, it may be necessary to literally flood [*sic*] a country with troops and to exert extreme pressure upon the population for years on end.[59]

In *The Nation in Arms*, Goltz also began to describe in some detail what a future *Volkskrieg* would entail. His vision of a future war excluded "decisive" battles such as Königgrätz and Sedan. The size of the armies

[52] Goltz, *Jena bis Pr. Eylau*, pp. 217–220. [53] Teske, *Goltz*, p. 35.

[54] Colmar von der Goltz, *Das Volk in Waffen* (Berlin: R. von Decker, 1883). This went through five editions before World War I, a sixth after, and was translated widely. A recent historian has called this book "the most significant work of military theory from Wilhelmine Germany." Gerd Krumeich, "The Myth of Gambetta and the 'People's War' in Germany and France, 1871–1914," in Förster and Nagler, *Total War*, p. 646.

[55] Colmar von der Goltz, *The Nation in Arms*. Revised edition (trans. Philip Ashworth) (London: Hugh Rees, 1906), p. 5. Based on the 5th German edition (1898).

[56] Ibid., p. 21. [57] Ibid., p. 9. Emphasis added.

[58] Ibid., p. 26. [59] Ibid., p. 465.

produced by nations in arms, as well as well-placed fortifications, would slow the pace of operations and make such battles impossible. Further, Goltz believed the large modern armies would be able to stretch out across entire border areas, making flanking movements difficult if not impossible. He envisioned that only after a period of encounter battles would any movement be restored in a future war:

> Only when, after the greatest of exertions on both sides, a crisis supervenes, followed on one side by inevitable exhaustion, events begin to move more rapidly. *It is absolutely certain that in a future war events will not march with anything like the rapidity peculiar to our last campaigns.*[60]

Unlike Moltke, Goltz feared that once the passions of the people had been roused, a negotiated peace would be difficult to bring about. Instead, he believed that only the moral pressures of the conflict would cause one side eventually to collapse. After destroying an enemy's army, he believed that the enemy's capital and important provinces should be occupied. If this failed to bring about peace, Goltz recommended: "There remains the last means, namely, heavy pressure upon the most prosperous and sensitive districts, or the occupation of the whole country and the cutting off of its communication with the outside world."[61]

Thus, for Goltz, the *Volkskrieg* of the future would be a much more trying conflict than Moltke hoped for. The Franco-German War had convinced the other European powers that they needed to raise mass armies and to utilize their resources to the utmost. The states of Europe had become "nations in arms" capable of prolonged resistance during warfare. Consequently, Goltz rejected the traditional German vision of a war won rapidly by means of a few great "decisive" battles. Instead, he envisioned a long-drawn-out war that continued until one belligerent had reached the end of its resources. Victory in such a conflict would not be the result of a peace negotiated after a few great battles, but would come through exhaustion. The side that was better prepared, that could more effectively harness the resources of its people, would emerge from a future *Volkskrieg* as the victor.

Colmar von der Goltz worked throughout his career to implement his ideas about warfare. Goltz was not merely a man of letters, he was a serving officer. As he advanced up the ladder of command in the German army, he was often in a position to put his ideas about preparing Germany for a future war into practice. As a corps commander from 1902 to 1907, Goltz was solely responsible for the training of his troops. He used his position to implement many of his ideas within his corps

[60] Ibid., p. 159. Emphasis in original. [61] Ibid., p. 468.

district, particularly the training of reserve officers.[62] In 1911, Goltz took steps towards implementing his ideas for youth training by unifying the various youth organizations of Germany into the Jungdeutschlandbund. Goltz saw this organization as a means of preparing Germany's young men for military service and of controlling the dangerous forces of a nation in arms. Consequently, he set forth a set of principles by which its members should live. This Jungdeutschland-Gesetz emphasised "truthfulness, frugality, reliability, respect for others, healthy living, politeness, and chivalry," all values that reinforced respect for authority.[63] Throughout his career, Goltz used every opportunity to prepare Germany better for the difficult war ahead by applying his ideas of a nation in arms.[64]

Other interpretations of the impact of *Volkskrieg*

The concept of "people's war" was not the province of Moltke and Goltz alone. Indeed, the subject of *Volkskrieg* occupied the minds of many German military intellectuals prior to the outbreak of World War I. In the years after the Franco-German War, German soldiers continued to write about the subject. In the early 1890s, the army opened its archives of the Franco-German War to researchers. A number took advantage of this and published works that focused on the second phase of the war. However, unlike Moltke, these authors did not conclude that German officers would have to rethink their basic assumptions about strategy and, unlike von der Goltz, these writers did not draw the radical conclusions drawn by him about how different future war would be. These writers recommended instead relatively minor improvements that would enable the army to fight more efficiently. Two writers in particular from this group stand out – Fritz Hoenig and Georg Cardinal von Widdern.

In 1893, Fritz Hoenig, a retired officer and well-known military writer,[65] published the first of a six-volume account of the second phase of the Franco-German War, entitled *Der Volkskrieg an der Loire im Herbst*

62 Teske, *Goltz*, pp. 58–59.

63 [Bruno] von Mudra, "Generalfeldmarschall Colmar Freiherr von der Goltz," introductory essay to *Das Volk in Waffen*. 6th edition (Berlin: R. v. Decker, 1925), p. xxv; Teske, *Goltz*, p. 69.

64 Goltz's two-year service period was finally introduced in 1893 in the teeth of much conservative opposition. Lamar Cecil, *Wilhelm II: Prince and Emperor, 1859–1900* (Chapel Hill: University of North Carolina Press, 1989), pp. 201–205.

65 Between 1875 and 1902, Hoenig published fifteen some-odd works of military history and theory and countless articles. Hoenig's career as a military writer is analysed in Joachim Hoffmann, "Der Militärschriftsteller Fritz Hoenig," *Militärgeschichtliche Mitteilungen* 1/70 (1970), pp. 5–25.

1870.[66] Prior to this book, Hoenig, who had served as a battalion adjutant in the 2nd Army during the war, had written a number of other accounts of the conflict which mainly focused on the war's tactical lessons.[67] His interest in the phenomenon of *Volkskrieg* had been piqued by his experiences during the war, and he had begun researching the campaign of the 2nd Army in 1871, shortly after the war's conclusion. However, only in 1892 was he given the access to the official documents necessary to complete his study.[68]

Hoenig believed that the German army had hitherto paid insufficient attention to the campaign on the Loire, representing it merely as a "struggle between two opposing armies" rather than the *Volkskrieg* which it really was. He held that interpreting the second phase of the Franco-German War strictly as a conflict of army against army missed the "change in the character of war." To ignore this change, argued Hoenig, meant seriously underestimating the enemy's [i.e., France's] will and ability to resist in a future conflict.[69] Hoenig wrote that certain nations had the necessary political willpower and the necessary resources to resist to their utmost. Based on the experience of the Franco-German War, he felt that France would show the same powerful will and ability to resist in a future war, even if faced with severe defeats at the outset of a war. He wrote, "southern France . . . can organize powerful forces and conduct considerable resistance even when all of northern France, including Paris, is subdued."[70] German strategists ignored this fact at their peril.

Hoenig charged that the German strategic leadership had made just this mistake in their initial approach to dealing with the armies of the Government of National Defence, and Hoenig hoped his history of the war would be a critique from which officers could learn and prepare for future wars.[71] In his opinion, the German leadership in 1870 had made the error of believing that France's ability to resist had been removed when the Imperial armies were destroyed. They did not believe France would be capable of raising new forces. Therefore, when reports came in of new French forces being formed in the provinces, Germany's leaders

66 Fritz Hoenig, *Der Volkskrieg an der Loire im Herbst 1870* (6 vols.) (Berlin: E. S. Mittler, 1893–99). Hoenig's work largely served as the basis for Lonsdale Hale's *The 'People's War' in France 1870–1871* (London: Hugh Rees, 1904).

67 Fritz Hoenig, *Zwei Brigaden* (Berlin: E. S. Mittler, 1882) and *24 Stunden Moltkes'cher Strategie entwickelt und erläutert an den Schlachten von Gravelotte und St. Privat* (Berlin: E. S. Mittler, 1891).

68 Count A. Bothmer, review of *Der Volkskrieg an der Loire, United Services Magazine* NS, VII (1893), p. 1032. Bothmer also noted that the principal commanders of the German campaign were deceased by 1892, making "a criticism of their doings . . . easier for the author than it would have been immediately after the campaign."

69 Hoenig, *Volkskrieg*, I, pp. 5–6. 70 Ibid., p. 8. 71 Ibid., pp. iii, 7.

discounted them. Hoenig faulted the leadership for not taking the threat more seriously and for not doing more to ascertain the whereabouts or strength of these forces.[72] He further believed that the German response, when it came, was too weak. He again put this down to an underestimation of the enemy as well as to the shortcomings of some of the German higher commanders.

Indeed, Hoenig's work consisted of a long critique of the German command in 1870–71. In all, he felt that the German leadership was taken completely by surprise by the continued French resistance after the defeat of the Imperial armies, and that they reacted slowly and ineffectively to the threat posed by the newly formed French armies and to the partisan threat to the German lines of communication. After underestimating the French threat, Hoenig felt that some commanders (most notably the Grand Duke of Mecklenburg-Schwerin) then began to overestimate them after a few setbacks.[73] Further, the German response to the French armies on the Loire was poorly coordinated.[74] Hoenig maintained that a more robust initial German response to the fresh French armies would have dealt them a blow from which they would never have recovered. With stronger leadership, Hoenig argued, the whole campaign on the Loire could have been ended almost before it had even begun. Thus, for Hoenig, a future war would have to be waged ruthlessly from the beginning and aim at stamping out enemy resistance as quickly as it arose.

In the same year that Hoenig's first volumes appeared, a retired cavalry colonel, Georg Cardinal von Widdern, began publishing his multivolume history of the partisan war on the German lines of communication in 1870–71.[75] Cardinal had served during the war with the *Etappendienst* guarding the German supply lines and had later become an instructor at various war schools in the new Reich. Like Hoenig, Cardinal believed that the next war would in all likelihood be a *Volkskrieg* similar to the second phase of the Franco-German War. In particular, he felt that the war's second phase had shown just how vulnerable modern armies were to partisan warfare. Cardinal wrote that, as the size and complexity of armies increased, so did their reliance upon fixed lines of communication. He maintained that the German army should learn from its experience in the

[72] Ibid., pp. 27–29. Generalleutnant von Podbielski, Moltke's *Generalquartiermeister*, described the French forces as a "mob," incapable of serious operations, p. 339.
[73] Ibid., p. 10. [74] Hoenig, *Volkskrieg*, VI, p. 334.
[75] Georg Cardinal von Widdern, *Deutsch-französischer Krieg an den rückwärtigen Verbindungen der deutschen Heer und der Etappendienst* (6 vols.) (Berlin: Eisenschmidt, 1893–99).

Volkskrieg, and, like Hoenig, intended his work to be a guide from which officers could learn.[76]

At the heart of Cardinal's work was the opinion that Germany must better prepare its armed forces for the *Kleinkrieg*, or partisan war,[77] which was sure to accompany any future war. He noted that in 1870–71 the German army maintained a force of over 110,000 troops and close to 70 artillery pieces to cover the long lines of communication through which the supplies for Germany's 454,000 man field army came. Thus for every four fighting troops, one was necessary to guard the flow of supplies.[78] Cardinal also noted that in the Franco-German War this task had fallen to the troops of the Landwehr, a force which he believed was unsuited to fight this difficult type of conflict. Cardinal felt that the Landwehr officers had been out of active service for too long to be able to respond to the demands of such a tactically challenging task. He maintained also that the troops were too old to fight the mobile war demanded by the nature of the *Kleinkrieg*.[79]

Although Cardinal recognized the changed nature of war and the likelihood that the next war would be similar to the *Volkskrieg* of the last, he, like Hoenig, did not feel large changes were needed in the German army. Cardinal wanted the army to train its officers to fight the *Kleinkrieg* as well as the more glamorous mobile war. He recommended that Germany assign more active-duty troops and a few higher-level officers to the *Etappendienst* so that the German army would be better prepared for the attacks against its communications which he believed must come in a future conflict.[80] Therefore, like Hoenig and most other German officers, Cardinal felt the German army needed only to tinker with its formula to overcome the changes in warfare brought about by the reappearance of the *Volkskrieg*.

Thus, the works by Hoenig and Cardinal were at heart quite different from those of Goltz. While all three saw the *Volkskrieg* on the Loire as a foreshadowing of future conflicts, Hoenig and Cardinal stressed the deficiencies of the German army, rather than the capabilities of the French

[76] The concluding volume even offered "Taktische Aufgaben aus dem Gebiet des Kleinen Krieges," from which officers could practice what they had learned. *Der Krieg an den rückwärtigen Verbindungen*, V, pp. 77–84.

[77] The terms "*Kleinkrieg*" and "*petite guerre*" were generally used to describe partisan warfare. Cardinal assumed that the *Kleinkrieg* of the future would be more systematic than in the past and would be carried out by larger and better prepared formations.

[78] *Der Krieg an den rückwärtigen Verbindungen*, I, pp. iv–v.

[79] Ibid., III, pp. 56, 73.

[80] Ibid., V, pp. 23–49. See also his *Der Kleine Krieg und der Etappendienst. Kriegsgeschichtliche und taktische Studie* (4 vols.) (Leipzig: Eisenschmidt, 1892–1907).

improvised armies.[81] In the end, Hoenig and Cardinal felt French successes could be better explained by German failings. As Dennis Showalter has noted, "this was a comfortable answer. It implied that the situation could have been prevented by measures within German control."[82] While Hoenig and Cardinal hoped that German officers would learn from the mistakes of the campaign on the Loire, they did not feel the Germans were incapable of winning another *Volkskrieg*. Moreover, Hoenig and Cardinal tended to conflate the traditional concept of *Volkskrieg* as a partisan war with the new concept of *Volkskrieg* as a battle between whole industrialized nations in arms developed by Moltke and Goltz. Thus, unlike Goltz, they did not feel a thoroughgoing program of reform was needed, and, despite the sometimes controversial nature of their works, Hoenig and Cardinal reflected more clearly the interpretation of the Franco-German War generally accepted by the rest of the German army.

Conclusions

Looking back nearly 130 years, it is obvious today that the second phase of the Franco-German War pointed more precisely to the way of the future than the great victories of the first phase. This phase displayed many features of the much greater *Volkskrieg* which would come forty-five years later. Although recent research has called into question the amount of public support for the policies of the Government of National Defense,[83] the French clearly strove hard to achieve near total mobilization and to create a nation in arms, even if they fell somewhat short of their goals. The government attempted to follow a "scorched earth" policy, issuing orders to destroy anything of value lest it fall into enemy hands. Manpower mobilization called a large proportion of the male population to the colors. French partisan activity brought forth reprisals against civilians from the German army, creating an upward spiral of violence remembered by both sides long after the war's end. The German army also deliberately targeted

[81] Many of Hoenig's other works stressed German shortcomings during the war. In particular, Hoenig's quest for historical accuracy regarding the battle of Gravelotte (18 August 1870) landed him in front of an *Ehrengericht* for allegedly maligning the character of General Schwarzkoppen. See Fritz Hoenig, *Meine Ehrenhandlung mit dem Oberst und Flügeladjutant von Schwarzkoppen und dem Oberst und Abteilungschef im Generalstabe von Bernhardi* (Berlin: n.p. 1902).

[82] Showalter, "Goltz and Bernhardi," p. 309.

[83] Sanford Kanter, "Exposing the Myth of the Franco-Prussian War," *War and Society* 4, 1 (1986), pp. 13–30; and Krumeich, "Myth of Gambetta," pp. 641–655. While the views of both authors on the support enjoyed by the government might be true, there is no doubting that the armies of Gambetta caused the Germans considerable difficulties and that the second phase of the war represented a distinct departure from the conditions of the war's first phase.

the civil population of fortresses under siege in an effort to bring resistance to an end sooner. With the Franco-German War, war in Europe had ceased to be a war of government against government and became one of nation against nation.

Thus, although the Franco-German War appeared to be a spectacular victory for the Germans and appeared to secure German military dominance of Europe, in fact, the war sowed the seeds of the destruction of the Second German Empire. The war's first phase showed the world the worth of an army based on conscription, while the second phase of the war demonstrated the ability of a modern nation-state to mobilize considerable resources, both manpower and industrial, and to continue resistance even after suffering a severe military defeat. These lessons were not lost on Germany's enemies, and they quickly instituted conscription and built up the structure of a "nation in arms" along Gambetta's model in their countries. After 1871, Germany could no longer count on its enemies being unprepared. Any future European conflict would pit the resources of whole nations against one another.

This shift in warfare was recognized by a number of clear-sighted German military commentators. Foremost amongst these was the intellectual father of the Wilhelmine army, Helmuth von Moltke the Elder. Moltke's war plans from 1872 onwards, as well as his public writings, reflected his understanding of how the rise of *Volkskrieg* affected Germany. His solution to Germany's growing strategic dilemma was to work more closely with Germany's diplomats, both in peacetime and in war, to ensure that Germany fought under the most favorable conditions possible and to negotiate a peace as quickly as possible once war had broken out.

Moltke, however, remained generally optimistic about the outcome of any future war. He believed that a well-trained German army could inflict enough punishment on its enemies to force them to the negotiating table. Consequently, Moltke did not see the necessity of rethinking the German army's operational approach: the *Kaiserheer* would still aim to defeat its opponents in great, "decisive" battles; only now, the goal Moltke hoped to achieve from such battles was more limited than during his earlier wars.

Moltke's ideas about *Volkskrieg* were supported, to a greater or lesser extent, by a number of young writers, who also focused their research on the implications of the second phase of the Franco-German War. The writings of Colmar von der Goltz – one of Wilhelmine Germany's most prominent military intellectuals – centered on how Germany should prepare itself for the task of fighting and winning another *Volkskrieg* and how the popular forces unleashed by a nation in arms could be controlled by a conservative government. His solution was to institutionalize Gambetta's improvisations – to prepare Germany in peacetime for the utmost exertion in wartime. By preparing before the outbreak of war, Goltz hoped that Germany would be able to fight at its peak of efficiency from the beginning of any conflict and that the passions of a people in arms would thus be channeled by the responsible authorities. However, Goltz painted a darker picture of future war than did Moltke. He saw a future *Volkskrieg* as a long-drawn-out struggle that would be ended by exhaustion, rather than a quick decisive battle. Hoenig and Cardinal were less radical in their demands for army reform than Goltz, calling for small improvements rather than fundamental change. Each author, however, believed that, with suitable changes in place, Germany could prevail in a future *Volkskrieg*.

Unlike Moltke, though, Goltz, Hoenig, and Cardinal were not in positions of authority when they wrote their books on the *Volkskrieg* in France. All three authors took a minority view on the lessons of the Franco-German War. Goltz was even disciplined by the Kaiser for proposing to reduce the terms of service. Hoenig too was censured. His attempts at "de-mystifying" the Wars of Unification landed him in front of a court of honor. Despite this, however, Goltz, Hoenig, and Cardinal had at least the tacit backing of the authorities. Goltz had reached his conclusions while writing the official history of the war and his historical books were written using the archives of the army. Hoenig and Cardinal, as well, were given access to the official records and to the private papers of many of the higher commanders for their works – a fact not missed by observers. Given the scope of access these men had to official records, and the protection given them by the army leadership (every military work had to clear the censors at the General Staff before publication), the historical works of these men could rightly be seen as semi-official accounts.

Yet, despite the warnings of these authors, the German army before 1914 focused, as a whole, on the Franco-German War's first phase and used this to support a short-war strategy. Moltke the Elder's successors as Chief of the General Staff planned to defeat the French and Russian armies in a few great battles. His successors cut diplomats from Germany's war plans and planned instead for the German military to impose a "victor's peace" upon both France and Russia. In short, the German strategic leadership after Moltke the Elder ignored the implications of the changed nature of warfare.

One of the most important reasons for this rejection can be found within the writings of the very men who stressed how warfare had changed. While Moltke rather quietly emphasized the shift in warfare and Goltz spoke a bit louder, the research of Hoenig and Cardinal undermined their arguments. Both Hoenig and Cardinal recognized that warfare in the future would be different. However, their works, by examining German errors in 1870–71, maintained that only minor changes would be necessary to deal with a future *Volkskrieg*. To these authors, change in warfare did not require an abandonment of Germany's traditional approach to war. Thus, their work supported the rejection of Goltz's radical approach and supported the more conventional thinking of men such as Alfred von Schlieffen.

In ignoring the fact that the Franco-German War represented a shift in warfare, the German strategic leadership before 1914 fatally weakened Germany. Believing that the army could win the next war without outside assistance, the General Staff cut both the Ministry of War and the Foreign Ministry out of its planning process. The result was a fragmentation rather than an integration of Germany's higher authorities. Not knowing the full details of Germany's war plan, the Ministry of War would not support the army increases demanded by the General Staff. Not knowing the army's full war plan, the Foreign Office could take no steps to ease Germany's diplomatic situation before the conflict. Once Germany's plan had failed and the *Volkskrieg* rejected by the General Staff had set in, Germany was forced, like Gambetta in 1870, to improvise its war effort.

2 The (re)birth of *Ermattungsstrategie*

One of Wilhelmine Germany's most important strategic commentators was not a serving soldier, but rather an academic – Hans Delbrück. The sixty-some-odd years of his career spanned the bellicose life of the Kaiserreich – from its foundation through the Franco-Prussian War to its demise through World War I. During that period, Delbrück played a key role in many areas of Wilhelmine society. He was at once a teacher at one of the most important universities in Germany (Friedrich-Wilhelms-Universität in Berlin), editor of the influential journal *Preußische Jahrbücher*, member of the Freikonservative Partei in the Prussian Landtag and later in the Reichstag, and writer of numerous works on history and contemporary affairs.[1] Most importantly for this study, Delbrück was a sharp critic of German strategic and operational thinking in the years before World War I, believing it to be close-minded in its approach to learning lessons from the past.[2]

At roughly the same time as Moltke the Elder and Colmar von der Goltz were questioning the army's continued adherence to *Vernichtungsstrategie* by examining the consequences of the *Volkskrieg* of 1870/71, Delbrück was challenging the intellectual underpinnings of the German army's approach to war from another direction. The young professor went so far as to attempt to form a new strategy (or rather, in his view, recall an old strategy) to deal effectively with the new reality of *Volkskrieg*. The resulting debate would eventually draw in most of the army's intellectuals, and if

[1] Peter Paret saw him as a forerunner of the modern "national security" specialist. Peter Paret, "Hans Delbrück on Military Critics and Military Historians," *Military Affairs* (Fall 1966), pp. 148–149.

[2] Despite playing such an important role in German society before World War I, Delbrück has never been the subject of a thorough biography, as has been noted by Arden Bucholz and others. Several studies of limited aspects of his career have been subjects of monographs. See, Arden Bucholz, *Hans Delbrück and the German Military Establishment: War Images in Conflict* (Iowa City: University of Iowa Press, 1985); and Sven Lange, *Hans Delbrück und der 'Strategiestreit': Kriegführung und Kriegsgeschichte in der Kontroverse 1879–1914* (Einzelschriften zur Militärgeschichte No. 40 Herausgegeben vom Militärgeschichtlichen Forschungsamt) (Freiburg: Rombach, 1995).

Delbrück's ideas were not fully accepted, the discourse would at least provide Germany's soldiers with the intellectual basis for an alternative strategy in 1914.

The *Strategiestreit* and *Ermattungsstrategie*

In 1879, Delbrück, at the time a young academic at the University of Berlin, published a review of Frederick the Great's "Military Testament," which had just been published for the first time in an annotated version.[3] In his review Delbrück took the editor, Major Adalbert von Taysen, to task for several points. Aside from some minor historical inaccuracies, Delbrück found Taysen's editing to be heavy handed and most damningly, that Taysen misunderstood the central point of the "Testament."

Frederick's "Military Testament," written in the autumn of 1768 and originally part of his "Political Testament," called for a *Detachmentskrieg* to be waged in case of a war with Austria – Prussian forces would seize Austrian territory and fight a defensive battle from prepared positions, with the ultimate goal of wearing down the Austrian forces by means of numerous small-scale encounters. In his comments to the edition, Taysen stated that the "Military Testament" only outlined a campaign plan for the next encounter with Austria and could not in any way be considered an elaboration of Frederick's general philosophy of war. Taysen maintained that Frederick normally sought decision through large-scale battle, not through occupying enemy territory and destroying enemy crops. To Taysen, Frederick sought to win his wars through great decisive battles which annihilated the enemy's armed forces, just as Napoleon and Moltke would do in the future. Delbrück argued precisely the opposite – Frederick's "Military Testament" was not a campaign plan for the next war but a general statement of Frederick's approach toward war. Delbrück further declared that "Frederick had at all times . . . looked upon 'battle' as an evil, which one must subject oneself to only in the case of the utmost necessity,"[4] and that "Frederick's aversion to battle [outlined in the 'Testament'] was in no way something new, but rather it was an improvement of a previously held conviction."[5]

Delbrück's strident criticism of Taysen's editorial views and his unique interpretation of Frederick the Great brought him into conflict with the military. His review received an immediate challenge from one of Taysen's colleagues in the General Staff. In the next issue of the *Zeitschrift für*

[3] Hans Delbrück, Review of *Das militärische Testament Friedrichs des Grossen*, in *Zeitschrift für preußische Geschichte und Landeskunde* 16 (Jan.–Feb. 1879), pp. 27–32.
[4] Ibid., p. 31. [5] Ibid., p. 32.

preußische Geschichte und Landeskunde, Colmar von der Goltz wrote an "Antikritik" rejecting Delbrück's analysis.[6] Delbrück responded in turn, defending his views in the same issue.[7] For the next thirty years, Delbrück and the military sparred, ostensibly over interpretations of Frederick the Great's strategy; each article by one side brought forth a response from the other with each side only slowly coming closer to the view of the other. The list of Delbrück's opponents reads like a "Who's Who" of Wilhelmine military intellectuals: Colmar Freiherr von der Goltz, Theodor von Bernhardi and his son Friedrich, Rudolph von Caemmerer, Fritz Hoenig, Wilhelm Scherff, and Alfred von Boguslawski – most of whom taught at the Kriegsakademie and reached the rank of general. By criticizing a key figure in the panoply of the German military, Delbrück succeeded in uniting an otherwise fragmented officer corps against him.[8] Delbrück's debate with the military has been well covered elsewhere,[9] thus it is not necessary to explore it in great depth here. It is important, however, for this study in two ways: first, from this *Strategiestreit* Delbrück's idea of *Ermattungsstrategie* developed fully; second, implied within Delbrück's interpretation of Frederick the Great's strategy was a criticism of the military's conception of contemporary war.

Based on his research into the writings of Carl von Clausewitz,[10] Delbrück came to believe that Clausewitz had posited, shortly before his death, not the one form of strategy normally accepted by Delbrück's contemporaries (*Vernichtungsstrategie*), but rather two forms of strategy.

6 Colmar Freiherr von der Goltz, "Antikritik," *Zeitschrift für preußische Geschichte und Landeskunde* 16 (May–June 1879), pp. 292–304. Goltz at the time was serving as an instructor at the Kriegsakademie and in the Military History Section of the General Staff. Hermann Teske, *Colmar Freiherr von der Goltz: Ein Kämpfer für den militärischen Fortschritt* (Göttingen: Musterschmidt, 1957), pp. 32–37.

7 Hans Delbrück, "Duplik," *Zeitschrift für preußische Geschichte und Landeskunde* 16 (May–June 1879), pp. 305–314.

8 For an introduction to the lively debates of this period, see Antulio J. Echevarria II, *After Clausewitz: German Military Thinkers Before the Great War* (Lawrence: University Press of Kansas, 2000); and Eric Dorn Brose, *The Kaiser's Army: The Politics of Military Technology in Germany during the Machine Age, 1870–1918* (Oxford: Oxford University Press, 2001).

9 Delbrück himself gives an overview in his *History of the Art of Warfare: The Modern Era*, IV, *The Dawn of Modern Warfare* (trans. Walter J. Renfroe Jr.) (Lincoln: University of Nebraska Press, 1985), pp. 378–382. See also Bucholz, *Delbrück*, pp. 52–85; and Lange, *Delbrück, passim.*

10 This thesis came from Delbrück's reading of two important pieces by Clausewitz, his "Über das Fortschreiten und den Stillstand den kriegerischen Begebenheiten" (later published by Delbrück in *Zeitschrift für preußische Geschichte und Landeskunde* 15 (May–June 1878), pp. 233–241) and his final notes to *On War*, Carl von Clausewitz, "Two Notes by the Author on his Plan for Revising *On War*" (trans. Michael Howard and Peter Paret) (Princeton: Princeton University Press, 1976), pp. 69–71). These remain even today the subject of much conjecture and debate. See Azar Gat, "Clausewitz's Final Notes," *Militärgeschichtliche Mitteilungen* 1 (1989), pp. 45–50.

Delbrück believed that Clausewitz was in the process of editing *On War* to reflect this new discovery, but this editing was interrupted by his call to Poland in 1830 and his subsequent death.

The first of the strategies elaborated by Clausewitz formed the core of the unedited *On War* and consisted of his interpretations of Napoleon's strategy. This he called *Niederwerfungsstrategie* (strategy of annihilation), and was based on his experiences in and research on the twenty years of Revolutionary and Napoleonic warfare. At the core of this strategy is the *Schlacht*, the "large-scale battle." Clausewitz observed that Napoleon always sought an encounter with his enemy that would result in a decisive victory, that is, a battlefield victory that would produce political results. To achieve this decisive victory, Napoleon aimed to annihilate his opponent's army in a great battle. To Napoleon, the "battle" was everything: "To march 5 miles a day, to fight, to rest – this is his entire art of war . . ."[11] Thus, Clausewitz outlined his first strategy: "the object is to overthrow the enemy – to render him politically helpless or militarily impotent, thus forcing him to sign whatever peace we please . . ."[12]

Based on the experiences of the Napoleonic Wars, *Niederwerfungsstrategie*, or *Vernichtungsstrategie* as it came to be known, formed the basis for military strategy after 1815. Soldiers, particularly Prussian soldiers, had learned a hard lesson at the hands of the Emperor of the French and were determined not to repeat their past mistakes. The old careful approach to warfare of the seventeenth and eighteenth centuries gave way to a less restricted way of war that sought to defeat totally an enemy's forces in battle, and thus dictate, rather than negotiate, peace. German strategists embraced this form of warfare, and "proved" its validity with the defeat of the Austrian armies in 1866 and the Imperial French armies in 1870. Wilhelm Groener admitted after World War I how deeply ingrained this idea had been in the German army before 1914:

> The officer corps had formed its ideas through the study of the wars of Napoleon and Moltke. These were fought in the style of the *Niederwerfungsstrategie*: a rapid flowing of the army over the enemy territory; the war's decision in a few, mighty strokes; a peace in which the defenceless enemy was forced to accept the conditions of the victor without demur.[13]

[11] Hans Delbrück, "Die Strategie des Perikles erläutert durch die Strategie Friedrichs des Großen," *Preußische Jahrbücher* 64 (1889), p. 265.

[12] Clausewitz, "Note of July 1827," in *On War*, p. 69. Quoted by Delbrück, "Perikles," p. 261.

[13] Wilhelm Groener, "Delbrücks Lehre, das Heer und der Weltkrieg," in Emil Daniels and Paul Rühlmann, eds., *Am Webstuhl der Zeit: Eine Erinnerungsgabe Hans Delbrück dem Achtzigjährigen von Freunden und Schülern dargebracht* (Berlin: Reimar Hobbing, 1928), p. 44.

German historians and strategists, however, looked further back for their inspiration than Napoleon, claiming that Frederick's approach to war foreshadowed and heavily influenced Napoleon's.

Thus, when Delbrück challenged this view of Frederick as the forerunner of Napoleon, he challenged the accepted wisdom of the military establishment and the basis for their approach to warfare. In his "Antikritik" to Delbrück's "Kritik," Goltz espoused the General Staff view of Frederick, arguing that the King "held the tactical decision to be the surest way to impose his will, and that he in no way had an aversion to [battle]."[14] Goltz went on to provide illustrations to show that Frederick sought "battle" whenever possible, and concluded, "the possibility of beating the enemy appeared to Frederick as valid a reason to seek battle as it did to Napoleon."

Delbrück could not accept this view of Frederick's strategy. To the *Niederwerfungsstrategie* espoused by Goltz and the military establishment, Delbrück outlined what he believed to be Clausewitz's second type of strategy – *Ermattungsstrategie* (strategy of attrition). Delbrück believed that towards the end of his life, Clausewitz had realized that by focusing purely on *Niederwerfungsstrategie*, he was excluding the experiences of earlier warfare from his supposedly universal theory of war. The campaigns of the pre-revolutionary period were not noted for the decisiveness of their battles, but rather the opposite. Clausewitz observed that commanders before Napoleon avoided costly large-scale battles and preferred to rely upon maneuver and smaller engagements to achieve their, generally more limited, goals. Clausewitz, according to Delbrück, recognized that there were circumstances where the motives of a nation did not warrant annihilating an enemy's armed strength completely and also (more importantly for this study) that there were times when a nation's limited strength made the total annihilation of an enemy army, and with it a dictated peace, almost impossible. Delbrück believed that Clausewitz showed the time for *Ermattungsstrategie* was when a nation had only "modest political goals, weak motives, [or] *limited strength*."[15]

Delbrück argued that Frederick followed *Ermattungsstrategie* not because his will was any weaker than Napoleon's but because he was constrained by the conditions of his age. Delbrück repeated his assertions that Frederick fought battles only when forced to by circumstances and added reasons why this was so: "Frederick did not have enough money or soldiers, or rather not enough reliable soldiers, to conduct war in the style of Napoleon. Therefore, he only entered into battle if

[14] Goltz, "Antikritik," p. 299.
[15] Clausewitz, *On War*, p. 99. As quoted in Delbrück, "Perikles," p. 262.

there was no other means of reaching his goal."[16] Frederick's army was in no way up to the campaigns of Napoleon's. It was made up of professional soldiers, impressed men, and prisoners of war. The army of Frederick was exactly that – a dynastic force, not a national force as under Napoleon. Soldiers, held in line only by "iron discipline," deserted whenever possible, making fighting war as under Napoleon – living off the land, fighting in broken terrain, pursuing a beaten foe – impossible. In short, according to Delbrück's analysis, Frederick's Prussia did not have the ability to annihilate its enemies, and thus he had to look for alternative strategies.

The most systematic exposition of *Ermattungsstrategie* came in Delbrück's "Die Strategie des Perikles erläutert durch die Strategie Friedrichs des Großen," first published serially in *Preußische Jahrbücher* in 1889.[17] Delbrück held that under certain circumstances, most notably in the days of Frederick, it was not possible to wage *Vernichtungsstrategie*. When these circumstances prevailed, Delbrück hoped to show that means other than great battles must be used to win a war. Operations other than "large-scale battle," he termed "maneuver." These included occupying an enemy's territory, destruction of an enemy's commerce and trade (especially through blockade when possible), destruction of key industries and crops, and smaller military engagements. In between the two "poles" of pure maneuver and decisive battle, Delbrück placed "small-scale battles" (*Kleingefechte*) and "sieges of fortresses."[18] He believed that, depending upon circumstances prevailing at the time, commanders moved between the two poles of battle and maneuver.[19] When a commander possessed insufficient forces to pursue a *Vernichtungsstrategie*, victory, Delbrück wrote, "depends upon who is first exhausted, but not only who first reduces the strength of the enemy, but even more so who is better able 'to keep the last dollar in his purse.'"[20]

Thus, a commander following *Ermattungsstrategie* followed a variety of methods by which he compelled the enemy to do his will. "Large-scale battle" was only one, usually shunned, element. Occupation of enemy territory, destruction of enemy trade, and the wearing down of enemy forces through small battles took the place of great battles. Delbrück continually stressed that a commander was compelled by the conditions

[16] Delbrück, "Duplik," p. 308.

[17] See n. 25. "Perikles" was later published as a pamphlet. *Die Strategie des Perikles erläutert durch die Strategie Friedrichs des Grossen* (Berlin: Walter & Apoland, 1890).

[18] Delbrück, "Perikles," pp. 267–268.

[19] Ibid., p. 270. Hence, Delbrück's alternative name for *Ermattungsstrategie*, *die zweipolige Strategie*.

[20] Ibid.

of his time to fight one strategy or the other. To Delbrück, Frederick was a great captain because he realized the limitations imposed upon him by his age and fought intelligently within those limitations.[21] Thus, in developing his ideas about *Ermattungsstrategie*, Delbrück introduced the importance of context to strategic theory. He maintained that each "great captain" applied a particular strategic approach that fitted the capacities and constraints of his time. While Delbrück clearly believed that certain strategic concepts could be translated from one period of history to another, he warned, most dramatically in "Perikles," that to do so blindly would result in disaster.

* * *

The publication of "Perikles" marked the beginning of a new period in the *Strategiestreit* between Delbrück and his military critics.[22] In "Perikles," Delbrück elaborated fully for the first time his new interpretation of Clausewitz and his ideas about *Ermattungsstrategie*. In "Perikles," he linked *Ermattungsstrategie* not only to Frederick the Great, but to other historical figures as well. Delbrück tried to establish that *Ermattungsstrategie* was not limited to warfare of the eighteenth century but operated at other times as well – in short, that it was a strategic principle which could not simply be ignored by modern soldiers. "Perikles" drew even greater response from the military, and the debate expanded off the pages of specialist journals onto the pages of national newspapers. Delbrück's ideas were attacked by military writers in the *National-Zeitung*, the *Norddeutsche Allgemeine Zeitung*, the *Voßische Zeitung*, the *Dresdener Tageblatt*, and the *Straßburger Post*, to name some of the more prominent papers.[23] Contrary to the wishes of the soldiers, the expansion of the debate onto the pages of the national press brought Delbrück's ideas to a much wider audience than previously and merely prolonged the debate.[24]

Nowhere in the writings of the debate did Delbrück explicitly criticize the military's views on contemporary war. The debate always stuck rigidly to historical topics. However, Delbrück's analysis of Frederick's strategy and his new interpretation of Clausewitz threatened the military

[21] Hans Delbrück, "Die methodische Kriegführung Friedrichs des Grossen," *Preußische Jahrbücher* 54 (1884), p. 196.

[22] Lange also recognizes this date as the beginning of a new phase of the debate. However, he believes it is a separate phase because of the growing support for Delbrück's ideas. Lange, *Delbrück*, pp. 98–113.

[23] Clippings from these newspapers are contained in the Staatsbibliothek zu Berlin, Delbrück Nachlass, Folder 93/1.

[24] The debate was even picked up by foreign armies. See the Austro-Hungarian *Reichswehr*, 14 February 1892; and Spenser Wilkinson's "Recent German Military Literature," *United Services Magazine*, NS, 5 (1892), p. 668. It is clear from reading Wilkinson's survey, however, that he had not actually read Delbrück's works, only those of his opponents.

in two ways. First, by challenging the veracity of the army's historical interpretation, Delbrück called into question, albeit indirectly, its view of warfare. History played a crucial role in the Wilhelmine army, especially as officers with combat experience retired. Moltke the Elder himself put forward the view that "long-range strategy could be developed with common sense and knowledge of military history."[25] Accordingly, in 1890, military history stood second only to tactics in number of hours per week (four) in the curriculum of the Kriegsakademie, and the continuity between the wars of Frederick the Great, Napoleon, and Moltke was emphasised.[26] At the Kriegsakademie, and within the army in general, students applied historical examples to modern situations, a process called the applicatory method. Officers focused not on seeking historical truth but rather on examples which illustrated their current ideas. A prominent General Staff officer, Maximilian Yorck Graf von Wartenburg, wrote, "we study military history not to recapture historical events, nor to use the opportunity to repeat past occurrences . . . but to choose what is valuable to us and to say how it went and why."[27] Delbrück's questioning of a central figure of the army's interpretation of military history thus challenged their view of modern war. Friedrich von Bernhardi admitted as much in 1892, saying that Delbrück's writings represented a "judgment on modern strategy through historical research and public opinion."[28]

Delbrück, however, not only called into question the army's analysis of history but also the army's understanding of Clausewitz. This represented a more direct attack on their current approach toward war. After the Wars of Unification, Moltke had thrust Clausewitz into the center of German military thought, by declaring *On War* one of the greatest influences on

[25] Steven E. Clemente, *For King and Kaiser! The Making of the Prussian Army Officer, 1860–1914* (New York: Greenwood Press, 1992), p. 181.

[26] Ibid., pp. 179–180.

[27] Maximilian Graf Yorck von Wartenburg, *Napoleon als Feldherr* (2 vols.) (Berlin: E. S. Mittler, 1885), I, p. 1. Yorck, who served as military history instructor at the Kriegsakademie from 1897 to 1898, was tipped as a possible successor to Schlieffen but was killed during the Boxer Rebellion. Bernhard Schwertfeger, *Die grossen Erzieher des deutschen Heeres: Aus der Geschichte der Kriegsakademie* (Potsdam: Akademische Verlagsgesellschaft Athenaion, 1936), p. 138; Arden Bucholz, *Moltke, Schlieffen and Prussian War Planning* (Providence, RI: Berg, 1991), p. 188.

[28] Friedrich von Bernhardi, "Mittheilung zum Streit über die strategische Theorie und Praxis Friedrichs des Grossen," *Beilage zur Allgemeine Zeitung* 65 (1892), p. 6, quoted in Lange, *Delbrück*, p. 101. Bernhardi was later an instructor in military history at the Kriegsakademie and Chief of the Military History Section of the General Staff. Walter K. Nehring, "General der Kavallerie Friedrich von Bernhardi – Soldat und Militärwissenschaftler," in Dermont Bradley and Ulrich Marwedel, eds., *Militärgeschichte, Militärwissenschaft und Konfliktsforschung: Eine Festschrift für Werner Hahlweg* (Osnabrück: Biblio Verlag, 1977), pp. 295–308.

his life.[29] Indeed, however much he changed his approach afterwards, Moltke's direction of the campaigns in 1866 and 1870–71 owed much to his interpretation of Clausewitz's analysis of Napoleon's methods. After 1871, his reading of Clausewitz became the predominant view within the army, and *On War* was increasingly used by soldiers to support their own ideas about modern warfare.[30] By attacking the prevailing view of Clausewitz, Delbrück assailed one of the main theoretical underpinnings of German strategic thought.

Moreover, Delbrück applied his reasoning not only to historical events, but to contemporary affairs as well. Early in his career, Delbrück had drawn the distinction between the functions of a "military historian" and those of a "military commentator." He argued that a "military historian" had the task of merely presenting the facts of an event in the past and putting these events into a historical context. On the other hand, he believed that a "military commentator" had the obligation, when discussing historical events, not merely to tell what happened, but also to tell what should have been done – in other words, to draw lessons from history applicable to the present day.[31] Delbrück placed himself in the former category, and most studies of his thought have accepted his statement and have focused on his work as a historian.[32]

Delbrück, though, lived in a period of great international tension, as Europe went through a series of diplomatic crises and an arms race before World War I. As editor of *Preußische Jahrbücher*, he had the opportunity to comment on current affairs and on current military matters. Throughout the 1890s and the early 1900s, he published analyses on wars around the world and on the growing tension within Europe. These commentaries, as well as his reviews of works of military theory, placed Delbrück at the center of the various debates on contemporary strategy which were engaging the German military in the years before World War I. Further, these commentaries show that Delbrück believed his concept of

[29] Eberhard Kessel, *Moltke* (Stuttgart: K. F. Koehler, 1957), p. 108.

[30] See Antulio J. Echevarria II, "Borrowing from the Master: Uses of Clausewitz in German Military Literature before the Great War," *War in History* 3, 3 (1996), pp. 274–292.

[31] Delbrück outlined these categories in a review essay entitled "Clausewitz" in *Zeitschrift für Preußische Geschichte und Landeskunde* 15 (Mar.–Apr. 1878), pp. 217–231. A portion of this essay was translated and published by Peter Paret. Paret, "Hans Delbrück on Military Affairs." See also Felix Gilbert, "From Clausewitz to Delbrück and Hintze: Achievements and Failures of Military History," *Journal of Strategic Studies* 3, 3 (1980), pp. 11–20. While both Paret and Gilbert recognize Delbrück's role as a "military commentator," neither examines his analysis of contemporary events.

[32] Even Bucholz's recent translation of a number of Delbrück's columns from the *Preußische Jahrbücher* fails to make explicit the connection between his commentary on contemporary affairs and the *Strategiestreit*. See *Delbrück's Modern Military History* (ed. and trans. Arden Bucholz) (Lincoln: University of Nebraska Press, 1997).

Ermattungsstrategie was very applicable to contemporary affairs and demonstrate that, despite declaring himself a military historian, Delbrück also engaged in work as a military commentator.[33]

Delbrück saw quite early that the division of Europe into two opposing camps would make a future war extremely dangerous for Germany. In September 1897, he published a column in the *Preußische Jahrbücher* on this issue, in which he wrote of the strategic implications of the growing Anglo-German antagonism. To Delbrück, the recent war between Turkey and Greece had confirmed once again the strength of the two power blocs on the Continent. He wrote: "The two blocs, the Dual Alliance and the Triple Alliance, appear to be as far from each other as a decade ago."[34] However, Delbrück felt that the international situation was made all the more perilous by the growing Anglo-German antagonism over trade, which had just been exacerbated by Kaiser Wilhelm's ill-considered telegram to President Kruger of the Transvaal Republic. This antagonism made the prospect of a future war for Germany even more dangerous in Delbrück's opinion. While Germany had hoped Great Britain would fear a Russo-French victory more than a German victory, the situation was clearly changing. Growing German industrial and trade strength made Great Britain feel threatened. Wilhelm's telegram made the situation even worse and made the prospect of Great Britain entering into an alliance with the French and Russians in case of a general European war even more likely. In this essay, Delbrück wrote that if this came to pass the next war could very well be a long-drawn-out affair, writing "only the unthinking conclude that the next war will be short merely because the last ones were . . ." Having the British, with their great financial strength and their seapower, for an enemy would therefore be disastrous for Germany.[35]

In the wake of the Bosnian annexation crisis in 1908, Delbrück returned to this danger of a war stemming from the continuing Anglo-German tension. He declared the position of Great Britain to be crucial in deciding whether or not war was imminent in the wake of the crisis. Delbrück wrote, "England stands today as a special opponent and rival of the German Empire."[36] This condition had come

[33] Both Paret in his "Hans Delbrück on Military Affairs" and Felix Gilbert in his "From Clausewitz to Delbrück and Hintze" recognize Delbrück's role as a "military commentator." However, neither has examined his analysis of contemporary events.

[34] Hans Delbrück, "Auswärtige Politik; die hohen Staatsvisiten," *Preußische Jahrbücher* 90 (Oct.–Dec. 1897), p. 175.

[35] Ibid., pp. 176–177.

[36] Hans Delbrück, "Danger of War," in *Delbrück's Modern Military History*, p. 91 (originally published as "Kriegsgefahr," *Preußische Jahrbücher* 135 (Jan.–Mar. 1909), pp. 163–182).

about because the English people were "filled with fear and antipathy against Germany, and fear is perhaps the greatest cause of war throughout world history."[37] He was pessimistic about German chances if faced with war between Germany and Austria on one side and France, Russia, Italy, and Great Britain on the other. Delbrück again stressed that Germany could not count on winning a war quickly, feeling it would be impossible to defeat France before Russian troops posed a significant threat to Germany. While Delbrück felt that Germany and Austria might be able to hold their own in the field against their continental enemies, he feared with Britain in the war the conflict would develop into another Seven Years War, which would lay ruin to much of Europe.[38]

In the years leading up to World War I, Delbrück continued to give similar warnings about the course of a future general European war. For example, in December 1913 he wrote:

> France is so well armed that even in a struggle limited to Germany and France our success would be very hotly contested. Certainly we would defeat our western neighbor in the end, *but only after facing a long, tenacious resistance.* However, if we enter into a war against France, we will undoubtedly have to deal also with Russia and possibly also with England.[39]

While Delbrück did not shrink from the prospect of war, he obviously considered it to be a more difficult undertaking than many of his contemporaries. In general, he supported German armaments programs as a means of keeping the peace, but cautioned against going to war lightly.[40] In his December 1913 essay, Delbrück wrote that Germany should only contemplate war when there remained no other way to protect its national honor.[41]

In addition to commenting on the prospective course of a future war while examining the growing tensions in Europe, Delbrück wrote extensively on the course of various conflicts around the world. From these wars, like his contemporaries in the army, he drew conclusions about the possible course of a future European war. The first conflict to come under Delbrück's inspection was the Second Anglo-Boer War. In January 1900, Delbrück wrote, "the Boer War is not only politically an important event, but it also appears that it must also have a great effect on Europe's

[37] Ibid., p. 94. [38] Ibid., p. 97.

[39] Hans Delbrück, "Die Alldeutschen," *Preußische Jahrbücher* 154 (Oct.–Dec. 1913), p. 574; Paul Rohrbach, "Delbrück als Prophet," in Daniels and Rühlmann, *Am Webstuhl der Zeit*, p. 57. Emphasis added.

[40] For example, Hans Delbrück, "Die Armee-Reform"; "Die Armee-Vorlage"; and "Heeresstärken," in "Politische Correspondenz," *Preußische Jahrbücher* 70 (July–Dec. 1892).

[41] Delbrück, "Die Alldeutschen," p. 575.

armies . . ."[42] In this essay, he went on to examine General Sir Redvers Buller's actions at the battle of Colenso and to discuss what he saw as the failings in British strategy and training, as well as the danger of taking false lessons from the war.

Despite the success of the Boers in defensive battles, Delbrück believed that one should not conclude that the defensive had become the decisive form of warfare. Fighting in South Africa had shown clearly just how modern weapons had made overcoming a defender more difficult. However, like many of his contemporaries, Delbrück maintained that defensive action alone could not decide a battle; offensive action was still necessary to bring a battle to its conclusion. He believed that the experiences from South Africa showed that, given the power of modern weapons in defense, a combination of defensive and offensive action was needed to win battles in future wars. He wrote:

> The principle value of the offensive remains the same. However, where the offensive can no longer work, one must work toward a combination of the offensive and defensive, i.e., the commencement of the offensive at the moment the advantage of the defensive is exhausted.[43]

The task of the modern general was to know when that crucial moment had come.

The Russo-Japanese War offered Delbrück another opportunity to comment on contemporary warfare and strategy. After the initial encounters of the war, Delbrück wrote that the Russian commander, General Alexei Kuropatkin, was obviously not up to date with modern warfare. Delbrück felt Kuropatkin should fight a war based on the operational ideas of Moltke, i.e., the Russians should launch a concerted attack against the Japanese on more than one front at a time.[44] Further, he argued that the Russians had not learned the importance of firepower and relied too greatly on the bayonet.[45] As the war wore on, the lack of decisive battles surprised Delbrück, and this caused him to raise the idea that perhaps the age of *Ermattungsstrategie* had returned. Delbrück made the point that neither the Japanese nor the Russians seemed to have the ability to exploit any battlefield victory they might achieve. In his opinion, if this condition continued, the war would be decided, as in the time of

[42] Delbrück, "Die Lehren des Transvaal-Krieges," *Preußische Jahrbücher* 99 (Jan.–Mar. 1900), p. 366.

[43] Ibid., p. 372.

[44] Delbrück cited Rudolph von Caemmerer's *Die Entwicklung der strategischen Wissenschaft im 19. Jahrhundert* (Berlin: Wilhelm Baensch, 1904) as his source for the correct interpretation of Moltke's strategic ideas. "Der Krieg," *Preußische Jahrbücher* 118 (Oct.–Dec. 1904), p. 557.

[45] Hans Delbrück, "Die Schlacht bei Mukden," *Preußische Jahrbücher* 120 (Apr.–June 1905), pp. 176–177.

Frederick, "by the side which has the 'last dollar in the wallet' [*wer den letzten Taler in der Tasche behält*], by the side which can maintain half a million soldiers in the field the longest."[46]

Even before the Russo-Japanese War, Delbrück, in a lengthy review of Ivan Bloch's *The Future of War*, had raised the idea that a return to the days of *Ermattungsstrategie* might be imminent. In general, he rejected Bloch's thesis, believing it still possible to wage war in pursuit of national goals. Delbrück did, however, raise the question of whether future wars would be decided by one or a few great battles, as was believed by his military contemporaries. In doing so he wondered whether a return to the style of warfare dominant in the eighteenth century, i.e., *Ermattungsstrategie*, was likely in the future. He wrote:

> It falls upon the commander to decide whether the basic law of war, the forceful annihilation of the enemy forces, operates any longer today. In the end, theory cannot easily solve problems like this; they can only be solved by experience. However, if we accept that Bloch is correct, the impossibility, or better said the uselessness, of battle in warfare would in no way be proved. We would only be returned to the standpoint of the strategy of the 16th to 18th century . . . and one would seek by means of small-scale battles to come to the gradual exhaustion of the enemy. . . .[47]

* * *

Contrary to Delbrück's own statements that his views on *Ermattungsstrategie* should be considered purely of historical interest, his writings on contemporary affairs in his column in the *Preußische Jahrbücher* show Delbrück applying his ideas about strategy to current affairs. Like Moltke, Delbrück increasingly feared the consequences of a general European war. As Europe went through a series of diplomatic crises in the years before 1914, he concluded, like Colmar von der Goltz, that the next war would not be won as quickly as the Wars of Unification; the forces arrayed made such a result impossible. Instead, he came to believe the next war would be long and characterized by the lack of decisive battles – much like Frederick the Great's Seven Years War.

Delbrück's commentary on international affairs was complemented by his analysis of the various wars that took place before World War I.

[46] Hans Delbrück, "Der Krieg," *Preußische Jahrbücher* 120 (Apr.–June 1905), p. 560. Delbrück had used exactly this phrase – "wer den letzten Taler in der Tasche behält" – in describing Frederick's strategy. See "Perikles," p. 270. Intriguingly, Alfred von Schlieffen expressed his opinion similarly. Schlieffen to Bernhard von Bülow, 27 March 1905, quoted in Heiner Raulff, *Zwischen Machtpolitik und Imperialismus: Die deutsche Frankreichpolitik 1904–05* (Düsseldorf: Droste, 1976), p. 128.

[47] Hans Delbrück, "Zukunftskrieg und Zukunftsfriede," *Preußische Jahrbücher* 96 (1899), p. 215.

Delbrück paid particularly close attention to how modern weapons and the size of modern armies changed the nature of war. While examining the Second Anglo-Boer War, Delbrück was inclined to discount the revolutionary effect of modern weapons. The Russo-Japanese War, however, showed quite clearly how warfare had changed from the 1870s. In Manchuria, despite winning great battles (at Mukden, the Japanese inflicted about 100,000 casualties upon the Russians, or one-third of the Russian forces involved), the Japanese were unable to bring about the complete defeat of the Russians. This caused Delbrück to question seriously whether or not in the immediate future Great Powers could be defeated decisively on the battlefield. Events on battlefields around the world reinforced Delbrück's belief that wars of the future might be wars of exhaustion, where the power, or power bloc, with greater resources would be able to stay the course longest and, hence, be winner by default.

The military response

The reaction of military intellectuals to Delbrück's ideas was far from the uniform front portrayed by most accounts.[48] As Delbrück's critique of the military took place on two levels, so did the military response. One school, by far the largest, attacked both Delbrück's historical and theoretical critiques. After the publication of "Perikles," Friedrich von Bernhardi spearheaded this school.[49] In 1892, Bernhardi published a work in which he rejected both Delbrück's historical interpretation and his views on Clausewitz.[50] In his memoirs, Bernhardi wrote that he attacked Delbrück because "at the time there lay the danger that unquestioning people [*urteilslose Menschen*] might be dazzled by the originality of [Delbrück's] opinions."[51]

Another school within the army accepted, to a certain degree, Delbrück's historical analysis, but had difficulties with his strategic

[48] Arden Bucholz's *Delbrück* and Gordon Craig's "Delbrück: The Military Historian," in Peter Paret, ed., *Makers of Modern Strategy from Machiavelli to the Nuclear Age* (Princeton: Princeton University Press, 1986), pp. 326–353, tend to portray Delbrück's military opponents as a uniform bloc. The most recent and thorough account of the *Strategiestreit*, Lange's *Delbrück*, is somewhat more nuanced but still falls into the same pattern.

[49] At the time, Bernhardi was in charge of the General Staff's history of Frederick's 1742 campaigns; published as Grosser Generalstab, *Die Kriege Friedrichs des Grossen: Der Erste Schlesische Krieg, 1740–1742* (2 vols.) (Berlin: E. S. Mittler, 1892–93). Other members of this school include Alfred von Boguslawski and Wilhelm Scherff.

[50] Friedrich von Bernhardi, *Delbrück, Friedrich der Grosse und Clausewitz. Streiflichter auf die Lehren des Professor Dr. Delbrück über Strategie* (Berlin: E. S. Mittler, 1892).

[51] Friedrich von Bernhardi, *Denkwürdigkeiten aus meinem Leben* (Berlin: E. S. Mittler, 1927), p. 143.

interpretations. Rudolph von Caemmerer was one example of this group.[52] Caemmerer represented a school within the German army (headed by Sigismund von Schlichting) that accepted the periodization of military history. To them, the German Wars of Unification represented a new strategic era, dominated by the ideas of Moltke rather than Napoleon.[53] In their view, improvements in technology and the increased size of armies between the Napoleonic Wars and the Wars of Unification changed the strategic conditions so much that one could not speak of Napoleon and Moltke following the same strategic approach. This view was heavily attacked by many other military writers.[54] Delbrück's periodization of military history offered reinforcement to their own interpretation. While Caemmerer could accept Delbrück's analysis of history, he rejected Delbrück's interpretation of Clausewitz, believing that Delbrück had read too much into Clausewitz. Caemmerer believed that Clausewitz wrote *On War* as a practical tool for contemporary and future soldiers and statesmen. Delbrück, on the other hand, believed that Clausewitz intended his book to be a dialectic work which explained the nature of war throughout the ages.[55]

This second school had two other important members, Max Jähns and Reinhold Koser. In 1891, Jähns, a former instructor at the Kriegsakademie, published the third volume of his influential *Geschichte der Kriegswissenschaft*.[56] In this work, Jähns virtually agreed with Delbrück's historical interpretation of Frederick. He wrote that Frederick, although he had attempted to follow *Vernichtungsstrategie* in his early campaigns, had been forced by the circumstances of his time to abandon such an approach to war.[57] Another member of the Kriegsakademie

[52] Another member of this school was Fritz Hoenig. See his "Die ein- und zweipolige Strategie," *Deutsche Heeres-Zeitung* 70, 18 and 19 (1892). Cf. Lange, *Delbrück*, p. 106.

[53] Sigismund von Schlichting's *Taktische und strategische Grundsätze der Gegenwart* (3 vols.) (Berlin: E. S. Mittler, 1898–99) and Caemmerer, *Die Entwicklung der strategischen Wissenschaft* are the prime works of this school. Indeed, Delbrück himself largely accepted Schlichting's views on modern strategy.

[54] See Antulio J. Echevarria, "Neo-Clausewitzianism: Freytag-Loringhoven and the Militarization of Clausewitz in German Military Literature Before the First World War" (Princeton University, Ph.D. Thesis, 1994); and Daniel Hughes, "Schlichting, Schlieffen, and the Prussian Theory of War in 1914," *Journal of Military History* 59 (April 1995), pp. 257–278.

[55] Hans Delbrück, Review of *Die Entwicklung der strategischen Wissenschaft im 19. Jahrhundert*, *Preußische Jahrbücher* 115 (1904), pp. 347–348.

[56] Max Jähns, *Geschichte der Kriegswissenschaft*, III: *Das XVII. Jahrhundert seit dem Auftreten Friedrichs des Grossen* (Munich: R. Oldenbourg, 1891). Lange views the publication of Jähns' book as the beginning of a new phase of the *Strategiestreit* because it represented a break in the ranks of the military. Lange, *Delbrück*, p. 98.

[57] Jähns, *Geschichte der Kriegswissenschaft*, III, pp. 2017–2031. The similarities between Jähn's interpretation and Delbrück's were noted by Gustav Roloff in "Eine vermeintliche neue Auffassung der Strategie Friedrichs des Grossen," *Beilage zur Allgemeine Zeitung* 16 (1892), pp. 1–4.

staff, Reinhold Koser, began in 1904 to publish a number of works on Frederick which also came close to accepting Delbrück's historical interpretations.[58] Both authors, however, steadfastly rejected the idea that their interpretations of Frederick were identical to Delbrück's, in large part because they rejected Delbrück's strategic interpretation.[59]

In the end, the writings of Caemmerer, Jähns, and Koser proved that Delbrück's interpretation of Frederick had achieved a degree of grudging acceptance from many military intellectuals.[60] Delbrück's interpretation of Clausewitz and his *Ermattungsstrategie*, however, continued to be rejected by military writers. While some officers, most notably Jähns and Koser, came close to confirming Delbrück's beliefs about Frederick, they refused to become closely associated with them because of Delbrück's strategic ideas. Others, such as Caemmerer and Hoenig, accepted in principle Delbrück's periodization of military history but also continued to reject his strategic interpretation. In the end, the debate was brought to a close by World War I. Delbrück's ideas remained disputed but had begun to achieve a degree of acceptance from a skeptical military.

Conclusion

Although Hans Delbrück claimed to be merely a military historian and not a military commentator, his long-running debate with the intellectuals of the Wilhelmine army and his analysis of contemporary affairs in the *Preußische Jahrbücher* proved this assertion to be false. His unique interpretation of the wars of Frederick the Great led him to define a strategic system that was at odds with the view prevalent in the army at the time. Delbrück attempted in his writings to show that the strategy chosen by a *Feldherr* was dictated by the conditions of his time rather than his military genius. Thus, Frederick followed a strategy that was designed not to overthrow his opponents in great battles, as Napoleon and Moltke would do in the nineteenth century, but to wear down his enemy's ability and will to continue the war through a series of actions. To Frederick, the occupation of an enemy province would be at times of far greater value than a victorious battle. Delbrück called this strategy *Ermattungsstrategie*, a name, with its connotations of weakness, that was guaranteed to put off the military.

58 Reinhold Koser, *Die Geschichte Friedrichs des Grossen* (4 vols.) (Berlin: Cotta, 1914); Koser, "Die preussische Kriegsführung im Siebenjährigen Kriege," *Historische Zeitschrift* 92 (1903), pp. 239–273.

59 Max Jähns, "Über den Wandel der strategischen Anschauungen Friedrichs des Grossen," *Allgemeine Zeitung*, 23 February 1892, pp. 4–7; Reinhold Koser, "Zusatz," *Historische Zeitschrift* 93 (1904), pp. 456–458.

60 Lange, *Delbrück*, p. 98.

Delbrück went much further than challenging the military's interpretation of Frederick the Great. He also questioned their reading of Clausewitz, whose *On War* served as the intellectual basis for their view of *Vernichtungsstrategie* since it was brought to prominence by Moltke the Elder. Delbrück claimed to have derived his concept of *Ermattungsstrategie* from Clausewitz's writings. If his strident criticisms of the army's view of Frederick was not enough to set military writers against him, his view of Clausewitz offered a direct challenge to the military's competence that could not be ignored.

Delbrück also turned his penetrating eye to contemporary affairs in his column in the *Preußische Jahrbücher.* Reading these columns shows several important things. First, Delbrück's analysis of the alliance system in Europe led him to believe that a general European war could not be won quickly. By the early years of the twentieth century, he recognized that the size of armies involved would prohibit a rapid, decisive victory. Further, with Great Britain allied with Germany's enemies, Germany would face the difficulties of naval blockade as well as an indecisive land conflict. With this being the case, Delbrück feared the consequences of any war. These conclusions were reinforced by his analysis of contemporary conflicts. The course of the Anglo-Boer War and of the Russo-Japanese War provided further worrying evidence about the course of future conflicts. Although he was always careful in how he phrased it, Delbrück believed that a future war would in all likelihood require Germany to follow a strategy of attrition much like Frederick had been forced to do in the Seven Years War.

The effects of Delbrück's thirty-five-year *Strategiestreit* with the intellectuals of the Wilhelmine army are of course difficult to measure. The debate certainly achieved prominence in pre-World War I Germany and beyond. By the early 1890s, it had spilled from specialized journals to the pages of national newspapers and it had involved most of Germany's important military intellectuals. Additionally, it is clear from the files of Delbrück's correspondence that he carried on his debates in private as well as in public with a good number of German officers.[61] Further, the debate coincided with the growing doubts of some of Germany's strategic planners, most notably Moltke the Elder and Moltke the Younger. While it is clear that by the outbreak of World War I Delbrück had brought a number of writers around to his side, especially regarding his historical

61 The Delbrück Nachlass at the Staatsbibliothek zu Berlin contains letters from Paul Bronsart von Schellendorf, Rudolph von Caemmerer, Colmar von der Goltz, Fritz Hoenig, Max Jähns, Egon von Gayl, Sigismund von Schlichting, and Alfred von Schlieffen to name a few of the more prominent. See Horst Wolf, *Der Nachlaß Hans Delbrück* (Berlin: Deutsche Staatsbibliothek, 1980).

analysis, many opponents still existed. Even with doubts, however, the German military on the whole was not ready to jettison its reliance on great battles to destroy their opponents, and could not ultimately see beyond this aspect of Delbrück's *Ermattungsstrategie*.

There were a number of important consequences of this debate. First, it forced the German army as a whole to re-examine its assumptions about warfare. Even if they rejected most of Delbrück's analysis, they were nevertheless exposed to an opposing point of view. That Delbrück was allowed to voice his opinions in army journals shows that at least some soldiers believed the debate was a worthwhile exercise.[62] Further, this debate prepared the groundwork for an intellectual shift that had to take place after the failure of Germany's short-war strategy in 1914. Many of Delbrück's concepts, combined with the ideas of Moltke the Elder and Goltz, would resurface in the strategy of Erich von Falkenhayn during his tenure as Chief of the General Staff.

[62] In 1887, "*Premierlieutenant a.D.*" Hans Delbrück published an essay on Frederick the Great in a supplement to the General Staff's official journal. "Über den Feldzugsplan Friedrichs des Grossen im Jahre 1757," *Beiheft zum Militär-Wochenblatt* 1887.

3 The short-war belief

More than ninety years after his death, Generalfeldmarschall Alfred Graf von Schlieffen remains one of Imperial Germany's most intriguing figures. Schlieffen's fifteen years as Chief of the Great General Staff left his stamp not just on the *Kaiserheer* but also on the Reichswehr and the Wehrmacht. Despite never having written a comprehensive work of theory (his ideas are scattered throughout his official documents and in a few short articles published after his retirement), he has inspired countless books and articles in support of his ideas and many which argue that his theories brought ruin to Germany and much of Europe. Certainly, few personalities in Wilhelmine Germany have provoked as much ink, and as much acrimony, as Alfred von Schlieffen.

Following World War I, the memory of Schlieffen and his strategic ideas was elevated to almost mythic heights. (Culminating, perhaps, with the foundation of a *Schlieffenverein* in 1921.[1]) Many of the officers who had served under Schlieffen felt that had the German army followed his teachings during the war, defeat would not have occurred. The books written by these men in the interwar period aimed at propagating their interpretation of Schlieffen's ideas, with the aim of preventing another occurrence of the stalemate and defeat of World War I. That many of these officers had risen to great prominence during war lent credence to their assertions.[2] After the war, Schlieffen was venerated as "one of the greatest soldiers who had ever lived."[3]

[1] "Satzungen der Vereins der Angehörigen des ehemaligen Generalstabes," 22 February 1921; and "Bericht über die erste Zusammenkunst der Vereinigung Graf Schlieffen," 16 March 1921 in BA/MA, Wilhelm Dommes Nachlass, N512/14.

[2] For examples of this work, see Wilhelm Groener, *Das Testament des Grafen Schlieffen* (Berlin: E. S. Mittler, 1927); Groener, *Der Feldherr wider Willen: Operative Studien über den Weltkrieg* (Berlin: E. S. Mittler, 1931); Wolfgang Foerster, *Graf Schlieffen und der Weltkrieg* (Berlin: E. S. Mittler, 1925); Foerster, *Aus der Gedankenwerkstatt des Deutschen Generalstabes* (Berlin: E. S. Mittler, 1931); and Eugen Ritter von Zoellner, "Schlieffens Vermächtnis," *Militär-Wissenschaftliche Rundschau*, Special Issue (1938).

[3] Erich Ludendorff, *Meine Kriegserinnerungen 1914–1918* (Berlin: E. S. Mittler, 1919), p. 18.

In reaction to these hagiographical studies, accepted opinion of Schlieffen and his ideas swung in the opposite direction. In 1956, Gerhard Ritter published his study of the Schlieffen plan, which he subtitled *Critique of a Myth.*[4] Jehuda Wallach followed with his even more biting critique in 1967.[5] Both men saw Schlieffen as dogmatic and blind to the strategic realities of his day. They place upon him, as the author of the famous "Schlieffen Plan," the blame for Germany's adherence to the short-war belief. It is these critical interpretations of Ritter and Wallach that today represent the "accepted" view of Schlieffen.[6]

Yet despite the volumes written about him (or perhaps because of), Schlieffen and his strategic ideas remain in many ways paradoxical. For instance, Schlieffen and his followers adamantly denied that he sought to establish a school of his own within military theory. As late as the 1960s, German historians found it necessary to establish that a distinct Schlieffen school of thought existed.[7] However, his ideas clearly influenced a generation of General Staff officers. Through his staff rides and tactical problems, he tried to inculcate the officers of the General Staff with a type of "system," which promised, if it was followed, victory. Additionally, his infamous plan called for the *Feldherr* to exercise firm control over the *Feldheer.* Yet in his staff rides and autumn maneuvers, Schlieffen consistently allowed junior officers freedom of action to act as they saw fit. And last, the Schlieffen Plan called for an immediate offensive at the war's outbreak. While in his last *Kriegsspiel,* Schlieffen displayed restraint and stood on the defensive until the enemies' plans became clear, rather than rushing headlong into the offensive.

4 Gerhard Ritter, *Der Schlieffenplan: Kritik eines Mythos* (Munich: R. Oldenbourg, 1956). Published in English as *The Schlieffen Plan: Critique of a Myth* (London: Oswald Wolff, 1958).

5 Jehuda L. Wallach, *Das Dogma der Vernichtungsschlacht: Die Lehren von Clausewitz und Schlieffen und ihre Wirkungen in zwei Weltkriegen* (Frankfurt: Bernard und Graefe, 1967). Published in English as *The Dogma of the Battle of Annihilation: The Theories of Clausewitz and Schlieffen and their Impact on the German Conduct of Two World Wars* (Westport, CT: Greenwood Press, 1986).

6 For similar views, see Jay Luvaas, "European Military Thought and Doctrine, 1870–1914," in Michael Howard, ed., *The Theory and Practice of War* (London: Cassell, 1965), pp. 71–77; L. L. Farrar, Jr., "The Short War Illusion: The Syndrome of German Strategy, August–December, 1914," *Militärgeschichtliche Mitteilungen* 2 (1972), pp. 39–52; Martin Kitchen, "The Traditions of German Strategic Thought," *International History Review* 1, 2 (1979), pp. 163–190; Stephan van Evera, "The Cult of the Offensive and the Origins of the First World War," *International Security* 9, 1 (1984), pp. 58–107; Gunther Rothenberg, "Moltke, Schlieffen, and the Doctrine of Strategic Envelopment," in Peter Paret, ed., *The Makers of Modern Strategy* (Princeton: Princeton University Press, 1986), pp. 296–325; Holger Herwig, *The First World War: Germany and Austria-Hungary, 1914–1918* (London: Arnold, 1997), pp. 46–52.

7 See Emanuel von Kiliani, "Die Operationslehre des Grafen von Schlieffen und ihre deutschen Gegner," *Wehrkunde* 10 (1961), pp. 71–76, 133–138.

Fig. 2 Alfred Graf von Schlieffen, author of Germany's war plan

Perhaps most intriguing, however, was his continued adherence to the belief that Germany could fight and win a short war. The evidence that the changing nature of warfare was having a great impact on how future war would be conducted was overwhelming by the end of the nineteenth century. As we have seen, the fears of a future *Volkskrieg* had a profound influence on Helmuth von Moltke the Elder and his war plans. Moltke's suspicions were reinforced by the writings of a number of other military intellectuals, who painted a picture of future war not being won by the traditional means of one or two great "decisive" battles, but rather through a long-drawn-out struggle that would only end with the complete exhaustion of one of the belligerents. It was clear to astute observers before 1914 that the traditional German strategic approach, *Vernichtungsstrategie*, needed to be replaced by something else and that German operational doctrine needed to be updated. However, despite all this, Moltke the Elder's successors as Chief of the General Staff remained committed to *Vernichtungsstrategie* and the belief that a future war could be won quickly. This belief was reflected in the plans drawn up by Schlieffen and Moltke the Younger and put into practice in August 1914. Why, despite the evidence of the second phase of the Franco-German War and the critiques offered by Hans Delbrück, did Schlieffen and Moltke the Younger not come up with plans that reflected Germany's strategic realities more accurately?

Schlieffen and Germany's strategic situation

Germany's strategic situation worsened as Alfred von Schlieffen took over as Chief of the Great General Staff in 1892. Just as Schlieffen took up his duties, France and Russia signed a military convention that obligated one to come to the aid of the other if attacked by Germany.[8] Although Moltke the Elder had thought such an alliance likely since the end of the Franco-German War, Otto von Bismarck's complex system of alliances had kept the possibility from becoming a concrete reality.[9] Now, with Bismarck gone, Germany's foreign policy degenerated, and Germany let slip the opportunity to renew the Reinsurance Treaty with Russia that

[8] The convention pledged France to deploy an army of 1.3 million troops against Germany, while Russia was to deploy 700,000–800,000 against Germany by the 14th mobilization day. See George F. Kennan, *The Fateful Alliance: France, Russia and the Coming of the First World War* (Manchester: Manchester University Press, 1984), esp. pp. 271–272, and William C. Fuller, *Strategy and Power in Russia 1600–1914* (New York: The Free Press, 1992), pp. 350–362.

[9] See Wolfgang Mommsen, *Grossmachtstellung und Weltpolitik: Die Aussenpolitik des Deutschen Reiches, 1870–1914* (Frankfurt: Ullstein, 1993).

would have kept Russia and France apart.[10] Where Moltke had to make contingency plans, Schlieffen now had to make definite plans for a war on two fronts against enemies superior in number to the German army.

To counter the Franco-Russian alliance, Germany could count on the support of two allies – Austria-Hungary and Italy – with whom Germany had formed the Triple Alliance in 1882.[11] However, Schlieffen did not have high hopes for aid from either country. Italy was never a firm member of the alliance, and although plans were made to transport three Italian army corps to the Franco-German border in the event of war, Schlieffen never really believed that this help would be forthcoming.[12] He also did not expect much from Austria-Hungary. The German General Staff Chief never really believed the relatively small Austro-Hungarian army to be effective, and regardless, it would have enough to do to look after itself against the Russians.[13]

Even with aid from Germany's allies, Schlieffen still expected the conditions under which the war would be fought to be very unfavorable for the German army. In 1892, Schlieffen calculated that the *Kaiserheer* would be outnumbered by its foes five to three.[14] Moreover, both the French and the Russians possessed powerful fortresses behind which their armies could shelter.[15] Early in his time as Chief of the General Staff, Schlieffen came to the conclusion that an offensive in the east against Russia stood little chance of bringing about a rapid victory.[16] In addition to the difficulty of breaching the Russian fortress line, Schlieffen felt that it would be extremely difficult to force the Russian army into a "decisive" battle. First, Schlieffen reasoned that a combined Austrian and German pincer attack on the salient of Russian Poland stood little chance of encircling

[10] Rainer Lahme, *Deutsche Aussenpolitik, 1880–1894. Von Gleichgewichtspolitik Bismarcks zur Allianzstrategie Caprivis* (Göttingen: Vandenhoeck & Ruprecht, 1990), pp. 100ff.

[11] Germany had formed an alliance with Austria-Hungary in October 1879 and this had been enlarged to include Italy in 1882.

[12] Schlieffen assumed that at best the Italian army would tie down one-tenth of the French army at the outbreak of war. However, he did not believe that Italy would live up to its treaty obligations. Alfred von Schlieffen to his sister Marie, 13 November 1892, reprinted in Alfred von Schlieffen, *Briefe* (ed. Eberhard Kessel) (Göttingen: Vandenhoeck & Ruprecht, 1958), p. 296.

[13] As a consequence of his doubts about the Austrians, Schlieffen did not enjoy good relations with their General Staff. See Lothar Höbett, "Schlieffen, Beck, Potiorek und das Ende der gemeinsamen deutsch-österreichisch-ungarischen Aufmarschpläne im Osten," *Militärgeschichtliche Mitteilungen* 12 (1984), pp. 7–30.

[14] See Schlieffen to his sister Marie, 13 November 1892, in Schlieffen, *Briefe*, p. 296.

[15] See Albert Grabau, *Das Festungsproblem in Deutschland und seine Auswirkung auf die strategische Lage von 1870–1914* (Berlin: Junker und Dünnhaupt, 1935).

[16] Ritter, *Schlieffen Plan*, pp. 23–24; Foerster, *Gedankenwerkstatt*, pp. 25–26; Helmuth Otto, *Schlieffen und der Generalstab: Der preussisch-deutsche Generalstab unter der Leitung des Generals von Schlieffen 1891–1905* (East Berlin: Deutscher Militärverlag, 1966), pp. 150–162.

the Russians because the two advancing wings would be too widely separated. Consequently, the Russians could simply withdraw their troops. Further, the Russians would be withdrawing toward their supply base while the Austro-German force would be getting further away from their bases.[17]

However, the situation in the west was different. There, the French army was not as large as its Russian counterpart and it did not possess the space available in Russia. Circumstances there offered some scope for a repetition of Moltke the Elder's victories of 1870. However, there were problems with this. Following their defeat in the Franco-German War, the French had gone to great lengths to fortify their border with Germany.[18] Already in 1879, Moltke the Elder complained that this "hermetically sealed" border would make a German breakthrough extremely costly.[19] The French had adopted a defensive strategy and intended to wait behind their strong border fortifications for a German offensive.[20] This meant that, in order to defeat the French, the Germans would have to advance into France. The French forts, however, ensured that a breakthrough would take time, a luxury Germany did not possess after the Franco-Russian Military Convention of 1892. While the German army was occupied breaking through the fortified border, the Russian army would have the time to mobilize and fall upon the vulnerable German rear. Even if the German army could break through quickly, it would still take time to defeat the French army in the field, again allowing the Russians sufficient time to invade from the east.

In 1895, Generalmajor Martin Köpke, an *Oberquartiermeister* in the General Staff, wrote a memorandum assessing the problems of a war against France. Köpke's report echoed many of the fears of his predecessors in the General Staff like Moltke the Elder and Colmar von der Goltz. He recognized the difficulties the Germans would face in breaking through the fortified French border and believed that the attackers

[17] [Wilhelm] Dieckmann, "Der Schlieffenplan," unpublished manuscript in BA/MA, W10/50220, pp. 10–11; Foerster, *Gedankenwerkstatt*, p. 49; Dennis Showalter, "The Eastern Front and German Military Planning, 1871–1914 – Some Observations," *East European Quarterly* 15, 2 (1981), pp. 168–170.

[18] See Guy Le Hallé, *Le système Séré de Rivières ou le témoignage des Pierres* (Louvier: Ysec, 2001).

[19] Kaiser Wilhelm I to Bismarck, 2 October 1879, reprinted in Ferdinand von Schmerfeld, ed., *Graf Moltke. Die Aufmarschpläne 1871–1890* (Berlin: E. S. Mittler, 1929), p. 80.

[20] Ritter wrote that "Schlieffen guessed the enemy's intentions with astonishing accuracy" in 1905. Ritter, *Schlieffen Plan*, p. 42. In fact, German intelligence had obtained portions of the French deployment plans, which gave them an accurate picture of Plans XIV and XV (1898–1906). Helmuth Greiner, "Welche Nachrichten besass der deut. GGS über Mobilmachung und Aufmarsch des franz. Heeres in den Jahren 1885–1914," unpublished manuscript in BA/MA, W10/50267.

could only expect minor successes after expending great effort over a long period of time. Given the strategic situation, Köpke was pessimistic about German chances in a future war, writing:

> the signs show clearly enough that a future war will look very different from that of 1870/71. We cannot expect rapid victories with decisive effect . . . Large-scale position warfare, battles with long, well-fortified fronts, sieges of large fortified areas must be victoriously conducted, or else we will not be able to achieve a victory over the French. Hopefully, we will not be deficient in the necessary preparations, both in the intellectual and the material senses, and we will be well trained and well armed for these forms of warfare when the decisive moment comes.[21]

The long-drawn-out war predicted by the likes of Köpke, Moltke the Elder, and Goltz was just the thing that Schlieffen believed Germany could not win. Schlieffen firmly believed that in such a war the superior resources of Germany's enemies must come to be decisive. Moreover, like Moltke, Schlieffen feared the effect of a long war on the social structure of Germany, and believed that the demands of modern war would cause Germany's economic and social system to collapse if a war continued for too long.[22] He believed that a long war such as the Russo-Japanese War would be unthinkable in Western Europe:

> such a war is impossible today, when the existence of a nation is founded upon an unbroken flow of trade and industry and when the gears that have been brought to a halt must be brought back into motion by the means of a rapid decision [*eine rasche Entscheidung*]. A strategy of exhaustion [*Ermattungsstrategie*] is impossible when the maintenance of millions necessitates the expenditure of milliards.[23]

Thus, to Schlieffen, Germany's next war would *have* to be solved by the traditional German means of victory – a great battle that annihilated the enemy's armed forces and allowed Germany to dictate peace to a defenseless enemy.

Until his retirement in 1906, Schlieffen struggled to find a satisfactory way out of this strategic dilemma. However, Schlieffen was in an even worse position than Moltke the Elder to solve the problem of a future *Volkskrieg*. The victor of Königgrätz and Sedan could call upon his substantial reputation as a strategist to push his ideas through the

[21] Martin Köpke, "Eine deutsche Offensive gegen Frankreich nach ihren Bedingungen, Richtungen und Aussichten," August 1895, quoted in Dieckmann, "Schlieffenplan," p. 55. This passage was also quoted in Stig Förster, "Der deutsche Generalstab und die Illusion des kurzen Krieges, 1871–1914. Metakritik eines Mythos," *Militärgeschichtliche Mitteilungen* 54 (1995), p. 75.

[22] See Schlieffen, "Kriegsspiel 1905," in Robert T. Foley, ed., *Alfred von Schlieffen's Military Writings* (London: Frank Cass, 2002), p. 126; Ritter, *Schlieffen Plan*, pp. 46–47.

[23] Schlieffen, "War Today," in Foley, *Schlieffen's Military Writings*, p. 200.

complex system of competing bureaucracies that was the government of Imperial Germany.[24] Indeed, during his tenure as Chief of the General Staff, Moltke the Elder was quite successful at expanding the remit and authority of the General Staff.[25] Schlieffen, however, suffered from the damage done to the political position of the General Staff by the activities of his immediate predecessor, Alfred von Waldersee.[26] Waldersee had used his position to gain personal political power, and when he was removed from his office, rival institutions grasped the opportunity to clip the wings of the General Staff.[27] In part, Schlieffen's appointment was due to the fact that he was seen as a safe choice to succeed the troublesome Waldersee. The relatively junior Schlieffen was not well known outside a small circle within the General Staff, and he had few interests outside the army.[28] Thus, Schlieffen came to the position at a political disadvantage. Not only did the influence of other organizations increase *vis-à-vis* the General Staff, but he also commanded no real following with the army or the government.[29]

The political weakening of the General Staff and his relative obscurity made it more difficult for Schlieffen to face the challenges of Germany's worsening strategic situation. The fragmented and competitive nature of the Imperial German governmental system made any attempt to develop a German grand strategy challenging. There was no body that attempted to coordinate foreign, domestic, and defense policy. Thus, while the General Staff developed Germany's war plans, it did so in a political vacuum, without formal consultation with the civil political authorities.[30] This systemic weakness was exacerbated by Schlieffen's political weakness and his

[24] Eberhard Kessel, *Moltke* (Stuttgart: K. F. Koehler, 1957), pp. 646ff.

[25] Arden Bucholz, *Moltke, Schlieffen and Prussian War Planning* (Oxford: Berg, 1993), pp. 58–93.

[26] On Waldersee's machinations, see Walter Goerlitz, *History of the German General Staff, 1657–1945* (trans. Brian Battershaw) (New York: Praeger, 1957), pp. 103–126.

[27] Upon taking up his position, Schlieffen was required to reprimand Waldersee's lieutenants publicly, a clear signal that other institutions were calling the shots. Schlieffen, *Briefe*, pp. 291–292; and Alfred Graf von Waldersee, *Denkwürdigkeiten des General-Feldmarschalls Alfred Graf von Waldersee* (ed. Heinrich Otto Meisner) (3 vols.) (Stuttgart: Deutsche Verlags-Anstalt, 1923), II, p. 189.

[28] See Goerlitz, *General Staff*, pp. 127–142; and Hugo Rochs, *Schlieffen* (3rd ed.; Berlin: Vossische Buchhandlung, 1926), pp. 13ff. Also, given the number of Schlieffen's relatives who were high-ranking officials within the Reich's bureaucracy, Schlieffen was seen as politically reliable. See Eberhard Kessel, "Einleitung," to Schlieffen, *Briefe*, pp. 28ff.; and Bucholz, *Prussian War Planning*, pp. 109ff.

[29] Foley, *Schlieffen's Military Writings*, pp. xviii–xxii.

[30] Gerhard Ritter, *The Sword and the Scepter: The Problem of Militarism in Germany*, vol. II: *The European Powers and the Wilhelmine Empire, 1890–1914* (Coral Gables, FL: University of Miami Press, 1972), pp. 118–136. See also, Stig Förster, "Der deutsche Generalstab und die Illusion des kurzen Krieges, 1871–1914. Metakritik eines Mythos," *Militärgeschichtliche Mitteilungen* 54 (1995), pp. 80–1.

narrow, purely military focus. Even within the army, Schlieffen's authority was not absolute. In the *Kaiserheer*, activities such as the development of force structure and doctrine were not clearly linked with war planning, and competing organizations had overlapping responsibilities. The General Staff drew up the deployment plans, and Schlieffen would become the *de facto* commander-in-chief of the German army at the outbreak of war. Yet, during peacetime, the Chief of the General Staff had no command functions. This fell to the commanders of the Reich's twenty army corps districts. These men trained their troops independently of one another and independently of the man who would command the army in wartime.[31] To make matters even more confused, the Ministries of War of the various states that made up the Second German Empire controlled the formation and equipping of units, and their Military Cabinets controlled officer promotions.[32] Thus, not only was there no official coordination of war planning and foreign policy, but even within the army, there were a variety of centers of authority competing with each other for bureaucratic power and control over defense policy. A politically weakened General Staff and a politically weak General Staff Chief had little prospect of constructing the grand strategy and the defense policy that was needed to face the challenges of a future *Volkskrieg*.

Schlieffen responded to this challenge not by forging closer links with other governmental institutions, but by focusing inward on areas he could control and influence.[33] Thus, he developed a two-fold approach to dealing with this situation, but an approach that was purely military in character. First, throughout his time as Chief of the General Staff, he pushed for army increases and for the development of modern weapons.[34]

[31] Paul Schneider, *Die Organisation des Heeres* (Berlin: E. S. Mittler, 1931), p. 66; Max van den Bergh, *Das Deutsche Heer vor dem Weltkriege: Eine Darstellung und Würdigung* (Berlin: Sanssouci, 1934), pp. 38ff.; Wiegand Schmidt-Richberg, "Die Regierungszeit Wilhelms II," in Militärgeschichtliches Forschungsamt, ed., *Deutsche Militärgeschichte 1648–1939*, Bd. III: *Von der Entlastung Bismarck bis zum Ende des Ersten Weltkrieges 1890–1918* (Munich: Bernard & Graefe Verlag, 1983), pp. 72–73.

[32] Heinrich Otto Meisner, *Der Kriegsminister, 1814–1914* (Berlin: Hermann Reinshagen Verlag, 1940); Rudolph Schmidt-Bückeburg, *Das Militärkabinett der preußischen Könige und deutschen Kaiser: Seine geschichtliche Entwicklung und staatsrechtliche Stellung 1787–1918* (Berlin: E. S. Mittler, 1933), pp. 152–240.

[33] Although Schlieffen enjoyed cordial relations with Friedrich von Holstein of the Foreign Office, his relationship with the heads of the German government's other institutions was strictly professional. Peter Rassow, "Schlieffen und Holstein," *Historische Zeitschrift* 173 (1952), pp. 297–313.

[34] See Reichsarchiv, *Der Weltkrieg 1914 bis 1918: Kriegsrüstung und Kriegswirtschaft*: Bd. I: *Die militärische, wirtschaftliche und finanzielle Rüstung Deutschlands von der Reichsgründung bis zum Ausbruch des Weltkrieges* (Berlin: E. S. Mittler, 1930), pp. 42ff.; and Ludwig Rüdt von Collenberg, "Graf Schlieffen und die Kriegsformation der deutschen Armee," *Wissen und Wehr* (1927), pp. 605–634.

A larger army would obviously allow for more flexibility in fighting a future war.[35] Better weapons would allow this army to do more. In particular, Schlieffen pushed hard for the development of mobile heavy artillery that would go some way to make up for the numerical inferiority of the German army and would help crack through the French and Russian fortifications.[36] Most importantly, however, Schlieffen attempted to deal with Germany's strategic dilemma by increasing the operational capabilities of the German army so that it would be able to fight more effectively than its enemies and give Germany some chance of winning the rapid, decisive victory he believed necessary.

Given that he did not believe Germany could survive a long war, Schlieffen believed that the war's outcome would be decided on the battlefield. Thus, all his energies were focused on bringing about a decisive battle early in any future war. As Schlieffen had no direct control over doctrine and training within the *Kaiserheer*, he had to rely upon the role that chiefs of staff would play in a future war. Each German unit from the division upwards possessed a chief of staff who would play a key role in commanding these units in wartime. These men, usually the best and the brightest officers within the army, exercised great influence over the decisions of the unit's commander.[37] Moreover, as the Franco-German War had shown, the General Staff Chief exercised his wartime command most efficiently through these subordinates. Schlieffen also assumed that at least some of the officers trained under him in the General Staff would go on to positions of high command in a future war.[38] Thus, Schlieffen attempted to develop within his subordinates in the General Staff a more or less uniform approach to war. He attempted to inculcate these officers with what we would today call the operational art in an effort to make up in quality for what he lacked in quantity.

[35] On the politics of army expansion in this period, see Stig Förster, *Der doppelte Militarismus: Die deutsche Heeresrüstungspolitik zwischen Status-Quo-Sicherung und Aggression 1890–1913* (Stuttgart: Franz Steiner, 1985); and Förster, "Alter und neuer Militarismus im Kaiserreich: Heeresrüstungspolitik und Dispositionen zum Kriege zwischen Status-Quo-Sicherung und imperialistischer Expansion, 1890–1913," in Jost Dülffer and Karl Holl, eds., *Bereit zum Krieg: Kriegsmentalität im wilhelminischen Deutschland, 1890–1914* (Göttingen: Vandenhoeck & Ruprecht, 1986), pp. 122–145.

[36] Curt Jany, *Geschichte der Königlich Preußischen Armee*, Bd. IV: *Die Königlich Preußische Armee und das Deutsche Reichsheer 1807 bis 1914* (Berlin: Karl Siegismund, 1933), pp. 314ff.; Eric Dorn Brose, *The Kaiser's Army: The Politics of Military Technology in Germany During the Machine Age, 1870–1918* (Oxford: Oxford University Press, 2001), pp. 74ff.

[37] On the role of the chiefs of staff, see Herbert Rosinski, *The German Army* (ed. Gordon Craig) (New York: Praeger, 1966), pp. 107–108.

[38] Schlieffen, "Tactical-Strategic Problems, 1903," in Foley, *Schlieffen's Military Writings*, p. 107.

Through his staff rides and wargames, Schlieffen taught his subordinates how to fight a modern, mass army. In response to the problems presented by the size of such armies, Schlieffen came up with a new concept of battle.[39] He viewed the clash of two modern armies as one huge battle spread over space and time, in which the smaller battles fought by the army corps, the *Teilschlachten*, would form the tactical encounters of traditional battles. These large numbers of battles that would take place far away from one another as the individual corps or groups of corps came into contact with the enemy would be welded together by the commander-in-chief into a *Gesamtschlacht* (complete battle). The individual *Teilschlachten* would be given significance by the commander-in-chief's plan. Just as a commander of old gave units particular goals on the battlefields of days past, a modern commander-in-chief would give specific goals to his army corps. Each would play a part in the overall plan. In Schlieffen's words: "The success of battle today depends more upon conceptual coherence than on territorial proximity. Thus, one battle might be fought in order to secure victory on another battlefield."[40] The army corps would, in essence, play the role once assigned to battalions or regiments in traditional battles.

This radical new vision of war was significant to Schlieffen's war plans. Given this vision, his war plans, in particular the famous Schlieffen Plan of 1905, must be seen as plans for what would, in essence, be gigantic battles. Although each individual army corps or army would be given independence to fight how it wanted, it was to be assigned its goals by the commander-in-chief, who might have used different means, but nonetheless directed the *Gesamtschlacht* as a commander might have directed a battle during the Napoleonic Wars. Schlieffen's war plans were thus designed to give structure to what would otherwise have been uncoordinated encounter battles. His war plans served to ensure that the sum of these battles was more than the sum of the parts.

Although he knew how he wanted the great, decisive battle to be fought in a future war, Schlieffen still faced the difficulty of how to bring such a battle about, and his war plans from 1892 to 1906 reflect his frustration at how to accomplish this. Schlieffen felt that he needed to fight a "decisive" battle in the west quickly in order to be able to shift forces to meet the Russian threat in the east. However, the French could not be relied upon to come out of their fortresses and fight in the open field,

[39] Schlieffen elaborated his operational approach fully in his "War Today," which appeared in *Deutsche Revue* in 1909. However, it is clear from the critiques of his wargames that he had striven to communicate his ideas to his subordinates during their training. See Schlieffen, "War Today," in Foley, *Schlieffen's Military Writings*, pp. 198–201 and his games in ibid., pp. 13–139, *passim*.

[40] Schlieffen, "War Today," in ibid., p. 198.

and, as Köpke's report showed, prizing the French from the safety of their fortifications would be a slow and costly process. Schlieffen's preferred means of dealing with this problem was to outflank the French fortress line by advancing through Luxemburg and Belgium. However, when Schlieffen first raised the possibility of such an advance in a memorandum in July 1893, it had to be rejected due to a lack of manpower and mobile heavy artillery.[41] Schlieffen, though, would return to the idea continuously for the next thirteen years.[42] By 1899, he felt that the German army was sufficiently strong to write the maneuver into German war plans as a contingency for the French not coming out of their fortresses to attack Germany.[43] By 1905, the German army had developed sufficiently and the strategic situation had altered dramatically enough for Schlieffen to make the maneuver the primary German war plan.

Indeed, the events of 1904/05 gave Schlieffen the hope that there was a strategic solution to Germany's dilemma. In 1904, Russia and Japan had gone to war in Korea. While most people in Europe expected a quick Russian victory once their army had reached the east,[44] the war, in fact, was a fiasco for the Russian army. Throughout the war, both sides grappled indecisively with one another, with the Russians generally coming off the worst. Slowly they were pushed deeper into Manchuria, and after losing Port Arthur and their Baltic Fleet in the battle of Tsushima and facing rebellion at home, the Russians were forced to come to a peace with Japan. Russian losses were substantial. At the battle of Mukden alone, the Russian army lost over 100,000 men.[45]

[41] Dieckmann, "Schlieffenplan," pp. 18ff. Despite its importance for future plans, this discussion by Schlieffen of an envelopment north of Verdun was not related in any other subsequent sources.

[42] Cf. Terence Zuber, "The Schlieffen Plan Reconsidered," *War in History* 6, 3 (1999), pp. 262–305, who argues that Schlieffen never seriously considered such an operation. This author's conclusions seem to be at odds with the conclusions reached by the very document upon which he bases much of his argument, Dieckmann's "Der Schlieffenplan." The very structure of Dieckmann's work indicates that he believed Schlieffen was working throughout his time as Chief of the General Staff toward a northern envelopment of the French fortifications. It begins with a section entitled, "Der Umgehungsplan" (The Outflanking Plan), in which Schlieffen's *Aufmarschpläne* were discussed until 1903. In these years, Schlieffen toyed with the idea of a shallow outflanking movement around the French fortifications. Dieckmann was to conclude his manuscript with a section entitled, "Der Umfassungsplan" (The Envelopment Plan), which, as its title suggests, would have taken Schlieffen's plans up to the famous memorandum of 1905 with its powerful right-wing envelopment.

[43] Robert T. Foley, "The Origins of the Schlieffen Plan," *War in History* 10, 2 (2003), pp. 253–263.

[44] Helmuth von Moltke, *Erinnerungen, Briefe, Dokumente, 1877–1916* (Stuttgart: Der Kommende Tag, 1922), p. 300.

[45] The interest shown by the General Staff in this war is illustrated by their exhaustive history of the conflict. See Historical Section of the Great General Staff, *The Russo-Japanese War* (trans. Karl von Donat) (5 vols.) (London: Hugh Rees, 1909–10).

The course of the war had a profound impact on Schlieffen's appreciation of Russian capabilities and, hence, on Germany's strategic situation.[46] In June 1905, Schlieffen wrote a long letter to the Chancellor describing the poor state of the Russian army. "For a long time," he wrote, "we have known that the Russian army possessed no effective leaders, that the majority of its officers were only of the most limited value, and that the troops had only limited training [*Ausbildung*]." However, Schlieffen wrote that most had believed these shortcomings would be compensated for to a certain degree by the steadiness and loyalty of the Russian troops. The war in the east had shown that this belief was false. Reportedly, Russian troops had little respect for their officers and did not obey orders. Further, the war had shown that their training was even worse than had been believed. Schlieffen concluded that the worth of the Russian army was minimal and that there was no prospect of it becoming an effective fighting force any time in the near future:

> the East Asian war has shown that the Russian army is less competent than had been previously assumed by informed opinion and that the war has worsened the Russian army rather than made it more efficient. It has lost all complaisance [*Freudigkeit*], all confidence [*Vertrauen*], and all obedience.
>
> It is very questionable whether or not an improvement will take place. The Russians lack enough self-awareness [*Selbsterkenntnis*] to carry this out. They see the origins of their defeat not in their own imperfections [*Unvollkommenkeiten*], but rather in the enemy's superiority in numbers and in the ineffectiveness of particular commanders. The Russian army lacks the men capable of carrying out the required reforms and who possess the necessary moral fortitude.[47]

Schlieffen's belief in the weakness of the Russian army now allowed him to contemplate seriously strategic options which had seemed unfeasible until this time. A window of opportunity had opened.[48] Schlieffen now felt that the bulk of the German army could be deployed in the west, with only a small force necessary in the east to defend against a greatly weakened and flawed Russian army.[49] Given that the French

46 The idea that Schlieffen "as chief of staff had never felt able to ignore the Russian threat" seems to be false in the light of his statements about the worth of the Russian army. Dennis Showalter, *Tannenberg: Clash of Empires* (Hamden, CT: Archon Books, 1991), p. 59.

47 Schlieffen to Bernhard von Bülow, 10 June 1905 in Foley, *Schlieffen's Military Writings*, p. 160.

48 The favorable strategic situation occasioned Schlieffen to advocate a pre-emptive strike against the French. See Heiner Raulff, *Zwischen Machtpolitik und Imperialismus: Die deutsche Frankreichpolitik 1904–05* (Düsseldorf: Droste, 1976), pp. 126–144. For an older analysis, see Walter Kloster, *Der deutsche Generalstab und der Präventivkriegs-Gedanke* (Stuttgart: Kohlhammer, 1932), pp. 34–44. Cf. Ritter, *Schlieffen Plan*, p. 46.

49 Schlieffen's opinions of the Russian army were supported by the reports of the German observers of the Russo-Japanese War. See BA/MA, PH3/653, "Berichte über russisch-japanischen Krieg," especially Otto von Lauenstein's damning report of 10 December 1905.

intended to remain on the defensive, protected behind their fortifications, Schlieffen needed to find a way to get at their army. Köpke's memorandum had painted a grim picture of how an attack through the French forts would develop and had reinforced an opinion already held by Schlieffen in 1893.[50] Thus, Schlieffen turned to one of his favorite operational concepts and the idea he had nurtured since 1893, a flanking maneuver.[51]

The result was the memorandum, "War Against France," or the "Schlieffen Plan" as it later became known, which Schlieffen completed in time for his retirement at the end of 1905. This document was taken up by Moltke the Younger and served as the basis, with some minor alterations, for Germany's primary war plan from 1906 to 1914. Schlieffen intended that almost the entire German army (thirty-three and a half corps) be deployed in the west, with most of this force being allocated to the right wing. This strong right wing was to advance through neutral Belgium and the Netherlands, into northern France and annihilate the French army in the process.[52] Once the French army was destroyed, Germany could dictate terms to a prostrate France and shift its forces east to deal with any Russian threat.[53]

Schlieffen's planning process, though, indicates that even with the advantages of a superior operational doctrine and the favorable strategic situation of 1905, he had his doubts about the feasibility of the undertaking. Gerhard Ritter's groundbreaking work, *The Schlieffen Plan* went into great detail about the process that eventually resulted in his final plan. In addition to publishing the final memorandum, Ritter also published the six drafts that Schlieffen wrote before finally finding one with which he was satisfied. These are very revealing, as they show his difficulty in finding a solution to Germany's expected two-front war. They demonstrate that right up to the moment he completed his memorandum, Schlieffen was undecided as to the best means of deployment.[54]

In addition to drafting his famous memorandum numerous times, Schlieffen also wargamed a variety of different scenarios during 1905, which indicates further his continuing unease. In the early months of the

50 Ritter, *Schlieffen Plan*, p. 22.

51 For an excellent detailed analysis of the plan's operational ideas, including the role of the possible encirclement of Paris and Moltke the Younger's use of the plan, see Terence M. Holmes, "The Reluctant March on Paris: A Reply to Terence Zuber's 'The Schlieffen Plan Reconsidered,'" *War in History* 8, 2 (2001), pp. 208–232.

52 Despite the moral indignation with which this move was greeted at the outbreak of the war (and, indeed, by some historians still today), violating Belgian neutrality was seriously considered by the Entente as well. See S. R. Williamson, "Joffre Reshapes French Strategy, 1911–1913," in Paul Kennedy, ed., *The War Plans of the Great Powers, 1880–1914* (London: George Allen & Unwin, 1979), pp. 133–154.

53 For the completed draft of the final plan, see Foley, *Schlieffen's Military Writings*, pp. 163–177.

54 Ritter, *Schlieffen Plan*, pp. 148–160.

year, Schlieffen carried out a wargame covering a possible war in the east in which the numbers of German forces were very inferior to those of the Russians. This game tested three scenarios for a Russian invasion of eastern Germany – one covered a Russian invasion by two armies from the Narev and the Niemen Rivers, another with a Niemen army advancing along both banks of the Vistula, and a third with the entire Russian army assembled at Warsaw for an advance on Berlin.[55]

In the summer of 1905, Schlieffen directed a complex staff ride in which he led the German side himself. Although recent commentators have seen no connection,[56] contemporaries of Schlieffen believed this staff ride to be an important test of his future war plan.[57] In this ride, almost the whole German army was deployed against France. The General Staff Chief intended to outflank the French army by advancing around their fortifications and thus bring about his desired decisive battle. Schlieffen outlined his plan of operation to his subordinates:

> after one has out-flanked the [French] position from the north, he faces a new position, a complete fortified system along the Lille–Maubeuge line and behind this La Fère, Laon, and Reims. Before he arrives at this line, he must pass Antwerp and his advance is split by Liège and Namur. When he has overcome completely these considerable difficulties, he will find the entire French army before him. It is therefore advisable to bring the whole German army, or at least all of the active army corps, on to a line from Brussels to Diedenhofen.
>
> From here, the German plan of operations is self-evident: One must stand firm at Metz–Diedenhofen and wheel left with the entire army, thereby always advancing right in order to win as much territory to the front and to the north as possible and in order to envelop the enemy, wherever he may be.[58]

Schlieffen selected three different solutions to play out from those offered by his subordinates leading the French army. First, Hugo Freiherr von Freytag-Loringhoven proposed that the French shift their forces further north with their left flank resting on Lille. The main force would attack west of Metz in the direction of Luxemburg–Namur–Brussels. Next, Cuno von Steuben put forward the plan that the French army would attack between Metz and Strassburg.[59] Finally, Hermann von

[55] Friedrich von Boetticher, "Der Lehrmeister des neuzeitlichen Krieges," in [Friedrich] von Cochenhausen, ed., *Von Scharnhorst zu Schlieffen, 1806–1906: Hundert Jahre preussisch-deutscher Generalstab* (Berlin: E. S. Mittler, 1933), p. 309. Unfortunately, no detailed description of this Kriegsspiel seems to have survived.

[56] Zuber, "Schlieffen Plan Reconsidered," pp. 292–293.

[57] Zoellner, "Schlieffens Vermächtnis," p. 52; Boetticher, "Lehrmeister," pp. 310–311; Erich Ludendorff, *Mein militärischer Werdegang* (Munich: Ludendorffs, 1933), p. 100.

[58] Zoellner, "Schlieffens Vemächtnis," pp. 49–50.

[59] See BA/MA, PH3/663, "Grosse Generalstabsreisen 1905 und 1906," which contains Steuben's orders.

Kuhl wanted to launch a counterattack against the advancing German army at what he believed to be its most vulnerable point – the pivot at Metz–Diedenhofen. He proposed to send one French force to the west of the Moselle and another to the east. Each of these solutions resulted in the French army being forced away from its base of operations (Paris), and in its complete defeat, seemingly vindicating Schlieffen's proposed northern envelopment of the French fortress line. However, Schlieffen himself came up with a French response that he believed might upset his plans – the creation of a new army to counterenvelop the right wing of the advancing German army. Indeed, it was just such a solution that the French employed in 1914.[60]

Finally, in November and December, Schlieffen directed a wargame that tested the German deployment plan in a two-front war. This game differed significantly from his western staff ride of earlier in the year. German forces were split almost evenly between the two fronts, and the initial decision fell in the east. Moreover, German forces remained on the defensive on both fronts, allowing the Russians and French to invade German territory, and Germany formed an alliance with Belgium and the Netherlands as a result of French violation of Belgian neutrality.[61]

Though the above scenario was unlikely given the weakness of the Russian army in 1905,[62] it brings to light several important points and raises some interesting questions. First, along with the year's other wargames, it shows even more forcefully than the many drafts of the Schlieffen Plan just how far-reaching Schlieffen's ideas were before his final draft and how unsure he was of just how to wage a two-front war successfully. He was willing to entertain the idea of allowing the initiative to pass, at least initially, to his enemies, in part for political reasons, and to allow his enemies the opportunity of invading German territory. The game also shows that Schlieffen was at least somewhat sensitive to political

[60] Zoellner, "Schlieffens Vemächtnis," pp. 48ff.; Boetticher, "Lehrmeister," pp. 310ff.; Bucholz, *Prussian War Planning*, pp. 199ff.; and Wilhelm Groener, *Testament des Grafen Schlieffen*, pp. 89ff. and Maps 9–11. Freytag-Loringhoven, at the time of this staff ride in the Historical Section of the General Staff, went on to be the *Generalquartiermeister* and adviser to Erich von Falkenhayn from January 1915 to August 1916 and then the Chief of the Deputy General Staff until the war's end. Hermann von Kuhl, in 1905 a member of the 3rd Section of the General Staff, went on to be Chief of the General Staff of the 1st Army in 1914 and later Chief of Staff to *Heeresgruppe Kronprinz Rupprecht* from 1915 to 1918.

[61] This game was discussed at length in Ulrich Liss, "Graf Schlieffen's letztes Kriegsspiel," *Wehr-Wissenschaftliche Rundschau* 3, 15 (1965), pp. 162–166. For the full text of Schlieffen's critique, see Foley, *Schlieffen's Military Writings*, pp. 119–139.

[62] Indeed, Schlieffen described the scenario as "unlikely, or better said, impossible." Ibid., p. 119.

questions. He believed that once Belgium was invaded, the Netherlands would also feel their independence threatened and would feel compelled to enter the war.[63] Schlieffen was obviously not a "military technician, pure and simple," as Ritter believed.[64] His look at the reaction of the Low Countries shows he had an understanding of the political consequences of invading their territory, even if he chose ultimately to ignore it in his quest for a rapid victory.[65]

The wargaming carried out by Schlieffen in 1905 demonstrates not only his doubts, but also another important feature of his thinking. It demonstrates that Schlieffen was willing to abandon or alter the pre-war deployment plan if circumstances forced him to do so. During his summer staff ride, he did just this when the French opponents attacked Metz and Strassburg. If this happened, he intended to fight the decisive battle in Lorraine, rather than continue the advance of the right wing.[66] As Ritter and more recently Terence Zuber have pointed out, the destruction of the French forces was Schlieffen's ultimate goal, not the wheel through Belgium itself.[67] Thus, the plan of 1905 must be seen in the light of the strategic circumstances of the time. Schlieffen was convinced that, with the Russians so weak, the French would not leave the safety of their fortresses voluntarily. Thus, the German army would have to go in and root them out. The series of wargames played during 1905 convinced Schlieffen that the most effective means of defeating the French would be by means of a powerful outflanking wing through the Low Countries. Of course, if the strategic situation changed again, Schlieffen would certainly have reexamined his plans.

Moltke the Younger and the Schlieffen Plan

In January 1906, Schlieffen was succeeded by Helmuth von Moltke the Younger, the nephew of the famous victor of the Wars of Unification. From the beginning of his tenure as Chief of the General Staff, Moltke was beset with doubts and fears. First, he questioned his own ability to carry out the tasks of chief of the General Staff. More importantly, he worried that Germany would experience great difficulty winning a future

[63] Ibid., p. 130. [64] Ritter, *Sword and the Scepter*, II, p. 194.

[65] The French of course considered an invasion through Belgium but rejected it on the grounds that it would damage relations with Britain. Williamson, "Joffre," pp. 133–154, *passim*.

[66] Boetticher, "Lehrmeister," pp. 310–311.

[67] Ritter, *Schlieffen Plan*, pp. 55–56; Zuber, "Schlieffen Plan Reconsidered," p. 280. Schlieffen, however, had clearly become obsessed with this idea by the end of his life, and this was reflected in his fanciful 1912 memorandum.

war. He expressed these fears in an audience with the Kaiser in January 1905:

> At this point, we have behind us a period of peace that has lasted more than 30 years, and I believe that we have become very peaceful in our perceptions. How and whether it will be possible to command mass armies, as we have formed them, cannot be known to any man, in my opinion. Further, our enemy has become quite different; we will no longer have to deal, as previously, with an enemy army that we can meet with superior numbers, rather [we will have to deal] with a nation in arms. [A future war] will become a *Volkskrieg* that will not be settled by the means of one decisive battle, but rather it will be a long, difficult struggle with a nation that will not give in before the entire strength of its people is broken and until our nation, even if we are victorious, is almost completely exhausted.[68]

Moltke's pessimistic view was later reinforced by German intelligence, who concluded that the French had a clear outline of the German deployment plan. In a report concerning possible French reactions to the Schlieffen Plan, they concluded that this knowledge could possibly prompt the French army to withdraw into southern France to avoid the German encirclement maneuver. The author was not confident in the plan's chances of success. He wrote:

> in the future, one cannot reckon on such complete annihilations of the entire [enemy] field army as was achieved in 1870 through the catastrophes of Metz and Sedan. When sizable portions of the six-times stronger [French] field army of today (today 2 million men, 1870 340,000 men) escape the early defeats, the continuation of operations is not easy for the Germans. Strong forces will certainly be left behind in the French border fortifications. The advance of the main German forces will be outflanked from Paris and Lyon.[69]

While Schlieffen could rely upon his belief that the superiority of German doctrine was sufficient to allow the army to defeat any enemy in the field, Moltke the Younger could not. It was clear that he believed

68 Moltke to his wife, 29 January 1905, in Moltke, *Erinnerungen*, p. 308. For Moltke's fears about the future war, see Annika Mombauer, *Helmuth von Moltke and the Origins of the First World War* (Cambridge: Cambridge University Press, 2001), pp. 54ff.; and Förster, "Illusion," pp. 83–90.

69 Grosser Generalstab, "Aufmarsch und operative Absichten der Franzosen in einem zukünftigen deutsch-französischen Kriege," May 1910, BA/MA, PH3/256; Foerster, *Gedankenwerkstatt*, pp. 119–122. This report appears to have been a thought-piece on possible French reactions to the Schlieffen Plan. Cf. J. K. Tannenbaum, "French Estimates of Germany's Operational War Plans," in Ernest R. May, *Knowing One's Enemies: Intelligence Before the Two World Wars* (Princeton: Princeton University Press, 1984), pp. 153–156. The intelligence assessments of this period indicated that the French intended to deploy the bulk of their army along the border between Rethel and Belfort defensively. See Greiner, "Nachrichten," pp. 98–112.

Fig. 3 Kaiser Wilhelm II (left) with his Chief of the General Staff, Helmuth von Moltke the Younger, during the 1913 Imperial Maneuvers

after thirty years of peace, the German army would have difficulties in combat. Further, he felt that France would not necessarily oblige Germany's plans, and that the next war would drag on for a long time, ending only when one side was exhausted. Yet, he maintained Schlieffen's plan as the basis for his deployment plans right up to 1914, and, in fact, applied Schlieffen's idea more rigidly than Schlieffen himself intended. Why should this have been?

The best possible answer for this lies in Germany's changing strategic situation between 1906 and 1914. The weakness of Russia in the wake of the Russo-Japanese War had given the Schlieffen Plan a window of opportunity for success. However, Russia was able to rebuild its strength more rapidly than was believed possible and, in fact, emerged a greater danger than it had been before 1905. The General Staff observed this process with growing alarm.

By 1910, the reform of the Russian army was evident to German observers. In August, Moltke wrote to Chancellor Theobald von Bethmann Hollweg outlining the implications of the on-going Russian reorganization. In addition to raising seven new divisions in European Russia, "a considerable increase in the number of technical units, particularly aircraft and railroad formations, [had] taken place, so that the Russian army [would] soon be better equipped with such formations than the German army." Further, the Russians were changing their deployment plans. Four army corps were pulled back from the border and deployed deeper in Russia, creating a "central army" that could be deployed according to need "in east Asia, on the western border or in the Balkans."[70] Ultimately, this "central army" was to be composed of seven army corps (fifteen divisions), a considerable reserve force.[71]

The Russians had also greatly improved the combat capability of their army. In the aftermath of the Russo-Japanese War, they had equipped their army with modern field howitzers, providing their infantry corps with important firepower.[72] Moreover, large numbers of old and unsatisfactory officers were dismissed, and younger more able men were promoted.[73] The army's regulations had also been thoroughly re-written to reflect the lessons of the war and training procedures had been tightened up.[74] While the Germans still reported that Russian tactics and training were below the standards of the German army, they acknowledged the great strides which the Russian army had taken and the fact that it was a much more dangerous foe than had been the case in 1905.[75]

The Russians also introduced reforms into their mobilization procedures, which decreased the time needed to deploy their army. The numbers of active personnel in units was increased and the mobilization procedures for reservists were simplified. Perhaps most importantly, though, in the spring of 1913, the Russians introduced a "war preparation period" [*Kriegsvorbereitungsperiode*]. This allowed for the beginning

70 Moltke to Bethmann, 5 August 1910, PRO GFM 10/89 (*Russland 72geh/15*: "Militär und Marine Angelegenheiten Russland, 1 January 1907–").

71 Moltke to Bethmann, 14 November 1910, in ibid. See also David Stevenson, *Armaments and the Coming of War: Europe, 1904–1914* (Oxford: Clarendon Press, 1996), pp. 149ff.

72 Helmuth von Moltke, "Die wichtigsten Veränderungen im Heerwesen Russlands im Jahre 1913," 6 March 1914, BA/MA, PH3/657. By the war's outbreak each Russian corps was equipped with a battalion of 12 122 mm howitzers. Bruce I. Gudmundsson, *On Artillery* (Westport, CT: Paeger, 1993), p. 32.

73 Moltke to Bethmann, "Die militär-politische Lage Deutschlands," 2 December 1911, PRO GFM 11/68 (*Deutschland 121/secreta*: "Die Angelegenheiten der deut. Armee, 1886–1919"), p. 11.

74 Grosser Generalstab, "Die Kriegsbereitschaft Russlands," February 1914, PRO GFM 10/89 (*Russland 72geh/15*: "Militär und Marine Angelegenheiten Russland, 1 January 1907–").

75 Grosser Generalstab, "Mitteilungen über russische Taktik," 27 February 1913, BA/MA, PH3/657.

of the mobilization process with a secret order in times of international tension, greatly reducing mobilization time.[76]

Further, financed largely through French loans, the Russians were expending great sums of money on improving their railroad capabilities, a process that had grave implications for German security.[77] German intelligence estimated that the great building program, which was to begin in 1912, would result in the laying of over 10,000 kilometers of new track. By 1922, the Russian interior would be linked far better with its borders.[78] This program caused considerable alarm within the General Staff. Moltke wrote to Bethmann of the effects:

> This means that whereas now the Russian army deploys and has ready for operations half of its army on the western border by the *13th* mobilization day and two-thirds by the *18th* mobilization day, *after the completion of the railway construction plan,* [Russia will be able to deploy] two-thirds [of its army] already by the *13th* mobilization day and the entire strength by the *18th* mobilization day.[79]

Already by 1911, Russian improvements in mobilization procedures had meant that its army would complete its deployment to the western border in half the time it had taken in 1906.[80] Clearly, this railroad expansion program made the situation even more difficult for the Germans.

While in 1911 Moltke could still write that France was Germany's most dangerous enemy,[81] clearly Russia was becoming more and more of a threat. The internal improvements of the Russian army made it a dangerous enemy by making it more tactically and strategically flexible. Its defeat in the Russo-Japanese War had prompted an updating of its combat regulations, the dismissal of unsatisfactory officers, the purchase of modern, mobile artillery, resulting in a more tactically capable

[76] Grosser Generalstab, "Die Kriegsbereitschaft Russlands," February 1914, PRO GFM 10/89 (*Russland 72geh/15*: "Militär und Marine Angelegenheiten Russland, 1 January 1907–"); Gunther Frantz, *Russlands Eintritt in den Weltkrieg* (Berlin: Deutsche Verlagsgesellschaft für Politik und Geschichte, 1924), pp. 17–24; Stevenson, *Armaments and Coming of War*, pp. 153ff.

[77] D. N. Collins, "The Franco-Russian Alliance and Russian Railways, 1891–1914," *The Historical Journal* 16, 4 (1973), pp. 777–788; Stevenson, *Armaments and Coming of War*, pp. 323ff.

[78] Grosser Generalstab, "Der Ausbau des strategischen Eisenbahnnetzes in Russland," 27 November 1913, PRO, GFM 6/141 (*Russland 93/17*: "Eisenbahnen in Russland, 1 Jun 1912–31 Dez 1914").

[79] Grosser Generalstab, "Der Ausbau des strategischen Bahnnetzes in Russland. Ergänzung und Berichtigung der Ausarbeitung vom 15.Dezember 1913," 7 July 1914, in ibid. Emphasis in original.

[80] Moltke to Bethmann, "Die militär-politische Lage Deutschlands," 2 December 1911, PRO GFM 11/68 (*Deutschland 121/secreta*: "Die Angelegenheiten der deut. Armee, 1886–1919"), p. 10.

[81] Ibid., p. 6.

force. Moreover, the railroad building plan and improvements in mobilization procedures made the Russian army more strategically flexible. These reforms allowed the Russian army to deploy more men faster than had been the case in Schlieffen's day. These improvements also enabled Russia to form a large "central army" in the heart of Russia and to shift its forces further back from the border, making the Russian army less vulnerable to a sudden Austro-German pre-emptive strike and allowing the Russians to have a variety of deployment plans.[82] Needless to say, these were worrying developments for Moltke.

The inability to strike at Russia, as well as the fact that any war against Russia would certainly be long and indecisive, forced Moltke to concentrate on France.[83] Russia's growing strength and speed of mobilization made it a steadily growing threat to Germany and made a rapid victory in the west even more crucial than in Schlieffen's day. Only by coming to a quick reckoning with France could Germany have the forces necessary to deal with the formidable Russian "steamroller."

Needing a rapid victory in the west, Moltke adhered to the basic outline of Schlieffen's 1905 plan. However, his fears caused him to make important alterations to Schlieffen's original concept.[84] First, to protect against an expected French invasion of Alsace-Lorraine, he had deployed eight army corps in the 6th and 7th Armies along the border.[85] Perhaps more importantly, in reaction to his fears about the possibility of having to fight a long war, Moltke had changed the course of the advance of the German right wing. Schlieffen's plan had called for the strong German right wing to outflank the French border fortifications by advance through Belgium and the Netherlands. Instead, Moltke decided to limit the German advance to Belgian territory with the desire of keeping the Netherlands as an outlet to the world. In 1911, he wrote:

82 See Gunther Frantz, "Russlands Westaufmarsch seit 1880," *Wissen und Wehr* (1930), pp. 235–255.

83 In 1913, Moltke abandoned the *Grosser Ostaufmarsch* and concentrated solely on plans for the west. See Mombauer, *Moltke*, pp. 100–105; Showalter, "Eastern Front," pp. 170–176.

84 The claim that these changes caused the failure of the German plan in 1914 has been sufficiently refuted by historians. For the most recent and the most comprehensive treatment, see Mombauer, *Moltke*, pp. 90–101.

85 Ludendorff, *Werdegang*, pp. 126–129; Reichsarchiv, *Der Weltkrieg*, Bd. I: *Die Grenzschlachten im Westen* (Berlin: E. S. Mittler, 1925), pp. 61–63. Although this alteration was criticized after the war for not leaving enough forces on the right wing, given the logistical difficulties of the right wing in 1914, it is doubtful whether the German army would have been able to deploy and supply more units than they actually did in 1914. See Martin van Creveld, *Supplying War* (Cambridge: Cambridge University Press, 1977), pp. 109–141; and Michael Salewski, "Moltke, Schlieffen und die Eisenbahn," in Roland Foerster, ed., *Generalfeldmarschall von Moltke: Bedeutung und Wirkung* (Munich: Oldenbourg, 1991), pp. 94–100.

Naturally, it is important that the right wing be as strong as possible during an advance through Belgium. However, I cannot agree that in order to carry out the envelopment Dutch neutrality needs to be violated as well as Belgian. A hostile Netherlands at our rear could have disastrous consequences for the advance of the German army to the west, especially if England were to use the violation of Belgian neutrality to enter the war against us. If the Netherlands remains neutral, she secures our rear, as England could not violate Dutch neutrality after having declared war on us for a violation of Belgian neutrality – she cannot commit the same violation of the law for which she declares war against us. Moreover, it would be a great value for us to have in the Netherlands a country whose neutrality allows us to have imports and supplies. She must be the windpipe through which we can breathe.[86]

This restriction of the advance to Belgium, however, caused severe constraints on the German deployment, as the right wing could not use the important rail lines of the Dutch Maastricht area. The German 1st and 2nd Armies, in total almost 600,000 troops with attendant supplies, were now forced to pass through a corridor only 12 miles wide.[87] Moltke's alteration made the immediate seizure of the intact Belgian railroads an absolute necessity. To this end, the General Staff devised a plan to take the Belgian fortress of Liège with its crucial rail junction by a *coup de main* at the outbreak of the war. When this plan, judged by Ritter to be "verging on the fantastic,"[88] was originally drawn up in 1908, it was intended to be launched on the 11th mobilization day. In the years before the war, however, the launch date was reduced to the 5th mobilization day, putting more and more time pressure on the German mobilization plan.[89] Having to take Liège on the fifth day meant that the German forces earmarked for the attack would have to start their advance within hours of the mobilization order being issued.[90] With the details of the plan worked out in such minute detail and with the time pressures imposed by the *coup de main* on Liège, it is no wonder that Moltke blanched at the prospect of having to scrap the entire plan in August 1914.[91]

86 Moltke, "Comments by Moltke on the Memorandum, *c.*1911," in Foley, *Schlieffen's Military Writings*, p. 179.

87 Bucholz, *Prussian War Planning*, p. 266.

88 Ritter, *Sword and the Scepter*, II, p. 221.

89 Gerhard Tappen to Ernst Kabisch, 14 April 1937, BA/MA, Tappen Nachlass, N56/5. Tappen professed to have no knowledge as to why the change in the time frame took place.

90 Moltke kept the details of the Liège plan secret from everyone outside the army. Bethmann did not find out the details until 31 July. Ritter, *Sword and Scepter*, II, p. 267.

91 In August 1914, when it seemed as if France would remain neutral, Moltke was asked by Kaiser Wilhelm to scrap his western deployment and deploy against Russia instead. This caused Moltke great stress and resulted in a minor breakdown. See Moltke, *Erinnerungen*, pp. 19–23; Mombauer, *Moltke*, pp. 219–226.

Recent research has shown clearly that Moltke had grave doubts about Germany's ability to conclude a future war rapidly. This begs the question why did he not scrap the plan and prepare Germany for a long war. An answer to this can be found in the changing strategic situation. While the General Staff may have believed France to be the more dangerous enemy in 1914, Russia was rapidly taking its place. When Russia's railway building and army reform were completed in 1922, it would be a far greater threat to Germany. These reforms would enable Russia to mobilize and deploy a massive army almost as quickly as the Germans could mobilize their forces. Convinced that a general European war was inevitable, Moltke pushed for war as soon as possible, believing that once Russian military reforms were completed, Germany's slim prospects of success would diminish even further.[92] However, even with the Russian reorganization incomplete it was still a far more dangerous foe than it had been in 1905. Germany needed to defeat France quickly in order to be able to meet this eastern threat, and only an offensive strategy offered even the slightest prospects of a rapid French collapse. Consequently, in July 1914, Moltke seized upon the assassination of Archduke Franz Ferdinand as the pretext needed to launch Germany's war and set in motion the plan that he hoped, but perhaps did not expect, would bring about France's fall.[93]

Conclusion

Alfred von Schlieffen and Helmuth von Moltke the Younger have been roughly handled by recent historians. Martin Kitchen described Schlieffen as a man obsessed with the "minutiae of military planning," who believed that the "uncertainties of warfare . . . could be eliminated as far as possible by careful planning and technical experience."[94] On the other hand, according to one historian, Schlieffen's successor, Moltke

[92] See his statements in the "Kriegsrat" of December 1912, which were recorded by Admiral Georg von Müller in his diary. Quoted in John C. G. Röhl, *The Kaiser and his Court: Wilhelm II and the Government of Germany* (Cambridge: Cambridge University Press, 1994), pp. 162–163. Moltke's timing for the war was also influenced by the reorganization of the Belgian army begun with their Army Law of 1913, which would have resulted in a field army of almost 350,000 men. This obviously would have made the advance through Belgium much more difficult and time consuming. See "Denkschriften über England, das engl. Expeditionskorps, Belgien und Italien," August 1911–April 1914, BA/MA, PH3/528.

[93] Annika Mombauer, "A Reluctant Military Leader? Helmuth von Moltke and the July Crisis of 1914," *War in History* 6, 4 (1999), pp. 417–446.

[94] Kitchen, "Traditions," pp. 170–171.

the Younger, was "unprepared by education and experience to understand war planning." This meant that he was unable to develop a "clear defense policy during the years 1906–1911."[95] According to recent historians, the shortcomings of these men led both to cling to a strategy that had no hope of success.

From the evidence available, however, it is clear that both men had sound reasons for maintaining war plans based on the traditional German approach to warfare, despite their doubts about the efficacy of following a *Vernichtungsstrategie*. For Schlieffen, there were several reasons. First, he believed that Germany simply could not survive a long war and, hence, a future war would have to be short. He felt that by making the German army operationally more capable than its enemies, the army could follow its traditional strategic approach. Second, Schlieffen believed that the Russo-Japanese War had shown that the Russian army, although it might be large, was by no means capable of fighting a modern war. Having never had much respect for the Russians, Schlieffen now believed that their army would not be able to reform itself in the foreseeable future. These conditions suggested to Schlieffen that a short war was indeed a possibility for Germany in 1905. However, a short war would only be possible if they could come to grips with the French army. As the French intended to remain on the defensive, the German army had to take the battle to them. Extensive wargaming in 1905 had demonstrated that this could be accomplished by outflanking the fortified Franco-German border.

Moltke the Younger had very different reasons for sticking with a plan that assumed an expeditious German victory. The years after Schlieffen's retirement had seen a significant change in Germany's strategic situation. The Russian army reform, which Schlieffen was convinced would not take place, occurred in fact with surprising alacrity. Moreover, not only did the Russians rebuild the strength they had lost during the war with Japan, they increased dramatically the capabilities of their army. The German General Staff believed that reforms begun around 1910 would be complete by 1922 at the latest, and would make the Russian army almost invulnerable. With no prospect of being able to fight a short campaign in the east and with the growing threat of the Russian army, Moltke the Younger had no choice but to focus German efforts in the west. To meet the Russian advance that would come in any war, he had to defeat the French forces quickly. This meant that he had to carry out an offensive strategy, regardless of his doubts about the ability of the German army to defeat France quickly. Again, the only way that offered even the faintest prospect of accomplishing this was to avoid fighting through

95 Bucholz, *Prussian War Planning*, pp. 217, 225.

the fortified border area, i.e., to outflank the French positions and keep the war in the free field where the Germans would be able to fight the kind of war at which they excelled – *Bewegungskrieg*. Thus, Moltke used the international crisis that arose from assassination of Archduke Franz Ferdinand as a pretext for launching what amounted to a pre-emptive strike against France before the growth of the Russian army put paid to all prospects of a German victory.

4 The rise of *Stellungskrieg*

On 1 August 1914, Kaiser Wilhelm II signed the order mobilizing the German army. After years of intense preparation, the German army was finally going to war. German military leaders believed their army would never be better prepared. At the beginning of the crisis in early July, the Prussian Minister of War, Generalleutnant Erich von Falkenhayn, had assured the Kaiser that the German army was fully ready for conflict,[1] while the Chief of the General Staff, Generaloberst Helmuth von Moltke, stressed that the timing would never be better.[2] After forty years of theorizing about war, the time had come to put German military ideas to the test; with great anticipation, German military theorists laid down their pens and took up their swords.

The Kaiser's order set in motion the detailed workings of the Schlieffen/Moltke Plan. A series of long-prepared and meticulously planned events began. The mobilization order arrived at the Ministry of War at 5:20p.m., only 20 minutes after it had been signed. By 5:25, the necessary telegrams were already being dispatched.[3] The next several weeks were spent in a state of organized confusion, as officers and men reported to their wartime posts and units assembled for the advance into France, all according to the detailed plans drawn up before the war.[4] Over 11,000 trains carried the army to the offensive. Between 2 and 18 August, 2,150 trains (one

[1] Erich von Falkenhayn to the *Parlamentarischer Untersuchungsausschuß* (the Reichstag commission investigating Germany's failure in the war) quoted in Erwin Hölzle, ed., *Quellen zur Entstehung des Ersten Weltkrieges: Internationale Dokumente, 1901–1914* (Darmstadt: Wissenschaftliche Buchgesellschaft, 1978), Document 131, p. 308; For Falkenhayn's role during the outbreak of war see, Holger Afflerbach, *Falkenhayn: Politisches Denken und Handeln im Kaiserreich* (Munich: Oldenbourg, 1994), pp. 147–171.

[2] For Moltke's role in the July Crisis and during the outbreak of war, see Annika Mombauer, *Helmuth von Moltke and the Origins of the First World War* (Cambridge: Cambridge University Press, 2001), pp. 182–226.

[3] Ernst von Wrisberg, *Heer und Heimat 1914–1918* (Leipzig: K. F. Koehler, 1921), p. 4. A state of *drohende Kriegsgefahr* (imminent threat of war) had been declared on 31 July. The German ultimatum to Russia expired at 4:00p.m. on 1 August and the Kaiser signed the mobilization order at 5:00p.m.

[4] On the mobilization process, see Hermann Rahne, "Die militärische Mobilmachungsplanung und -technik in Preußen und im deutschen Reich (Mitte des 19. Jahrhunderts

every 10 minutes) crossed the Hohenzollern Bridge in Cologne. In all, the Germans assembled and deployed close to 4 million men and over 850,000 horses. The years of preparation seemed to pay off, as the mobilization proceeded like clockwork. A fortnight after the mobilization order was issued, the *Westheer* was declared *operationsbereit.*[5]

The first few days after mobilization also saw the war's first encounters as German troops entered Luxemburg and Belgium. On 3 August, Luxemburg fell without resistance.[6] Belgium, though, offered more difficulty. The taking of the fortress of Liège, with its rail network so crucial to the German deployment, took longer than planned. However, the fortress was eventually neutralized sufficiently to allow the troops of the German right wing to pass, creating just a small bump in the road for the advancing Germans.[7] By 20 August, the powerful German right wing stood ready to advance into France and crush the French army in a swift, decisive campaign.

At first, the plan created by Schlieffen and modified by Moltke seemed to be succeeding. The powerful German thrust through Belgium aimed at the French left wing took the French command by surprise. Committed to their own offensive in Alsace-Lorraine, they possessed few reserves readily available for deployment against the German right, and the German armies advanced deep into France pursuing the weak French left wing and with it the recently landed British Expeditionary Force (BEF). The pre-war emphasis on *Bewegungskrieg*, with its fluid battles and grand envelopments seemed to be paying off. The German command was overjoyed and convinced of their impending victory against the French. The Imperial Headquarters celebrated victory after victory and daily anticipated another Sedan.[8]

However, in a story well told, the German advance was brought to a halt on the Marne River in a series of battles lasting from 5 to 9 September, and

bis zur Auslösung des zweiten Weltkrieges)" (2 vols.) (Karl-Marx-Universität, Leipzig, Dissertation, 1972), I, pp. 113–184.

[5] Reichsarchiv, *Der Weltkrieg*, Bd. I: *Die Grenzschlachten im Westen* (Berlin: E. S. Mittler, 1925), pp. 128–154; Hermann von Staabs, *Aufmarsch nach zwei Fronten auf Grund der Operationspläne von 1871–1914* (Berlin: E. S. Mittler, 1925), pp. 41–42. The *Ostheer* had been declared *operationsbereit* three days earlier.

[6] *Der Weltkrieg*, I, pp. 106–108. [7] Ibid., pp. 108–120.

[8] This feeling of impending victory was particularly strong amongst the Kaiser's entourage, while the professional military were a bit more guarded in their optimism. See the diaries of the head of the Kaiser's headquarters, Plessen, and those of the head of his Naval Cabinet, Müller. Hans von Plessen, "Tagebuch," 24 August – 7 September 1914, BA/MA, W10/51063 and Admiral Georg Müller's diary entries reprinted in *The Kaiser and His Court: The First World War Diaries of Admiral Georg von Müller* (ed. Walter Görlitz, trans. Mervyn Savill) (London: MacDonald, 1961), pp. 25–28; For Moltke's reaction, see Gerhard Tappen, *Bis zur Marne* (Oldenburg: Stalling, 1920), p. 18.

the German right wing was forced to retreat by redeployed French forces and the BEF.[9] With this retreat came the end of the Schlieffen/Moltke Plan and also the end of Helmuth von Moltke's career as the strategic head of the German army. In the sarcastic words of the Prussian Minister of War, "Schlieffen's notes [had] come to an end, and with this, Moltke's wits."[10] On 14 September, Falkenhayn took up the reins of Germany's strategic direction from the shattered Moltke. Thus to Falkenhayn fell the task of taking the German army into poorly charted and largely unknown territory – *Stellungskrieg* (position warfare) and *Ermattungsstrategie*.

The German army at war

Although the German army went to war in August 1914 with a high reputation, it had not fought a war in over forty years. The army's reputation stemmed initially from its successes in the Wars of Unification and was sustained by its peacetime emphasis on professional excellence. Probably no other army dedicated as much time to the training and the development of its officers. This emphasis was reflected in the myriad of professional journals, societies, and schools that had developed after 1870. This emphasis was also reflected in the debates over tactics and strategy which developed in the years before World War I. The professionalism of the German officer corps would be a crucial element in their reaction to the changes in warfare which manifested themselves in 1914. The intellectual openness of the officer corps allowed for a relatively rapid response to the tactical and technical problems of *Stellungskrieg*. However, before this could occur, one of the elements which fostered this climate of intellectual flexibility in the peacetime German army created difficulties for the smooth wartime operation of the army.

As Chapter 3 has shown, the Wilhelmine German army could best be characterized during peacetime as a "polycracy," with many different centers of authority competing with one another for power.[11] The corps commanders, the Ministry of War, the Military Cabinet, and the General Staff all possessed important, often overlapping, powers during

[9] The best analysis of the battle of the Marne remains Sewell Tyng, *The Campaign of the Marne 1914* (Oxford: Oxford University Press, 1935). For more recent treatments, see Mombauer, *Moltke*, pp. 250–271; and Hew Strachan, *The First World War*, Vol. I: *To Arms* (Oxford: Oxford University Press, 2001), pp. 242–262.

[10] Quoted in Hans von Zwehl, *Erich von Falkenhayn: Eine biographische Studie* (Berlin: E. S. Mittler, 1926), p. 66.

[11] I borrow this term from Hans-Ulrich Wehler, who used the phrase *authoritäre Polykratie* to describe the structure of Wilhelmine government. *Das Deutsche Kaiserreich* (Göttingen: Musterschmidt, 1973), pp. 69–77.

peacetime, but none had clear authority over the others.[12] Additionally, the *Kaiserheer* was in fact made up of several armies, as the armies of Bavaria, Württemberg, and Saxony all existed as autonomous institutions during peacetime. While this structure allowed many competing views of warfare and doctrine to develop before the outbreak of World War I, it also meant that the German army entered the war with a command structure which was open to challenge from within.

The outbreak of war was meant to simplify the German command structure. With the declaration of war, Kaiser Wilhelm II assumed command of the various contingents (i.e., the Bavarian, Württemberg, and Saxon armies) of the Imperial army as the *Oberster Kriegsherr* (Supreme Warlord) under Article 63 of the German Constitution. Wilhelm was to be advised on matters of strategy by the Chief of the Prussian General Staff and by the Imperial Chancellor, in August 1914 Helmuth von Moltke and Theobald von Bethmann Hollweg, respectively. In reality, the Emperor abdicated his command functions to the Chief of the General Staff, who issued orders under Wilhelm's name often without prior consultation. Thus, the Chief of the General Staff became the *de facto* director of Germany's war, able to issue orders with Imperial approval over a wide area. Armed with this authority, the General Staff was able to move into areas which had previously been the remit of other organizations.[13]

It would be a mistake, though, to see the General Staff as an all-powerful organization, especially at the beginning of the war. Several competing organizations still wielded considerable power and many of the army's commanders held considerable personal authority. At the war's outbreak, the German army's twenty-five army corps and fourteen reserve corps formed eight armies, with seven deployed in the west and one in the east. The commanders of these armies were drawn from the high nobility (Crown Prince Wilhelm, Crown Prince Rupprecht, and Albrecht Duke of Württemberg) and from high-ranking officers who had often held important posts in the pre-war army (Josias von Heeringen and Karl

[12] On the tensions between the various higher authorities within the army see "Die Entwicklung des Verhältnisses zwischen Generalstab und Kriegsministerium," unpublished manuscript in BA/MA, W10/50211; Heinrich Otto Meisner, *Der Kriegsminister 1814–1914* (Berlin: Hermann Reinshagen Verlag, 1940); Rudolf Schmidt-Bückeburg, *Das Militärkabinett der preussischen Könige und deutschen Kaiser: Seine geschichtliche Entwicklung und staatsrechtliche Stellung, 1787–1918* (Berlin: E. S. Mittler, 1933). On the role of corps commanders, especially in training [*Ausbildung*], see Paul Schneider, *Die Organisation des Heeres* (Berlin: E. S. Mittler, 1931), pp. 13–27.

[13] See Friedrich Hossbach, *Die Entwicklung des Oberbefehls über das Heer in Brandenburg, Preussen und im Deutschen Reich von 1655–1945* (Würzburg: Holzner, 1957), pp. 56–71; and Holger Afflerbach, "Wilhelm as Supreme Warlord in the First World War," *War in History* 5, 4 (1998), pp. 427–449.

von Einem had each served as Prussian Minister of War). The very real personal authority of these army commanders was further strengthened by the tradition of mission-command within the German army,[14] which delegated command authority from the Supreme Command (*Oberste Heeresleitung* or OHL) to subordinates, and this tradition was often invoked by army commanders within the first weeks of the war to carry out their own strategic schemes that sometimes ran counter to the OHL's directions.[15]

Moreover, the General Staff had little or no influence on diplomacy and foreign policy, a task that still fell to the Chancellor and the Foreign Office. While Bethmann Hollweg went to war with the Imperial Headquarters and representatives from the Chancellery and the Foreign Office were permanently assigned to liaise with the General Staff, old habits died hard, and each institution continued to operate with minimal consultation with the other. Additionally, frictions during the July Crisis and the early days of the war meant that the two institutions eyed each other with a higher degree of hostility than normal.[16] Thus, developing a truly "strategic" policy, that is, one that combined the military and diplomatic spheres, continued to be a problem.

Most pernicious for Moltke, however, were the Military Cabinet and the Ministry of War. The head of the Military Cabinet, Generaloberst Moriz von Lyncker, and the Prussian Minister of War, Erich von Falkenhayn, were close advisors of the Kaiser. Both accompanied the Imperial Headquarters into the field in 1914 and were in a position to influence events. In Falkenhayn, Moltke found someone within the headquarters willing to criticize his strategic decisions vocally and prominently.[17] In Lyncker, Moltke found someone willing to listen to

[14] See Martin Samuels, "Directive Command and the German General Staff," *War in History* 2, 1 (1995), pp. 22–40. The position of Wilhelm and Rupprecht as crown princes of Germany and Bavaria, respectively, allowed them to play a political role. Wilhelm, in particular, was kept unusually well informed about events. See the diary of Major von Redern, the Ia of the Operations Section, BA/MA, W10/50676. On Rupprecht, see Frederick Campbell, "The Bavarian Army, 1870–1918: The Constitutional and Structural Relations with the Prussian Military Establishment" (Ohio State University, Ph.D. Thesis, 1972), pp. 226–240.

[15] See Mombauer, *Moltke*, pp. 227ff.; Holger Herwig, *The First World War* (London: Arnold, 1997), pp. 99–101.

[16] On Bethmann's rocky relationship with the military at the war's outbreak, see Gerhard Ritter, *The Sword and the Sceptre: The Problem of Militarism in Germany*, vol. II: *The European Powers and the Wilhelminian Empire, 1890–1914* (trans. Heinz Norden) (Coral Gables, FL: University of Miami Press, 1970), pp. 263ff.

[17] See the diary and reports of the Bavarian military plenipotentiary in the OHL, Karl Ritter von Wenninger, printed in Bernd F. Schulte, "Neue Dokumente zu Kriegsausbruch und Kriegsverlauf 1914," *Militärgeschichtliche Mitteilungen* 1 (1979), pp. 123–185.

Falkenhayn's criticisms.[18] When Moltke's strategy seemed to be going badly, each of these individuals was in a position to make important changes. The result was Moltke's dismissal and Falkenhayn's promotion when the German armies were forced to retreat at the battle of the Marne in early September.[19]

The new Chief of the General Staff

Like Helmuth von Moltke the Younger, Erich von Falkenhayn's reputation suffered the severe criticisms of his contemporaries after the war. From this criticism emerges the picture of a hesitant, weak leader, who lacked the strength of will necessary to take difficult decisions. Max Bauer, who served in the OHL through Falkenhayn's tenure and who recognized some of Falkenhayn's better qualities, nevertheless judged him unfit for high command. After the war, he wrote:

> Falkenhayn had great merits. His ability to work was unlimited. He understood easily, comprehended quickly, had a good memory, and made decisions rapidly. However, be it because he lacked a certain foundation or be it because he lacked the intuition of a *Feldherr*, [these decisions] were often half measures in which he frequently vacillated. Additionally, he was very clever and understood men, how to retain and use them, without them knowing it . . . All in all, he was of uncommon nature and would have made an excellent statesman, diplomat, or politician, but the position of *Feldherr* suited him least.[20]

Another member of his staff, Wilhelm Groener, came to a similar conclusion. He wrote that Falkenhayn was "lacking in confidence, vacillating, and easily influenced by others."[21] Others saw Falkenhayn as pessimistic and, hence, not dedicated to winning the war.[22]

Undoubtedly, Falkenhayn's appointment as Chief of the General Staff came as a surprise to his contemporaries.[23] At 53, he was younger than

[18] Groener wrote, "after the move to Luxemburg, two enemy camps formed, the General Staff in the Kölner Hof and the Military Cabinet and the Ministry of War in the Hotel Brasseur." Paper presented to the Mittwochsgesellschaft, 11 January 1933 in USNA, Groener Papers, M-137, Roll 13.

[19] For accounts of this process, see Afflerbach, *Falkenhayn*, pp. 179–189; and Mombauer, *Moltke*, pp. 260–271.

[20] Max Bauer, *Der grosse Krieg in Feld und Heimat* (Tübingen: Osiander'sche Buchhandlung, 1921), p. 58.

[21] Wilhelm Groener, "Die Strategie Falkenhayns. Herbst 1914," Paper presented to the Mittwochsgesellschaft, 29 May 1935, USNA, Groener Papers, M-137, Roll 13.

[22] Plessen characterized Falkenhayn as a "terrible pessimist." Plessen, "Tagebuch," 25 September 1914.

[23] For examples see Gerhard Tappen, "Kriegstagebuch," 15 September 1914, BA/MA, NL Tappen, N56/1; and August von Cramon, *Unser österreichisch-ungarischer Bundesgenosse im Weltkriege* (Berlin: E. S. Mittler, 1920), p. 76.

the army's corps and army commanders, and his experience in the Great General Staff was very limited.[24] Falkenhayn, however, had been tipped as early as 10 August as a possible replacement for Moltke by the Chief of the Military Cabinet, and it was Lyncker and his deputy, Oberst Ulrich Freiherr von Marschall, who were instrumental in convincing the Kaiser to call Falkenhayn to the post.[25] Additionally, Falkenhayn was trusted enough by the Kaiser and his Military Cabinet to retain his position as Minister of War when he took up the post of Chief of the General Staff, an important consolidation of two powerful offices.[26] However, despite this support from high places, Falkenhayn was never able to shake off the image of the "outsider."

Indeed, Falkenhayn had certainly not followed an "ordinary" career for a German officer, and this would have great impact on his time as Chief of the General Staff. After attending cadet school, he was commissioned in the Oldenburg Infantry Regiment Nr. 91 in 1880. Though he graduated from the Kriegsakademie near the top of his class, Falkenhayn spent only three years (1893–96) in the Great General Staff in Berlin. In 1896, he left Prussian service for China, where he remained for six years, working first as an instructor for the Chinese army, then on the staff of the German expeditionary force during the Boxer Rebellion, and finally as a representative of the German government after the Rebellion. During the war, Falkenhayn's enemies circulated the rumor that he had had to leave the army and flee Germany due to gambling debts.[27] As his most recent biographer has shown, Falkenhayn's true reason was ambition. China offered a chance to break out of the boredom of peacetime garrison duty and to be exposed to the wider world.[28]

Due to his time spent in China and his limited experience in the Great General Staff, many of his fellow officers saw Falkenhayn as an interloper and charged that he did not belong to the so-called "Schlieffen School." In December 1914, this fact was used against Falkenhayn in an attempt to have him removed from the post of Chief of the General Staff. Major Hans von Haeften, then adjutant to Moltke and later the president of the Reichsarchiv, said in a discussion with Bethmann that Falkenhayn lacked

24 Reichsarchiv, *Der Weltkrieg*, Bd. V: *Der Herbst-Feldzug 1914* (Berlin: E. S. Mittler, 1929), p. 8.

25 Erich von Falkenhayn, diary entry for 10 August 1914, quoted in Zwehl, *Falkenhayn*, p. 61; Wilhelm Solger, "General von Falkenhayn als Chef des Generalstabes des deutschen Feldheeres," unpublished manuscript in BA/MA, W10/50709, p. 2.

26 From the very beginning this was looked upon unfavorably by some in the army. See Plessen, "Tagebuch," 15 September 1914.

27 For example, see Erich Ludendorff to Helmuth von Moltke, 2 January 1915, printed in Egmont Zechlin, "Ludendorff im Jahre 1915. Unveröffentliche Briefe," *Historische Zeitschrift* 211 (1970), p. 325.

28 Afflerbach, *Falkenhayn*, p. 45.

Fig. 4 Erich von Falkenhayn (left), the new Chief of the General Staff

training in the "Schlieffen tradition" because he "had only served in the General Staff under Schlieffen for a short period." Haeften maintained that because of this failing, Falkenhayn did not have the trust of the army.[29] These criticisms were taken up after the war by historians.[30]

Even Falkenhayn's supporters acknowledged that he held different operational ideas from those taught in the General Staff during Schlieffen's time. Wilhelm Heye, later the successor of Hans von Seeckt as the Chief of the *Reichswehr Heeresleitung* and strong supporter of Falkenhayn throughout the war, wrote of his time serving under Falkenhayn on the staff of the XVI Army Corps:

> I owe much to v. Falkenhayn from my time in Metz. One could learn a tremendous amount from him on General Staff rides, in winter wargames, and during maneuvers, despite the fact that it was immediately obvious even to us young General Staff officers that he lacked the schooling in operations taught by the genial Schlieffen . . . The opinions of [Falkenhayn] and his students in Metz on operational problems almost always differed sharply. Therefore, it was not astonishing to me that also during the war Falkenhayn's operational methods, as for example at Verdun, found so little acceptance from the other army commanders, especially not from his rival Ludendorff, Schlieffen's best student.[31]

Falkenhayn's surviving comments on staff problems issued while he was Chief of Staff to the XVI Army Corps show his impatience with some of the assumptions of Schlieffen's old students now under his command and demonstrate that even before the war he was developing his own tactical and operational ideas.[32]

Indeed, Falkenhayn prided himself on his independence. His duties in China allowed him to operate outside the normal constraints of a German officer, and before the outbreak of war he often spoke of returning to the Far East.[33] Moreover, Falkenhayn clearly relished his experiences outside Schlieffen's Great General Staff and believed that these gave him a wider outlook. He described himself as an autodidact and boasted, perhaps as a swipe at Schlieffen, that his education was based on experience rather than theoretical study.[34] Gerhard Ritter noted that Falkenhayn's time

[29] Quoted in Ekkehart P. Guth, "Der Gegensatz zwischen dem Oberbefehlshaber Ost und dem Chef des Generalstabes des Feldheeres 1914/15: Die Rolle des Majors v. Haeften im Spannungsfeld zwischen Hindenburg, Ludendorff und Falkenhayn," *Militärgeschichtliche Mitteilungen* 1 (1984), p. 90.

[30] For examples, see Wolfgang Foerster, *Graf Schlieffen und der Weltkrieg* (Berlin: E. S. Mittler, 1925), p. 86; and Solger, "Falkenhayn," p. 2.

[31] Wilhelm Heye, "Lebenserinnerungen Teil I (1869–1914)", unpublished manuscript in BA/MA, Heye Nachlass, N18/1, pp. 279–280.

[32] See Falkenhayn's comments to the solutions for the *Schlußaufgaben* issued in 1909 and 1910 in "German General Staff Problems, 1892–1913," unpublished manuscript in USNA, RG 165, Box 620.

[33] Afflerbach, *Falkenhayn*, pp. 86–98.

[34] Zwehl, *Falkenhayn*, pp. 7–8.

in China "had broadened his political horizons and given him a certain worldliness uncommon in the German officer corps."[35] The experience certainly opened his mind to a broader array of strategic and operational ideas than most of his contemporaries.

Despite later criticisms, Falkenhayn's time in China was to prove crucial to his career. In China, he came to the attention of Kaiser Wilhelm II and Heinrich, Prince of Prussia. Upon his return to Germany, Falkenhayn spent several years in posts typical for an officer of his rank. In 1913, he was suddenly thrust into the top echelons of the army due in large part to Imperial favor. The Kaiser, in a move that caused considerable consternation in the army, named him to replace Josias von Heeringen as Prussian Minister of War. The hitherto obscure 52-year-old Generalmajor was to replace the longest serving general in the army. Not since Albrecht von Roon in 1859 had a Generalmajor been appointed to such a senior position. Accordingly, Falkenhayn was simultaneously advanced from Generalmajor to Generalleutnant, jumping over the heads of around thirty more senior Generalmajore – a move that caused a further stir and created additional ill-feeling toward Falkenhayn.[36]

As Minister of War, Falkenhayn played a prominent role in the July Crisis, urging the Kaiser toward war at every opportunity, and, as Minister of War, he took to the field at the war's outbreak as a member of the Imperial Headquarters.[37] However, his presence in the headquarters was unwelcome to some. Perhaps because Falkenhayn was seen as a threat to Moltke, many General Staff officers expressed the opinion that the Minister of War's place during wartime was in Berlin, where administrative matters could be dealt with, not in the field. Consequently, Falkenhayn was not kept officially informed about the course of operations and played no role in the operational decisionmaking prior to his appointment as Chief of the General Staff.[38]

Though he had not been kept in close touch with the army's operations, Falkenhayn was able to remain in unofficial contact with the front. Through these contacts, he developed an unfavorable impression of

[35] Ritter, *The Sword and the Scepter*, vol. III: *The Tragedy of Statesmanship – Bethmann Hollweg as War Chancellor (1914–1917)* (trans. Heinz Norden) (Coral Gables, FL: University of Miami Press, 1972), p. 42.

[36] Falkenhayn was, however, promoted initially *ohne Patent*, meaning his rank did not advance him in seniority. Only on 27 January 1914 was he given his *Patent*. See Falkenhayn's "Personal-Bogen," in USNA, M-137, Roll 13.

[37] A copy of a portion of Falkenhayn's diary from the July Crisis has recently reappeared in the material returned to Germany from the former Soviet Union. The entries, from 27 July to 4 August 1914, show clearly Falkenhayn's desire for war in July 1914. BA/MA, W10/50635. See also Afflerbach, *Falkenhayn*, pp. 148ff.

[38] On the policy to keep Falkenhayn out of the decisionmaking process, see Hermann Ritter Mertz von Quirnheim to Reichsarchiv, 4 January 1934, BA/MA, W10/51523.

Moltke's handling of the war. Thus, he came to the General Staff determined to correct the wrongs he saw in Moltke's leadership. First and foremost, this meant to Falkenhayn a firmer control over the war's operations.[39] To this end, the new General Staff Chief immediately moved the OHL from Luxemburg to Charleville-Mézières to be closer to the front-line formations. From there, Falkenhayn intended to exercise stricter control over the army's tactical formations.[40]

Indeed, Falkenhayn was in a better position than Moltke to impose his will on the army. As both Chief of the General Staff and Minister of War, he brought two competing organizations, a significant portion of the army's bureaucracy, under a unified command. For the first time in many years, army planning and administration were under the control of one man. Hans von Zwehl, who as Falkenhayn's authorized biographer had access to his now-missing personal papers, wrote that even before the war Falkenhayn had harbored the ambition of reunifying the General Staff with the Ministry of War.[41] Now, in September 1914, he seemed to have achieved his goal. Falkenhayn believed that by retaining both positions, he could better the relationship between the two organizations and affect a more efficient running of the war.[42] In addition to Falkenhayn's control over the army bureaucracy, his good relationship with the Military Cabinet, and indeed with the Kaiser himself, ensured that there would be little meddling from above in his direction of operations.[43]

The Second OHL

Falkenhayn took over the OHL at a difficult time. The shock of the defeat at the battle of the Marne and the seeming failure of the pre-war plan shook an organization that was already straining under the stress of Moltke's slow breakdown. Perhaps because of this tension, Falkenhayn made few major personnel changes when he took over as Chief

[39] Falkenhayn was not alone in his criticism of Moltke's command style. On 4 September 1914, Wenninger reported to Munich that many were fed up with Moltke's *laissez-faire* leadership. Schulte, "Neue Dokumente," p. 166.

[40] Erich von Falkenhayn, *General Headquarters and its Critical Decisions, 1914–1918* (London: Hutchinson, 1919), p. 10; Redern, "Tagebuch," 25 September 1914.

[41] Zwehl, *Falkenhayn*, pp. 53–54. Indeed, Falkenhayn is reported to have said in October 1914 that one of the war's lessons was that the General Staff should be subordinated to the Ministry of War. Wrisberg, *Heer und Heimat*, p. 21.

[42] Falkenhayn, *General Headquarters*, p. 2. The OHL's *Bürooffizier*, Friedrich Mewes, noticed a significant improvement in the relations between the General Staff and the Ministry of War, especially between Tappen and Wrisberg. Mewes to Reichsarchiv, 7 December 1920, BA/MA, W10/51063.

[43] Groener called Falkenhayn the "expressed favorite of the Military Cabinet." Groener, "Die Strategie Falkenhayns," p. 4. For his relationship with the Kaiser, see Afflerbach, "Wilhelm as Supreme Warlord," pp. 433–443, passim.

of the General Staff. Although Hermann von Stein, the *Generalquartiermeister*, was removed from the OHL and given a corps command, most of Moltke's original staff remained.[44] The operations officer, Oberst Gerhard Tappen, stayed at his post, as did the other important section chiefs. Falkenhayn, however, entered his position determined to impose his command over the somewhat self-willed staff. Even Falkenhayn's critics credit him for his energy in reinvigorating the OHL following the Marne crisis.[45] One observer wrote, "we all lost our heads a bit – with one exception – Falkenhayn. A practical man, a Gneisenau, who leads us from retreat to victory!"[46]

Although Falkenhayn did not make many personnel changes when he took over as Chief of the General Staff, the day-to-day running of the OHL changed considerably. An extraordinarily hard-working man, Falkenhayn entered into the position determined to take all important decisions personally, later writing that from the day he was named Chief of the General Staff until his resignation in 1916, he "assumed sole responsibility for Germany's conduct of the war."[47] Unlike Moltke, Falkenhayn was resolved not to delegate his authority unduly, and accordingly he broke up the clique of staff officers who had exercised considerable power under his predecessor.[48] Moreover, Falkenhayn was naturally reserved and was loath to share his mind with his subordinates. Under Falkenhayn, the staff officers of the OHL would assume the role of advisors rather than decisionmakers. Although he developed a small circle of advisors, the new General Staff Chief never took them completely into his confidence. His distance from even his closest staff earned him the sobriquet, *der einsame Feldherr*, or "the lonely commander."[49]

Over time, a circle of advisors developed around the new General Staff Chief, with whom he debated, often quite vehemently, different courses of action. Although the composition of this group changed from time

44 Stein was replaced by Generalmajor von Voigts-Rhetz, who died of a heart attack shortly after assuming the position. Voigts-Rhetz was replaced by Generalmajor Adolph Wild von Hohenborn (see below).

45 *Der Weltkrieg*, V, pp. 8–9; Theobald von Bethmann Hollweg, *Betrachtungen zum Weltkriege* (2 vols.) (Berlin: Reimar Hobbing, 1921), II, p. 44.

46 Wenninger to his wife, 10 October 1914, in Schulte, "Neue Dokumente," p. 177.

47 Falkenhayn, *General Headquarters*, p. 1.

48 It was claimed a type of camarilla had developed in the OHL under Moltke, composed of the heads of the Operations, Intelligence, Political, and Central Sections of the General Staff (Tappen, Hentsch, Dommes, and Fabeck). See Eugen Ritter von Zoellner's report in Konrad Krafft von Dellmensingen, "Kriegstagebuch," 16 September 1914 in BA/MA, W10/50642. See also Mewes to Reichsarchiv, 7 December 1920, BA/MA, W10/51063; Wilhelm Groener, *Lebenserinnerungen* (ed. Friedrich Frhr. Hiller von Gaertringen) (Göttingen: Vandenhoeck & Ruprecht, 1957), p. 188; Wenninger, "Tagebuch," 14/15 September 1914, in Schulte, "Neue Dokumente," p. 174.

49 Hermann Ziese-Beringer, *Der einsame Feldherr: Die Wahrheit über Verdun* (2 vols.) (Berlin: Frundsberg-Verlag, 1934).

to time, several officers remained close to Falkenhayn throughout his tenure. The first of this group was the OHL's operations officer, Gerhard Tappen. Almost universally disliked,[50] Tappen was once described condescendingly by Falkenhayn as his "registrar."[51] Despite this remark, as Tappen's diary shows, he functioned as a sounding board for Falkenhayn's ideas throughout the war and on occasion exercised considerable influence over the General Staff Chief.

Falkenhayn frequently discussed events with his operations officer, and the two often disagreed violently as to the proper course of action. Tappen later described these exchanges:

> General von Falkenhayn's opinions were often very difficult to determine. He would sometimes mention an idea that perhaps did not correspond at all to his real opinion merely to arouse my opposition. When it sometimes then came to a really exciting and unrefreshing argument, he would finally say, after I had expressed my opinion sharply, that this was his opinion also. During these sessions, I often had the feeling that it would have to come to a complete break between us.[52]

This tension led on at least one occasion to Tappen proffering his resignation.[53]

The second figure in Falkenhayn's inner core of advisors was an old friend, Generalmajor Adolph Wild von Hohenborn.[54] In November 1914, Wild was assigned to the OHL to replace the recently deceased Voigts-Rhetz as *Generalquartiermeister*. Although the traditional role of a *Generalquartiermeister* was to see to the smooth operation of the lines of communication, Wild wrote to his wife about the different nature of his appointment: "Falkenhayn . . . said to me that he needs someone who can advise and support him, be his second conscience, someone who can help him bear the responsibility."[55] Wild functioned in this role as an

[50] Max Bauer described Tappen to his wife: "We all hate . . . [him] with all our hearts. He possesses all the terrible properties – egotism, arrogance, insincerity, ignorance and stupidity to the highest degree." Bauer to his wife, 17 November 1915, quoted in Adolf Vogt, *Oberst Max Bauer: Generalstabsoffizier im Zwielicht 1869–1929* (Osnabrück: Biblio, 1974), p. 595. For other examples see Fritz von Loßberg, *Meine Tätigkeit im Weltkrieg 1914–1918* (Berlin: E. S. Mittler, 1939), pp. 127–128; Rauch to his wife, 11 January 1915, BA/MA, W10/51305.

[51] Falkenhayn once remarked to Groener, "in operational matters, Tappen has absolutely no influence over me. However, he is an excellent registrar for me . . ." Groener, *Lebenserinnerungen*, p. 188. See also Afflerbach, *Falkenhayn*, p. 232.

[52] Gerhard Tappen, "Kriegserinnerungen," unpublished manuscript in BA/MA, W10/50661, pp. 92–93.

[53] Ibid., p. 165. Following a particularly violent argument concerning the attack on Verdun, Falkenhayn told Tappen, "I will not have a second Chief next to me."

[54] Plessen, no fan of Falkenhayn, was opposed to Wild being named *Generalquartiermeister* because of his closeness with Falkenhayn. Plessen, "Tagebuch," 10 November 1914.

[55] Wild to his wife, 10 November 1914, BA/MA, Wild Nachlass, N44/3.

Fig. 5 Adolph Wild von Hohenborn, one of Falkenhayn's close advisors and from January 1915 Minister of War

"unofficial advisor" throughout Falkenhayn's time as Chief of the General Staff, even after he left the OHL. Falkenhayn's continued trust in Wild was shown when he named Wild to take over as Minister of War in January 1915 after intrigues had forced Falkenhayn to give up his position of Minister of War.[56]

[56] "the personality of the new Minister of War, Lieut.-General Wild von Hohenborn, guaranteed the maintenance of [the cooperation between the General Staff and the Ministry of War]." Falkenhayn, *General Headquarters*, p. 3. Wild's close relationship with Lyncker must also have helped maintain smooth relations between the higher authorities of the army. See Wild to his wife, 11 November 1914, BA/MA, N44/3.

Fig. 6 Hugo Freiherr von Freytag-Loringhoven, one of Falkenhayn's close advisors

Wild's successor as *Generalquartiermeister*, Generalleutnant Hugo Freiherr von Freytag-Loringhoven, was the last of Falkenhayn's inner circle. Freytag, who before and after the war distinguished himself as a military writer, often discussed operations with Falkenhayn and participated in the OHL's evening "Whisper Club," at which recent events were discussed.[57] Despite their frequent discussions, however, Freytag ultimately concluded that his influence over Falkenhayn was limited. After

57 Hugo Freiherr von Freytag-Loringhoven, *Menschen und Dinge, wie ich sie in meinem Leben sah* (Berlin: E. S. Mittler, 1923), pp. 269–270.

the war he wrote, "the final decisions were always [Falkenhayn's] exclusive property . . . Basically he lacked a truly trusted helper with whom he could have talked everything over."[58]

Outside of these three advisors, the other members of the OHL functioned largely as specialists within their areas of responsibility. Their influence over operational decisions varied, but was usually quite limited. Oberst Wilhelm Groener, as the head of the railway section, played an important role in planning and as such was never far from the decisionmaking center. Others played important roles in assessing the lessons of *Stellungskrieg*. Oberst Max Bauer was responsible for "heavy artillery." Together with Oberst Fritz von Loßberg,[59] who functioned as the operations officer on the Western Front when the OHL moved to the east in spring 1915, and with Hauptmann Christian Harbou, Bauer updated the army's regulations during the summer of 1915 taking into account the lessons of the war to that date.[60]

In the short term, Falkenhayn's decision to keep the core of Moltke's staff in place when he assumed command may have helped steady an army shaken by setback, but in the long term it created tensions which diminished the effectiveness of the OHL and made it difficult for Falkenhayn to command the fractious German army. Falkenhayn's command style was the opposite of Moltke's. While Moltke had allowed his junior staff officers great latitude in decisionmaking, Falkenhayn reserved all decisions for himself. His unwillingness to involve his staff in his decisions clearly caused resentment, even amongst those closest to him such as Tappen. Added to the sense of resentment at a newcomer imposing his style upon an organization with a set method of operation came problems caused by Falkenhayn's personality. Although contemporaries are almost unanimous in praising his ability to work hard, most were less complimentary about his interpersonal skills. Some recalled his biting sarcasm, and most felt that they never really understood what was in Falkenhayn's mind.[61]

58 Ibid., p. 269.

59 Loßberg was described as a "creature of Falkenhayn's" (!) by a disgruntled Max Hoffman, *War Diaries and Other Papers* (trans. Eric Sutton) (2 vols.) (London: Martin Secker, 1929), I, p. 88.

60 Bauer, *Der grosse Krieg*, p. 86; Martin Samuels, *Command or Control? Command, Training and Tactics in the British and German Armies, 1888–1918* (London: Frank Cass, 1995), pp. 158–170. (See Chapter 7.)

61 On Falkenhayn's personality, see Hermann Ritter Mertz von Quirnheim to Reichsarchiv, 15 November 1933, BA/MA, W10/50705; Heye, "Lebenserinnerungen," I, pp. 280–284; Wilhelm Solger, "Falkenhayn," in Friedrich von Cochenhausen, *Heerführer des Weltkrieges* (Berlin: E. S. Mittler, 1939), pp. 93–101; Groener, *Lebenserinnerungen*, p. 187. See also the synopsis of the "psychological profile" drawn up by the Reichsarchiv in BA/MA, W10/50709.

His poor working relationship with this staff had serious implications for his ability to conduct the war. The German army of World War I relied upon its network of staff officers to communicate not just official orders, but also the real intentions of these orders.[62] In addition to formal means of communication, staff officers relied on an informal system, one based on personal relationships built up over years of working together, to transmit ideas and opinions.[63] As a relative newcomer to the General Staff, Falkenhayn had few of these personal ties to staff officers in the field. This made him all the more reliant upon his subordinates in the OHL. By alienating these officers, he cut this crucial informal communication cord. Unable, or unwilling, to understand some of Falkenhayn's more radical operational and strategic ideas, his staff officers did not work to ensure their acceptance within the wider army. As we shall see, in time, this would have grave implications for Falkenhayn's ability to conduct the war as he desired.

Falkenhayn's first strategic decisions

The German defeat at the battle of the Marne marked the failure of German plans and left the army in a precarious position. Before being replaced as Chief of the General Staff, Moltke had ordered a general retreat. The armies of the right wing (1st and 2nd) withdrew to the Aisne River, while the 3rd, 4th, and 5th Armies were withdrawn to a line running from Reims to north of Verdun. Moltke also ordered that the 6th and 7th Armies end their attempts to break through the French position to the south and set up defensive positions. In keeping with pre-war ideas, this retreat was to be a purely temporary measure, designed to buy time to bring up sufficient forces to renew the offensive on the right wing. To this end, Moltke initially ordered the 7th Army to the extreme right flank of the army. Pressure from Entente forces, however, forced him to deploy the 7th Army to fill the hole that had arisen between the retreating 1st and 2nd Armies.[64]

When Falkenhayn replaced Moltke on 14 September, this strategic redeployment had been largely completed. The 1st Army stood on the

[62] See Walter Goerlitz, *History of the German General Staff, 1657–1945* (trans. Brian Battershaw) (New York: Praeger, 1957), pp. 150–203.

[63] The diaries of staff officers during the war are replete with examples of this informal communication system, particularly once the war settled into *Stellungskrieg*. For examples, see Hoffmann, *War Diaries*; Adolph Wild von Hohenborn, "Kriegstagebuch," Wild Nachlass, BA/MA, N44/2; and Hermann von Kuhl, "Kriegstagebuch," BA/MA, W10/50652.

[64] Reichsarchiv, *Der Weltkrieg*, Bd. IV: *Der Marne Feldzug – Die Schlacht* (Berlin: E. S. Mittler, 1926), pp. 448–485. On Moltke's reaction to the defeat, see Mombauer, *Moltke*, pp. 260–271.

Aisne River with its right flank on the Oise. The 7th Army had been brought up from Alsace to fill the gap between the 1st and the 2nd Armies and it too stood on the Aisne. The 2nd Army's right flank connected with the 7th north of Reims and the 3rd, 4th, and 5th Armies held a line running from Prosnes east to Verdun. Each army had established field positions and seemed in a good position to repel any frontal attacks from the enemy. The real weakness of the German army came from its extreme right wing. There, the 1st Army's right flank was left hanging unprotected, vulnerable to envelopment by French forces being shifted from the south.[65]

The new German command needed to come up with an alternative plan of operation to restart the stalled offensive and defeat the French before the situation in the east became unmanageable. Groener believed that the German high command had the following options in mid-September 1914:

1. To try once again to throw back the French through an immediate frontal "mass attack" [*Massenangriff*] before the French could effect an envelopment of our right wing.
2. To go on the defensive behind the Aisne and to secure the right wing with large numbers of reserves.
3. To continue the retreat and thereby effect a complete regrouping of the German forces in order to undertake a new operation against the left flank of the French army.[66]

The new Chief of the General Staff believed that a speedy decision could still be reached on the Western Front,[67] and during the night of 14/15 September, he drew up a new plan of operation, choosing Groener's third option. Falkenhayn resolved to carry out a withdrawal to protect the vulnerable right flank and buy further time for a strategic regrouping. He intended to order the 1st Army to "break off from the enemy and to establish . . . the line Artems–La Fère–Nouvion Catillon." Falkenhayn planned with this maneuver to secure his right flank from French envelopment, await the arrival of the 6th Army, which was in transit from Lorraine, and to buy time to regroup the German forces for another assault on the French left wing. This renewed offensive would begin on 18 September with the 5th Army and would proceed "in echelon" over the next few days, culminating in the 6th Army's envelopment of the French forces from the extreme right wing.[68]

[65] *Der Weltkrieg*, V, pp. 17–20. [66] Groener, *Lebenserinnerungen*, p. 179.

[67] Wenninger to Bavarian Ministry of War, 14 September 1914, in Schulte, "Neue Dokumente," pp. 175–76.

[68] Erich von Falkenhayn, "Operationsplan am 15.9.14," quoted in a letter from the Reichsarchiv to Tappen, 26 February 1926, BA/MA, N56/3; *Der Weltkrieg*, V, pp. 20ff.

Falkenhayn was dissuaded, however, from this plan by Tappen, who returned from a tour of the front on 15 September. Tappen put forward a number of arguments to convince Falkenhayn not to institute his initial intentions. First, he believed the French to be exhausted and argued that only one final push was needed to decide the campaign. Further, Tappen argued that German morale was already shaken by the withdrawal after the defeat at the Marne and that any additional withdrawals would have an adverse effect on the morale of the German troops.[69] Although he did not completely agree with Tappen's assessment, Falkenhayn was generally convinced by his arguments and agreed to scrap the plan of the fifteenth.[70]

Tappen's reasoning displays several important characteristics that would reappear throughout the war. His assumptions, which became Falkenhayn's as well, would have far-reaching consequences. First, Tappen, and Falkenhayn with him, underestimated French will power and their ability to continue to resist. At the same time, both men overestimated German strength, which by this point was ebbing away quickly. Based on these beliefs, Falkenhayn was convinced that the French were at the end of their strength and that only one final push was needed to win the war. The General Staff Chief would again seriously underestimate the strength of his enemies before the French offensive in the autumn of 1915 and at the beginning of his offensive at Verdun in early 1916. Additionally, both men overestimated the moral effect of a withdrawal upon their own troops. This belief caused them to rule out any withdrawal, even tactical, by German forces. By November, this idea was translated into a policy that solidified the trench line. Falkenhayn would write: "Hold what you have, and never voluntarily surrender a square foot of land in the west."[71]

More immediately, Falkenhayn accepted Tappen's opinion that the French were nearly exhausted and that they offered no pressing threat

[69] There is some evidence to suggest this belief came from the 1st Army itself. On 21 September 1914, Tappen told Hermann Ritter Mertz von Quirnheim, the Ia of the 6th Army, that the 1st Army had declared its troops would not bear further retreat. Mertz to Reicharchiv, 24 January 1924, BA/MA, W10/51177.

[70] *Der Weltkrieg*, V, p. 21. Herbert Rosinski judged this decision to be the real beginning of trench warfare, writing, "it is the 15th [of September], the morning on which Falkenhayn decided against a return to the mobile strategy of the first weeks, *that must be considered the real turning point of the war.*" Herbert Rosinski, *The German Army* (ed. Gordon Craig) (New York: Praeger, 1966), p. 138. Italics in the original.

[71] Falkenhayn to Colmar von der Goltz, 16 November 1914, quoted in *Der Weltkrieg*, V, p. 585. Falkenhayn's policy may also have been influenced by the Kaiser's view on retreat. On 7 September, he had ordered: "Attack for as long as possible – under no circumstances take a step back." Quoted in Mombauer, *Moltke*, p. 228.

to the army's right wing. With this threat gone, he believed there was sufficient time to bring up the 6th Army without having to execute a strategic withdrawal. From 15 to 19 September, various orders to renew the offensive went forth from the OHL. Bülow's army group (1st, 2nd, and 7th Armies) was allowed to undertake its planned offensive. The 3rd, 4th, and 5th Armies were ordered to renew their assaults on the existing French positions.[72] These new attacks were to go forward quickly, "with the intention of passing under the enemy long-range artillery, overrunning the French infantry positions and capturing as quickly as possible the numerous enemy artillery pieces." These attacks were not intended to be decisive in themselves; rather they were to weaken the French further, to prevent them from shifting additional forces to their left wing, and to demonstrate to the Entente that the German offensive strength was not exhausted.[73]

Although he had rejected a tactical withdrawal, Falkenhayn remained committed to a battle along the lines dictated by pre-war operational doctrine. The General Staff Chief now decided to carry out a grand flanking maneuver that would have done any adherent to the operational ideas of Schlieffen proud.[74] The ultimate decision was to come from the intervention of the 6th Army on the right wing, which had begun its redeployment on 17 September. He informed the Bavarian Crown Prince Rupprecht, the commander of the 6th Army, that "the main goal of the [6th] Army must be . . . to achieve the decision of battle [*Schlachtentscheidung*] on the right wing of the army as soon as possible."[75] However, by the eighteenth, the French were again threatening the German right with envelopment with units from quieter areas of the front.[76] This forced Falkenhayn to set the 6th Army a secondary task. Falkenhayn wrote, "6th Army must use the first arriving units . . . to throw back the enemy force which has recently arrived on the right flank of the army and thereby take over the task of securing the army's right flank."[77] The General Staff Chief hoped, however, that the French units would be in no condition to put

72 *Der Weltkrieg*, V, pp. 34–55.

73 [Wilhelm] Solger, "Die Umstellung der Ob.Heeres-Ltg. vom Bewegungs- zum Stellungs-Krieg (IX./X. 1914)," (Forschungsarbeit zu Band V), unpublished manuscript in BA/MA, W10/51151, pp. 8–9, 11–12.

74 Jehuda Wallach, *The Dogma of the Battle of Annihilation* (Westport, CT: Greenwood Press, 1986), pp. 128–129.

75 Falkenhayn to 6th Army, 18 September 1914, quoted in Solger, "Umstellung," p. 15.

76 *Der Weltkrieg*, V, p. 61.

77 Falkenhayn to 6th Army, 18 September 1914, quoted in Solger, "Umstellung," p. 15. See also Konrad Krafft von Dellmensingen, "Kriegstagebuch," 18 September 1914, in BA/MA, W10/50643.

up a determined fight. He informed Rupprecht that the French units were now hopelessly "mixed with one another" and that many French units on their left wing had previously been defeated by the 6th Army in Lorraine.[78]

The French, however, were not as exhausted as Tappen and Falkenhayn believed, and the German attacks were unsuccessful in preventing them from transferring troops to their left wing. Using their better rail communications, they were able to shift their forces faster than the Germans.[79] Thus, as the first units of the 6th Army arrived on the German right wing, they were thrown immediately into battle to defend against a French envelopment. The 6th Army's secondary task, the protection of the right wing, became of necessity its primary task. For the next several weeks, the two opponents fed units, stripped from quieter sections of the front, on to the western flank piecemeal, in an attempt to outflank each other.[80]

After the failure of the 6th Army to decide the issue with a flank attack, Falkenhayn again returned to the idea of building a strong strike force on the extreme right wing. As part of this attempt, the 4th Army was rebuilt out of the III Reserve Corps which had recently been freed for further action with the fall of Antwerp, and four reserve corps which had been formed after the war's outbreak by volunteers.[81] This new attack was supplied liberally with the heavy artillery freed by the capture of Antwerp.[82] On 10 October, Falkenhayn assigned the 4th Army its tasks: "The 4th Army is to advance, *without regard for casualties*, with its right wing resting on the coast, first on the fortresses of Dunkirk and Calais . . . then to swing south . . . at St. Omer."[83] In conjunction with the 6th Army, the 4th Army was to smash the vulnerable left flank of the Entente forces and thereby deal the enemy an "annihilating blow."[84]

[78] Kronprinz Rupprecht von Bayern, *Mein Kriegstagebuch* (ed. Eugen von Frauenholz) (3 vols.) (Berlin: E. S. Mittler, 1929), I, p. 127.

[79] Ministère de la Guerre, *Les Armées Françaises dans la Grande Guerre* Tome I\Vol. IV: *La Bataille de l'Aisne, la Course à la Mer, la Bataille des Flandres, les Opérations sur le Front Stabilisé* (Paris: Imprimerie Nationale, 1933), pp. 147–176. German efforts to transfer troops from their left to their right wing were hampered by damage done to the rail network in France and Belgium. Adolph Sarter, *Die deutschen Eisenbahnen im Kriege* (Stuttgart: Deutsche Verlags-Anstalt, 1930), pp. 88ff.

[80] For the details of this stage in the "race to the sea," see *Der Weltkrieg*, V, pp. 69–118; and Strachan, *First World War*, I, pp. 262–280.

[81] Kriegsministerium, MI Nr. 3531/14 A1, 16 August 1914, in USNA, Documents of the Royal Prussian Military Cabinet, M-962, Roll 3; Wrisberg, *Heer und Heimat*, pp. 15–19.

[82] This artillery force amounted to twenty batteries of heavy field howitzers, twelve batteries of 21 cm howitzers, and six batteries of 10 cm cannon. *Der Weltkrieg*, V, p. 282.

[83] Quoted in *Der Weltkrieg*, V, p. 279. Italics added.

[84] Mertz to Reichsarchiv, 24 January 1924, BA/MA, W10/51177.

By 21 October, Falkenhayn's offensive was in progress. However, the desired results were again lacking. The 4th Army, composed mainly of hastily trained recruits, moved only slowly forward. Once again, the enemy was not as weak as the OHL had believed and was able to hold off the German attacks from hurriedly prepared defensive positions. Yet the 4th and 6th Armies continued attacking, in the belief that the enemy was near collapse, suffering severe casualties in frontal attacks poorly supported by artillery preparation.[85] From mid-October to the beginning of November, the 4th Army suffered 39,000 dead and wounded and 13,000 missing. The 6th Army lost 27,000 casualties and 1,000 missing.[86]

By early November it had become clear that the campaign would not be decided in Flanders. However, refusing for the moment the growing pressure to shift the main German effort to the east, Falkenhayn decided to continue operations at Ypres. Instead of attempting to win a "decisive" battle, the General Staff Chief now aimed at a more limited goal. He instructed the 4th Army to seize Ypres, "the central point of the enemy's defensive position," and Mount Kemmel. Although this would only be a "local result," Falkenhayn believed it would be of great value to the overall situation on the Western Front.[87]

It soon became clear, however, that even this limited goal would be more difficult than anticipated. On 8 November, Falkenhayn informed the Kaiser that operations in Flanders had come to a standstill, "the barbed wire cannot be crossed." Despite being pressured by the 4th and 6th Armies to continue the offensive,[88] two days later he told the Kaiser that he intended to call off the operations in Flanders as soon as the town of Ypres had been taken. The General Staff Chief felt that the Germans "could no longer reckon on any great success" in the west.[89] The German troops were exhausted and the ammunition for the heavy

[85] For the most recent account from the German perspective, which strips away much of the myth surrounding this battle, see Karl Unruh, *Langemarck: Legende und Wirklichkeit* (Koblenz: Bernard & Graefe, 1986).

[86] *Der Weltkrieg*, V, p. 401.

[87] AOK 4, "Kriegstagebuch," 4 November 1914, quoted in "Die deutsche Oberste Heeresleitung im Westen von 4.–28. November 1914" (Forschungsarbeit zu Bd. VI), unpublished manuscript in BA/MA, W10/51159, p. 2 (hereafter, "Die OHL im Westen"); Mertz, "Tagebuch," 12 November 1914, BA/MA, W10/51177; Tappen, "Kriegstagebuch," 4 November 1914; Afflerbach, *Falkenhayn*, pp. 194–195.

[88] At a meeting of the army Chiefs of Staff, Falkenhayn was told by the Chiefs of Staff of the 6th and 4th Armies (Konrad Krafft von Dellmensingen and Emil Ilse, respectively) that they could advance if reinforced and urged Falkenhayn not to give up the offensive. Konrad Krafft von Dellmensingen, "Kriegstagebuch," 12 November 1914, in BA/MA, W10/50644; "Die OHL im Westen," p. 15.

[89] Plessen, "Tagebuch," 8 and 10 November 1914; Falkenhayn, *General Headquarters*, pp. 33–34.

artillery was almost completely spent.[90] In the end, even the limited goal of capturing Ypres eluded the Germans, and Falkenhayn was forced to order the *Westheer* onto the defensive while he dealt with the growing threat in the east.[91]

The campaign's failure could be put down to a number of factors, some of which were temporary. The German attacks, though supported by the siege train freed by the fall of Antwerp, lacked munitions and thus could not be properly supported by heavy artillery. Second, the four reserve corps employed were inadequately trained and led, and were completely incapable of the demands of conducting a breakthrough of a prepared enemy position, even one as primitively prepared as the position at Ypres.[92] Third, the attacks generally proceeded without proper artillery preparation or support, the infantry believing speed to be more important than careful preparation. Crucially, the Ypres offensive had demonstrated to Falkenhayn clearly and forcefully the difficulties of attempting a "decisive" battle under the conditions of 1914.

The new General Staff Chief's attempt at bringing the war to a successful conclusion in the west had failed. The French had matched his flanking movements at each step and neither side had been able to gain an advantage. Further, the French troops were not as exhausted as Falkenhayn and Tappen continually held, and German troops were more fatigued than either believed. Wherever the opposing sides met each other, progress came to a halt and improvised field positions arose. All attempts to break through these positions were repulsed with great loss. By the end of the Ypres campaign, the German army was exhausted. Since the beginning of the war, it had suffered some 800,000 casualties, including some 116,000 dead.[93] With the failure to bring the war rapidly to a close in the west, Germany now faced the nightmare of a two-front war against roughly equal opponents. Moltke the Elder's great fear, a *Volkskrieg* of indeterminate duration, had come to pass.

[90] By 12 November, the German army had munitions remaining for only six more days of combat. Redern, "Tagebuch," 12 November 1914; Mertz recalled that on at least one occasion German officers had to threaten their men with pistols to get them out of the trenches to attack the enemy. Mertz to Reichsarchiv, 24 January 1924, BA/MA, W10/51177. In ten days of combat around Ypres, the attacking units had suffered 160,000 casualties. Plessen, "Tagebuch," 16 November 1914.

[91] Despite the "decisive" victory at Tannenberg, the Russians were threatening to knock Austria-Hungary from the war. The best efforts of the German units in the east were having little effect against the Russian "steamroller." Reinforcement was necessary to stabilize the front and inflict a setback upon the Russians. See *Der Weltkrieg*, VI, pp. 34–218; Herwig, *First World War*, pp. 106–113.

[92] Falkenhayn was to be heavily criticized for his decision to use these new corps in offensive operations. See Afflerbach, *Falkenhayn*, pp. 195–196.

[93] Herwig, *First World War*, p. 119.

Falkenhayn's new strategic direction

The failure at Ypres had far-reaching consequences. First, the inability to break through the primitive Entente trenches meant that mobility could not be restored to the front. Over the next several months, these primitive trenches would become increasingly sophisticated and even more difficult to break through. Second, the failure of the offensive and the high casualties caused Falkenhayn to rethink fundamentally German strategy. Although the Reichsarchiv's claim that he went through an "inner change" at this stage that led him to question his ability as Chief of the General Staff is overstated, clearly the failure of all his attempts to bring the war rapidly to a decisive end had a great impact upon him.[94] Wild wrote to his wife that Falkenhayn, "carries with difficulty the weight of the responsibility of being both Minister of War and General Staff Chief, and is not sure of himself."[95]

From this experience, however, the General Staff Chief reached important conclusions about the future course of the war. Already by early November he was convinced that "decisive," war-winning battlefield victory along the lines of pre-war doctrine was not possible with the forces at Germany's disposal in the west. The question then arose, whether or not to shift the focus of German efforts to the east, a strategy favored by a number of German leaders, most notably the commanders of the German forces in the east, Paul von Hindenburg and Erich Ludendorff. With respect for Russia's military potential and the vast space into which its armies could withdraw, the General Staff Chief rejected this. Not for the last time, Falkenhayn raised the specter of Napoleon's experience in Russia as a justification for not becoming involved deeply in the east.[96] Moreover, Falkenhayn also questioned whether a decisive battlefield victory in the east was any more likely than in the west given the strategic and tactical conditions prevailing at the time.

The day he called off the offensive at Ypres, Falkenhayn responded to Hindenburg's request for additional troops. In his letter, the General Staff Chief expressed his doubts as to whether or not Germany could expect anything more than limited gains under the current conditions.[97] He wrote that it would be easier for him to send reinforcement to the east when

94 *Der Weltkrieg*, VI, p. 437; Afflerbach, *Falkenhayn*, pp. 211–212. The Reichsarchiv's claim may also have been an attempt to cast aspersions upon Falkenhayn's subsequent strategic decisions.

95 Wild to his wife, 10 November 1914, N324/44. The failure at Ypres also led others in the army to question Falkenhayn's competence, see Afflerbach, *Falkenhayn*, pp. 211–217.

96 Falkenhayn, *General Headquarters*, pp. 14, 35.

97 Ibid., p. 35.

a well-found hope exists that within the realm of possibility the arrival of new forces in the east could bring about a final decision. However, at the moment this hope does not exist. In the best case, we would succeed in pushing the enemy back behind the Narew and Vistula River lines and force him to abandon Galicia. However, this does not constitute a war-winning decision [*Kriegsentscheidung*], although I cannot dispute that such a result could be of wide-ranging political significance.[98]

The clear difficulties of finding a military solution to the war with the forces at Germany's disposal led Falkenhayn to take a radical step. He now asked the Chancellor to find a diplomatic solution to Germany's strategic situation, admitting that there was no military solution.[99] Like Moltke the Elder before him, Falkenhayn recognized that Germany's military strength did not suffice to achieve battlefield victories against all its enemies simultaneously. Consequently, the new General Staff Chief had returned to an idea from Moltke the Elder's war plans; military success would serve as a springboard for a negotiated peace with at least one of Germany's enemies.

On 18 November, Falkenhayn met with Bethmann and asked him to conclude a separate peace with one of Germany's enemies. The General Staff Chief believed that this was the only way in which sufficient forces could be collected to achieve a "decisive" victory against the remaining enemies. Bethmann later conveyed the content of the conversation to the Under State Secretary for Foreign Affairs, Arthur Zimmermann:

This is how General von Falkenhayn judges the situation:

As long as Russia, France and England stay together it is impossible for us to defeat our opponents in such a way that we can make a decent peace. On the contrary we would run the risk of slowly exhausting ourselves. Either Russia or France must be detached. If we can succeed in causing Russia to make peace – and in first line this is what we should try to do – then we will be able to defeat France and England so decisively that we could dictate the peace . . . It is, however, to be expected with certainty that if Russia should make peace, France would also sing a different tune. Then, if England were not completely acquiescent we would wear her down, starving her out by means of a blockade based in Belgium, even though some months would be necessary to do so.[100]

98 Falkenhayn to Hindenburg, 18 November 1914, quoted in *Der Weltkrieg*, VI, p. 95.

99 Herwig, *First World War*, p. 117. Herwig's statement that this was the "first time in German history" that a Chief of Staff asked a Chancellor to negotiate a peace is a bit too sweeping. Clearly, Moltke the Elder worked closely with Bismarck. As Chapter 1 has shown, he also wrote into his war plans after 1870 the necessity of coming to terms with his enemy after initial victories, a task which would fall to Germany's diplomats.

100 Bethmann to Zimmermann, 18 November 1914, printed in Paul R. Sweet, "Leaders and Policies: Germany in the Winter of 1914–1915," *Journal of Central European Affairs* 16, 3 (1956), p. 232.

Falkenhayn felt that the "psychological moment for contact with Russia would be at hand if General Hindenburg should succeed in defeating the Russians in the battles now taking place." With Russia out of the picture, Germany could concentrate its forces, and perhaps count on Austro-Hungarian aid, to defeat its enemies in the west.[101]

Falkenhayn's conversation with Bethmann revealed the General Staff Chief's views about Germany's enemies. Clearly, he felt that peace could be obtained easily with Russia and that between the two countries there was no deep conflict. He also believed that, if a negotiated peace could be agreed with Russia, it was likely France would follow. Great Britain was another matter. Falkenhayn believed that Britain was Germany's main enemy and that Britain's *Vernichtungswille*, or "desire for annihilation," and hatred for Germany meant a negotiated peace between the two nations was almost impossible.[102] Only after its continental allies had been defeated could Britain itself be truly engaged.[103]

Indeed, Falkenhayn's conclusions took him much further than Moltke the Elder's ideas. He had, in essence, come to a strategy reminiscent of Delbrück's *Ermattungsstrategie*. Delbrück had demonstrated that Clausewitz had shown the time for *Ermattungsstrategie* was when a nation had only "modest political goals, weak motives, [or] limited strength."[104] To the new General Staff Chief, it was clear that Germany only possessed "limited strength." Without the capacity necessary to defeat its enemies totally, Falkenhayn believed that Germany would have to convince at least one enemy that the price of continuing the war was too great to pay. After November 1914, he no longer aimed at a dictated peace brought about by a decisive battlefield victory, at least in the first stage of the war. Instead, the General Staff Chief now aimed at detaching at first France or Russia from the anti-German coalition by means of a combination of military and diplomatic action. With one front gone, Germany's other enemies would either be convinced to negotiate a peace or sufficient military forces would be available to produce victory. Rather than the great

[101] Fritz Fischer, *Germany's Aims in the First World War* (New York: Norton, 1967), pp. 184ff.; and Ritter, *The Sword and the Scepter*, vol. III: *The Tragedy of Statesmanship*, pp. 45–45. Cf. Afflerbach, *Falkenhayn*, pp. 198–210, who stresses the anti-British nature of Falkenhayn's strategy.

[102] Falkenhayn's view that Britain would fight on even after its continental allies had been defeated was shared by his predecessor, Moltke the Younger. See Hermann von Kuhl, *Der Weltkrieg 1914–1918*, I (Berlin: W. Kolk, 1929), p. 165. On the general topic of German attitudes toward Britain, see Matthew Stibbe, *German Anglophobia and the Great War, 1914–1918* (Cambridge: Cambridge University Press, 2001).

[103] Falkenhayn wrote that Britain planned to win the war by following a strategy of "starvation and attrition." Falkenhayn, *General Headquarters*, pp. 23–24; Afflerbach, *Falkenhayn*, pp. 198–210.

[104] Hans Delbrück, "Die Strategie des Perikles," *Preußische Jahrbücher* 64 (1889), p. 263.

warwinning battles predicted by pre-war theory, victories on the battlefield would serve a more limited political goal – they would convince Germany's enemies that the price of continuing the war was too high to pay. With Germany's continental enemies gone, it would be free to fight a long war against its real enemy, Great Britain. However, Falkenhayn would meet almost as much difficulty in carrying out this radical strategy from his own side as he did from enemy counter-moves.

5 Competing strategic visions

While the consequences of the failure of Germany's war plan and the inability to break through the Entente line during the offensive at Ypres were clear to Falkenhayn, others within the German government and army did not draw the same radical conclusions. Indeed, most within Germany remained wedded to the traditional pre-war theory of warfare, one that placed "decisive" battlefield victories at its heart. Although Falkenhayn's strategic ideas were similar to those of the greatly respected Moltke the Elder, they also bore a great similarity to Hans Delbrück's despised concept of *Ermattungsstrategie*. As such, they were bound to get a rocky reception. The strategy advocated by Falkenhayn in late 1914 seemed to many to be a strategy of despair, and as such was rejected forcefully by many diplomats and officers unwilling to admit that Germany did not have the resources necessary to win the current *Volkskrieg* on its own terms. The result of this division over strategic approach was a deep schism within the German strategic leadership, which erupted into a bitter feud in late 1914. In the short term, this dispute nearly paralyzed the German high command. In the long term, it poisoned the working relationship between the two men necessary to carry out an effective strategy of attrition – the heads of the military and the civilian government, Erich von Falkenhayn and Theobald von Bethmann Hollweg.

* * *

When Falkenhayn outlined his new strategy to Bethmann in November 1914, the General Staff Chief held out some hopes that the offensives then being conducted by German and Austro-Hungarian troops would encourage the Russians to entertain moderate German peace proposals.[1] However, it is clear from his conversation with Bethmann that Falkenhayn believed Germany's main enemies lay in the west. He felt that between Russia and Germany there existed no real conflict of interests and that a

[1] For details of OberOst's Lodz offensive (11 to 25 November), Reichsarchiv, *Der Weltkrieg*, Bd. VI: *Der Herbst-Feldzug 1914* (Berlin: E. S. Mittler, 1929), pp. 104–226.

peace between the two nations could be concluded with little difficulty.[2] The General Staff Chief hoped that local military success would further the political agenda for peace. Moreover, he felt that by following a policy of peace with only minimal annexations, peace could be negotiated with France after Russia was removed from the war. Great Britain was another story. Falkenhayn viewed Britain as Germany's main enemy, and believed that Britain's *Vernichtungswille* and hatred for Germany would rule out any negotiated peace between the two nations. Instead, Germany would have to fight a long war against Britain utilizing the resources of the whole Continent.[3] Indeed, as early as August 1914, he had written in his diary "without the defeat of England this war will be lost for us."[4]

Not everyone in the German strategic leadership agreed with Falkenhayn's opinions, however. Not long after his conversation with the General Staff Chief, Bethmann traveled to the headquarters of Generalfeldmarschall Paul von Hindenburg and Generalleutnant Erich Ludendorff's Oberbefehlshaber Ost (OberOst) in Posen.[5] There, he found two highly capable, ambitious, and popular officers who maintained the traditional view that the military was capable of setting the conditions for peace on its own, without any assistance from the Foreign Office. These men believed that Russia could, and should, be defeated militarily, allowing Germany to dictate peace on its terms. This was to be accomplished in a time-tested manner. Despite the evidence of the war to date, Hindenburg still felt that the military overthrow of Russia was possible, if not through a single great battle, a "Sedan" in his words, then "through a series of such and similar battles."[6] Already dissatisfied with Falkenhayn's handling of the war and offended by his lack of regard for their strategic ideas, Hindenburg and Ludendorff argued that OberOst should be reinforced and that Germany's main effort should shift from the west to the east, and only after Russia had been militarily defeated should Germany concern itself with its Western enemies.[7]

2 Falkenhayn's most recent biographer has shown the extent to which his upbringing and family memories of the Napoleonic period helped make Falkenhayn a Russophile. Holger Afflerbach, *Falkenhayn: Politisches Denken und Handeln im Kaiserreich* (Munich: Oldenbourg Verlag, 1994), pp. 10–11.

3 Ibid., pp. 198–210.

4 Quoted in Hans von Zwehl, *Erich von Falkenhayn: Eine biographische Studie* (Berlin: E. S. Mittler, 1926), p. 211.

5 On 1 November 1914, the command of the 8th Army was redesignated *Oberbefehlshaber über die gesamten Streitkräfte im Osten des Reiches*, or "Supreme Commander, German Forces in the East of the Empire," OberOst for short. Under the command of Hindenburg were the 8th and 9th Armies and various *Landwehr* and fortress units. *Der Weltkrieg*, VI, pp. 37–38.

6 Paul von Hindenburg, *Out of My Life* (London: Cassell and Co., 1920), p. 132.

7 *Der Weltkrieg*, VI, pp. 415–416.

Fig. 7 The proponents of the traditional German way of war – OberOst, Paul von Hindenburg (left) and Erich Ludendorff (right), with Kaiser Wilhelm II (center)

Indeed, the belief that Germany's main effort should now shift to the east was strong amongst German soldiers. On the Eastern Front, the conditions were much different than on the Western. Rather than static trench warfare, war in the east maintained a more mobile character. The great distances and poor communications network did not permit a continuous trench line, and, thanks to the training of Schlieffen and Moltke the Younger, Germans excelled at fighting a *Bewegungskrieg*. The battles of Tannenberg (26 to 31 August) and the Masurian Lakes (9 to 14 September) demonstrated this, as well as ensured that the names of Hindenburg and Ludendorff would be on the lips of every German. Moreover, in addition to creating the myth of Hindenburg's and Ludendorff's military genius, this victory reinforced the opinion common in the German army that the Russians were incompetent soldiers. Understandably, to many German officers, a *Bewegungskrieg* in the east fought along traditional lines seemed preferable to a long, attritional *Stellungskrieg* in the west, and pressure grew on Falkenhayn from within the army to shift the main German effort to the Eastern Front.[8]

[8] Even some of the officers of his own staff felt this way. See Wild's memorandum of late December 1914 recommending the employment of the four new corps in the east

Falkenhayn resisted strongly this shift of emphasis. In addition to his belief that Germany's main enemy was in the west, the General Staff Chief did not believe in OberOst's basic strategic approach. As we have seen, the failure in the west had convinced the General Staff Chief that "decisive" battles on the model of Königgrätz or Sedan were no longer possible. Already in mid-November, Falkenhayn had rejected reinforcing OberOst on these grounds.[9] Further, the General Staff Chief believed that the Russian army could easily withdraw into the expanses of its country and avoid any "decisive" engagement.[10] Moreover, in late 1914, Falkenhayn feared that any withdrawal of units from the Western Front would dangerously weaken the German position there. He wrote that a transfer of troops to the east "would certainly be without any value if in the meantime the western enemies were successful in crushing our western forces or only even in forcing us to give up the North Sea coast."[11] Citing similar reasons, Falkenhayn refused the Austro-Hungarian Chief of Staff's request for reinforcement as well.[12] An added, but unarticulated, motive was Falkenhayn's reluctance to contribute to the rising popularity of Hindenburg and Ludendorff by pandering to their strategic ideas.

Regardless of opinion, by the end of November the German army was incapable of any further offensive action. The war to date had exhausted the German army. Between the war's outbreak and the end of the Ypres offensive on 18 November, the German army had suffered 800,000 casualties, including 116,000 dead, or nearly half the strength of its field army.[13] German soldiers on the Western Front were so weary of battle that on some occasions during the Ypres offensive officers had to drive their men at pistol point out of the trenches into the attack.[14] Further, there existed no appreciable reserve of artillery munitions.[15] Until sufficient reserves could be built and the German army rested, the question of where to place the emphasis of the German war effort remained merely a staff problem.

in BA/MA, W10/51151; and Wilhelm Groener's diary entry for 20 November 1914 in Wilhelm Groener, *Lebenserinnerungen* (ed. Friedrich Freiherr Hiller von Gaettringen) (Göttingen: Vandenhoeck & Ruprecht, 1957), pp. 203–204.

9 Falkenhayn to Hindenburg, 18 November 1914, quoted in *Der Weltkrieg*, VI, pp. 95–96.

10 Erich von Falkenhayn, *General Headquarters and its Critical Decisions 1914–1916* (London: Hutchinson, 1919), p. 14.

11 Falkenhayn to Hindenburg, 18 November 1914, quoted in *Der Weltkrieg*, VI, p. 96.

12 Falkenhayn to Conrad, 18 November 1914, quoted in ibid., p. 95.

13 Holger Herwig, *The First World War: Germany and Austria-Hungary 1914–1918* (London: Arnold, 1997), p. 119; Richard Bessel, *Germany After the First World War* (Oxford: Clarendon Press, 1993), p. 6.

14 Mertz to Reichsarchiv, 24 January 1924, BA/MA, W10/51177.

15 On 12 November, the First General Staff Officer (Ia) of the Operations Section of the OHL recorded in his diary that there existed artillery ammunition for only six more days of fighting. Major von Redern, "Tagebuch," 12 November 1914, BA/MA, W10/50676.

However, the issue remained just under the surface, and Falkenhayn's handling of the Ypres offensive combined with his evident rejection of the German army's "traditional" strategic approach, caused many to question his competence to be Chief of the General Staff. While the German army was rebuilding in December 1914, those resolved to see the war brought to an end by means of a great decisive battle in the east formed an anti-Falkenhayn cabal. Centered on the ambitious OberOst, these men were determined to see Falkenhayn replaced as Chief of the General Staff by someone inculcated with the "proper" strategic ideas. The situation was brought to a head by the creation of four new army corps during December 1914, which would be ready for employment by 20 January. During December and early January, OberOst increased their efforts to gain the new force for employment in the east and to bring Falkenhayn down. As the new force neared its completion, the power struggle between OberOst and Falkenhayn became ever more viscous and ever more personal.

Appealing to differing motives, the energetic officers of the OberOst worked feverishly behind the scenes to reach their goals, and Falkenhayn soon developed powerful enemies. Finding members for this *fronde* was not difficult for the "easterners." By December 1914, many within the army were clearly dissatisfied with the progress of the war, and they tended to blame Falkenhayn for some of the more spectacular failures. There was a general feeling that Falkenhayn was too junior and lacked the necessary experience and authority to lead the German army.[16] For years, the post of Chief of the General Staff had been filled by men of great stature within the German army – men such as Helmuth von Moltke the Elder and his nephew and Alfred Graf von Schlieffen. These men commanded great respect, something the junior Falkenhayn lacked. These fears about Falkenhayn's suitability to lead the army seemed to be highlighted by the results of his first strategic decisions.

In particular, Falkenhayn's conduct of the Ypres offensive, with its terrible casualties, had shaken the confidence of several important army commanders. Already during the offensive, Bavarian Crown Prince Rupprecht, commander of the 6th Army, had clashed with the General Staff Chief over the battle's progress, and this mistrust continued into the new year.[17] The commander of the 3rd Army, Karl von Einem, was also

[16] See Groener, *Lebenserinnerungen*, pp. 205–206; Josef Stürgkh, *Im deutschen Grossen Hauptquartier* (Leipzig: Paul List, 1927), pp. 81ff.

[17] Falkenhayn, not satisfied with the progress being made by the 6th Army, created a new army group outside of Rupprecht's command to continue the offensive. Rupprecht was so offended that he considered appealing Falkenhayn's decision directly with the Kaiser. Kronprinz Rupprecht, *Mein Kriegstagebuch* (ed. Eugen von Frauenholz) (3 vols.) (Berlin: E. S. Mittler, 1929), I, pp. 232ff.

dissatisfied with Falkenhayn's conduct of the war,[18] and the German Crown Prince Wilhelm, who commanded the 5th Army, went so far as to write to his father advising that Falkenhayn should be replaced by Hindenburg.[19]

Now Falkenhayn's poor relationship with his staff in the OHL began to have a detrimental effect on his ability to command the fractious army. The fact that Falkenhayn did not enjoy the full support of his immediate staff and that he did not have a following of young General Staff officers deployed with the army made it difficult for him to counter the growing ill-feeling among the commanders of the field army. Indeed, it appears that some of Falkenhayn's closest staff were secretly criticizing their chief's handling of the war.[20] To make matters worse, OberOst did have the informal network that Falkenhayn lacked, and they increasingly used these personal connections in their feud with the General Staff Chief.

In addition to the army leadership, many within the political leadership began to doubt Falkenhayn's suitability to be Chief of the General Staff, most dangerously the Chancellor. Bethmann had been won over by the officers of OberOst at their meeting on 6 December. Already shaken by what he saw as Falkenhayn's undue pessimism and perhaps fearful of Falkenhayn's bureaucratic power, Bethmann came to believe that he should be removed from his position as Chief of the General Staff and restricted to his duties as Minister of War. Further, he was convinced by OberOst that the emphasis in Germany's military effort should shift to the east, where a traditional strategy could be followed.[21] Bethmann was supported in this belief by the Under Secretary of State for Foreign Affairs, Arthur Zimmermann, who argued that Russia was a more dangerous enemy than those in the west and should be dealt with first.[22]

18 For examples, see Karl von Einem, "Kriegstagebuch," 20 November 1914 and 10 January 1915, BA/MA, N324/12. A much-edited version of Einem's diary was published after the war as *Ein Armeeführer erlebt den Weltkrieg* (ed. Junius Alter) (Leipzig: v. Hase and Koehler, 1938).

19 Paul Herre, *Kronprinz Wilhelm: Seine Rolle in der deutschen Politik* (Munich: C. H. Beck, 1954), pp. 55–56.

20 See Helmuth von Moltke's comments about information coming from the OHL, Moltke to an anonymous military colleague, 12 January 1915, printed in Helmuth von Moltke, *Erinnerungen Briefe Dokumente, 1877–1916* (ed. Eliza von Moltke) (Stuttgart: Der Kommende Tag, 1922), p. 409.

21 Falkenhayn did indeed have a tendency to interfere in areas more properly left to the Reich's political leadership. Karl-Heinz Janßen, *Der Kanzler und der General: Die Führungskrise um Bethmann Hollweg und Falkenhayn (1914–1916)* (Göttingen: Musterschmidt, 1967), pp. 21ff.; Zwehl, *Falkenhayn*, pp. 166–167; Sweet, "Leaders and Policies," p. 235.

22 Zimmermann to Bethmann, 27 November 1914, reprinted in Sweet, "Leaders and Policies," pp. 236–239. Zimmermann's memorandum was in response to Bethmann's letter

Upon his return to Berlin, Bethmann began agitating for Falkenhayn's replacement as Chief of the General Staff. Generaloberst Hans von Plessen, the Kaiser's Adjutant General and commander of the Imperial Headquarters, recorded in his diary on 8 December: "At [the Kaiser's] request, I traveled to see the Chancellor. He is very apprehensive about our future. Has no trust in Falkenhayn. Wants Ludendorff instead. Falkenhayn shall be only Minister of War."[23] Again, on 10 December, Bethmann pushed the matter with the army authorities. Plessen found him arguing with Generaloberst Moriz Freiherr von Lyncker, the head of the Kaiser's Military Cabinet.[24] The Chancellor again put forward the argument that "Falkenhayn should be limited to the post of Minister of War and Ludendorff should become Chief of the General Staff."[25]

Indeed, by attacking the unification of two important army bureaucracies under Falkenhayn, the Chancellor was playing a shrewd game. If Bethmann had criticized the General Staff Chief directly on operational matters, the soldiers of the Kaiser's headquarters would certainly have resented the interference of a civilian in strictly army business. Instead, Bethmann attacked Falkenhayn at the political level and was able to awaken in soldiers a degree of unease about Falkenhayn's position. Since at least the Franco-German War, the Ministry of War and the General Staff had gradually grown apart and had become rivals, and their independence from one another had become a matter of convention if not law.[26] Now, the Chancellor was arguing "the great increase in authority that the unification in one person of the offices of Minister of War and Chief of the General Staff means a great danger, especially in such a difficult man as Falkenhayn."[27]

of 19 November outlining Falkenhayn's strategic ideas. On Zimmermann's eastern ideas, see also Gerhard Ritter, *The Sword and the Scepter: The Problem of Militarism in Germany*, vol. III: *The Tragedy of Statesmanship – Bethmann Hollweg as War Chancellor (1914–1917)* (trans. Heinz Norden) (Coral Gables, FL: University of Miami Press, 1972), pp. 45–48.

23 Hans von Plessen, "Tagebuch," 8 December 1914, BA/MA, W10/51063.

24 The Military Cabinet was responsible for officer assignments. See Rudolf Schmidt-Bückeburg, *Das Militärkabinett der preußischen Könige und deutschen Kaiser* (Berlin: E. S. Mittler, 1933).

25 Plessen, "Tagebuch," 10 December 1914. Both Lyncker and Plessen defended Falkenhayn at this stage. Plessen gave him the credit for rebuilding the army, a task which he believed was accomplished so efficiently because Falkenhayn was at once Minister of War and Chief of the General Staff.

26 On the tensions between the army's bureaucracies, see Heinrich Otto Meisner, *Der Kriegsminister 1814–1914* (Berlin: Hermann Reinshagen Verlag, 1940), *passim*; and Gordon Craig, *Politics of the Prussian Army* (New York: Oxford University Press, 1956), pp. 219–299 *passim*.

27 Quoted in Hans von Haeften's "Tagebuch," reprinted in Ekkehart P. Guth, "Der Gegensatz zwischen dem Oberbefehlshaber Ost und dem Chef des Generalstabes des Feldheeres 1914/15: Die Rolle des Majors v. Haeften im Spannungsfeld zwischen Hindenburg, Ludendorff und Falkenhayn," *Militärgeschichtliche Mitteilungen* 1 (1984), p. 89.

Fig. 8 The Imperial Chancellor, Theobald von Bethmann Hollweg

Having won over a number of key officers to his side, including Hans von Plessen, Bethmann finally broached the subject of dismissing Falkenhayn with the Kaiser on 3 January 1915.[28] The Chancellor marshaled his arguments and claimed that "the objections to the office-accumulation are all the greater, as public opinion, the important political circles, and, as I know definitely, a greater part of the army possess no great trust in General v. Falkenhayn." As a successor, Bethmann recommended Ludendorff. The Kaiser, however, would not hear of dismissing Falkenhayn. While Crown Prince Wilhelm had made him aware of the objections to the unification of the two key offices in the army, the Kaiser "claimed to know nothing of the mistrust of General von Falkenhayn." Further, Wilhelm declared that Falkenhayn still possessed his full trust and confidence and that he could never countenance the appointment of Ludendorff, a "dubious character, eaten away by personal ambition," in the Kaiser's words, as Chief of the General Staff.[29] It looked as if the campaign to unseat Falkenhayn and to shift German strategy to the east had failed. Indeed, Bethmann's attack on what Wilhelm saw as his "command authority" had actually done harm to the effort to remove Falkenhayn from one of his posts. According to Plessen's diary, the Kaiser had already decided to name Generalleutnant Adolph Wild von Hohenborn Minister of War and restrict Falkenhayn to his post of General Staff Chief.[30] After his meeting with Bethmann, Wilhelm determined to keep Falkenhayn in both his posts.

Despite the setback, the campaign against Falkenhayn was not yet dead. OberOst now made full use of their personal communication network within the army to reinvigorate the failing battle. To coordinate their anti-Falkenhayn campaign, OberOst employed an energetic young General Staff officer, Major Hans von Haeften, to work behind the scenes, and Haeften was able to keep the campaign alive even after the Kaiser's initial command. In addition to being an intelligence officer in OberOst, Haeften was also the personal adjutant of Moltke the Younger, who following his dismissal had been named Deputy Chief of the General Staff and stationed in Berlin. Haeften's positions gave him access to the highest levels of the Reich's government and army and allowed him to travel

28 As his diary clearly demonstrates, Plessen's opinion of Falkenhayn had varied considerably over time. Plessen at first did not like Falkenhayn, but then his handling of the army after the Marne won Plessen's grudging respect. However, the refusal to shift his focus to the east turned Plessen against Falkenhayn. By the end of December, he was supporting the Chancellor and OberOst. Plessen, "Tagebuch," 30 December 1914.

29 Bethmann to the Under State-Secretary of the Reich Chancellery, Arnold Wahnschaffe, 7 January 1915, quoted in Afflerbach, *Falkenhayn*, pp. 222–223.

30 Plessen, "Tagebuch," 2 January 1915.

relatively freely from front to front. The young General Staff officer was fanatically wedded to the traditional concept of a "decisive" military victory, which he believed could be carried out in the east. Moreover, like many in OberOst, he carried a great deal of personal animosity toward Falkenhayn.[31] From 5 to 8 January, he traveled to the Western Front to brief his friends on the staffs of the armies there on the situation on the Eastern Front and to organize their opposition to Falkenhayn. Through their staffs, Haeften was able to convince the leaders of the *Westheer*, particularly Crown Prince Rupprecht and Crown Prince Wilhelm, that the Eastern Front should be reinforced as soon as possible in order to seek a "decisive" battle there. After Haeften's briefing, these leaders acknowledged that "it is obvious that the new corps should not be employed in the west, but rather in the east," and the 6th Army even put forward the opinion that they could make at least one additional corps available for service in the east.[32]

Also in early January, Haeften was able to bring Moltke into the fray against Falkenhayn. Now posted to Berlin with little meaningful to occupy his time, the former General Staff Chief was anxious to regain influence within the army.[33] Like Bethmann, Moltke decided to attack Falkenhayn on the political level. On 8 January 1915, he wrote to the Chancellor, providing him with much-needed military support:

> There is no question . . . that the unification of the offices of Chief of the General Staff and Minister of War in one hand is judged as unfavorable by a wide circle of the nation. I personally hold the unification for undesirable. The General Staff and the Ministry of War are two authorities, which must form a balance to one another if they are to work in a useful way. Additionally, the Minister of War belongs in Berlin at the center of his effectiveness. The unification of both offices is personally comfortable for the holder; when he meets opposition, he can decide dictatorially. This has recently been demonstrated in the question of the formation of the new corps. As I have heard, the Ministry of War, and Falkenhayn as Minister of War, was against their formation and for a reinforcement of our *Westheer*, while General v. Falkenhayn the Chief of the General Staff ordered their formation. In this case, I would have followed the Ministry of War's opinion.[34]

[31] See Guth, "Gegensatz," pp. 75–111, *passim*. Max Hoffmann, OberOst's Ia, spoke of Falkenhayn as the "evil angel of the Fatherland." See his diary entry for 1 December 1914, in Max Hoffmann, *War Diaries and Other Papers* (trans. Eric Sutton) (London: Martin Secker, 1929), p. 51. Also Ludendorff openly spoke of his hatred for Falkenhayn. See his letter to Moltke, 2 January 1915, printed in Egmont Zechlin, "Ludendorff im Jahre 1915. Unveröffentlichte Briefe," *Historische Zeitschrift* 211 (1970), pp. 324ff.

[32] Haeften, "Tagebuch," 8 January 1915, in ibid., p. 93.

[33] See Annika Mombauer, *Helmuth von Moltke and the Origins of the First World War* (Cambridge: Cambridge University Press, 2001), pp. 275–281.

[34] Moltke to Bethmann, 8 January 1915, printed in Moltke, *Erinnerungen*, pp. 395–396.

Moltke put forward Generaloberst Karl von Bülow to be Falkenhayn's successor, as he believed Ludendorff to be too young for the post. The fact that Moltke had held the position of Chief of the General Staff at once gave his arguments greater force and allowed him to go further in his criticisms of Falkenhayn. He was able to suggest that Falkenhayn's new strategy was incorrect and that Russia should first be defeated "decisively" before the situation in the west was tackled.

In the next few days, Moltke supported his arguments with several additional letters to Bethmann and the Kaiser. The topic of his letters was the serious shortfall in foodstuffs Germany was facing. The subtext of the missives was that Germany could not win a long war. Therefore, the war would have to be ended quickly. In Moltke's eyes, the only way this could be accomplished was by a traditional battlefield victory fought in the east. He wrote: "According to my deepest convictions, the war's decision lies in the east." There, he believed it was still possible to deliver a knockout blow to the Russian army and force a peace upon a defenseless Russia.[35]

Despite the intrigues against him, Falkenhayn stood firm in his beliefs and, in keeping with the strategy he outlined to the Chancellor in November, the General Staff Chief declared in January 1915, "the war will be decided here in the west at Calais."[36] Falkenhayn continued to believe that conditions did not allow for a "decisive" victory. Therefore, he still felt that the only way to bring the war to an end was through some sort of separate peace with one of Germany's enemies. He was under no illusions about what could be accomplished with only four and a half corps. Unlike OberOst, Falkenhayn was convinced that "the nine divisions in training . . . would not be sufficient to effect a real decision in either the West or the East."[37] However, the opposition to his western strategy and the weakness of Austria-Hungary made him pause to consider a *limited* eastern offensive. On 2 January, he now told Franz Conrad von Hötzendorf, the Austro-Hungarian Chief of Staff, that he would decide within three weeks whether or not he would deploy his new army corps in the east.[38]

Also in early January, the frustrated General Staff Chief finally struck back at his tormentors in an effort to silence his most violent critics. First, a number of German units, formed with a number of Austro-Hungarian

[35] Moltke to Bethmann, 10 January 1915, and Moltke to Kaiser Wilhelm, 10 January 1915, printed in ibid., pp. 399–406. See also Mombauer, *Moltke*, pp. 280–282.

[36] Quoted in Janßen, *Der Kanzler und der General*, p. 41.

[37] Falkenhayn, *General Headquarters*, p. 43.

[38] Gerhard Tappen, "Kriegstagebuch," 2 January 1915, BA/MA, N56/1; Janßen, *Der Kanzler und der General*, p. 66; Afflerbach, *Falkenhayn*, p. 231.

units into the so-called *Südarmee*, were sent to the Austro-Hungarian section of the Eastern Front from OberOst as reinforcements.[39] Although he did not believe this force would accomplish much, it was intended to end his ally's cries for reinforcement and provide them with assistance for their forthcoming offensive in the Carpathians. Second, in an attempt to quell OberOst's insubordination once and for all, Falkenhayn ordered the separation of the Hindenburg/Ludendorff team. On 8 January, Ludendorff was ordered to report to Alexander von Linsingen's *Südarmee* as Chief of Staff. Further, on 11 January, the General Staff Chief traveled to Posen to meet Hindenburg and attempt to come to some form of understanding with OberOst.[40]

However, Hindenburg was in no mood to compromise with Falkenhayn after the latter had just transferred his Chief of Staff, and Falkenhayn's attempt to sideline his most vocal critic – Ludendorff – was met with hefty opposition, which brought the power struggle between OberOst and Falkenhayn to a head. Ludendorff's first reaction to this transfer was to request to be relieved of his duties as Chief of Staff and be given a division instead, and he immediately wrote to the Military Cabinet. However, at Hindenburg's behest, Ludendorff withdrew this request.[41] Now Hindenburg took up the fight for his former Chief of Staff. At his meeting with Falkenhayn, Hindenburg demanded Ludendorff's return and a shift of strategy to the east. When Falkenhayn refused, Hindenburg informed him that the army no longer had confidence in him and the Field Marshal advised that he resign immediately. Additionally, Hindenburg informed Falkenhayn he had written to the Kaiser saying exactly the same thing. All Falkenhayn's attempts to mollify Hindenburg and to get him to refrain from sending his letter were in vain.[42]

True to his word, in rapid succession, Hindenburg wrote first to the head of the Kaiser's Military Cabinet, Lyncker, and then to the Kaiser himself. The Field Marshal called for Falkenhayn's replacement, Ludendorff's return to OberOst, and the employment of the new corps in the east. Haeften recorded Hindenburg's words in his diary: Hindenburg felt that it was his duty as the oldest general in the army to inform the Kaiser that "with a few strokes of the pen, [he] could bring calm, security, and trust to the nation again through the reinstatement of Moltke to his previous position as Chief of the General Staff, through the return

[39] Reichsarchiv, *Der Weltkrieg*, Bd. VII: *Die Operationen des Jahres 1915: Ereignisse im Winter und Frühjahr* (Berlin: E. S. Mittler, 1931), pp. 10ff.

[40] Ibid., pp. 13–14; Tappen, "Kriegstagebuch," 12 January 1915.

[41] Ludendorff to Moltke, 9 January 1915, in Zechlin, "Ludendorff im Jahre 1915," pp. 326ff.; Erich Ludendorff, *Meine Kriegserinnerungen* (Berlin: E. S. Mittler, 1919), pp. 89–90.

[42] Afflerbach, *Falkenhayn*, p. 226; Haeften, "Tagebuch," 12 January 1915, in Guth, "Gegensatz," pp. 96–97.

of Ludendorff to his position as chief of staff in Posen, and through the employment of the new corps in the east." He further declared that he could no longer work with Falkenhayn and gave the Kaiser an ultimatum – either Falkenhayn was dismissed or he would resign.[43]

Like Bethmann's intervention earlier in the month, Hindenburg's *démarche* only enraged the touchy Kaiser. To Wilhelm, Hindenburg's letter smacked of insubordination and even of a threat to the monarchy. The Kaiser and his headquarters maintained that a German field marshal could not resign in the face of the enemy; he could only be dismissed by his Kaiser.[44] Further, Wilhelm was very sensitive to Hindenburg's growing popularity with the German public, and in Hindenburg's letter was an implied threat to appeal to public opinion if the Kaiser did not do as Hindenburg desired.[45] The angry Wilhelm compared Hindenburg with Wallenstein, and his first response was to order Hindenburg's dismissal and court martial.[46] With difficulty, his staff dissuaded him from such a course. Moreover, Bethmann intervened once again and informed the Kaiser that he "could no longer bear responsibility for the political situation if the Kaiser dismissed Hindenburg."[47]

Hindenburg's letter brought forth a deluge of support. Once again, Haeften was able to bring Moltke into the fray. Moltke first wrote to Hindenburg encouraging him to stand fast in the face of the Kaiser's anger, promising that "I stand or fall with you."[48] Moltke then wrote to the Kaiser two letters in which he used words as strong as Hindenburg's: "General v. Falkenhayn is, in my firm opinion, neither in his character nor in qualifications suitable to be Your Majesty's principal advisor in military affairs in these difficult times. – His person constitutes a serious danger to the Fatherland." Moltke went on to say that a western strategy, as advocated by Falkenhayn, could only lead to minor successes and that only an eastern strategy could result in any meaningful victory. Like Hindenburg, Moltke threatened resignation if Falkenhayn were not replaced.[49]

At the same time as Moltke was writing to support Hindenburg, Haeften and OberOst were able to call upon a wide range of others, including many in the Imperial family. First, Crown Prince Wilhelm, who

43 Haeften, "Tagebuch," 12 January 1915, in Guth, "Gegensatz," pp. 96ff.
44 Plessen, "Tagebuch," 14 to 16 January 1915.
45 Janßen, *Der Kanzler und der General*, p. 76.
46 Axel Freiherr Varnbüler von und zu Hemmingen to Carl von Weizsäcker, 29 May 1916, published in Janßen, *Der Kanzler und der General*, pp. 291–292.
47 Bethmann to Lyncker, 14 January 1915, in ibid., p. 79.
48 Moltke to Hindenburg, 14 January 1915, printed in Moltke, *Erinnerungen*, pp. 409–410. Cf. Haeften, "Tagebuch," 17 January 1915, in Guth, "Gegensatz," p. 99.
49 Moltke to Wilhelm, 15 and 17 January 1915, printed in Moltke, *Erinnerungen*, pp. 410–416.

had spoken against Falkenhayn for some time, was consulted when Hindenburg's letter arrived. According to Plessen, although the Crown Prince sympathized with the Kaiser's anger, he "blew the same horn as Hindenburg."[50] A visit by another of the OberOst conspiracy, Elard von Oldenburg-Januschau, to 5th Army headquarters on 16 January resulted in an additional letter of support for Hindenburg from the Crown Prince.[51] Further, another of the Kaiser's sons who had served on the staff of OberOst, Prince Joachim, paved the way for Haeften to meet Kaiserin Augusta Victoria on 18 January. At their meeting, Haeften informed the Kaiserin of the contents of Hindenburg's letter to the Kaiser and of the danger he believed Falkenhayn represented to Germany. The Kaiserin sent Haeften back to Berlin carrying a letter from her to her husband, in which she urged the Kaiser to acquiesce to Hindenburg's demands.[52]

While support for Hindenburg was coming in from all around the Reich, the Kaiser's staff were taking steps to resolve the leadership crisis. Wilhelm had been greatly taken aback by the actions of his subordinates. Yet at the same time, as offended as he was, he had to take seriously their opinions, and from this finally came a compromise that brought order once again to the German army. On 15 January, the Kaiser discussed the matter with his two closest aides, Plessen and Lyncker. Lyncker, who was Falkenhayn's firmest supporter, advised the Kaiser to defuse the situation by sending Hindenburg a "soothing letter" and maintained that "there existed no basis for relieving [Falkenhayn] of his position." The three men determined, however, that Falkenhayn should give up his post of Minister of War and confine himself to the duties of Chief of the General Staff. On 16 January, the Kaiser met Falkenhayn alone and informed him of this. Falkenhayn's favorite candidate, Adolph Wild von Hohenborn, was named as his replacement. Further, the Kaiser and his General Staff Chief determined that three of the four reserve corps would be employed in the east and that these would be reinforced by a corps from the west. Almost as an afterthought, Ludendorff was transferred back to OberOst.[53]

This compromise seemed to defuse the situation. Yet, the perceived insubordination of his generals and the intervention of his family in his "command authority" had angered Wilhelm greatly. Although he was dissuaded by his aides from cashiering Hindenburg, Wilhelm let his disfavor be known to the Field Marshal by issuing a Cabinet Order forbidding

[50] Plessen, "Tagebuch," 14 January 1915.
[51] Janßen, *Der Kanzler und der General*, p. 77; Haeften, "Tagebuch," 16 Janaury 1915, in Guth, "Gegensatz," p. 99.
[52] Haeften, "Tagebuch," 18 January 1915, in Guth, "Gegensatz," pp. 101–102.
[53] Plessen, "Tagebuch," 15 and 16 January 1915; Afflerbach, *Falkenhayn*, pp. 227–228.

Hindenburg to resign even when Falkenhayn remained as Chief of the General Staff.[54] Additionally, he wrote a scathing letter to Moltke threatening him with dismissal, although at the last minute he ordered Plessen to ask Moltke not to open the letter.[55]

It was Haeften, however, who bore the brunt of Wilhelm's wrath. Haeften arrived in Imperial Headquarters carrying the Kaiserin's letter on 20 January, after the issue had been settled. Wilhelm complained that "now the ladies room becomes involved in this issue also. The behavior of Field Marshal v. Hindenburg is completely unheard of."[56] The Kaiser ordered Haeften to submit to a questionnaire, the results of which would determine whether or not a court martial was warranted. However, before the Kaiser could fully vent his rage, Plessen intervened and had Haeften transferred to an out-of-the-way position in Cologne.[57]

Both sides were able to claim victory in the "leadership crisis." On paper, at least, OberOst seemed to win most of their goals. Falkenhayn no longer held two high-level posts, Ludendorff was back again with OberOst, and four army corps were gained as reinforcement for the Eastern Front. Finally, OberOst could go ahead with their much-anticipated offensive as soon as the reinforcements arrived.

However, their victory was at a great cost. Falkenhayn, who seemed to have lost a great deal, in fact had emerged from the crisis strengthened in his position. He retained the most important of his posts, Chief of the General Staff, and with it the strategic direction of the war. He had even been promoted to General der Infanterie. Further, his candidate, Wild von Hohenborn, was put into the position of Minister of War and was to remain in the headquarters with Falkenhayn rather than return to Berlin. Perhaps most importantly, however, Falkenhayn retained the favor of the Kaiser.[58] Throughout the crisis, Wilhelm had stood by his Chief of the General Staff. The conduct of the anti-Falkenhayn cabal had clearly filled him with distaste, and often angered him greatly. While he had never liked Ludendorff (a "dubious character, eaten away by ambition"), he formed a very poor opinion of Hindenburg as well. It was only the vigorous intervention of his staff that prevented the Kaiser from cashiering the insubordinate Hindenburg. In his final tirade, Wilhelm had informed

[54] This was delivered to OberOst by Lyncker's deputy, Ulrich Freiherr von Marshall, on 18 January. Janßen, *Der Kanzler und der General*, p. 79; Haeften, "Tagebuch," 18 January 1915, in Guth, "Gegensatz," pp. 100–101.

[55] Plessen, "Tagebuch," 23 and 24 January 1915.

[56] Quoted in Afflerbach, *Falkenhayn*, p. 229.

[57] Plessen, "Tagebuch," 21 January 1916; Guth, "Gegensatz," pp. 105–107; Ritter, *Sword and the Scepter*, III, pp. 55–56.

[58] See Holger Afflerbach, "Wilhelm II as Supreme Warlord in the First World War," *War in History* 5, 4 (1998), pp. 427–449.

Haeften that Hindenburg "sees mere figments of his imagination" and that a close aide had found the Field Marshal "a completely worn out, frail old man."[59] Finally, the results of OberOst's "Winter Battle" (7 to 21 February) vindicated Falkenhayn. After some initial successes, the German forces were forced to give up their gains in the face of stiff Russian counterattacks and the terrible eastern winter weather. While the Russians suffered high losses, so too did the Germans.[60]

* * *

The "leadership crisis" that beset the German army in late 1914/early 1915 was perhaps unique in modern warfare. Hindenburg's challenge to Kaiser Wilhelm in January 1915 was certainly, in the words of the well-known historian Gerhard Ritter, "unprecedented in Prussian military history."[61] Never before had a German officer challenged his superior officer and his Kaiser in such a manner. However, never before had a German officer enjoyed so much popular support as did Hindenburg in early 1915, and he was prepared to appeal to this mass support to get his way if need be. This fact changed the relationship between the Kaiser and his generals fundamentally. For the rest of the war, Wilhelm knew he faced redundancy if ever a figure as popular as Hindenburg were to come to the High Command.

However, this unique command situation without a doubt fitted the unique military situation in which Germany found itself. While previous authors have seen this crisis largely in personal and political terms,[62] it in fact represents the playing out of an important split in German military thought which had begun even before the war's outbreak. The failure of Germany's initial plans to win the war in a few rapid, decisive battles represented the failure of the "traditional" German approach to warfare and left Germany in a precarious strategic position. Germany now found itself surrounded by enemies who possessed far greater resources, both in terms of manpower and material. Additionally, mass armies armed with rapid-fire weapons and artillery created an operational difficulty that further complicated the strategic picture.

To Falkenhayn, these challenges called for a new way of thinking about warfare. The General Staff Chief believed that Germany did not have the resources necessary to win the war outright. Therefore, he abandoned

[59] Quoted in Afflerbach, *Falkenhayn*, p. 230.

[60] On the "Winter Battle," see *Der Weltkrieg*, VII, pp. 260ff.; Herwig, *The First World War*, pp. 135ff.

[61] Ritter, *Sword and the Scepter*, III, p. 52.

[62] Cf. Janßen, *Der Kanzler und der General*; Ritter, *Sword and the Scepter*, III; and Heinz Kraft, *Staatsräson und Kriegsführung im kaiserlichen Deutschland 1914–1916* (Göttingen: Musterschmidt, 1980).

the traditional German army approach of attempting to deal its enemy an annihilating blow through which peace could be dictated to a beaten enemy. Instead, he concentrated on trying to find a political solution to the war. In Falkenhayn's approach, the military still played a key role, but military power was to be subordinated to diplomacy. Much like Moltke the Elder twenty-five years earlier, Falkenhayn envisioned limited military successes leading to political success. However, peace was not to be dictated to a prostrate foe and would as a consequence have to be moderate.

This approach, a "strategy of attrition," was rejected completely by the officers of OberOst.[63] These men remained wedded to the traditional German approach to warfare. Unlike Falkenhayn, who did not believe a "decisive" victory was possible after November 1914, OberOst still maintained that battles along the lines of a Königgrätz or a Sedan could be fought. Following a "strategy of annihilation," they hoped to win the war militarily before concluding peace, and they bent all their efforts toward accomplishing this strategy. The personal animosity of those in OberOst toward Falkenhayn was largely a result of this profound division in professional opinion.

In a very real sense, the Chancellor was stuck in the middle of these two opposing approaches. Although Falkenhayn's strategic approach gave the Reich's chief political leader more control over the outcome of the war, Bethmann shied away from such responsibility. While coming to an agreement with Russia was more difficult than Falkenhayn imagined, the Chancellor's attempts to separate Russia from the Entente in late 1914 were half hearted at best.[64] Instead, he pinned his hopes on OberOst and their promised military solution to Germany's strategic dilemma.[65]

The real outcome of the leadership crisis of late 1914/early 1915 was an unworkable command structure. Although Falkenhayn seemed to emerge victorious from the crisis, the bad blood created between him and the Chancellor during the bitter feud did not bode well for his vision of the military and political power of Germany working together to achieve peace. Moreover, OberOst proved successful in convincing much of the senior military and political leadership that the war could still be won by

[63] Hans Delbrück, "Falkenhayn und Ludendorff," *Preußische Jahrbücher* 180 (1920), pp. 249–281.

[64] On Bethmann's diplomatic initiatives in this period, see Rudolph Stadelmann, "Die Friedensversuche im ersten Jahre des Weltkrieges," *Historische Zeitschrift* 156 (1937), pp. 489ff.; L. L. Farrar, *Divide and Conquer: German Efforts to Conclude a Separate Peace, 1914–1918* (New York: Columbia University Press, 1978), pp. 13–34.

[65] Bethmann was aware, however, of the risks of supporting OberOst. He said, "with Falkenhayn, we risk losing the war strategically; with Ludendorff politically." Quoted in Janßen, *Der Kanzler und der General*, p. 253.

traditional means and that Falkenhayn's new strategic approach was a liability. Indeed, even his closest subordinates seemed unwilling to support Falkenhayn's new strategy. Although the Kaiser had left Germany's strategic reins in his hands, the continued existence of the popular Hindenburg and Ludendorff team represented a continued threat to Falkenhayn's position. This threat and the rejection of his strategy by a substantial portion of his military subordinates meant that the normally taciturn Falkenhayn became even more reluctant to share his ideas. Thus, the bitter feud made creating a new *operational* approach to complement his new strategic approach all the more difficult.

6 Attack in the east

Although Falkenhayn emerged largely victorious over the opponents of his strategy in early 1915, he was still forced to give up to OberOst most of the reserves that he had so painstakingly pulled together for an offensive on the Western Front. Before he could launch a western offensive, even the limited offensive envisioned by his strategy, the General Staff Chief would need to come up with new forces. Fortunately, the Ministry of War was hard at work forming new units, and in early 1915 Falkenhayn was soliciting plans from the Chiefs of Staff of the *Westheer* for an offensive on the Western Front.[1] However, before he could implement his plans, events forced him reluctantly to intervene on the Eastern Front with all the reserves he could muster. Ironically, after his bitter feud with the "easterners" in the German political and military leadership, the General Staff Chief was now forced by circumstances to try out his new strategic ideas and to develop his new operational approaches in the east.

* * *

In both the west and the east, the opening offensives of the Central Powers in 1914 had failed. While in the west the German armies still held significant portions of French territory and all but a slender portion of Belgium,[2] the Austro-Hungarian forces had not fared quite as well in the east. Due in part to faulty deployment, the Habsburg forces neither conquered Serbia nor defeated the Russian forces arrayed against them. In fact, the Austro-Hungarian forces had not only failed to achieve their initial goals but had been driven with great losses from Serbia and from Austrian Galicia.[3] Within three weeks of the beginning of the Austro-Hungarian offensive against the Russians, they had suffered over 300,000

[1] See Chapter 7 below.

[2] Although the Germans only occupied 6 percent of the territory of France, the area they occupied had accounted for 64 percent of France's pre-war pig-iron production, 58 percent of its steel output, and 40 percent of its coal. Gerd Hardach, *The First World War, 1914–1918* (London: Allen Lane, 1977), pp. 87–88.

[3] For a narrative of the beginning stages of the war, see Reichsarchiv, *Der Weltkrieg 1914 bis 1918*, Bd. I: *Die Grenzschlachten im Westen* (Berlin: E. S. Mittler, 1925) and Bd. II: *Die Befreiung Ostpreußens* (Berlin: E. S. Mittler, 1925). For the Austro-Hungarian side,

casualties and prisoners of war, close to a third of the strength of the Austro-Hungarian army at the war's outbreak. A further 120,000 men were trapped in the besieged fortress of Przemysl.[4]

A series of ill-fated offensives in the autumn and winter failed to alter the situation in Austria-Hungary's favor. Though Przemysl was relieved on 10 October 1914, it was besieged again when the Austro-Hungarian forces were forced to pull back by Russian counterattacks. Despite their best efforts, the combined offensives of the OberOst and the *Armee-Oberkommando* (AOK), the Austro-Hungarian General Staff, came to nothing but the attrition of the Habsburg army.[5]

By the early spring of 1915, Austria-Hungary was in serious trouble. The offensives of the past several months had reduced the army to a shell of its pre-war capability. Already in December, Conrad had told the Austrian Foreign Minister, Leopold von Berchtold, that, "the best officers and non-commissioned officers have died or have been removed from service, likewise the core of the rank and file." Further, he believed that unless something radical was done soon Austria-Hungary "could no longer master the military situation."[6] In the opinion of most Austro-Hungarian military leaders, the old Habsburg army had ceased to exist after the failure of the winter offensive. Indeed, from this point onwards, the Austrian official history refers to the army as merely a collection of *Landsturm* and militia.[7] Contemporary German assessments of the worth of the Habsburg troops were equally damning.[8]

The great losses of the winter offensives were further exacerbated by Russian successes. The Austrians had been unable to relieve the besieged fortress of Przemysl or to push the Russians back from the Carpathian Mountains. On 22 March, Przemysl's governor, Hermann Kusmanek von Burgneustädten, ordered the surrender of the fortress, and its garrison of 120,000 went into Russian captivity. Shortly before the fall of Przemysl, the commander of the Russian Southwest Front, General N. Y. Ivanov, had been ordered by the Russian high command to complete

Bundesministerium für Landesverteidigung, *Oesterreich-Ungarns Letzter Krieg 1914–1918*: Bd. I: *Das Kriegsjahr 1914* (Vienna: Verlag der Militärwissenschaftlichen Mitteilungen, 1931).

4 *Oesterreich-Ungarns Letzter Krieg*, I, pp. 319–320.

5 See Reichsarchiv, *Der Weltkrieg*, Bd. VII: *Die Operationen des Jahres 1915: Die Ereignisse im Winter und Frühjahr* (Berlin: E. S. Mittler, 1931) and Bundesministerium für Landesverteidigung, *Oesterreich-Ungarns Letzter Krieg*, Bd. II: *Das Kriegsjahr 1915 (Erster Teil)* (Vienna: Verlag der Militärwissenschaftlichen Mitteilungen, 1931) for full accounts of the offensives.

6 Franz Conrad von Hötzendorf, *Aus meiner Dienstzeit 1906–1918* (5 vols.) (Vienna: Rikola Verlag, 1925), V, p. 753.

7 *Oesterreich-Ungarns Letzter Krieg*, II, p. 271; Holger Herwig, *The First World War: Germany and Austria – 1914–1918* (London: Arnold, 1997), p. 137.

8 For example, see Gerhard Tappen, "Meine Kriegserinnerungen," unpublished manuscript in BA/MA, W10/50661, p. 106.

the destruction of the Austro-Hungarian army.[9] To accomplish this task, Ivanov intended to drive through the Carpathian passes to the Hungarian Plain. His thirty divisions, now reinforced by the force that had besieged Przemysl, slowly pushed the Austro-Hungarians back through the passes.[10] The Carpathian Mountains constituted the last natural obstacle before the Hungarian Plain, and once these crucial passes were lost, Conrad had no hope of stopping the Russians from taking Budapest. This fresh pressure caused Conrad to launch at his German ally increasingly shrill cries for help.

Initially, the OHL saw the AOK as too pessimistic and rebuffed Conrad's pleas.[11] On 25 March, Falkenhayn telegraphed Generalmajor August von Cramon, the German liaison officer with the AOK, for an assessment of the situation. Falkenhayn questioned how the intervention of two German divisions, as Conrad requested, could alter the situation.[12] Cramon replied the next day that it was no longer clear whether the Austrians, particularly the 3rd Army fighting in the Carpathians against superior Russian forces, could hold against further Russian attacks. In his opinion, the intervention of even a few German divisions would help to stabilize the situation.[13] To this end, two German divisions, called the *Beskidenkorps*, were dispatched in early April to shore up the threatened 3rd Austro-Hungarian Army.[14]

Conrad kept up his pleas for help even after the dispatch of the *Beskidenkorps*, threatening in a meeting with Falkenhayn in Berlin to sue for peace with Russia if further German help was not forthcoming.[15] Conrad's gloomy view of the situation was supported by Cramon. His

[9] Norman Stone, *The Eastern Front, 1914–1917* (London: Hodder and Stoughton, 1975), pp. 120–121.

[10] On Russian plans, see Jurij Daniloff, *Russland im Weltkriege 1914–1915* (Jena: Frommannsche Buchhandlung, 1925), pp. 450ff.

[11] "The Austrians appear to regard things very pessimistically." Gerhard Tappen, "Kriegstagebuch," 2 April 1915, BA/MA, N56/1.

[12] Falkenhayn to Cramon, 25 March 1915, OHL Nr. 632 OIb, BA/MA, W10/51388.

[13] Cramon to Falkenhayn, 26 March 1915 (no Akten Nr.), BA/MA, W10/51388. See also August von Cramon, *Unser österreichisch-ungarischer Bundesgenosse im Weltkriege* (Berlin: E. S. Mittler, 1922), pp. 7–13; and *Oesterreich-Ungarns letzter Krieg*, II, pp. 235–242.

[14] In fact, a number of German units and commanders had already been dispatched to aid Austro-Hungarian formations. The *Südarmee* was commanded by a German general, Alexander von Linsingen and was made up of Austrian and German units. Another German general, Remus von Woyrsch, commanded another mixed army to the north. The Austro-Hungarians feared, with good reason, that this increasing reliance on German troops and commanders would lessen their independence. See transcript of telephone conversations between Moritz Fleischmann (the Austrian liaison officer with OberOst) and AOK, 2 January 1915, BA/MA, W10/51373.

[15] Letter of Adolph Wild von Hohenborn (then Minister of War) to his wife, 3 April 1915, BA/MA, N44/3; and Hans von Plessen (commander of the Imperial Headquarters), "Tagebuch," 5 April 1915, BA/MA, W10/50656. Falkenhayn did not take Conrad's threat seriously.

Fig. 9 The Chief of the Austro-Hungarian General Staff, Franz Conrad Freiherr von Hoetzendorf

reports stressed the weakness of the Austrian forces and the growing necessity of German support. On 6 April, he wrote that the Austro-Hungarian forces could hold against a determined attack only if supported by German troops or commanded by German generals. His report concluded that further German support was "extremely desirable."[16] Falkenhayn came to the conclusion that if the Austro-Hungarian army could not hold the Carpathian line, the last meaningful natural obstacle before the Hungarian Plain, then Vienna would be lost within six weeks.[17]

Austria-Hungary's deteriorating military situation was made all the worse by the Central Powers' worsening diplomatic position. By the spring of 1915, Italy and Rumania were threatening to join the Entente against the Central Powers. All attempts to convince them to join the Central Powers floundered.[18] Both states possessed sizeable armies, and the entry of either into the war before the military situation in the east was stabilized could lead to disastrous results.[19] Falkenhayn believed that Austria-Hungary would be forced from the war if faced with the necessity of fighting another enemy.[20] This fact pushed the German General Staff Chief to intervene in the east. If a victory could be achieved against the Russians, perhaps Italy and Rumania could be persuaded not to enter the war. At the very least, Falkenhayn hoped an intervention by sizeable German forces would lead to an improvement in Austria-Hungary's military position.[21]

Thus, the severity of the military and diplomatic positions in April caused Falkenhayn to begin to plan, despite his previous feud with OberOst, a large-scale operation in the east. On 4 April, he telegraphed Cramon to enquire whether or not the railway lines and the general conditions in the area of Gorlice were good enough to support a "powerful thrust from the area of Gorlice in the direction of Sanok."[22] On 6 April,

16 Cramon to Falkenhayn, 6 April 1915, Nr. 460, BA/MA, W10/51388.

17 Stone, *Eastern Front*, p. 127.

18 See Z. A. B. Zeman, *A Diplomatic History of the First World War* (London: Weidenfeld and Nicolson, 1971), pp. 1–48.

19 Though the Italian Chief of Staff, Cadorna, boasted he could field a million troops within a month of receiving a mobilization order, the Italians were able to attack the Austro-Hungarians with only 460,000 men in June 1915. When Rumania finally entered in August 1916, it had an army of 623,000. Herwig, *First World War*, pp. 151–153, 218.

20 Tappen, "Kriegserinnerungen," pp. 94–95.

21 Erich von Falkenhayn, *General Headquarters and Critical Decisions, 1914–1916* (London: Hutchinson, 1919), pp. 78–81. Falkenhayn also believed a successful offensive would take troops away from the planned Russian offensive against Turkey, which intelligence had reported in April. Cramon to OHL, 21 April 1915 (no Akten Nr.), BA/MA, W10/50689.

22 Falkenhayn to Cramon, 4 April 1915 (no Akten Nr.), BA/MA, W10/51388. In fact, the chief of the *Feldeisenbahnabteilung*, Oberst Wilhelm Groener, had been ordered by Falkenhayn on 29 March to study the railroads in the Gorlice area in preparation for a possible German offensive. Wilhelm Groener, *Lebenserinnerungen* (ed. Friedrich

Cramon reported back that he believed the conditions favorable for a German attack of around four army corps supported by heavy guns in the second half of April.[23] For the next several days, Falkenhayn and his staff, who had been deeply involved in planning an offensive in the west, debated intervention in the east.[24] His operations officer, Gerhard Tappen, and the Minister of War, Adolf Wild von Hohenborn, argued that the German reserves should be held for use in the west. They believed that only in the case of an extreme emergency should German reserves be used in the east.[25] Finally, on 13 April, convinced of the perilous situation, Falkenhayn decided on the necessity of intervening in the east and sought the Kaiser's approval.[26]

However, in keeping with the strategic ideas he had developed in late 1914, Falkenhayn initially intended the operation to be limited in scale and in goals. The German General Staff Chief remained convinced that the war would ultimately be won on the Western, rather than the Eastern Front. Throughout his time as Chief of the General Staff, Falkenhayn never deviated from his belief that a traditional, "decisive" battlefield victory could not be won in the east, despite the insistence of OberOst. Thus, the intervention in the east was initially designed merely to improve the strategic position of the Austro-Hungarians to the point at which they could hold their front without substantial German aid, and consequently to free German forces for use on the Western Front. As the offensive progressed from victory to victory, however, Falkenhayn's goals would begin to grow, and the nature of the offensive in the east would change considerably.

This eastern operation was made possible by a reorganization of German forces in the spring of 1915 planned by Generalmajor Ernst von Wrisberg, the director of the General War Department of the Ministry of War. Wrisberg created a number of new divisions by removing each division's fourth regiment and by taking two guns from each artillery battery. In return for the lost fourth regiment, each division received

Frhr. Hiller von Gaertringen) (Göttingen: Vandenhoeck & Ruprecht, 1957), pp. 226–227. After the war, a great debate arose as to the originator of the idea for an attack from the area of Gorlice, with Conrad and Falkenhayn both claiming the honor. Conrad was extremely bitter that the honors seemed to fall to Falkenhayn. Franz Conrad von Hötzendorf, *Private Aufzeichnungen: Erste Veröffentlichen aus den Papierien des k.u.k. Generalstabs-Chefs* (ed. Kurt Peball) (Vienna: Amalthea, 1977), p. 93. For an overview of the topic, see Oskar Regele, *Feldmarschall Conrad: Auftrag und Erfüllung 1906–1918* (Vienna: Verlag Herlod, 1955), pp. 346–352.

[23] Cramon to Falkenhayn, 6 April 1915, Nr. 460, BA/MA, W10/51388.

[24] For Falkenhayn's western plans, see Chapter 7.

[25] Tappen, "Kriegstagebuch," 7 April 1915; Wild von Hohenborn to his wife, 13 April 1915, BA/MA, N44/3.

[26] Plessen, "Tagebuch," 13 April 1915. The Kaiser and Plessen both had doubts about the feasibility of the planned operation and feared the Western Front would be fatally weakened by the removal of forces.

2,400 recruits. This plan had the advantage of creating new units by mixing experienced troops with recruits, rather than creating a new division largely from scratch, and allowed for the formation of fourteen new divisions by March 1915.[27] While some were held as reserves on the Western Front, eight divisions were organized as a new army, the 11th Army. Originally formed to conduct a breakthrough operation in the west, the 11th Army received Hans von Seeckt, then a colonel and Chief of Staff of the III Corps, as its chief of staff.[28] Once the OHL had decided to employ the army in the east instead, August von Mackensen, the commander of the 9th Army and participant in the battle of Tannenberg, was named to command. On 14 April 1915, the OHL gave the 11th Army the task of carrying out the eastern offensive.

The 11th Army was to be assisted in its task by the strategic reserve of artillery, which had recently been formed by the OHL. Oberst Ernst Frahnert, the deputy chief of the Artillery Section in the OHL, was given the task of adjusting the organization of the German heavy artillery forces in the light of the rise of *Stellungskrieg*.[29] By stripping fortresses of their guns, by taking back into service recently retired cannon, and by an increased construction program, the OHL was able to equip the 11th Army with 466 "light" cannon and 156 "heavy" cannon, or 622 guns of all calibers. To the German guns were added a further 453 Austro-Hungarian artillery pieces, a considerable number by the standards of early 1915.[30] Additionally, each of 11th Army's corps was assigned two light, one medium, and one heavy trench mortar detachment (*Minenwerfer Abteilung*), as well as a number of 30.5 cm Austro-Hungarian howitzers.[31]

Falkenhayn's operational principles

Armed with the Kaiser's approval to commence operations in the east, Falkenhayn met Conrad in Berlin on 14 April to agree upon the

27 Ernst von Wrisberg, *Heer und Heimat 1914–1918* (Leipzig: Koehler, 1921), pp. 16–17 and *Der Weltkrieg*, VII, p. 303. Originally, the Minister of War believed that twenty-four new divisions could be formed in this manner. In the end, they were only able to build fourteen.

28 See Chapter 7.

29 Frahnert to Reichsarchiv, 20 January 1931, BA/MA, W10/51408. For an account of the artillery reorganization see Wrisberg, *Heer und Heimat*, pp. 36–43, 58–65; and [Richard] von Berendt, "Mit der Artillerie durch den Weltkrieg," *Wissen und Wehr* (1924), pp. 36–47, 185–197.

30 "Beispiele für Artillerie-Stärken bei Durchbruchsangriffen," BA/MA, W10/50160; *Der Weltkrieg*, VII, p. 372. Each field artillery battery was assigned 1,200 rounds, each heavy field howitzer battery 600 rounds, and each 21 cm mortar battery 500 rounds for the first phase of the offensive.

31 Oskar Tile von Kalm, *Gorlice* (*Schlachten des Weltkrieges*, Bd. 30) (Berlin: Gerhard Stalling, 1930), p. 29.

particulars. On 16 April, he telegraphed Conrad with the final details and outlined the 11th Army's task:

> The German 11th Army, formed recently from eight infantry divisions and under the command of Generaloberst von Mackensen, will be transported to the area of the Austro-Hungarian 4th Army southeast of Krakow in order to advance from the general line Gorlice–Gromik, to break through the Russian position in cooperation with the 4th Army, and, eventually, to make the Russian Carpathian front west of the Lupow Passes untenable.[32]

The 11th Army was also to be assigned two Austro-Hungarian infantry divisions and a cavalry division, and the Austro-Hungarian 4th Army was to come under the orders of Mackensen. The 11th Army would receive its orders from the AOK, who would take "all important decisions in consultation with the German OHL."[33] Units of the 11th Army began transportation to the Eastern Front on 17 April and completed their deployment on 29 April. Mackensen's attack orders went to his corps on 29 April, with the attack to begin on 2 May. Thus, from the day of decision (13 April) to the day of attack (2 May) only twenty days elapsed. In this period, eight German divisions, a large park of artillery with munitions, and supplies sufficient to support a major offensive were transported east. In twenty days, Mackensen and Seeckt completed their operations plans. Speed was clearly one of Falkenhayn's goals.

In the course of the planning for the eastern intervention, important aspects of Falkenhayn's operational thinking began to emerge clearly. Perhaps foremost amongst these was Falkenhayn's insistence on strategic surprise, which explains in part his haste. From the beginning of the decision to intervene in the east, Falkenhayn had insisted on maintaining strict secrecy. In his initial query to Cramon on 4 April, he had even specified that the AOK was not to be informed of his plans.[34] Falkenhayn stated explicitly his belief in the importance of strategic surprise in a telegram to Conrad on 22 April, writing that he believed an essential element of the operation's success was that "Mackensen not lose the advantage of surprise."[35]

As the planning progressed, the OHL took elaborate measures to ensure secrecy. First, the transported troops were not informed of their

[32] Falkenhayn to Conrad, 16 April 1915, OHL Nr. 727 OIb, BA/MA, W10/50744.

[33] Ibid. The 11th Army was composed of the Guard Corps, XXXXXI Reserve Corps, X Corps, 119th Division, the 11th Bavarian Division, the Austro-Hungarian VI Corps, and the Austro-Hungarian 11th Cavalry Division.

[34] Falkenhayn to Cramon, 4 April 1915 (no Akten Nr.) BA/MA, W10/51388; OHL put little trust in the security measures of AOK. Tappen to Reichsarchiv, 2 July 1932, BA/MA, N56/5.

[35] Falkenhayn to Conrad, 22 April 1915, Nr. 754 OIb, BA/MA, W10/50689.

final destination and neither were most of the railroad officials.[36] The troops transported from the west were sent along northerly rail lines in an effort to make observers believe the troops were destined for Hindenburg's front in East Prussia. All unit designations were also obscured. In an effort to prevent spying in the immediate area of Gorlice, the local inhabitants were removed to the far rear of the battle area. Additionally, when German staff officers arrived to survey the positions their units would be occupying, they donned Austrian headgear so as not to give away their presence to the Russians. Also, German troops were to relieve Austro-Hungarian troops at night to minimize the chances of the Russians becoming suspicious at a great number of unit changes.[37] Last, Falkenhayn stressed to Conrad and to Mackensen that the attack should come as soon as the German forces had completed their deployment.[38]

Falkenhayn also proposed to keep the Russians guessing by carrying out a number of diversionary attacks. On 16 April, he ordered OberOst to execute an attack with the aim of "deceiving the enemy for as long as possible as to our intentions, as well as binding the enemy forces north of the Pilica."[39] OberOst began a series of demonstrations. On 2 May, the German 9th Army launched an unsuccessful gas attack and the 10th Army began a series of local offensives. The real success came, however, with the "invasion" of the Courland. Initially opposed by no serious forces, a weak German force succeeded in taking most of this barren area, including the antiquated fortress of Libau, and in threatening Riga. The Russian high command was forced to divert forces away from Galicia to defend Riga.[40]

Falkenhayn's deception campaign extended to the Western Front and to his ally's forces as well. The gas attack by the German 4th Army at Ypres on 22 April was designed to disguise the transfer of troops east, which explains in part the lack of reserves for exploitation.[41] Falkenhayn was

[36] Leonhard Graf von Rothkirch Freiherr von Trach, *Gorlice-Tarnow* (*Der große Krieg in Einzeldarstellungen*, H. 21) (Oldenburg: Gerhard Stalling, 1918), pp. 18–19.

[37] Trach, *Gorlice-Tarnow*, pp. 26–27; Kalm, *Gorlice*, pp. 21, 24, 27; Tappen, "Kriegserinnerungen," p. 97.

[38] Falkenhayn to Conrad, 22 April 1915, Nr. 754 OIb, BA/MA, W10/50689 and transcript of a telephone conversation between Falkenhayn and Seeckt, 27 April 1915, in Hans von Seeckt, *Aus meinem Leben 1866–1917* (ed. Friedrich von Rabenau) (Leipzig: v. Hase & Koehler, 1938), p. 119.

[39] Falkenhayn to OberOst, 16 April 1915, Nr. 726 OIb, BA/MA, W10/50744.

[40] Erich Ludendorff, *Meine Kriegserinnerungen 1914–1918* (Berlin: E. S. Mittler, 1919), pp. 109–112; Stone, *Eastern Front*, p. 172. In all, the Russians were forced to deploy nine infantry and nine cavalry divisions to face the German's five infantry and seven and a half cavalry.

[41] Falkenhayn, *General Headquarters*, pp. 84–85; Tappen, "Kriegserinnerungen," p. 99; *Der Weltkrieg*, VII, pp. 38–49.

more ambitious with Habsburg forces. In addition to local attacks along the Austro-Hungarian front, Falkenhayn proposed the Austro-Hungarian 3rd Army retreat in order to draw Russian forces deeper into the Carpathians. Falkenhayn hoped that Russian reserves would then be withdrawn from the front at Gorlice and that more Russian forces might be trapped by the coming operation.[42] Conrad refused this request; though in the end, Austro-Hungarian forces hardly needed a special order to withdraw.[43]

The 11th Army's tactical principles

On 27 April, Mackensen issued the 11th Army's "Guiding Orders." In this document, Mackensen outlined the tactical principles by which the 11th Army was to fight at Gorlice and for the remainder of the campaign in the east. This order owed much to Seeckt's experience with the limited offensives on the Western Front and represents a clear step forward in German ideas about the conduct of battle.[44] Mackensen stressed that the units of the 11th Army must at all costs maintain the momentum of their attacks: "The 11th Army's attack must be carried forward with all speed, if it is to fulfill its assignment." The continuous momentum of the attack was to be accomplished by "arraying the attacking infantry in deep columns [*Tiefengliederung*] and rapid following of the artillery fire." Mackensen did not foresee the army's attacking units making equal progress. His orders envisaged that those units ahead of others would support the general advance by continually moving forward and thus keep the Russians off balance.[45]

The 11th Army also paid particularly close attention to artillery preparation before the battle and artillery support during the battle. Mackensen intended to use the artillery as much as possible to batter his way into the Russian position and to kill and demoralize Russian defenders.[46] On

42 Falkenhayn to Conrad, 22 April 1915, Nr. 754OIb, BA/MA, W10/50689; Falkenhayn, *General Headquarters*, p. 82; *Oesterreich-Ungarns Letzter Krieg*, II, p. 306.

43 Through the second half of April, Russian attacks pushed the Austro-Hungarian units slowly back all along the Carpathian line. *Oesterreich-Ungarns Letzter Krieg*, II, pp. 261–267.

44 See Arthur Bullrich, "Die Schlacht bei Vailly am 30.X.1914 als Ausgangspunkt für die Erfolge bei Gorlice entscheidener neuer taktischer Grundsätze," unpublished manuscript in USNA, Seeckt Papers, M-132, Roll 20. Indeed, the orders were drafted by Seeckt, and his memoirs contain a facsimile of the original. Seeckt, *Leben*, between p. 120 and p. 121.

45 AOK 11 "Grundlegende Direktiven für den Angriff," Nr. 117 Ia, 27 April 1915, printed in [Hermann] von François, *Gorlice 1915: Der Karpathendurchbruch und die Befreiung von Galizien* (Leipzig: Koehler, 1922), pp. 34–35; excerpted in Kalm, *Gorlice*, pp. 32–33.

46 August von Mackensen, *Briefe und Aufzeichnungen* (ed. Wolfgang Foerster) (Leipzig: Bibliographisches Institut, 1938), p. 141.

Fig. 10 August von Mackensen (right), the commander of the 11th Army, with Gerhard Tappen, Falkenhayn's operations officer

29 April, when he issued his attack orders to his command, the commander of the 11th Army issued a special artillery order as well. For the first time in the war, the command of the army-level artillery was to be centralized in one officer only, General Alfred Ziethen.[47] Under Ziethen's direction, the evening of 1–2 May was given over by Mackensen to "harassing fire" [*Störungsfeuer*], designed to prevent the enemy from strengthening their positions, from shifting reserves, and to keep the enemy troops off balance. Additionally, flat-trajectory cannon were given the task of destroying Russian bunkers. This harassing fire was to slacken between 10:00 and 11:00p.m. and between 1:00 and 3:00a.m. to allow pioneer patrols to cut through the Russian barbed wire and reconnaissance patrols in time to assess the effect of the fire.[48]

Mackensen ordered that the full bombardment commence at 6:00a.m. on 2 May. This "barrage" was to continue for four hours until the infantry assault at 10:00. Though he gave the individual corps freedom of action regarding targeting, Mackensen outlined the employment of the various

[47] Previously, army-level artillery was assigned to the individual corps, usually to the corps that bore the attack's *Schwerpunkt*, to be used as they saw fit. Bruce I. Gudmundsson, *On Artillery* (Westport, CT: Praeger, 1993), p. 55; and Berendt, "Artillerie," p. 43.

[48] Kalm, *Gorlice*, pp. 35–36.

types of guns. Heavy flat-trajectory cannon were to be used in the last quarter of an hour before the infantry assault to hit potential concentration areas so that the Russian forward positions could not be reinforced. Howitzers were to bombard the enemy trenches and mortars were to target specific bunkers and wire entanglements. Additionally, the 11th Army's order stipulated that each corps was to assign a number of batteries to the front line. These batteries were to work closely with the attacking infantry to destroy enemy machine-gun nests and other strongpoints. Mackensen stressed the importance of close infantry/artillery cooperation and that the artillery was to follow the advancing infantry as quickly as possible. Artillery observers were to advance with the infantry and cooperate closely with them to break down enemy resistance. [49]

The breakthrough at Gorlice

The 11th Army's attack on 2 May was a resounding success. Except for minor points, all units achieved their pre-established goals and captured large numbers of Russian prisoners. By the evening of 2 May, the Russian first position and the village of Gorlice were in German hands. Falkenhayn's insistence on strategic surprise paid off handsomely. Despite knowing that German troops had replaced Austro-Hungarian troops in the area of Gorlice, the commander of the Russian 3rd Army, General Radko-Dmitriev,[50] focused as he was on penetrating the Carpathians, made no preparations to counter a German offensive. At the point of the breakthrough, the 11th Army's ten divisions were faced by five and a half second-rate Russian divisions. The 700-odd German guns were faced by 140 Russian light and 4 heavy artillery pieces.[51] OberOst's attacks against the Russian Northwest Front convinced its commander, General Michail Alexeyev, that a major attack was coming from the north. As a consequence, he refused to send reinforcements once the 11th Army attacked at Gorlice. Poor railroads meant that the Russians could not move reinforcements in quickly once the Germans had attacked.[52] Radko-Dmitriev's

[49] Ibid. The best account in English of the infantry/artillery cooperation at Gorlice is Bruce I. Gudmundsson, *Stormtroop Tactics: Innovation in the German Army, 1914–1918* (New York: Praeger, 1989), pp. 107–123. For an example of a corps' artillery order, see François, *Gorlice*, pp. 39–42.

[50] Radko-Dmitriev had been Bulgaria's diplomatic representative to Russia before the war. Upon the war's outbreak, he resigned this position to take a commission in the Tsar's service. For a synopsis of his varied career, see C. H. Baer, ed., *Der Völkerkrieg*, Bd. 6 (Stuttgart: Julius Hoffmann, 1915), pp. 238–240.

[51] Stone, *Eastern Front*, p. 130.

[52] N. N. Golovin, *The Russian Army in World War I* (Hamden, CT: Archon Books, 1969), p. 186.

reserve, the III Caucasian Corps, could not reach the battlefield until 4 May, too late to restore the position, but not too late to be destroyed by Mackensen's relentless attacks.[53]

While Falkenhayn's strategic surprise ensured the isolation of the Russian 3rd Army, Mackensen's operational technique ensured victory on the battlefield. The heavy concentration of Austro-Hungarian–German guns and mortars pounded the Russian positions with little Russian reply. Radko-Dmitriev's few guns were starved of ammunition and were no match for the accuracy or weight of the German guns.[54] Though pockets of resistance remained, German accounts are replete with stories of the German infantry walking into the Russian positions to be met with Russian soldiers beaten senseless by the shelling.[55] On the first day of the offensive, the 11th Army took 17,000 Russian prisoners and 8 guns.[56]

During the night of 2/3 May, Mackensen's artillery moved forward and his corps prepared for the next day's attack. Again, on 3 May, the 11th Army smashed through the Russian positions and took large numbers of prisoners. This pattern of rapid build-up and attack, Mackensen's "pursuit" of the Russians, continued without pause until 10 May, and provided the model for the remainder of the campaign in the east in 1915. Ordered by the high command to hold at any cost, Ivanov's Southwest Front could do little but throw units in piecemeal to be destroyed. Outflanked by the advancing Germans and pressured by the Austro-Hungarians in the Carpathians, on the tenth, he was finally given permission to withdraw to the San River. By this time, the Russian 3rd Army had lost 140,000 prisoners and 200 guns to the Germans. At the beginning of May, the Russian 3rd Army consisted of close to 200,000 men. A further 50,000 replacements were received by 10 May. Only 40,000 reached the new defensive position on the San.[57] Radko-Dmitriev described his army as "literally bled white."[58]

By 9 May, Falkenhayn was able to declare, "the German troops under Generaloberst von Mackensen have fulfilled their mission . . ."[59] A grateful Kaiser Wilhelm shifted his headquarters to Schloss Pless in Silesia and showered honors upon his men after celebrating with his customary

53 Anon., "Erinnerungen an Galizien 1915," *Wissen und Wehr* (1922), p. 167. The author was a staff officer with the 11th Army during the campaign.

54 Alfred Knox, *With the Russian Army, 1914–1917* (2 vols.) (London: Hutchinson, 1921), I, pp. 282–283. Cf. Stone, *Eastern Front*, pp. 144–164. Knox was the British military attaché to Russia during the war.

55 Kalm, *Gorlice*, pp. 50f.; Trach, *Gorlice-Tarnow*, pp. 39–52; François, *Gorlice*, pp. 50–51.

56 François, *Gorlice*, p. 63.

57 Stone, *Eastern Front*, p. 139.

58 Report of 10 May, quoted in Daniloff, *Russland im Weltkrieg*, p. 494.

59 Falkenhayn to Conrad, 9 May 1915, Nr. 1054r, BA/MA, W10/51380.

bottle of *Sekt*: Falkenhayn received the Order of the Black Eagle; Mackensen and Seeckt, as well as Archduke Friedrich and Conrad, received the Pour le Mérite; and Tappen was awarded the Knight's Cross of the House of Hohenzollern.[60] Mackensen became a hero overnight and was named by the press as the "master of the breakthrough" (the irony, however, of Schlieffen's onetime adjutant now being called the "master of the breakthrough" was not lost on some contemporaries).[61]

Indeed, Mackensen's tactical principles proved to be an effective approach to the battlefield conditions in the east in 1915 and complemented operationally Falkenhayn's new strategic approach. While the pre-war doctrine of flank attacks and envelopments sought to cut the enemy off from his lines of communication and cause the enemy force to collapse, Mackensen relied instead upon the ability of the German heavy artillery to inflict severe casualties upon the Russian defenders while breaking through the Russian trench system. However, given the fact that this process relied on heavy artillery, the 11th Army's advance was slow, and the Russians were able to withdraw to positions prepared in the rear. Thus, Mackensen's "pursuit" of the Russians was in reality a series of set-piece breakthrough battles, which cost the Russian defenders dearly each time they attempted to stand and face the advancing Austro-German force. The results, though, were the same as a traditional pursuit – the Russian army was relentlessly ground down and bled white.

Exploitation and strategic priorities

Despite the success of the breakthrough, as Wilhelm Groener noted on 15 May, it was time for the "second act" which would turn the tactical success into an "operational" victory.[62] Falkenhayn seemed in agreement with Groener despite declaring Mackensen's mission finished. The original mission of relieving military pressure on Austria-Hungary had been accomplished, but now Falkenhayn turned his sights on what was perhaps on his mind since intervening in the east – ensuring that Austria-Hungary was safe from future Russian threats.[63] Falkenhayn and Conrad agreed

[60] Plessen, "Tagebuch," 12 May 1915; Tappen, "Kriegstagebuch," 12 May 1915; Treutler to Bethmann Hollweg, 12 May 1915, PRO, GFM 34/2584 (*Weltkrieg geh.* Bd.15).

[61] Theo Schwarzmüller, *Zwischen Kaiser und "Führer": Generalfeldmarschall August von Mackensen* (Paderborn: Ferdinand Schöningh, 1996), p. 108.

[62] Diary entry for 15 May 1915, in Groener, *Lebenserinnerungen*, p. 232.

[63] After the war Falkenhayn wrote that his original aims were "the permanent crippling of Russia's offensive power . . . but in the first place the freeing of the allies' front from the pressure upon it." Falkenhayn, *General Headquarters*, p. 80. The surviving evidence indicates that this wider goal only came about after the success of the initial breakthrough.

on 13 May that Mackensen's next task was to reach the San River and retake the fortress of Przemysl – a defensive line which could be held quite easily by Austro-Hungarian forces.[64]

The strategic situation, however, militated against a rapid decision on future goals and against a rapid exploitation of the 11th Army's success. To the south, the Austro-Hungarian 7th Army had been attacked on 9 May and suffered serious losses to the Russian 9th Army.[65] Conrad wanted to shift troops south to Bukowina to reinforce his 7th Army. Accordingly, he requested Falkenhayn to transfer more troops from the west to cover the withdrawal of two Austro-Hungarian divisions from Galicia.[66] Falkenhayn replied that due to the "expected large English–French offensive southwest of Lille" no further German troops could be spared for the east. This long-anticipated Anglo-French offensive began on 9 May and broke with unexpected ferocity. For the time being, Falkenhayn felt unable to shift reserves from the west to the east. He questioned, however, Conrad's desire to send troops to Bukowina. He believed that "the decision lies in West Galicia" and that upon its success rested the fate of the remainder of the Austro-Hungarian Army.[67]

In addition to the Russian offensive in Bukowina and the Anglo-French attack in the west, the Central Powers expected Italy to declare war any day. Falkenhayn and Conrad were at loggerheads concerning how the Central Powers should react to this Italian move and this impasse dominated their discussions for most of mid-May.[68] Conrad was obsessed by the desire to punish the Central Powers' onetime ally and suggested that Germany and Austria-Hungary each send ten divisions to the coming Italian front.[69] Despite the fact that the Habsburg army was already overstretched, Conrad insisted forcefully that the Central Powers wage war against Italy offensively.[70]

Falkenhayn favored remaining on the defensive against Italy. Instead, he raised again the idea of launching an offensive against Serbia designed to knock Serbia out of the war once and for all and to open

64 *Der Weltkrieg*, VII, p. 426; *Oesterreich-Ungarns Letzter Krieg*, II, p. 372.
65 *Oesterreich-Ungarns Letzter Krieg*, II, pp. 357–361.
66 Conrad to Falkenhayn, 9 May 1915, Nr. 9991, BA/MA, W10/51380.
67 Falkenhayn to Conrad, 10 May 1915, Nr. 1072r, BA/MA, W10/50689; Reichsarchiv, *Der Weltkrieg*, Bd. VIII: *Die Operationen des Jahres 1915: Die Ereignisse im Westen im Frühjahr und Sommer, im Osten vom Frühjahr bis zum Jahresschluß* (Berlin: E. S. Mittler, 1932), pp. 55–78.
68 For an account of the acrimonious exchange between Conrad and Falkenhayn see, Tappen, "Kriegserinnerungen," pp. 105–107. Conrad's obsession with Italy was noted by Karl Graf von Kageneck, the German military attaché to Austria-Hungary. Kageneck to Reichsarchiv, 11 August 1931, BA/MA, W10/51408.
69 Conrad to Falkenhayn, 14 May 1915, Op. Nr. 10176, BA/MA, W10/50689.
70 Conrad, *Private Aufzeichnungen*, pp. 94–99.

communications with a beleaguered Turkey.[71] However, he remained convinced that before any other undertaking, Austria-Hungary must be made safe from any future Russian attack. Falkenhayn held that the Austro-Hungarian–German forces must first deal the Russians a powerful blow, which would push them behind the San and reduce their offensive capability. The German General Staff Chief envisioned the creation of a strong defensive position, which could be held with around thirty divisions, based on the line of the major rivers of the region. If this could be accomplished, it would free some twenty-five German and Austro-Hungarian divisions for use elsewhere.[72] However, this had not been achieved by late May and, consequently, Falkenhayn believed that the allied forces should remain focused on Galicia until their goals had been achieved. Conrad finally agreed to Falkenhayn's proposals, though he remained inclined to stop operations in Galicia and to shift troops to punish the Italians.[73]

In the end, the two General Staff Chiefs were overtaken by events. By 23 May, when Italy declared war against Austria-Hungary (though not against Germany), Mackensen's offensive in Galicia had begun to lose steam. Although Mackensen had been ordered on 13 May to throw the Russians behind the San and to retake Przemysl, he was forced to postpone the attack until 17 May. The 11th Army needed time to bring up sufficient supplies to renew the offensive, and the Austro-Hungarian armies flanking the predominantly German 11th Army had difficulty getting into position for the attack.[74] It was not until 25 May that the 11th Army had secured the San River line and had established bridgeheads across the river. The 3rd Austro-Hungarian Army on the 11th Army's southern flank had made little progress in retaking the fortress of Przemysl, and Mackensen was forced to divert units of the 11th Army to aid the Austro-Hungarians, while the remainder of his troops prepared defensive positions along the San. On 3 June, Przemysl was finally retaken by the 11th Bavarian Division.[75]

[71] "Vorschlag General v. Falkenhayns für die Führung der Operation der Verbündeten im Fall des sofortigen Eintritts Italiens in den Krieg," 18 May 1915, BA/MA, W10/50683.

[72] Falkenhayn to Conrad, 16 May 1915, Nr. 1224r, BA/MA, W10/50689 and "Bemerkungen General v. Falkenhayns zur Erwiderung General Conrads," 17 May 1915, BA/MA, W10/50683.

[73] Conrad to Falkenhayn, "Erwiderung auf die Denkschrift des Chefs des Generalstabes des deutschen Feldheeres Nr. 1224r," 17 May 1915, Nr.10285, BA/MA, W10/50683.

[74] *Der Weltkrieg*, VIII, p. 141; and Friedrich von Mantey, "In welchem Masse vermögen Verkehrsmittel den Ansatz und Verlauf militärischer Operation zu beeinflussen?," *Wissen und Wehr* (1939), pp. 37–51.

[75] François, *Gorlice*, pp. 145–180. Mackensen "laid" the recaptured fortress at Kaiser Franz Joseph's feet. ("Ich bitte Seiner k.u.k. apostolischen Majestät zu melden, daß die 11.Armee Przemysl Allerhöchstihm zu Füßen legt.") Quoted in Seeckt, *Leben*, p. 144; Herwig, *First World War*, p. 142.

Through late May, the Russians shifted more and more reserves to the Galician front. By 20 May, German intelligence had already discovered in Galicia Russian units originally intended for an offensive against Turkey (the so-called "Odessa Army"). Each day brought the knowledge of more of these units.[76] Although these newly introduced forces were not rated highly by German intelligence, they achieved local successes, especially against Austro-Hungarian forces, and, for some time, the Central Powers' position on the San was insecure.[77]

Reality forced Falkenhayn and Conrad to lay aside their strategic differences and agree upon a course of action. To deal with the Italian question, a specially formed German unit, the *Alpenkorps*, was transported to the Italian Front and three newly formed German divisions (101, 103, and 105) were sent to southern Austria-Hungary (Syrmia) to replace the five Austro-Hungarian divisions sent to the Italian Front.[78] The two agreed to stand on the defensive against Italy for the time being. To reinvigorate the slowed offensive in Galicia, OHL ordered additional German forces to the region: two and a half divisions were taken from the west, two divisions from OberOst, and two of the divisions destined for Syrmia were assigned to Mackensen's command.[79]

On 3 June, Mackensen received his new instructions concerning the conduct of the campaign. A reshuffling of forces took place, putting German units in the Austro-Hungarian 3rd and 4th Armies to strengthen their offensive power. Mackensen assumed command of these Austro-Hungarian armies in addition to his own 11th Army, that he might have "the strength to conduct an offensive against the Russian forces east of the San . . ."[80] AOK ordered *Heeresgruppe Mackensen* to "strike decisively" the enemy before him and to take the city of Lemberg.[81] Falkenhayn hoped that the capture of Lemberg, the city which on its capture in 1914 the Tsar proclaimed would always remain Russian, would "create a disastrous impression for the Russians throughout the whole east."[82]

Before Mackensen could go over to the offensive, however, preparations had to be made, once again causing delay. The Austro-Hungarian units under his command had to move into a suitable position and

[76] Nachrichtenabteilung Ost, "Vortragsnotizen," 20–29 May 1915, BA/MA, W10/51388.

[77] *Der Weltkrieg*, VIII, pp. 217–220; *Oesterreich-Ungarns Letzter Krieg*, II, pp. 383–386; Tappen, "Kriegserinnerungen," p. 108.

[78] Tappen, "Kriegserinnerungen," pp. 106–107; Falkenhayn, *General Headquarters*, pp. 94–95. The three German divisions in south Austria-Hungary had the task of defending against a possible Rumanian invasion and to guard against a possible problem with the south Slavs of this area of the Habsburg Empire.

[79] *Der Weltkrieg*, VIII, p. 202.

[80] "Direktiven für die Fortsetzung der Operationen in Galizien," 4 June 1915, AOK Nr. 11160, BA/MA, W10/51388; Mackensen, *Briefe*, p. 170.

[81] *Der Weltkrieg*, VIII, p. 203.

[82] Falkenhayn, *General Headquarters*, p. 101.

supplies had to be accumulated. Like the earlier offensives of the campaign, the Central Powers attacked with great amounts of artillery, designed to crush Russian positions and stun the defenders. The build-up of the needed supplies was delayed by the poor road and rail network of Galicia. While these preparations were progressing, the Russians counterattacked the Austro-Hungarian 3rd Army, causing delay in their preparations. Additionally, the Austro-Hungarian 4th Army had difficulty reaching its designated position.[83] As a result, *Heeresgruppe Mackensen* could not begin its offensive until 12 June.

Repeating the formula perfected in the previous month's fighting, *Heeresgruppe Mackensen* began a breakthrough operation on 12 June. Between 13 June and 22 June, they smashed through two Russian defensive positions as they had at Gorlice. As the powerful German 11th Army pierced the Russian positions, it "pulled" its neighboring units along through the breach. A small breakthrough quickly became a rout. By 22 June, *Heeresgruppe Mackensen* had captured Lemberg.[84] With Lemberg's fall came the end of the first phase of operations in the east and the end of one of the war's most successful campaigns. The Central Powers had advanced over 300 kilometers since 1 May and had relentlessly ground down the Russian army. From 1 May until 22 June, the 11th Army alone captured over 250,000 prisoners, 225 of the Russians' precious guns, and over 600 machine guns. The damage done to the Russians was so great that a British liaison officer described the Russian army as a "harmless mob."[85] It had cost the 11th Army 87,000 casualties, 12,000 of who were dead.[86] In his memoirs, Falkenhayn summed up what he saw as the outcome of his reluctant eastern venture up to 22 June:

> The threat to Hungary had been completely removed; Austria-Hungary was given the possibility of sending sufficient forces to the Italian front; Turkey was relieved from the danger of an attack upon the Bosphorus by the Russian Odessa Army; these and the pacification of Rumania and the resumption of connections with Bulgaria were the immediate and highly valuable consequences.[87]

Additionally, the operational principles employed by the German armies proved their worth. The combination of heavy artillery and close

[83] *Oesterreich-Ungarns Letzter Krieg*, II, pp. 451–452; 11th Army to OHL, 3 June 1915, Ia Nr. 2017, BA/MA, W10/51388. Mackensen complained of the weakness of the Austro-Hungarian forces and requested OHL pressure the AOK to reinforce the Austro-Hungarian 3rd and 4th Armies.

[84] The fall of Lemberg was seen by most as much more important politically than militarily. See Plessen, "Tagebuch," 22 June 1915. Mackensen earned his field marshal's baton for his success.

[85] Capt. J. F. Nielson, Report of 6 June 1915, quoted in Knox, *With the Russian Army* I, p. 287.

[86] *Der Weltkrieg*, VIII, pp. 236–237.

[87] Falkenhayn, *General Headquarters*, p. 104.

infantry/artillery cooperation succeeded in breaking through Russian positions time after time. No Russian trench position seemed to be able to withstand the onslaught. Although the Russians were normally able to withdraw before they could be encircled and destroyed by the advancing Germans, the process of the breakthrough caused them serious losses. German tactics caused a slow but steady hemorrhaging of the Russian Army, from which Falkenhayn hoped it would never recover.

A separate peace with Russia?

After the fall of Lemberg, it seemed the role of the powerful German assault group was at an end, and Falkenhayn began making plans to transport units back to the west. There, they would be useful in defending against the powerful Entente attacks and form the nucleus of an army that would attack the Western Allies.[88] In the west, the Entente again prepared for an offensive, and the OHL reckoned on an inferiority of 600 battalions.[89] The reintroduction of forces from the east seemed necessary to shore up the threatened front. Additionally, Falkenhayn conceived of plans for the "cleansing" of French forces from the small portion of German territory they occupied. The conduct of the operations in the east were again to fall prey to the requirements of other fronts.[90]

Falkenhayn soon altered his opinion, however. The Entente superiority in the west militated against Falkenhayn's planned small offensive in Alsace and the German forces seemed able to hold their own defensively against the Entente attacks. Additionally, despite the notable successes in Galicia, Falkenhayn, and many authorities of the Central Powers, came to believe that not enough had yet been achieved in the east.[91] As the campaign in the east progressed, the "permanent crippling" of Russian offensive power became an important goal of the OHL. The performance of Russian troops during the offensive from mid-May until 22 June had

[88] Groener, *Lebenserinnerungen*, p. 239; Tappen, "Kriegstagebuch," 18 June 1915.

[89] Falkenhayn to OberOst, 11 June 1915, Nr. 2398r, BA/MA, W10/51388.

[90] Tappen, "Kriegserinnerungen," pp. 113–114. Falkenhayn's idea of "cleansing" Alsace of French troops drew great attention from the Reichsarchiv after the war, and the Reichsarchiv seemed determined to prove that Falkenhayn intended this operation to be a "war deciding" offensive. Tappen indicated it was merely a secondary concern. Tappen to Reichsarchiv, 16 June 1932, BA/MA, N56/5. Other evidence supports Tappen. See Heymann to Reichsarchiv, 16 November 1932, BA/MA, W10/51352 (Heymann was involved in the operation's planning); Groener, *Lebenserinnerungen*, p. 249.

[91] Groener, *Lebenserinnerungen*, pp. 239–240; Tappen later wrote, "If the Russian army was destroyed, then a peace with Russia could be made and a decisive offensive in the west . . . could be launched." Tappen to Reichsarchiv, 16 June 1932, BA/MA, N56/5.

shown that the Russian army had been considerably weakened.[92] However, Falkenhayn did not believe that the Russian military had yet been "permanently crippled." He determined to keep the pressure on Russia through the summer to destroy what he believed to be the last of Russia's reserves.

In addition to wearing down Russia's army, Falkenhayn came to believe that Russia could be pressured into coming to terms with the Central Powers. As Chapter 4 has shown, shortly after the failure of the German campaign in 1914, Falkenhayn concluded that Germany could not win a long war against all the Entente powers, and that Germany should make strenuous efforts to detach Russia or France from the coalition. As Falkenhayn believed that between Germany and Russia there existed no real difference of interests, at least none necessitating war, he was again convinced that Russia could be brought to the peace table.[93]

Returning again to Moltke the Elder's idea that military success should serve as the springboard for a negotiated peace,[94] the General Staff Chief felt that by the summer of 1915 the time was right to approach Russia with a German offer of a separate peace.[95] As early as 3 June, he proposed Russia be offered an armistice in view of the military setbacks recently inflicted.[96] Bethmann, once again, held the moment to be inappropriate. After the fall of Lemberg, Falkenhayn renewed his drive for a separate peace, and operations were directed toward this goal. He intended further operations to demonstrate to the Russians that they could never defeat the Central Powers. The Russian army was to be destroyed and Russian Poland was to be conquered. Falkenhayn knew how important Poland was to Russia and he intended to use this territory as a bargaining chip in negotiations with his enemy.[97]

Conrad agreed with Falkenhayn's goals. On 21 July, in the midst of another highly successful campaign, he sent Falkenhayn a memorandum suggesting the time was right to offer Russia peace terms. He proposed

[92] Tappen wrote, "The worth of the Russian troops had fallen considerably. Their replacements, especially officer replacements, were barely trained and lacked weapons." "Kriegserinnerungen," p. 113.

[93] Holger Afflerbach, *Falkenhayn: Politisches Denken und Handeln im Kaiserreich* (Munich: Oldenbourg Verlag, 1996), p. 295.

[94] See Chapter 1.

[95] Indeed, Russian public opinion was severely shaken by the events of the past months. See Daniloff, *Russland im Weltkrieg*, pp. 516ff.

[96] Gerhard Ritter, *The Sword and the Scepter*, vol. III: *The Tragedy of Statesmanship – Bethmann-Hollweg as War Chancellor (1914–1917)* (London: Allen Lane, 1972), p. 68. Falkenhayn's desire for a moderate peace with Russia was shared by Plessen as well. "We must come to peace with Russia. Therefore, no great annexations." Plessen, "Tagebuch," 10 July 1915.

[97] Afflerbach, *Falkenhayn*, p. 300.

that Russia be offered special rights in the Dardanelles and perhaps even an alliance with the Central Powers. A peace with Russia, Conrad declared, would allow the transfer of sufficient forces to other theaters to decide the war. He stressed that Germany and Austria-Hungary should make all efforts to construct a "golden bridge" to Russia. Falkenhayn answered the next day, declaring that he had advised the German government along similar lines for some time and that he had forwarded Conrad's memorandum to Bethmann.[98]

Falkenhayn and Conrad's pressure for a separate peace met with no success, however. Though the German Foreign Office made some overtures to the Russians through a Danish intermediary, the Russians were unwilling to discuss peace terms, declaring they would stand by the Entente pledge of 5 September 1914 that no member would conclude a separate peace. The Chancellor felt that a publication of definitive terms, as Falkenhayn wanted, would be seen as a sign of German weakness by the Entente and the neutrals. Bethmann also realized that as long as there remained the prospect of the Entente opening the Dardenelles, Russia would have no reason for responding to German offers.[99] He suggested instead that, in order to keep the Russians well disposed to a peace offer, Falkenhayn should "conduct the war against Russia with 'benevolence' [*wohlwollend*]." As part of his "benevolent" conduct of the campaign, Falkenhayn ordered that no public celebrations of the capture of Warsaw were to be held.[100] By early August, however, the drive for a separate peace was slowing down and no amount of German military success seemed to be able to restart the process.[101]

The conquest of Russian Poland

By July 1915, Russian Poland formed a great salient in the Central Powers' line, its northern flank being formed by East Prussia and its southern by the recently reconquered Austrian Galicia. The Russians defended this portion of the front with formidable fortresses and with six armies. The Russians hoped that these powerful fortresses, upon which so much money had been spent before the war, would act as brakes on the

98 Ibid., pp. 300–301.

99 Rudolph Stadelmann, "Friedensversuche im ersten Jahre des Weltkriegs," *Historische Zeitschrift* 156 (1937), p. 525.

100 Wild von Hohenborn to his wife, 24 June 1915, BA/MA, N44/3. Wild believed that Falkenhayn must have misunderstood Bethmann. Herwig, *First World War*, p. 145.

101 For an overview of the attempts at peace in the east in 1915, see L. L. Farrar, *Divide and Conquer: German Efforts to Conclude a Separate Peace, 1914–1918* (New York: Columbia University Press, 1978), pp. 13–34; Fischer, *Germany's Aims*, pp. 184–214; and Ritter, *Sword and Scepter*, III, pp. 66–74.

coming German attack. Novogeogievsk, at the confluence of the Vistula and Narev Rivers, covered the approach to Warsaw with 1,680 guns and over a million rounds of ammunition. All told, Novogeogievsk, together with Ivanogorod, Dvinsk, Osoweic, Grodno, and Kovno, protected the frontiers of Russian Poland with a total of 5,200 old and 4,030 modern artillery pieces.[102] The two Russian fronts (the Northwest Front under Alexeyev and the Southwest Front under Ivanov) were arrayed in the salient placed under the command of Alexeyev at the beginning of the month. The two fronts defended the 1,300 km salient with six armies (including the armies so roughly handled by Mackensen in May), or eighty divisions, two-thirds of the whole Russian army.[103]

Falkenhayn, intent on not becoming too deeply engaged in what he regarded as a fruitless attack deep into Russia, intended to attack with a shallow envelopment and to cripple the Russian army in the process.[104] The General Staff Chief rejected the calls of OberOst and Conrad for a grand envelopment from Prussia in the north and Austrian Galicia in the south, aimed at encircling all the Russian forces in the Polish salient. Given the experience of the past months, he felt that the Russians would simply retreat faster than the arms of the German envelopment could advance.[105] Instead, he decided to rely upon the operational techniques perfected by Mackensen in the campaign. The Russian army would be broken up in a series of step-by-step offensives, which relied on artillery to destroy the Russian defenses and defenders.[106]

Accordingly, on 13 July, the Central Powers began attacking all along their line, in what was to be the largest German operation since the invasion of France. From the north, Gallwitz's *Armeeabteilung* advanced against the Russian 1st and 12th Armies on the Narev River and, with the German 9th Army attacking from the south, quickly threatened Warsaw.[107] *Armeeabteilung Woyrsch*, composed mainly of *Landwehr* units, attacked in the center to prevent the Russians from reinforcing the salient's flanks.[108] In the south, *Heeresgruppe Mackensen* (now the 11th

102 Stone, *Eastern Front*, pp. 74–75. 103 *Der Weltkrieg* VIII, p. 445.

104 Plessen, "Tagebuch," 28 June 1915.

105 Indeed, Alfred von Schlieffen reached the same conclusion when considering a similar plan put forward before the war. See Robert T. Foley, ed., *Alfred von Schlieffen's Military Writings* (London: Frank Cass, 2002), pp. 144ff.

106 For an overview of the bitter debate between Falkenhayn, OberOst, and Conrad see, Ludwig Rüdt von Collenburg, "Die Oberste Heeresleitung und der Oberbefehlshaber Ost im Sommerfeldzug 1915," *Wissen und Wehr* (1932), pp. 281–296; and Franz Uhle-Wettler, *Erich Ludendorff in seiner Zeit* (Berg: Kurt Vowinckel-Verlag, 1995), pp. 180–187.

107 Max von Gallwitz, *Meine Führertätigkeit im Weltkrieg 1914–1916* (Berlin: E. S. Mittler, 1929), pp. 268–378.

108 Wilhelm Heye, "Lebenserinnerungen des Generaloberst W. Heye: Teil II: Wie ich den Weltkrieg erlebte," unpublished manuscript in BA/MA, Nachlass Heye, N18/4, pp. 32ff.

Army, the 4th Austro-Hungarian Army, the 1st Austro-Hungarian Army, and the newly formed *Bugarmee*) received the order to break through the Russian position along the Vistula and Bug Rivers and advance northerly toward Brest-Litovsk to break Warsaw's lines of communication.[109] All told, nine German and Austro-Hungarian armies attacked the Russian salient.

Again, the Central Powers attacked with great material superiority, overwhelming Russian resistance with heavy artillery. (Gallwitz attacked on 13 July with 500 guns and 400,000 rounds of ammunition, a greater intensity of fire than at Gorlice.[110]) One Russian corps commander wrote of the experience, "The Germans plough up the battlefields with a hail of metal and level our trenches and fortifications, the fire often burying the defenders of the trenches in them. The Germans expend metal, we expend life."[111] As at Gorlice, the Russian artillery was unable to reply, being hopelessly out-gunned and out-classed, and the attacking infantry was often able to walk into battered Russian positions unopposed. Russian replacements were hurried into battle, some only having time for two or three weeks of training.[112]

Following the formula perfected in the previous months, the "phalanx Mackensen," as the Russian press called the Austro-German forces,[113] advanced remorselessly, if slowly. The Russians were unable to construct defensive positions strong enough to contain the formidable striking power of the Germans, and repeatedly the German armies broke through hastily constructed Russian positions.[114] The Russian high command faced the unenviable decision of retreating from Poland completely or of losing much of their army. Finally, on 22 July, General Alexeyev ordered a general retreat, which continued until September.[115] Everywhere important Russian positions fell to the Central Powers: Warsaw and Ivanogorod were taken on 4 August, Kovno was captured on 18 August, Novogeorgievsk fell on 19 August, Osoweic on 22 August, Brest-Litovsk on 26 August.

By September 1915, the Central Powers had driven the Russians from Poland. Additionally, OberOst's renewed offensive to the north had advanced deeper into Courland and into Russia itself, capturing the

109 Mackensen, *Briefe*, p. 189. 110 *Der Weltkrieg*, VIII, p. 284.

111 General Zuev (commander of the Russian XXIX Corps), quoted in Golovin, *Russian Army*, p. 227.

112 Ibid. For Gallwitz' breakthrough see, Gustav Meyer, *Der Durchbruch am Narew (Juli-August 1915)* (*Der große Krieg in Einzeldarstellungen* H. 27/28) (Oldenburg: Gerhard Stalling, 1919).

113 Daniloff, *Russland im Weltkrieg*, p. 505.

114 See Pehlmann, *Die Kämpfe der Bug-Armee* (*Der große Krieg in Einzeldarstellungen* H. 26) (Oldenburg: Gerhard Stalling, 1918).

115 Stone, *Eastern Front*, p. 181; Golovin, *Russian Army*, p. 224.

fortress of Kovno and Vilna and threatening Riga. The advance to Vilna cut the only Russian north–south railway, effectively cutting the Russian front in two.[116] The human cost to the Russians was just as great. From the beginning of May until the end of the year, the Russians lost over 2.2 million men, including over 1 million prisoners. In October 1915, the British military attaché in Russia reported that Russian divisions were down to 5,000 men.[117] In January 1916, German intelligence reckoned that Russian divisions only numbered 11,000 men, most of whom would be poorly trained, poorly equipped, and poorly led.[118]

By 31 August planning had begun on defensive positions along the newly captured ground, and the operations in Poland began to wind down.[119] The massive losses inflicted on the Russian army and its poor combat performance in the campaign convinced both Falkenhayn and Conrad that the Russian army was incapable of offensive action for the foreseeable future.[120] Though Russia had not been forced into a separate peace, the other more immediate goal of the Central Powers had been achieved. The Central Powers possessed, by early September, a seemingly defensible frontier. The offensive power of the Russian army had been broken and German forces could now be used elsewhere without fear of an Austro-Hungarian collapse.

Though small German and Austro-Hungarian offensives continued until the end of the year, the great campaign was over by early September.[121] On 6 September, the Bulgarians finally agreed to a military convention with the Central Powers and Falkenhayn's long-planned Serbian expedition could go ahead. Mackensen was again chosen to spearhead this combined Austro-Hungarian–Bulgarian–German invasion scheduled to begin in early October.[122] Additionally, the expected Anglo-French offensive in the west claimed more troops, and Falkenhayn began shifting troops west in anticipation of this attack and for a future

[116] Golovin, *Russian Army*, p. 188.

[117] Report of Lt.-Col. A. Knox, 12 October 1915, PRO, WO 106/1067.

[118] *Der Weltkrieg*, VIII, pp. 596–597.

[119] Tappen, "Kriegstagebuch," 31 August 1915.

[120] Reports even came in to OHL that Russian units were using women and children in the front line. Tappen, "Kriegstagebuch," 29 August 1915. See also Plessen, "Tagebuch," 26 August 1915. In January 1916, Falkenhayn informed Bethmann that the Russian army was incapable of any "large-scale offensives" for the immediate future. Bethmann, diary entry for 7 January 1916, quoted in Karl-Heinz Janßen, *Der Kanzler und der General: Die Führungskrise um Bethmann Hollweg und Falkenhayn 1914–1916* (Göttingen: Musterschmidt, 1967), p. 288.

[121] *Der Weltkrieg*, VIII, pp. 456–533; Bundesministerium für Landesverteidigung, *Oesterreich-Ungarns Letzter Krieg*, Bd. III: *Kriegsjahr 1915 (Zweiter Teil)* (Vienna: Verlag, der Militärwissenschaftlichen Mitteilungen, 1932), pp. 523–559.

[122] Volker Ullrich, "Entscheidung im Osten oder Sicherung der Dardanellen: das Ringen um den Serbienfeldzug 1915," *Militärgeschichtliche Mitteilungen* 2 (1982), pp. 45–63.

German offensive.[123] Conrad was finally free to deploy his troops against his arch-enemy, Italy.

Conclusion

By the end of 1915, the Central Powers stood at the height of their success. The campaigns begun in May 1915 had resulted in the conquest of Russian Poland, the weakening of the Russian army, and the destruction and occupation of Serbia. German and Austro-Hungarian victories had persuaded Bulgaria to enter into alliance with the Central Powers and Rumania at least to remain neutral. The defeat of Serbia opened secure land communications with Turkey and ensured that supplies could flow freely to aid against further Entente attacks. With Turkey secure, no Entente supplies would reach the stricken Russia through the Dardanelles. To the strategic leaders of Germany and Austria-Hungary, Falkenhayn and Conrad, their backs seemed protected, allowing them to entertain the thought of offensives elsewhere.

Despite these notable successes, Falkenhayn's conduct of the campaigns in the east in 1915 was highly criticized by historians after the war. Liddell Hart wrote that Falkenhayn's strategy in 1915 lacked decisiveness, and that "Falkenhayn's cautious strategy was to prove the most hazardous in the long run, and indeed pave the way for Germany's bankruptcy."[124] In a discussion about conclusions to draw from the 1915 eastern campaigns, the writers of the German official history agreed. They believed that Falkenhayn should have withdrawn forces from the Western Front sufficient to defeat Russia "decisively" enough to dictate peace terms, even if this meant a general withdrawal to shorten German positions in France. The consensus of opinion amongst the Reichsarchiv writers was that Falkenhayn lacked the strategic vision and the moral strength necessary to conduct the operations to a decisive end. Now the director of the Historical Section of the Reichsarchiv, Falkenhayn's bitter wartime enemy Hans von Haeften concluded that "Falkenhayn had led us to catastrophe."[125]

[123] Tappen, "Kriegstagebuch," 5 September 1915; Groener, *Lebenserinnerungen*, p. 249.

[124] B. H. Liddell Hart, *The Real War 1914–1918* (London: Faber & Faber, 1930), p. 150.

[125] "Protokoll über die Besprechung bei Herrn General von Haeften am 6.Dezember 1930," BA/MA, W10/51408. Present were the writers of vol. 8 of *Der Weltkrieg*, Wolfgang Foerster, Theobald von Schäfer, Wilhelm Solger, Günther Frantz, and Otto Klemp. It must be remembered that Haeften was a bitter opponent of Falkenhayn during the war and played a prominent role in the intrigues against him. (See Ekkehart P. Guth, "Der Gegensatz zwischen dem Oberbefehlshaber Ost und dem Chef des Generalstabes des Feldherres: Die Rolle des Majors v.Haeften im Spannungsfeld zwischen Hindenburg, Ludendorff und Falkenhayn," *Militärgeschichtliche Mitteilungen* 1 (1984),

Central to this criticism was Falkenhayn's decision to conduct a step-by-step offensive with limited goals in the east. This strategy was partly forced on Falkenhayn by the relative weakness of the Germans on the Western Front and the Central Powers' unstable diplomatic position. More than that, however, this strategy, as well as the strategy he would follow in the west, reflected what Falkenhayn believed to be Germany's material weakness.[126] As we saw in Chapter 4, Falkenhayn believed that Germany did not have the strength, even with a shortening of the front in the west, to defeat Russia or either of its other enemies decisively.[127] Convinced that "decisive" operations were not possible under the current conditions, he focused instead on what he believed to be achievable goals and tailored his strategy accordingly.

Although after the war he would be criticized for scattering his forces in diversionary operations, his critics missed the fact that these secondary operations were central components of Falkenhayn's strategy. To him, one goal remained constant throughout the operations in the east in 1915 – the securing of the Eastern Front from Russian threat through the destruction of the enemy's offensive power. To achieve this, Falkenhayn had to strike a careful balance between operations central to destroying the Russian army and side operations (like the conquering of the Russian Baltic region) which drained away German strength. These secondary operations, however, played an important role in Falkenhayn's strategy. They functioned as diversions, which kept the enemy guessing about the location of the real attack, and served to siphon off enemy reserves away from the main attack.

These diversionary attacks were essential in securing the necessary strategic surprise in early May when Mackensen's 11th Army attacked at Gorlice. The Russians, focused as they were on their own operations in the Carpathians, were unprepared for the German assault and had few reserves handy. The scarce Russian reserves were partially diverted by the German attack in the Courland, which convinced the commander of the Northwest Front that strong attacks would fall there rather than on the Southwest Front. Consequently, he refused to dispatch the necessary

pp. 75–111.) Indeed, much of the criticism leveled against Falkenhayn after the war was really a continuation of the acrimonious strategic debate and personal conflicts that went on during the war between Falkenhayn and Ludendorff and his followers.

126 Falkenhayn, *General Headquarters*, pp. 88–90; Tappen to Reichsarchiv, 16 June 1932, BA/MA, N56/5; Zwehl, *Falkenhayn*, p. 139.

127 In June 1915, Falkenhayn had examined this possibility, and the reporting officer, Generalmajor von Mertens, the general of engineers for the 10th Army, rejected it as impractical. Mewes to Reichsarchiv, 15 August and 8 September 1931, BA/MA, W10/51408. See Chapter 7 for a full discussion.

reinforcement. For a limited operation, the diversion in Courland reaped disproportionate results.

This concept of strategic surprise was considered by Falkenhayn to be essential to the success of the operations in the east. While this idea was by no means new in 1915, war in the west had shown how crucial it was to successful operations. Falkenhayn had learned by 1915 that an enemy, in strongly constructed positions, could easily bring up enough reserves to counter almost any attack if given enough warning. Consequently, in the eastern campaigns of 1915, the OHL went to elaborate lengths to hide its intentions from the enemy for as long as possible. This included, in addition to wide-ranging diversionary attacks, going so far as to keep the Austro-Hungarian AOK in the dark regarding German plans.

Another tool crucial to Falkenhayn's planned destruction of the Russian army was the liberal use of heavy artillery. Artillery provided the manpower-deficient but materially rich Germans with a cost-effective means for fighting the manpower-rich but materially deficient Russian army. The German advantage stemmed not just from a superiority in number of guns but also from superior technique. By 1915, the German army had made great tactical and technical developments in infantry/artillery cooperation. The Russians suffered horribly under the accurate German fire through the entire offensive, and German infantry was often called upon merely to mop up shattered Russian forces. In short, Falkenhayn's policy matched German strengths with Russian weaknesses, summed up succinctly by the commander of the Russian IXX Corps, General Zuev, "the Germans expend metal, we expend life."[128]

Between May and September 1915, Falkenhayn's strategy had succeeded in inflicting over 2 million casualties upon the Russians – the greatest number of casualties inflicted on an enemy in any campaign until that time.[129] (By contrast, though the figures are still highly disputed, in the course of the battle of the Somme in 1916, the British suffered 420,000 casualties, the French 200,000 and the Germans 465,000 or 1,085,000 all told.[130]) Worse, these casualties encompassed the trained manpower and, in German eyes more importantly, the trained and experienced officers essential for modern warfare. It is understandable that Falkenhayn (and Conrad) believed the Russian army incapable of any offensive action for the foreseeable future.

[128] Quoted in Golovin, *Russian Army*, p. 227.

[129] *Der Weltkrieg*, VIII, pp. 596–597; Golovin, *Russian Army*, p. 222. It is difficult to give an accurate count of Russian losses, as they were so high in 1915 that the Russians lost track themselves.

[130] Herwig, *First World War*, p. 204.

In part, the very success of Falkenhayn's strategy in the east in 1915 led to the criticisms of future historians. Falkenhayn's success had led to a diminution of the Hindenburg/Ludendorff star. As Wilhelm Groener noted in his diary after a conversation with the Kaiser in the summer of 1915: "His trust in Falkenhayn is unshaken and unshakeable. He [the Kaiser] believes in him [Falkenhayn], while he has no close connection with the personalities of the east [Hindenburg and Ludendorff]."[131] Hans von Haeften, and many other German officers, found Falkenhayn's methods of warfare repellent. In the summer of 1915, they longed for a return to grand envelopments, as Ludendorff advocated. Their post-war critique reflected their wartime opinions. Falkenhayn's choice of strategy, however, has been seconded by a more recent (and probably more objective) researcher than Liddell Hart or the Reichsarchiv, Norman Stone:

> Falkenhayn was a modern general, and had a more sensible view of the war than Ludendorff or Conrad. He knew that great manoeuvres, as in past wars, could not fit the present circumstances. The war in the East proved Falkenhayn to be right. What shook *Stavka* was not the ostensibly brilliant manoeuvring of Ludendorff – and certainly not that of Conrad – but the huge losses they suffered in set-piece soldiers' battles such as Gorlice, or Mackensen's bludgeoning before Lublin. They were much more costly, even than Tannenberg.[132]

One aspect of Falkenhayn's strategy in 1915, however, did not fare so well – that of forcing Russia into agreeing to a separate peace. Falkenhayn's idea of pummeling the Russians to the negotiating table came to no end. This was in part because the concept relied upon two factors out of Falkenhayn's control – the Chancellor and Russia's resolve. Falkenhayn could not force Bethmann into negotiations with the Russians and he clearly underestimated Russian will. In the end, he had to settle for a goal he could achieve – the crushing of Russian military power. Russia was not taken from the war, as Falkenhayn had desired since November 1914, but its offensive capability was seemingly crippled.

At the end of 1915, German successes in the east allowed Falkenhayn to concentrate on what was to him the decisive theater of combat, the Western Front. He took with him important lessons from the campaign in the east, which would see application in his strategy for defeating the western allies. Falkenhayn's insistence on strategic surprise was crucial to success in Poland. He would attempt to use it again in France. Diversionary attacks had been successful in deceiving the Russian command and in keeping large enemy forces tied up elsewhere. Falkenhayn would attempt this again in the west. Powerful artillery combined with close

131 Groener, *Lebenserinnerungen*, 245.
132 Stone, *Eastern Front*, p. 178; Cf. Afflerbach, *Falkenhayn*, pp. 312–313.

infantry/artillery cooperation had played a central role breaking through and destroying many Russian units, causing grievous harm to the capability of the Russian army. Artillery would play an even more crucial role in his campaign against the western allies. At Verdun the Germans would use more artillery, better supplied with ammunition and with improved infantry/artillery tactics. And last, Falkenhayn would again return to the idea of forcing one enemy into a separate peace by inflicting unacceptable damage on its army and by forcing it to fight for an important geographical feature.

7 Defense in the west

Falkenhayn's reluctant eastern venture in the spring and summer of 1915 had disturbed German plans for an offensive in the west. After Bethmann Hollweg's failure to bring about a separate peace with Russia in late 1914/early 1915, Falkenhayn had again turned to the west, in his eyes the most important theater.[1] In keeping with the strategy he had outlined in November 1914, the General Staff Chief hoped to launch an offensive there that would divide the two western allies and bring France to a separate peace. In order to do this, however, he had to find a solution to the tactical deadlock produced by the trenches, i.e., to find a way to break through the enemy positions and restore some sort of mobility to the war.

As 1915 began, the strategists of Germany and the Entente were thinking along similar lines. The results of previous offensives had convinced many leaders on both sides that if only a bit more pressure were applied, if only a bit more heavy artillery were employed, the enemy position could be broken through and mobility could thus be reintroduced to the war.[2] Once mobility had been restored, most strategists believed the war could be won quickly. To this end, both sides began preparing for an offensive that would break through the stalemate of the trenches.

The French, who had no second front to make demands upon their forces, put into motion the first major offensive of the year in early February in the Champagne region. There, they hoped to drive through the German position, capture the vital rail line 5 km behind the front, and cause the German northern front to collapse. Despite heavy losses, the French were unable either to pierce the strong German position or even to push the German front back the short distance needed to capture the Challerange–Bazancourt railway. The results of the month-long offensive

1 Erich von Falkenhayn, *General Headquarters and its Critical Decisions, 1914–1916* (London: Hutchinson & Co., 1919), pp. 42–43.

2 Konrad Krafft von Dellmensingen, *Der Durchbruch* (Hamburg: Hanseatische Verlagsanstalt, 1937), pp. 32–33.

were 240,000 French casualties,[3] and a new term in the German military vocabulary, *Trommelfeuer*, the continuous rain of heavy artillery shells upon the German positions.[4] By mid-March, the French were exhausted by their efforts and the initiative passed to the Germans.[5]

German breakthrough plans

The most pressing problem facing the OHL in early 1915 was reserves. After the failures of 1914, the German army needed time to rebuild. The reserves built up in January had been sent to the east against the General Staff Chief's better judgment, and Falkenhayn was forced to wait until early spring until additional units could be constructed. As we have examined in Chapter 6, the reorganization of the German army directed by the Ministry of War's General Ernst von Wrisberg offered the prospect of a large number of new divisions by the end of March.[6] Consequently, on 3 March, the 11th Army was formed by the OHL, with the intention of utilizing it for the nucleus of a western attack group. Falkenhayn gave General der Infantrie Max von Fabeck command of this new army and named Hans von Seeckt as his chief of staff. Both officers had extensive experience on the Western Front; Fabeck had commanded an army group during the Ypres offensive and Seeckt had planned the III Army Corps' successful assault on Vailly. With these new units coming into being and with experienced leaders on hand, Falkenhayn was able to return to his idea of a major offensive in France. Accordingly, he set the *Westheer*'s planning mechanism in motion, requesting plans for breakthrough operations from the armies on the Western Front.

By mid-March, Falkenhayn had received a number of plans, two of which seemed promising. On the same day as the 11th Army was formed, the OHL received the report of Generalleutnant Konrad Krafft von Dellmensingen, Chief of Staff to the 6th Army, which called for a breakthrough in the area of Arras. The goal of this operation was the splitting of the British and French forces and the pushing of the British forces

[3] Ibid., pp. 31–34. The Germans suffered only 45,000 casualties to the 240,000 French.

[4] Max Bauer, *Der grosse Krieg in Feld und Heimat* (Tübingen: Osiander'sche Buchhandlung, 1921), p. 85.

[5] On the *Winterschlacht* in the Champagne see Reichsarchiv, *Der Weltkrieg*, Bd. VII: *Die Operationen des Jahres 1915: Ereignisse im Winter und Frühjahr* (Berlin: E. S. Mittler, 1931), pp. 35–53; and Ministère de la Guerre, *Les Armées Françaises dans la Grande Guerre*, Tome II: *La Stabilisation du Front – Les Attaques Locales (14 Novembre 1914–1 Mai 1915)* (Paris: Imprimerie Nationale, 1931), pp. 410–481.

[6] Ernst von Wrisberg, *Heer und Heimat 1914–1918* (Leipzig: Koehler, 1921), pp. 16–17; *Der Weltkrieg*, VII, p. 303; Krafft, *Durchbruch*, p. 36. Originally, it was hoped that twenty-four new divisions would be formed. In the end, Wrisberg's reorganization resulted in only fourteen.

into the sea.[7] Ten days later, the OHL received a second promising plan from the 1st Army. Generalleutnant Hermann von Kuhl, Chief of Staff of the 1st Army and author of this plan, believed the most favorable area for a breakthrough to be along the border of the 1st and the 7th Armies. Kuhl planned to attack along a 20 km front from Vailly eastwards across the Aisne and achieve a breakthrough in the French line from Condé to Paissy. The 1st Army believed that a tactical breakthrough in this area would result in operations returning to the "free field," and that the operations could be extended from there to Paris.[8]

After examining the 1st Army's report, the new Minister of War, Adolf Wild von Hohenborn, expressed his doubts regarding the plan in a memorandum of 15 March. Wild believed that the OHL possessed sufficient forces to achieve a tactical breakthrough under the 1st Army's plan, but that the German strength was insufficient to turn the tactical success into an operational success. Wild believed the result of the operation would merely be a gain of "worthless" terrain, and not a "campaign decision" [*Feldzugsentscheidung*].[9] Indeed, Kuhl admitted to the same faults in his plan in a second memorandum to the OHL later in the month.[10] While Falkenhayn continued to consider the 1st Army's plan, especially as a diversionary attack,[11] attention shifted to the 6th Army's proposals.

As the task of carrying out and exploiting this breakthrough on the Western Front was to fall to the 11th Army, Falkenhayn gave verbally to Seeckt the mission of examining areas of the Western Front for the coming offensive when the staff of the 11th Army formed on 11 March.[12] On 16 March Seeckt received his written orders. Falkenhayn wrote: "The *Oberste Heeresleitung* has the intention to break through the Western Front after sufficient forces have been assembled." Seeckt was to "reconnoiter the terrain between Canal la Bassée and the Avre Brook near Roye for an operation with the goal of breaking through the enemy position north

7 Quoted in an untitled and unpublished manuscript of the Reichsarchiv in BA/MA, W10/50707, pp. 10–12 (hereafter, "Durchbruchspläne"). Although the original documents have been destroyed, this Reichsarchiv manuscript contains long excerpts from the original memoranda. This manuscript seems to have served as the basis for the chapter, "Erwägungen für einen kriegsentscheidenden Durchbruch im Westen," in *Der Weltkrieg*, VII, pp. 307–323. See also Krafft, *Durchbruch*, pp. 36–42.

8 AOK 1 to OHL, Ia Nr. 1182, 13 March 1915, in "Durchbruchspläne," pp. 20–23.

9 Adolph Wild von Hohenborn, 15 March 1915, in ibid., p. 25.

10 "Durchbruch im Westen," AOK 1 Ia Nr. 1221, 18 March 1915, in ibid., p. 32. This memorandum was submitted to the OHL by Kuhl personally, not as Chief of Staff of the 1st Army, and examines several possible breakthrough plans.

11 Gerhard Tappen was sent to the 7th Army for several weeks to serve as its chief of staff and to make a judgment on the 1st Army's plan. Tappen, "Kriegstagebuch," 7 March 1915, BA/MA, N56/1.

12 Hans von Seeckt, *Aus meinem Leben 1866–1917* (ed. Friedrich von Rabenau) (Leipzig: Hase & Koehler, 1938), p. 102.

of the Somme on a front 25 to 30 km wide and continuing to the sea."[13] The 11th Army's completed proposal was to be submitted by the end of the month. The OHL reserved for itself the right of preparing plans for the exploitation of the tactical breakthrough.

On 30 March, Seeckt submitted his report.[14] After examining the possibilities of a breakthrough along the 100 km stretch of front from Canal la Bassée to near Roye, he concluded that the area which offered the best tactical and operational conditions for a breakthrough was along a 25 km front running from north of Ficheux (just south of Arras) to south of Thiepval (just north of Albert). To Seeckt, this section of the front offered a number of advantages to an attacker. First, this section of front lay only around 65 kilometers from the coast. Second, Seeckt wrote that the enemy positions on this section of the front "appeared to be not more than average in strength, and in parts below average." Additionally, the area behind the front there was less developed than other areas of northern France; hence, there would be fewer areas upon which the enemy could form an effective center of renewed resistance. Last, as the attack developed, its left wing would be covered from an enemy counterattack to a certain degree by the Somme. Seeckt believed that a successful breakthrough in this section of the front would lead to the separation of the northern and southern portions of the Allied armies.

Seeckt's report also outlined the 11th Army's plan of attack and the forces necessary. He envisioned the initial breakthrough of the 25 km front being carried out by a "breakthrough army" [*Durchbruchsarmee*] of five corps. This *Durchbruchsarmee* would be supported by a second wave, designed to protect its flanks and keep up the momentum of attack; one army corps would follow behind its right wing, another behind its center, and two behind its left wing. While the right wing of the *Durchbruchsarmee* would advance in a northwesterly direction on Warlus and Couy en Artois, the center would drive on Avesnes le Comte and the left wing would cover the army from a southern attack. Seeckt also felt a second army of five corps would be necessary to carry the attack forward enough to split completely the Allied armies. When the attacking German forces reached Doullens (about 30 km from the German front line), he believed the objective of dividing the enemy armies would have been achieved. The breakthrough assault would have to be supported by large amounts of artillery. At least one heavy field howitzer battery for every 200 meters

[13] OHL to AOK 11, 16 March 1915, quoted in "Durchbruchspläne," p. 27.

[14] 11th Army, Ia Nr. 7g, 30 March 1915. The following paragraphs are drawn from the extracts of Seeckt's report in "Durchbruchspläne," pp. 52–59. See also *Der Weltkrieg*, VII, pp. 318–320.

of the front was necessary, in all 125 batteries. He further recommended an additional 30 heavy cannon and heavy howitzer batteries.

Through March and April, Falkenhayn took further steps to implement his offensive intentions in the west. On 29 March, Falkenhayn issued a directive covering defensive doctrine designed to make the *Westheer*'s positions stronger and allow the release of more troops to serve as an OHL reserve (a process to which he would return later in the year). This directive covered items from the construction of reinforced shelters for trench garrisons to the improvement of wire entanglements. Additionally, each corps was to prepare plans for an offensive in its sector.[15] The *Westheer* had been largely on the defensive for a considerable time, and this last element of Falkenhayn's directive indicates he felt it necessary to improve the offensive capability of the army, even if only through staff exercises.

Two days after this first directive, another entitled, "Training of the OHL Reserve," was issued by the OHL. Falkenhayn wrote, "The units standing behind the front as an OHL reserve are intended for use in an offensive." As such, they were to receive, "careful training in the area of technical attacks [*besonders sorgfältige Schulung in dem Gebrauch der technischen Angriffsmittel*]." Exercise areas, with model enemy trenches, were to be constructed behind the front lines to achieve these training goals. The directive specified that the training was to begin with small units and to progress ultimately to the division. Further, in an effort to spread the knowledge obtained in previous offensives by other units, Falkenhayn specified that these reserve units should study the reports of the 1st Army's successful limited offensives at Vailly and Soissons, as well as share knowledge amongst themselves.[16]

The plans for a breakthrough produced by the *Westheer* in March contain many similarities and provide an insight into the minds of the German military leadership in early 1915. Clearly, both the *Westheer*'s commanders and the OHL, despite the evidence of the recent French offensive, believed a breakthrough to be possible, if sufficient forces were properly employed. Seeckt's report of 30 March, what seems to be OHL's final plan, called for the breakthrough to be carried out by fourteen army corps, including eleven newly built corps. This compared with the seventeen army corps required by Krafft's plan and the nine and a half required

15 OHL Nr. 19305, 29 March 1915, BA/MA, W10/51308; *Der Weltkrieg*, VII, p. 316.

16 OHL, "Ausbildung der Reserven der Obersten Heeresleitung," Nr. 19500, 31 March 1915, BA/MA, W10/51308; *Der Weltkrieg*, VII, p. 317. This training scheme seems to have been separate from the formation of the *Sturmabteilung* in the VIII Army Corps, which would develop into the stormtroops of later in the war. See Bruce I. Gudmundsson, *Stormtroop Tactics: Innovation in the German Army, 1914–1918* (New York: Praeger, 1989).

by Kuhl's plan of 13 March. Additionally, each plan called for the initial breakthrough to be supported by large amounts of heavy artillery.

Propitious terrain, however, was more important than weight of forces to each of these authors. All three memoranda stressed the necessity of choosing the most favorable sector of front for the breakthrough attempt. Kuhl's opinion speaks for all three:

> The place where the breakthrough shall take place, must be so chosen that the tactical conditions are favorable, that a large portion of the enemy's troops will be defeated or pushed aside, and, especially, that the enemy will not be able to prepare another defensive position behind the broken position.[17]

Given their own experience at defense, the Germans were clear that the portion of the front picked for a breakthrough had to be carefully chosen. The enemy trench system must not be inordinately strong and the terrain had to be favorable to the attacker. All three authors chose a section of the front that offered few natural features upon which the enemy could fall back and reorganize their defense. The pressing need to choose the proper sector for a breakthrough led Falkenhayn to assign Seeckt, the Chief of Staff of the force intended to execute the offensive, the task of personally reconnoitering the front.

All three authors also identified other important elements in ensuring a successful breakthrough. First, each wrote of the necessity of a powerful diversionary attack, designed to tie down enemy forces far from the point of decision. Second, each stressed the importance of hitting the enemy quickly and powerfully with a surprise blow. In Krafft's words, the enemy position "must be completely smashed. The first blow must break in with elemental force [*mit elementarer Wucht*] and with all possible surprise . . ."[18] Kuhl wrote similarly and with reference to French attacks: "It must not come to the French procedure, one corps after the other being pushed against the enemy position. We must strive for surprise at all costs. The breakthrough must succeed suddenly."[19] Further, each author highlighted the importance of maintaining the momentum of the attack once the initial breakthrough had succeeded.

All three officers emphasized the importance of heavy artillery, particularly heavy howitzers with their high-trajectory fire, in breaking through an enemy trench system. However, they put far less importance on weight of artillery than did the Entente planners. Instead, after the experience of successful limited attacks at Vailly and Soissons, the German planners emphasized short but accurate bombardments, which focused on key

17 AOK 1 to OHL, Ia Nr. 1182, 13 March 1915, quoted in "Durchbruchspläne," pp. 18–19.
18 AOK 6 to OHL, 3 March 1915 in ibid., p. 9.
19 AOK 1 to OHL, Ia Nr. 1182, 13 March 1915 in ibid., p. 19.

enemy targets (strongpoints, enemy observation posts, enemy artillery, etc.). Such bombardments allowed for more selective targeting and also had the significant advantage of maintaining the element of surprise. Each plan called for close artillery/infantry cooperation, and Krafft even wrote of the importance of using aerial observation for the artillery, for which he recommended the employment of twenty aircraft squadrons.[20]

Throughout the planning in the spring of 1915, Falkenhayn had reserved for himself the responsibility of directing the exploitation of any breakthrough, merely giving the 11th Army the task of planning the breakthrough itself.[21] Thus, the General Staff Chief kept in his hands the strategic direction of the campaign. Unfortunately, with the evidence that has survived, it is difficult to determine exactly Falkenhayn's intentions in early 1915. However, given the strategy he outlined to Bethmann in November 1914 and the planning that was carried out by the *Westheer* some conclusions can be drawn.

First, as we have seen, Falkenhayn did not believe that the forces at Germany's disposal would allow for a "decisive" battle to be fought. He told the Chancellor plainly that at least one enemy would have to be detached from the anti-German coalition if Germany were to have any chance of winning the war. In the spring of 1915, evidence suggests that Falkenhayn was aiming to force France into a separate peace.[22] First, the General Staff Chief gave the 11th Army the task of "breaking through the enemy front . . . with the goal of driving to the sea."[23] In a comment to Kuhl's memorandum of 18 March, Falkenhayn wrote that if the British army could be divided from the French and forced to retreat from the Continent, "then the French would certainly be finished with their ally."[24] The plan devised by Seeckt clearly aimed at the separation of the forces of the two nations. However, we cannot know how Falkenhayn then planned to force the British from the Continent. Indeed, it is questionable if Germany would have had the forces necessary to reach even this limited goal. Seeckt's plan required fourteen army corps and numerous heavy artillery batteries just for the breakthrough and drive to the coast.[25] Despite the hopes raised by Wrisberg's reorganization plan the

[20] AOK 6 to OHL, 3 March 1915 in ibid., p. 13.
[21] Falkenhayn to AOK 11, 16 March 1915, quoted in ibid., p. 27.
[22] The General Staff Chief was convinced this could be accomplished. He told Groener on 24 March that "he expected the war to be over by the time the leaves fall [!]." Wilhelm Groener, *Lebenserinnerungen* (ed. Friedrich Freiherr Hiller von Gaertringen) (Göttingen: Vandenhoeck & Ruprecht, 1957), p. 533.
[23] Falkenhayn to AOK 11, 16 March 1915, quoted in "Durchbruchspläne," p. 27.
[24] Comment to Kuhl's memorandum, ibid., p. 36.
[25] Falkenhayn had originally refused the 6th Army's plan on the fact that it required too many units. Krafft, *Durchbruch*, p. 40.

OHL had built up a reserve of only sixteen divisions behind the Western Front by the middle of April;[26] clearly, not enough to carry out Seeckt's plan, let alone any exploitation.

In the end, despite all the preparation, Falkenhayn's plans for a breakthrough operation in the west were brought quickly to a halt by the deteriorating position of Germany's ally, Austria-Hungary. As we saw in Chapter 6, in April 1915, Falkenhayn was forced to send substantial reinforcements to the east, including the spearhead of his upcoming western operation, the 11th Army. The resulting offensive in Galicia drew in more and more German units as Falkenhayn sought to deal Russia a blow which would either bring it to the negotiating table or damage its army so much that it would be unable to threaten Austria-Hungary with an offensive for an extended period of time. The OHL was forced once again to allow the initiative in the west to pass to the Entente.

Defensive doctrine

Forced to postpone his plans for an offensive in the west and faced with increasing demands for troops in the east, Falkenhayn shifted from preparing for an attack and instead concentrated on securing, with the smallest number of troops, the Western Front from Entente assaults. The Entente attacks during the winter, especially those of the French in the Champagne, had at times come close to breaking through the German position and had forced the Germans to re-examine their defensive doctrine as early as March.[27] The plans for a major German offensive and the availability of plentiful reserves, however, had pushed plans for strengthening the *Westheer*'s defensive system to the background. The constant need for fresh troops as the offensive in the east progressed during the summer caused Falkenhayn to turn again to the question of defensive doctrine.

The German army's defensive system in the west had developed haphazardly since late 1914. Each of the *Westheer*'s armies developed its own unique trench system based on local conditions and experiences. In most cases, these systems reflected the pre-war emphasis on temporary field fortifications. Many positions lacked depth and were consequently vulnerable to powerful enemy attacks, particularly as the strength of the Western Allies' heavy artillery grew. Over the course of the spring and summer, the *Westheer* went through a period of reorganization designed to standardize defensive doctrine and strengthen the front.

[26] *Der Weltkrieg*, VII, p. 314.

[27] Martin Samuels, *Command or Control? Command, Training and Tactics in the British and German Armies 1888–1918* (London: Frank Cass, 1995), pp. 161–166.

Although the OHL did not change its policy of never giving up a foot of earth (*Halten was zu halten ist*), the German defense system became more flexible and the beginnings of the defense in depth of 1917/18 can be seen. After absorbing the lessons of the defensive battles in the winter, OHL ordered each of the *Westheer*'s armies in early April to create a second defensive position several kilometers behind the first, somewhat sheltered from the effects of enemy artillery.[28] Additionally, positions were to be constructed wherever possible on reverse slopes to remain unobserved by enemy artillery. The first defensive position became more elaborate as well. What had once been a simple trench became a more complex position, with strongpoints and garrisons behind the first trench. It had now become a "fortified zone," rather than a simple line of trenches.[29] The experiences of *Trommelfeuer* convinced the Germans that the enemy would often break in to the first position and that keeping large numbers of troops in the first trench only caused high casualties. Priority shifted from holding terrain at all costs to keeping the troops alive. Troops arrayed behind the first trench survived enemy attacks more easily and could be used to drive the enemy out with counterattacks.[30]

The success of these measures seemed proven by the poor results of the Entente offensives in Artois in May and June, and, increasingly, the safety of the German position in the west seemed assured to the OHL.[31] On 6 June, Falkenhayn traveled from Pless to the OHL's western headquarters in Mézières to begin an inspection of the front.[32] Upon his arrival, Falkenhayn found the 1st, 2nd, and 6th Armies involved in "severe" battles, but everywhere the German troops held their own against Entente

28 In January, this proposal had been rejected by the 2nd, 4th, 6th, and 7th Armies as unnecessary. AOK 6, I. Nr. 5747, 18 January 1915, BA/MA, W10/51308. A debate also began concerning whether or not to situate these positions on reverse slopes. See Samuels, *Command or Control*, pp. 159–170.

29 See AOK 3, "Experience Gained in the Winter Battle in Champagne from the Point of View of the Organization of the Enemy's Lines of Defence and the Means of Combating an Attempt to Pierce Our Line," 14 April 1915 (British translation), British Army Central Distribution Service (CDS) 303. (My thanks to Dr. Martin Samuels for access to his collection of CDS and SS documents.)

30 William Balck, *Die Entwickelung der Taktik im Weltkriege* (Berlin: R. Eisenschmidt, 1922), pp. 84–85. For an example of how the revised instructions were issued at corps level, see "The Lessons of the recent fighting in the Ban de Sapt," [German] XV Reserve Corps, Ia Nr. 1635, 17 July 1915, PRO, WO 157/1. See also Friedrich Seeßelberg, *et al.*, *Der Stellungskrieg 1914–1918* (Berlin: E. S. Mittler, 1926), pp. 102–230.

31 Reichsarchiv, *Der Weltkrieg*, VIII: *Die Operationen des Jahres 1915: Die Ereignisse im Westen im Frühjahr und Sommer, im Osten vom Frühjahr bis zum Jahresschluss* (Berlin: E. S. Mittler, 1932), pp. 55–78.

32 When the OHL relocated to Pless in May, it left behind a number of officers under the command of Fritz von Loßberg, then the Ia of the OHL, at its headquarters in Mézières to liaise with the *Westheer*. See Fritz von Loßberg, *Meine Tätigkeit im Weltkriege 1914–1918* (Berlin: E. S. Mittler, 1939), p. 148.

attacks. After meeting with the chiefs of staff of the *Westheer*, Falkenhayn was convinced that the Entente attacks would achieve no meaningful results and that the *Westheer* would be able to give up several units for use in the east (these would be replaced with fought-out units from the east).[33] On 10 June, Falkenhayn returned to Pless to direct the ongoing offensive in Galicia, convinced in the ability of the *Westheer* to ward off any Entente offensive, and the transfer of units took place.[34]

Falkenhayn's trip to the Western Front in early June brought a number of steps designed to strengthen the *Westheer*'s defensive position further and free additional troops for use "in other theatres." First, shortly after Falkenhayn's return to the east, several officers from the OHL in Pless were ordered to the west with important missions. On 20 June, Generalmajor von Mertens, the general of engineers of the 10th Army, was ordered by Falkenhayn to the west. The purpose of his mission is today somewhat hazy. The Reichsarchiv reported that Mertens' task was to establish a military line of demarcation for a future peace between Germany and the Entente.[35] This view is somewhat supported by Falkenhayn's ideas at the time concerning a separate peace (see below). However, the OHL's *Bürooffizier*, Major Friedrich Mewes, wrote that Mertens' mission was much more radical. He maintained that Mertens was sent to the west to identify a position upon which the *Westheer* could fall back and hold with far fewer troops.[36] Falkenhayn, driven by the requirements of his eastern offensive, seems to have considered seriously for a time a shortening of the Western Front, designed to free more reserves for employment in the east. While in the end Falkenhayn chose not to undertake a general withdrawal to a shorter position in the west, he still needed to find more troops to feed his eastern venture. Shortly after Mertens' return to the east, two more officers went from the OHL's headquarters at Pless to the Western Front as part of Falkenhayn's general reorganization.

On 3 July, General der Infantrie Eberhard von Claer and General der Artillerie Ludwig Lauter were sent by the OHL to the Western Front.[37]

[33] The orders were originally sent on 2 June but the transport of units was postponed until Falkenhayn visited the west. OHL to 4th Army, 2 June 1915, OHL Nr. 1948r; OHL to *Armee-Abteilungen Gaede* and *Falkenhausen*, 2 June 1915, OHL Nr. 1950r, BA/MA, W10/51388.

[34] Tappen, "Kriegstagebuch," 10 June 1915.

[35] *Der Weltkrieg*, VIII, p. 610.

[36] Mewes to Reichsarchiv, 15 August and 8 September 1931, BA/MA, W10/51408. Mewes' suggestion that the Reichsarchiv query Majors Harbou and Geyer about Mertens' mission seems not to have been pursued.

[37] Eberhard von Claer, Inspector General of Fortresses from 1913, became *General vom Ingenieur- und Pionierkorps im Grossen Hauptquartier* at the war's outbreak and Ludwig Lauter, the Inspector General of Artillery since 1911, became the *General der Fussartillerie im Grossen Hauptquartier* in August 1914.

Claer's task was to referee the debate that had developed within the western OHL over the *Westheer*'s various defensive systems and recommend a single, common system to be used by all armies on the front.[38] Lauter's mission was to examine the artillery of the *Westheer* and to update the artillery training procedures and manuals, taking into account the most recent lessons and requirements of position warfare.[39] Re-establishing a common infantry and artillery doctrine in the armies of the *Westheer* would go a long way toward creating a more secure front, and bring Falkenhayn the troops he needed for his offensive in the east.

Over the course of 1915, much attention had been paid to creating a new infantry defensive doctrine, but the equally important artillery doctrine had been neglected. Under the direction of Lauter, the artillery of the *Westheer* was to be overhauled. The experiences of the previous battles on the Western Front had taught the importance of artillery in defense, and, through the summer, the OHL issued directives on the proper employment of artillery in defensive battles. The Germans had admitted that their artillery had been "unable to combat the effects of the French artillery on our [defending] infantry." However, the German defensive artillery was able to obtain

> very successful results against the enemy's infantry, either by directing a heavy fire against the infantry positions from which the attack was issuing, and thus bringing it to a standstill, or else by directing a rapid and concentrated fire against the attack itself.[40]

The artillery of the *Westheer*'s armies, reinforced when necessary from the OHL artillery reserve, would assemble at threatened points and be parceled out to subordinate formations as necessary. The combined fire of the guns would be crucial to destroying the attacking enemy infantry as they left their trenches and to cutting the attacking troops off from their rearward communications.[41] New techniques of observation and planned fire were introduced, including specialized ranging detachments behind the German lines designed to facilitate counter-battery fire.

38 Bauer, *Krieg*, p. 86; and Eberhard von Claer, "Meine Tätigkeit als Chef des Ingenieur- und Pionierkorps und General-Inspekteur der Festungen sowie als General vom Chef des Ingenieur- und Pionierkorps im Großen Hauptquartier," *Vierteljahreshefte für Pioniere* (November 1937), pp. 204–206. For a full discussion of the debates on defensive doctrine in 1915, see Samuels, *Command or Control*, pp. 159–170. G. C. Wynne's *If Germany Attacks: The Battle in Depth in the West* (London: Faber and Faber, 1939) offers an interpretation based almost solely on Loßberg's memoirs.

39 *Der Weltkrieg*, VIII, pp. 98–99; Loßberg, *Meine Tätigkeit*, pp. 157–158. Loßberg recorded that Claer earned himself the sobriquet, "Grabenschreck," or "Terror of the Trenches."

40 AOK 3, "Experiences Gained in the Winter Battles in Champagne," CDS 303.

41 OHL, "Barrage Fire in case of Attack and the Necessary Expenditure of Ammunition," Nr. 3550, 11 July 1915, PRO, WO157/3.

Lauter ensured that each army was employing its artillery most efficiently and that pre-war training manuals were updated to reflect the most recent lessons of *Stellungskrieg*.[42]

As the reorganization of the *Westheer* progressed, Falkenhayn again traveled to the west. On 29 July, he conducted a meeting with all the Chiefs of Staff of the *Westheer*, which gives us important clues to Falkenhayn's strategic thinking in the summer of 1915. Falkenhayn opened by thanking the Chiefs in the name of the Kaiser for their good work in warding off the Entente attacks and in giving the *Ostheer* the breathing room necessary to conduct operations. During this meeting, Falkenhayn expressed his belief that the Western Allies would not attack any time in the near future and that, if they did, the "Iron Wall" in the west, strengthened by the recent reorganization, would undoubtedly hold firm. Falkenhayn opined that the French did not have the necessary will to undertake a major offensive and that the British were too preoccupied with events in Gallipoli. A German attack in the west, Falkenhayn's wish, was also ruled out in the near future – operations in the east would not be concluded for some time.[43] Based on these beliefs, the General Staff Chief ordered additional units to be withdrawn from the west for use in the east.[44]

Falkenhayn remained convinced through the summer that the Entente would not launch a major offensive in the near future and that the reorganized *Westheer* could defend against any Entente attack. Indeed, there is evidence to suggest that in the summer of 1915 Falkenhayn believed that, far from planning an offensive, the French were ready for peace. On 30 June, he sent a memorandum to Bethmann and the Foreign Office outlining his assessment of the French. In its conclusion Falkenhayn wrote:

> France's victims in this war are so many that the government can bear the responsibility for them neither before the people of France nor someday before history. Soon [the French government] will be faced with the question of whether, despite all outside help, the ending of resistance is a more fitting path for the future of the nation than the continuation of this hopeless war.[45]

The failure of the French to launch a great relief offensive in August reinforced Falkenhayn's belief that the French were incapable of a further

42 The change in artillery doctrine necessitated altering some long-held beliefs about the employment of artillery. See Major Justrow, "Die artilleristische Waffe," in Seeßelberg, *Stellungskrieg*, pp. 254–281; and also Major Dr.-Ing. Karl Becker, "Schiesstechnik und Ballistik," in ibid., pp. 282–291. The heavy artillery [*Fußartillerie*] arm, which was trained for *Festungskrieg*, made the adjustment easier than the field artillery [*Feldartillerie*].

43 "Die Besprechung in Metz am 29.Juli 1915," BA/MA, W10/51312, contains the war diary entries for the chiefs of staff participating in the conference. See also *Der Weltkrieg*, VIII, pp. 100–101, which relies upon the diary entries of Hermann Ritter Mertz von Quirnheim.

44 Tappen, "Kriegstagebuch," 30 July 1915.

45 *Der Weltkrieg*, VIII, pp. 609–610.

great effort.[46] Indeed, he remained firm in this belief, despite the growing evidence of a coming offensive offered by the 6th and 3rd Armies, until he had seen the offensive with his own eyes on 25 September.

Accordingly, Falkenhayn continued to focus his effort in the east and to strip the *Westheer* of its reserves. However, many German leaders were still fearful of another powerful Entente offensive; both Crown Prince Wilhelm and Crown Prince Rupprecht complained about the weakness of the *Westheer.*[47] By 22 September, on the eve of a major Entente offensive, the OHL reserve on the Western Front had been reduced to four infantry divisions and two independent infantry brigades. Additionally, the Guard Corps and the staff of the X Corps with its 20th Division had arrived in Belgium in mid-September for rest after the campaign in Russia and were available as a reserve in an emergency. The OHL artillery reserve, crucial to any defensive battle, consisted of thirteen modern heavy batteries and eleven older heavy batteries. Facing this meager reserve of four full-strength divisions, three tired divisions, and two brigades, the OHL intelligence reckoned that the French and English possessed a reserve of fifty divisions.[48]

The *Herbstschlacht* in the Champagne

Despite Falkenhayn's confidence that the French did not have the will to launch another great offensive, the commander of the 3rd Army, Generaloberst Karl von Einem, believed otherwise. Shortly after Falkenhayn's meeting with the Chiefs of Staff, the German 3rd Army began noting French preparations for a major offensive.[49] In early August, Einem noted French preparations in the Champagne, but wrote, "we calmly and confidently await the attack."[50] Throughout the month, the offensive preparations in front of Einem's 3rd Army as well as in front of Crown Prince Rupprecht's 6th Army became more and more apparent and more threatening. By the end of the month, Einem began reorganizing his army

46 Falkenhayn, *General Headquarters*, p. 166.

47 Reichsarchiv, *Der Weltkrieg*, Bd. IX: *Die Operationen des Jahres 1915: Die Ereignisse im Westen und auf dem Balkan vom Sommer bis zum Jahresschluss* (Berlin: E. S. Mittler, 1933), pp. 17, 27.

48 *Der Weltkrieg*, IX, p. 100; Loßberg, *Meine Tätigkeit*, pp. 161–162. The Guard Corps had suffered 21,000 casualties in the Russian campaign and was in the process of inducting recruits.

49 This offensive has been called "one of the worst-kept secrets of the war." Richard Griffiths, *Marshal Pétain* (London: Constable, 1994, first published 1970), p. 14.

50 Karl von Einem, "Kriegstagebuch," 11 August 1915, BA/MA, N324/12. Einem's diary was published in edited form after the war as *Ein Armeeführer erlebt den Weltkrieg* (ed. Junius Alter) (Leipzig: v. Hase & Koehler, 1938). As the published version omits many details, I have used the original.

to strengthen threatened points on his front. He also began requesting infantry and artillery reinforcement from the OHL.[51] On 7 September, General Lauter, the OHL's artillery officer, arrived to examine the 3rd Army's artillery preparations and requirements. Convinced of an impending French offensive, Lauter recommended an immediate reinforcement of ten heavy artillery batteries.[52] Falkenhayn, however, continued to believe the French preparations to be a feint, and in response to the 3rd Army's requests for reinforcement, he offered only limited artillery and infantry reinforcement and more artillery ammunition.[53]

As September progressed, however, French intentions became clearer. From the beginning of the month, French deserters reported the coming offensive. One deserter confessed that a major offensive was to begin between 14 and 21 September. These rumors were supported by reports from German agents. By the 16th, the 3rd Army had identified, in addition to the two previous corps, three new French corps on its front and large numbers of French heavy batteries.[54] Further, the French began pushing their trenches closer to the German positions in an effort to reduce the distance the infantry had to cover during an assault.[55] All evidence pointed to a coming major French offensive, and the OHL's Intelligence Section reported on 7 September that they expected a French offensive, with a main attack in Champagne and a diversionary attack in Artois, any day.[56] Even Falkenhayn's normally skeptical operations officer, Gerhard Tappen, began to believe that an offensive was impending.[57]

In fact, against Einem's 3rd Army stood Noël de Castelnau's *groupe d'armées du centre*, composed of two French armies, the 2nd under Fernande de Langle de Cary and the 4th under Philippe Pétain. Castelnau's army group had been preparing an offensive since early July and had accumulated a powerful striking force. Einem's 8 divisions faced 27 French divisions and the 3rd Army's 600 some artillery pieces were overwhelmed by the 683 heavy and 1,443 light French guns. The French also massed cavalry divisions behind the infantry in order to exploit the

51 Loßberg, *Meine Tätigkeit*, pp. 162–163.
52 Einem, "Kriegstagebuch," 5 and 7 September 1915; Oberstleutnant a.D. Muths, "Die deutsche schwere Artillerie im August bis Dezember 1915," Appendix 3 to "Forschungsarbeit zu Band IX," BA/MA, W10/51353, p. 10.
53 Falkenhayn, *General Headquarters*, p. 166; *Der Weltkrieg*, IX, pp. 32–34.
54 Einem, "Kriegstagebuch," 31 August to 16 September 1915.
55 Arndt von Kirchbach, *Kämpfe in der Champagne (Winter 1914–Herbst 1915) (Der große Krieg in Einzeldarstellungen* H. 11) (Oldenburg: Gerhard Stalling, 1919), p. 70.
56 Hauptmann a.D. Krogh, "Kriegstagebuch," 7 September 1915, BA/MA, W10/51305.
57 Tappen, "Kriegstagebuch," 5 September 1915. On the 21st, however, he wrote that commanders of the *Westheer*'s armies seemed excessively nervous.

Fig. 11 Generaloberst Karl von Einem, commander of the 3rd Army in the *Herbstschlacht*

expected breakthrough. At the French *Schwerpunkt*, the German VIII Reserve Corps faced five French corps.[58]

The French, determined not to repeat the mistakes of earlier offensives, paid meticulous attention to preparations for this attack. Since early August, the French had followed a policy of rotating their assault divisions into the front line, giving them enough time to become familiar

[58] Ministère de la Guerre, *Les Armées Françaises dans la Grande Guerre*, Tome III: *Les Offensives de 1915–L'Hiver de 1915–1916* (Paris: Imprimerie Nationale, 1923), p. 310; "Beispiele für Artillerie-Stärken bei Durchbruchsangriffen," BA/MA, W10/50160.

with the terrain but not enough time to suffer serious casualties.[59] Joffre hoped that this great accumulation of troops supported by masses of artillery, as at Gorlice, would give the little extra needed to punch through the German lines into open ground. Stealing another page from Falkenhayn's book, Joffre believed a powerful diversionary attack in Artois to be important in keeping the Germans guessing as to the location of the main attack. The greatly weakened *Westheer* was shortly to be attacked by a vastly superior enemy.[60]

At 7:00a.m. on 22 September, the French opened their *Trommelfeuer* in the Champagne and in Artois. Einem recorded in his diary on the same day that he awaited the French infantry attack at any moment. In fact, the firing on the 22nd signaled the beginning of a 72 hour bombardment that in the end obliterated many German positions, wiped out their garrisons, swept away the German wire, destroyed artillery observation posts, and cut rearward communications. The bombardment also extended far beyond the forward trenches in an effort to hinder the Germans in bringing forward reinforcements. The rail facilities at Bazancourt and Challerange were destroyed and 3rd Army's headquarters was attacked by French aircraft. The Germans observed an average of thirty to thirty-five French batteries directed against each German division. For three days, the smoke and dust kicked up by the French fire blocked out the sun above the position of the German 3rd Army.[61]

In all, the French 2nd and 4th Armies fired close to 3.4 million artillery rounds (including almost 600,000 heavy rounds) on the 3rd Army's positions during their preparatory bombardment.[62] The *Trommelfeuer* fell heaviest against Generalleutnant Fleck's VIII Reserve Corps, where the French intended to concentrate their main effort.[63] French preparations over the previous month had convinced the 3rd Army that the main French blow would fall in the VIII Reserve Corps' sector (and on its neighbor, the 21st Reserve Division of the 5th Army) and efforts had been made to reinforce this position. Here Einem collected most of his artillery

[59] AOK 3, *Die Champagne-Herbstschlacht 1915* (Munich: Albert Langen, 1916), pp. 24ff.

[60] Joseph Joffre, *The Memoirs of Marshal Joffre* (trans. T. Bentley Mott) (2 vols.) (London: Geoffrey Bles, 1932), II, pp. 354ff.; *Les Armées Françaises*, III, pp. 275–278; Griffiths, *Pétain*, pp. 13–14.

[61] AOK 3, *Die Champagne-Herbstschlacht*, pp. 31–39; Kirchbach, *Kämpfe in der Champagne*, pp. 74–77; *Der Weltkrieg*, IX, pp. 48–49.

[62] *Les Armées Françaises*, III, p. 537. Ironically, the French blamed insufficient ammunition for the failure of the offensive. p. 548.

[63] The VIII Reserve Corps was composed of the Division Liebert (15th Reserve Division), the 50th Infantry Division, and the Division Ditfurth (16th Reserve Division). It held a front of around 20 km. Fleck had distinguished himself in command of an army group during the previous French offensives in the Champagne.

reserve, and upon the opening of the French *Trommelfeuer*, further heavy artillery reinforcement arrived from the OHL.[64]

Despite the beginning of the French bombardment on 22 September, Falkenhayn remained skeptical of French intentions. The General Staff Chief had left Pless on 21 September for the west to judge for himself the seriousness of the situation. On the 24th, in a discussion with Einem, he repeated his belief that the French did not have the will to launch a major offensive.[65] Several French probing attacks against VIII Reserve Corps were repulsed on the 24th, reinforcing his opinion.[66] Crown Prince Rupprecht later recalled that Falkenhayn expressed to the Kaiser the view that the 3rd Army saw things "far too black."[67] Nevertheless, the General Staff Chief took a number of steps to reinforce the 3rd Army. First, he placed the 5th Infantry Division, which had been ear-marked for the Serbian campaign, at the disposal of the 3rd Army.[68] Then, from 22 to 24 September, twenty-three heavy batteries were transferred to the 3rd Army from various areas of the front.[69]

At 9:15a.m. on 25 September, the long-awaited French infantry offensive began. As expected, the attack fell heaviest against the VIII Reserve Corps and its neighbor, the 5th Army's 21st Reserve Division. Here, five German divisions were attacked by nineteen French divisions with almost three times the number of guns.[70] The efforts of the French preparatory bombardment had paid handsome dividends. In many areas, the attacking French infantry found the German positions to be almost completely destroyed and the remaining defenders to be too stunned to offer meaningful resistance.[71] Indeed, many German defenders were caught by French infantry in their dugouts before they could man their positions.[72]

64 Kirchbach, *Kämpfe in der Champagne*, pp. 75–76; *Der Weltkrieg*, IX, pp. 49–50; Muths, "Artillerie," p. 10.

65 Einem, "Kriegstagebuch," 24 September 1915, "I spoke to Falkenhayn and made him aware of the very serious situation. He was of the opinion, however, that the French did not have the guts . . ."

66 Tappen, "Kriegstagebuch," 24 September 1915; *Der Weltkrieg*, IX, p. 51.

67 [Wilhelm] Solger, "Die Leitung des deutschen Westheeres im September und Oktober 1915 seit dem Begin der Herbstschlacht in der Champagne und im Artois," unpublished manuscript in BA/MA, W10/51353, p. 1.

68 After the war, Einem wrote that he believed the 5th Infantry Division was released to the 3rd Army far too late in the battle. Einem to Reichsarchiv, 17 September 1932, BA/MA, W10/51352.

69 *Der Weltkrieg*, IX, p. 50.

70 Noël de Castelnau, "Rapport d'ensemble sur les opérations offensives de Champagne (Septembre 1915)," 1 November 1915, *Les Armées Françaises*, III, *Annexes* IV, Annexe Nr. 3019.

71 AOK 3, *Die Champagne-Herbstschlacht*, pp. 55ff.; Kirchbach, *Kämpfe in der Champagne*, p. 86; Report of 14 Corps d'Armée, Nr. 144, 1 October 1915, *Les Armées Françaises*, III, *Annexes* III, Annexe Nr. 2513.

72 *Der Weltkrieg*, IX, p. 61.

The bombardment had also done a good job of cutting German communications, making it difficult for the German infantry to call in artillery support or request reinforcements. Supported by a gas attack, the French quickly broke into the German position and began rolling up the trenches. Before noon, several French corps had made deep penetrations into the German position, overrunning completely the first German line. The French command poured reserves into the initial breaches.[73]

As the French attacks began on the morning of the 25th, Falkenhayn and the Kaiser, who were on a tour of the *Westheer*'s armies, were preparing to leave Montmedy for the 5th Army's headquarters at Stenay, 60 km away. Before they left Montmedy, the *Westheer*'s morning reports arrived at around 10:00a.m., forwarded by Loßberg from Mézières.[74] The contents of the initial reports confirmed Falkenhayn's previous opinion of the French intentions. The 3rd Army reported that in its sector the French artillery fire continued as before. The 3rd Army staff, whose communications with its units had been severely restricted by the effects of French artillery fire, was unable to determine whether or not a French attack had taken place during the night or in the early hours of the morning. The 6th Army reported that although infantry attacks had taken place, they appeared "to be insignificant."[75]

By the time Falkenhayn and the Kaiser had arrived at Stenay, the staffs of the 6th and 3rd Armies had begun to realize the scale of the Entente operations, and Falkenhayn found grave reports waiting for him. The 6th Army reported to the OHL at 12:30p.m. that the enemy had broken into its position in a number of places and that all its reserves had been committed to battle. Rupprecht wrote, "further immediate reinforcement is necessary."[76] At 12:15, 3rd Army called its neighbor, the 5th Army, with an urgent request for reinforcement, saying that the "enemy has broken through in the area of Souain-Somme Py." As the 5th Army's XVIII Reserve Corps was already heavily engaged in battle, Crown Prince Wilhelm refused the 3rd Army's request.[77] Further, a tense telephone conversation took place between Falkenhayn and Einem and his Chief of Staff, Generalleutnant Ritter von Höhn, in which Falkenhayn felt it necessary to remind Einem that the Kaiser expected "every man to do his duty."[78] Falkenhayn soon left Stenay for the OHL headquarters at Mézières.

73 *Les Armées Françaises*, III, pp. 372–373. 74 Loßberg, *Meine Tätigkeit*, p. 164.

75 AOK 3 and AOK 6, "Morgenmeldung, 25 September 1915," printed in Solger, "Die Leitung des deutschen Westheeres," p. 2.

76 AOK 6, "Mittagsmeldung, 25 September 1915," in ibid., p. 3.

77 "Niederschrift eines Fernspruchs oder Fernspräches von AOK 3 and AOK 5, 25 September 1915, 12:15," printed in ibid., p. 4.

78 Einem, "Kriegstagebuch," 25 September 1915.

Falkenhayn began to take steps to reinforce the threatened sectors even before he left Stenay. He ordered the 192nd Infantry Brigade from reserve behind the 7th Army to the 6th Army and the 56th Infantry Division from *Armeeabteilung Falkenhausen* to the 3rd Army. After arriving at Mézières, he ordered the Guard Corps to be transported from its rest areas south of Brussels to the 6th Army and the X Army Corps headquarters with its 20th Infantry Division from its rest area south of Antwerp to the 3rd Army. Later, he rerouted the 192nd Infantry Brigade to the 3rd Army. Einem also received a battalion of heavy field howitzers from the 7th Army.[79] It would, however, take several hours for these reinforcements to arrive, and until that time, the 6th and 3rd Armies were left to their own devices.[80]

As the day progressed, the extent of the French penetration in the 3rd Army's sector slowly became known to the OHL, and it became apparent that the most threatening attack was in the 3rd Army's sector rather than in Artois. The VIII Reserve Corps' 15th Reserve Division and 50th Infantry Division had been forced back to their second defensive position (*R-Stellung*), and its 16th Reserve Division had also been badly shaken.[81] All local counterattacks had failed to re-take the divisions' initial positions. Throughout the day, Einem rushed reserves as they arrived forward to stem the breach, but they were only barely able to hold the VIII Reserve Corps' incomplete *R-Stellung*;[82] in some areas the VIII Reserve Corps had even been pushed out of its forward-most positions within the *R-Stellung*.[83] Each of the corps' divisions had lost close to 5,000 men and the 50th Infantry Division had lost a number of its guns.[84] After the first day, the VIII Reserve Corps' commander, Generalleutnant Fleck, was so

79 *Der Weltkrieg*, IX, pp. 66–68. The X Army Corps' 20th Infantry Division was still in transit from the Eastern Front.

80 Communications between the Operations and the Intelligence Sections of the OHL seem to have been exceedingly poor. Despite being repeatedly warned of the impending French attack by the Intelligence Section, the Operations Section had developed no contingency plan. Major Hessig of the Intelligence Section recalled that in the crucial first few hours of the attack, personnel from the Operations Section flooded his office with requests for information about enemy strengths along the front. Hessig to Rauch, 4 July 1929, BA/MA, W10/51305.

81 The 16th Reserve Division (Division Ditfurth) had even shown itself skittish before the battle. Its commander, Generalmajor Ditfurth had found it necessary to issue an order restricting the use of artillery as the division had been calling in fire whenever the enemy showed any signs of attack. 16th RD, Ia Nr. 215, 11 August 1915, PRO, WO157/3.

82 On the condition of the *R-Stellung*, see AOK 3, *Die Champagne-Herbstschlacht*, pp. 16–17.

83 "Ferngespräch zwischen Höhn und Knobelsdorf, 5:30p.m., 25 September 1915," from the Akten of the 5th Army, quoted in Solger, "Die Leitung des deutschen Westheeres," p. 16.

84 *Der Weltkrieg*, IX, p. 73; Loßberg, *Meine Tätigkeit*, p. 168.

shaken by the French attack that he recommended a general withdrawal of his corps early in the evening.[85]

Indeed, there is some evidence to show that not only Fleck, but the command of the 3rd Army as well was badly shaken by the events of the day and were unable to come to grips with the fast moving situation. The 3rd Army's written reports for the day seem to indicate that its staff had little grasp of the day's battle and are worth quoting at some length. At 1:50p.m., the 3rd Army reported:

> This morning, extraordinarily strong infantry attacks, wave after wave, took place along the entire front of the XIII Reserve Corps and the VIII Reserve Corps . . .
>
> Attack on the 23rd Reserve Division was defeated. At 24th Reserve Division and Division Liebert the enemy has broken in to the position in a few places. Details are lacking.
>
> The 50th Infantry Division is maintaining its position. The left wing of Division Ditfurth has been somewhat pushed back.

In fact, by 11:00a.m., both the 15th Reserve Division and the 50th Infantry Division had been pushed completely out of their first and into their second positions. At 3:05p.m., the 3rd Army reported again to the OHL. Once again, its report showed little appreciation of the situation:

> XII Reserve Corps has beaten back very strong attack and have taken around 600 prisoners. Situation of the VIII Reserve Corps is unclear. Commanding General reports that a good portion of the foremost position has been lost and perhaps also much artillery. Rearward position will hold. Artillery is lacking.

Two further reports in the evening and night showed a similar lack of understanding of the situation by Fleck's VIII Reserve Corps. While this confusion was somewhat understandable given the great destruction of the communications network by French artillery, the 3rd Army could easily have gained a clearer picture of the confused situation by sending a representative from its staff to the front line.[86] No attempt seems to have been made to do this, despite the fact that the 5th Army had already sent its intelligence officer to the VIII Reserve Corps.[87]

This command muddle persuaded Falkenhayn, who was already dissatisfied with the 3rd Army, that changes were necessary. First, the 3rd Army was placed under the command of *Heeresgruppe Deutscher Kronprinz* on the afternoon of the 26th.[88] As the 5th Army was attacked as

[85] *Der Weltkrieg*, IX, p. 71.

[86] 3rd Army's reports for 25 September 1915 are printed in Solger, "Die Leitung des deutschen Westheeres," pp. 3–15.

[87] Höhn to Reichsarchiv, 15 July 1923, BA/MA, W10/51353.

[88] *Heeresgruppe Deutscher Kronprinz* had been formed in early August out of the 5th Army and *Armeeabteilungen Strantz*, *Falkenhausen*, and *Gaede*.

well, Falkenhayn felt that Wilhelm could better coordinate the defense of both armies.[89] The 5th Army's staff had also shown more initiative in dealing with the crisis. In addition to the intelligence officer from the 5th Army's staff, Crown Prince Wilhelm himself sought to make contact with the VIII Reserve Corps on the 25th to steady their shaken nerves, and his Chief of Staff, Generalleutnant Constantin Schmidt von Knobelsdorf, visited the threatened areas of the front.[90] It is quite probable that OHL received more information about the plight of the VIII Reserve Corps on the 25th from the 5th Army than from the 3rd Army.

This change in the command arrangements provided Falkenhayn with the opportunity to make changes within the 3rd Army staff as well. In the afternoon of the 26th, Falkenhayn telephoned 3rd Army headquarters to inform them of their new command relationship with the 5th Army. Einem's Chief of Staff, Höhn, was senior to Crown Prince Wilhelm's Chief of Staff, and consequently, told Falkenhayn that he refused to serve under a junior.[91] As a further notice of his dissatisfaction with the 3rd Army, Falkenhayn replaced Höhn immediately with Fritz von Loßberg.

Loßberg left Mézières with Falkenhayn's admonition to hold on to the remaining positions at all costs ringing in his ears and arrived at 3rd Army's headquarters at Vouziers around 3:30p.m. on the 26th. Immediately upon his arrival, he answered a call from General Fleck, asking if the planned withdrawal of VIII Reserve Corps was still to take place the next day. Loßberg replied, "The VIII Reserve Corps must stand and die in its current position."[92] Shortly thereafter, Loßberg visited Fleck's headquarters to see the situation for himself. There he met Schmidt von Knobelsdorf who also felt a personal visit necessary to calm the frayed

89 *Der Weltkrieg*, IX, pp. 72–73. Einem later wrote that he felt greatly insulted by this move, but realized it was the best way to get badly needed reinforcements from 5th Army. Einem to Reichsarchiv, 17 September 1932, BA/MA, W10/51352.

90 Kronprinz Wilhelm, *Meine Erinnerungen aus Deutschlands Heldenkampf* (Berlin: E. S. Mittler, 1923), p. 142.

91 Höhn to Reichsarchiv, 15 July 1923, BA/MA, W10/51353. Einem wrote that Falkenhayn, not Höhn, bore the responsibility for the 3rd Army's desperate position as he had weakened the *Westheer* far too much pursuing his campaign in Russia. Einem, "Kriegstagebuch," 26 September 1915.

92 Loßberg, *Meine Tätigkeit*, pp. 167–168. Loßberg wrote that Höhn had given permission for the VIII Reserve Corps to withdraw, and that this decision had caused Falkenhayn to dismiss him. After the war, Höhn denied ever giving such permission. Höhn to Reichsarchiv, 15 July 1923, BA/MA, W10/51353. Einem also later denied ever acquiescing to a withdrawal. Einem to Reichsarchiv, 17 September 1932, BA/MA, W10/51352; see also his diary entry for the day, Einem, "Kriegstagebuch," 26 September 1915, in which he wrote that he learned of Fleck's plans from Knobelsdorf. The Id of VIII Reserve Corps, Förster, wrote that Fleck had already given the orders for a withdrawal by the time Loßberg arrived at 3rd Army headquarters. Förster to Nathusius, 5 October 1932, BA/MA, W10/51352.

nerves of the corps staff. The two army chiefs left after a short reconnaissance convinced that the VIII Reserve Corps would hold its current position (the original *R-Stellung*) with the reinforcements now arriving. Loßberg then left to tour the 3rd Army's remaining units.[93]

After reconnoitering the 3rd Army's position and examining the arriving reinforcements, Loßberg determined the 3rd Army's defensive position needed greater depth to withstand the renewed French attacks. Upon losing their first position on the 25th, the VIII Reserve Corps had fallen back on its incomplete *R-Stellung*. This position had the advantage, however, of being situated on the reverse slope of the Py Valley, and hence, was sheltered from French observation.[94] Loßberg ordered this position to be held with a few troops and artillery observers. Artillery was now to take over the burden of the battle. The French attacks were to be checked in the first instance by artillery fire called in by the observers in the front line.[95] Once a French attack started, the German guns were to cut the advancing French infantry from its rear and lay down a barrage on the trenches from which the French were attacking.[96]

Behind the front line, Loßberg arrayed strongpoints, machine gun and field gun placements, and garrisons for counterattacks, which were designed to support the first position. The creation of a new *R-Stellung* several kilometers behind the new front line further strengthened the 3rd Army's new position.[97] These steps, combined with the arrival of the 5th Infantry Division, the 56th Infantry Division, the 20th Infantry Division, and artillery reinforcements over the next several days, created a new defensive system that was far stronger than the original.[98]

By the time Tappen reached Mézières from Pless on 27 September, the immediate crisis had passed and he could record that, "in general, everything is in order."[99] Over the next several weeks, the French continued

93 Loßberg, *Meine Tätigkeit*, p. 172.

94 On the French observation difficulties, see Langle de Cary to Joffre, 4th Army Nr. 5075, 12 November 1915, in *Les Armées Françaises*, III, *Annexes* IV, Annexe Nr. 3069; Castelnau, "Rapport," p. 103.

95 *Der Weltkrieg*, IX, p. 97.

96 AOK 3, *Die Champagne-Herbstschlacht*, pp. 68–73. Through the course of the battle the 3rd Army fired some 1,564,000 field gun rounds and almost 400,000 heavy artillery rounds. *Der Weltkrieg*, IX, p. 97.

97 These defensive measures introduced by Loßberg presaged many of the doctrinal changes introduced into the *Westheer* by Paul von Hindenburg and Erich Ludendorff in 1917. Cf. Timothy Lupfer, *Leavenworth Paper 4: The Dynamics of Doctrine: The Changes in German Tactical Doctrine During the First World War* (Fort Leavenworth: US Army Command and General Staff College, 1981).

98 Wynne, *If Germany Attacks*, pp. 90–96; Samuels, *Command or Control*, pp. 168–169.

99 Tappen, "Kriegstagebuch," 27 September 1915. By 4 October, Falkenhayn had declared the danger of a French breakthrough to be over. Bethmann to Jagow, AS5157, 4 October 1915, PRO, GFM 34/2587 (*Weltkrieg geh.*, Bd. 23).

their attacks, but gained only minor successes against the strengthened positions of the 3rd Army. By 14 October, the French operation, which had come so tantalizingly close on the first day to breaking through the German position, was over. Falkenhayn's belief in the defensive strength of the *Westheer* proved correct. The *Westheer* had, in fact, survived the initial period with only local reserves. The divisions brought from the east only began to arrive on the Western Front on 5 October.[100] The two attacking French armies had suffered greatly in their efforts to break through the German defensive system, losing close to 150,000 men.[101] The Germans, however, suffered too; the defenders had lost around 17,000 officers and 80,000 men.[102]

Conclusion

The French offensive in September made a deep and lasting impression on the General Staff Chief. After the war, Freytag-Loringhoven wrote that Falkenhayn had given his orders with "unshakeable calm" during the first crucial hours of the offensive.[103] Gerhard Tappen painted a different, and probably more accurate, picture. When he arrived from Pless on 27 September, Tappen found Falkenhayn "very dejected." In a letter to the Reichsarchiv, Tappen wrote, "the impression [of the *Herbstschlacht*] was so deep and enduring on General Falkenhayn that he made reference to the battle during the attack on Verdun."[104] Falkenhayn's reaction was brought on by a number of factors. First, his assessment of the Entente had been proved wrong by the power of the attacks on 25 September. His policy of stripping the *Westheer* for troops to use in the east – first in his offensive in Russia, then for his campaign in Serbia – had nearly brought catastrophe to the Germans on the Western Front. The experience brought home forcefully the necessity of maintaining a sufficient reserve to deal with such contingencies. Additionally, as Wilhelm Solger of the Reichsarchiv remarked, the setback in the Champagne came almost a year to the day from when Falkenhayn took over as Chief of the General Staff from Helmuth von Moltke under very similar circumstances.[105] This

100 The XI Army Corps was the first formation from the east to arrive. "Die grossen Transportbewegungen vom Ost- zum Westkriegschauplatze im September/Oktober 1915" (Vorarbeit zu Bd. IX), unpublished manuscript in BA/MA, W10/51313.

101 *Les Armées Françaises*, III, p. 538.

102 *Der Weltkrieg*, IX, p. 97; Loßberg, *Meine Tätigkeit*, p. 185.

103 Hugo Freiherr von Freytag-Loringhoven, *Menschen und Dinge, wie ich sie in meinem Leben sah* (Berlin: E. S. Mittler, 1923), pp. 288–289.

104 Tappen to Reichsarchiv, 16 June 1932, BA/MA, N56/5. See also Falkenhayn, *General Headquarters*, p. 172.

105 Solger, "Die Leitung des deutschen Westheeres," pp. 17–18.

memory must have made the shock of the initial French success all the more jarring.

The impact of the *Herbstschlacht* went beyond the emotional, however, it also had important implications for German plans. Despite possessing vastly superior forces and attacking after an intense three-day bombardment, the French were unable to achieve a meaningful result. Falkenhayn reached certain conclusions from this. At the strategic level, the failure of the French offensive reinforced his opinions about both France and its army. Already in June, Falkenhayn believed that the French nation was nearing the end of its material and moral strength. Now, the failures of the French army in the *Herbstschlacht* bolstered his belief that their army was a flawed instrument and that it too was nearing the end of its strength.[106]

The experience of the *Herbstschlacht* also added to the lessons drawn from the Eastern Front regarding Falkenhayn's new operational approach. Seemingly in contrast to the experience in the east, the French failures demonstrated the ability of weak forces to hold against overwhelming odds if they possessed strong defensive positions. Indeed, the effect of the German artillery firing from good defensive positions was devastating to the attacking French troops during the battle.[107] The OHL put French casualties at 200,000 by 2 October.[108] Indeed, the events of September proved to the General Staff Chief that a "mass attack" could not work under the battlefield conditions of late 1915. He later wrote:

> the lessons to be deduced from the failure of our enemies' mass attacks are decisive against any imitation of their battle methods. Attempts at a mass break-through, even with the extreme accumulation of men and material, cannot be regarded as holding out the prospects of success . . .[109]

Thus, unlike his ideas in early 1915 and unlike the evidence of the campaign in the east, by the end of the *Herbstschlacht*, Falkenhayn was convinced that a breakthrough was impossible given the tactical conditions prevailing on the Western Front in late 1915.[110] The plans drawn up early in the year would have to be scrapped.

106 Tappen to Reichsarchiv, 15 May 1931, BA/MA, N56/5; Falkenhayn, *General Headquarters*, p. 209.

107 Falkenhayn, *General Headquarters*, p. 173.

108 Tappen, "Kriegstagebuch," 2 October 1915.

109 Falkenhayn, *General Headquarters*, pp. 212–213 (see Chapter 8).

110 Tappen to Reichsarchiv, 16 June 1932, BA/MA, N56/5; Falkenhayn, *General Headquarters*, p. 174. Pétain reached a similar conclusion, declaring, "The Battle of Champagne demonstrates the difficulty, if not the impossibility of carrying in one thrust successive enemy positions . . ." Philippe Pétain, "Rapport sur les opérations de la IIe armée et enseignements à en tirer," IIe Armée PC Nr. 5668, 1 November 1915, *Les Armées Françaises*, III, *Annexes* IV, Annexe Nr. 3041, p. 168.

After defeating Russia and Serbia and successfully fending off serious Entente attacks in the west, the challenge Falkenhayn faced at the end of 1915 was to develop a synthesis of the seemingly contradictory strategic and operational lessons he had gained in the war to date in order to form a new means of bringing the war to an end on German terms. The result of this process would be a strategic and operational approach unique in the annals of warfare – the battle of Verdun.

8 Verdun: the plan

As 1916 began, the German strategic situation was stable if not favorable. Through the course of 1915, the German armies had advanced deep into Russia and had seemingly crushed the Russian offensive capability. Serbia had been dealt an even heavier blow, as a combined German–Austro-Hungarian–Bulgarian force occupied the country and ejected the remnants of the Serb army from the Continent. The destruction of Serbia opened rail communications with Turkey, thus helping to shore up this beleaguered ally. In Italy and on the Western Front, the Central Powers had warded off powerful Entente offensives and looked likely to be able to hold off any similar attacks for the foreseeable future.

However, Erich von Falkenhayn was no closer to achieving the goals he had set in November 1914. Despite suffering crippling losses in the summer of 1915, Russia had spurned Germany's advances for a separate peace. In the west, the German General Staff Chief had been unable to carry out an offensive aimed at dividing the western allies and forcing France to the negotiating table. Consequently, Germany was forced to maintain substantial strength on both fronts and could not accumulate sufficient forces to defeat any one enemy in a great "decisive" battle, as pre-war doctrine prescribed.

Despite the stable strategic situation, both Falkenhayn and Conrad were in agreement that the war would have to be ended by 1917. The two General Staff chiefs saw that their nations would soon reach the end of their resources. In early January, Falkenhayn informed Bethmann that "because of our economic and internal political conditions, it is extremely desirable to bring the war to an end before the winter of 1916/17."[1]

[1] Theobald von Bethmann Hollweg, diary entry for 7 January 1916, quoted in Karl-Heinz Janßen, *Der Kanzler und der General: Die Führungskrise um Bethmann Hollweg und Falkenhayn, 1914–1916* (Göttingen: Musterschmidt, 1967), p. 288. Similar thoughts were expressed by many of Germany's other strategic leaders. See Gerhard Tappen, "Besprechung mit dem Generalleutnant a.D. Tappen im Reichsarchiv am 6.IX.1932," BA/MA, Tappen Nachlass, N56/5, p. 5 (hereafter, Tappen, "Besprechung"). Wilhelm

In an audience with the Kaiser in late January 1916, the General Staff Chief told the assembly that "time [is] against us. Our allies, Austria and Turkey, [cannot] carry on the war beyond autumn of this year."[2] Conrad expressed similar thoughts, telling Falkenhayn that "the Central Powers cannot take the risk of allowing the war with the well-provided Entente to become a war of exhaustion, rather it must be, the sooner the better, brought to a decision through a large-scale action."[3] This being so, both leaders began to plan offensives which they hoped would end the war before the resources of their respective nations ran out.

After the experience with the Chancellor and the Foreign Office during the Russian campaign in 1915, however, the German General Staff realized that he would have little cooperation from the civil authorities in his plan to bring at least one of Germany's enemies to the negotiating table. Once again, poor personal relations exacerbated structural problems within the strategic decisionmaking system of the Kaiserreich. Therefore, Falkenhayn believed that military means would have to be found to entice one of the Entente into a separate peace with Germany.

Falkenhayn had always viewed the Western Front as the decisive theater of war.[4] As Chapter 6 has shown, he was only drawn into an offensive in the east because of Austria-Hungary's desperate situation. With Russia substantially weakened, Falkenhayn now believed he could turn his attentions again to the west without fear of a Russian threat to either eastern Germany or Austria-Hungary. Thus, while Conrad planned to knock Austria-Hungary's arch-enemy, Italy, out of the war, Falkenhayn in late 1915 turned his attention back to the Western Front.[5] There, he

Groener, *Lebenserinnerungen* (ed. Friedrich Frhr. Hiller von Gaertringen) (Göttingen: Vandenhoeck & Ruprecht, 1957) (diary entry for 24 December 1915), p. 545; Hans von Plessen, "Tagebuch," 3 December 1915, BA/MA, W10/50676. However, Adolf Wild von Hohenborn held a contrary view. He reported to Bethmann in early December 1915, "We can still wage a long, long war!" Adolf Wild von Hohenborn, "Kriegstagebuch," 11 December 1915, BA/MA, Wild Nachlass, N44/2.

2 Georg von Müller, *The Kaiser and his Court: The First World War Diaries of Admiral Georg von Müller* (ed. Walter Görlitz, trans Mervyn Savill) (London: MacDonald, 1961) (diary entry for 24 January 1916), p. 129.

3 Bundesministerium für Landesverteidigung, *Oesterreich-Ungarns Letzter Krieg 1914–1918*, Bd. III: *Das Kriegsjahr 1915 von der Einnahme von Brest-Litowsk bis zur Jahreswende* (Vienna: Verlag der Militärwissenschaftlichen Mitteilungen, 1932), pp. 590–591.

4 Erich von Falkenhayn, *General Headquarters and its Critical Decisions 1914–1916* (London: Hutchinson, 1919), p. 24; Hugo von Freytag-Loringhoven, *Menschen und Dinge, wie ich sie in meinem Leben sah* (Berlin: E. S. Mittler, 1923), p. 284; Tappen to Reichsarchiv, 16 June 1932, BA/MA, N56/5.

5 This division of effort was much criticized after the war. See Georg Wetzell, "Konnte im Jahre 1916 deutscherseits eine Kriegsentscheidung angestrebt werden und war der Gedanke, sie bei Verdun zu suchen, berechtigt?" (Paper presented to the Reichswehrministerium, 1926), unpublished manuscript in BA/MA, W10/51528; and more recently,

hoped to take the offensive for the first time since 1914 and force an end to the war.

The strategic situation on the Western Front 1915–16

Although several powerful Entente offensives had dented the German lines in the west during the course of 1915, the German position remained largely the same as at the end of 1914. The Western Front still consisted of a trench system that ran unbroken from just south of Ostend in the north to Pfetterhausen on the Swiss border. Behind their respective trenches, 119 German divisions faced 96 French and 43 British divisions. Additionally, each side could draw upon significant reserves. By mid-January 1916, the Germans maintained a reserve of 25 divisions in the west, while the French reserve consisted of 24 divisions and the British of 3.[6]

As Falkenhayn again contemplated a major offensive in the west, the Intelligence Section of the OHL drew up a number of reports assessing the manpower available to the Entente armies. In mid-November 1915, they estimated the French army, including the 1916 Class, which had not yet reached the front, to be around 3 million men, 500,000 of whom were in replacement depots behind the front. This number was 400,000 less than had been available at the war's outbreak, indicating to the Germans that French strength had peaked. The Intelligence Section further estimated that, under everyday conditions, the French were losing 70,000 men per month. At this rate of "wastage," German intelligence anticipated that by September 1916 the French army would be experiencing severe shortages and would be forced to call up its younger classes earlier and earlier to meet the expected shortfall in manpower.[7] Of course, any offensive action would only speed this process.

Assessing the British strength proved to be somewhat more problematic for the Intelligence Section, as it lacked a clear picture of the British army's final structure. At the end of November 1915, they reckoned that

Holger Herwig, *The First World War: Germany and Austria-Hungary, 1914–1918* (London: Arnold, 1997), pp. 204ff.

6 Reichsarchiv, *Der Weltkrieg*, Bd. X: *Die Operationen des Jahres 1916 bis zum Wechsel in der Obersten Heeresleitung* (Berlin: E. S. Mittler, 1936), pp. 11–12, 52–53; James B. Edmonds, ed., *Military Operations: France and Belgium, 1916*, vol. I (London: Macmillan, 1932), pp. 18–19.

7 Nachrichtenabteilung West, Report dated 14 November 1915, quoted in "Die Beurteilung der Kampfkraft der französischen Armee durch die deutsche OHL zwischen dem 1.1 und 29.8.16," BA/MA, W10/51521, p. 4 (hereafter, "Beurteilung I"). The Intelligence Section believed that the 200,000 men of 1917 Class would be used up by September 1916. This meant that the French would be forced to call up their 1918 Class in June 1916 to be ready to meet the shortfall in September.

the British army had a strength of close to 950,000 men, with 270,000 regulars, 400,000 in the Kitchener formations, and 170,000 in Territorial formations. To this number, 60,000 Indians and 47,000 Canadians had to be added. German intelligence estimated the British would have either 35 $\frac{1}{2}$ or 36 $\frac{1}{2}$ divisions plus 6 cavalry divisions on the Western Front in early 1916. While their report also stated that the British army would eventually reach around 70 divisions, the Intelligence Section did not know when this would occur or where these divisions would be deployed.[8]

Thus, the Germans faced a numerically superior foe in the west – a strong French army with generally good reserves and a British army which had not yet reached its peak strength. Added to this numerical superiority of the enemy, the Entente experience in 1915 had shown just how difficult it was to break through a well-constructed defensive system. The Entente had attempted on three separate occasions in 1915 to break through the German defensive lines by employing overwhelming force. Although the lack of ready German reserves almost allowed the French to achieve an operational breakthrough in late September 1915, each Entente offensive had merely resulted in high casualties, especially to the attacker, and minor gains in territory.[9] These experiences spoke against the success of a German breakthrough attempt, while the large numbers of Entente reserves ensured that, even if the Germans succeeded in breaking through their lines, any exploitation would be impossible.

Offsetting the material factors, however, were morale and skill. In early 1915, Falkenhayn judged the French army to be deficient in both these categories and the British to be lacking in the latter, but the German army to possess both in abundance. Indeed, even before the war, Falkenhayn, together with many other German leaders, had judged the French harshly, believing France to be a nation in long-term decline.[10] As early as June 1915, he had reported to the Chancellor that France did not have the necessary will to continue the war for much longer and that France was nearing the end of its resources.[11] In September, Falkenhayn told the Kaiser that "the French are at the end of their strength and in no condition

8 "Die Beurteilung der Kampfkraft der englischen Armee durch die deutsche OHL. Ende 1915," BA/MA, W10/51521 (hereafter, "Beurteilung II").

9 During the *Herbstschlacht* in 1915, the French suffered around 250,000 casualties and the Germans around 150,000. Peter Graf von Kielmannsegg, *Deutschland und der Erste Weltkrieg* (Frankfurt: Akademische Verlagsgesellschaft Athenaion, 1968), p. 97.

10 Holger Afflerbach, *Falkenhayn: Politisches Denken und Handeln im Kaiserreich* (Munich: Oldenbourg, 1994), pp. 68–71; Tappen later said, "before the war, we had always said that the French would have no reserves with which to fill their holes." Tappen, "Besprechung," p. 18.

11 Reichsarchiv, *Der Weltkrieg*, Bd. VIII: *Die Operationen des Jahres 1915: Die Ereignisse im Westen im Frühjahr und Sommer, im Osten vom Frühjahr bis zum Jahresschluss* (Berlin: E. S. Mittler, 1932), pp. 609–610. See Chapter 7.

to attack."[12] The utter failure of the French offensives in 1915 only served to reinforce his low estimation of the French and his high evaluation of the German soldier. Although after the war Falkenhayn was criticized for this underestimation of the French,[13] his opinion was shared by others in the German high command at the time. In early December 1915, Adolph Wild von Hohenborn characterized the French as "weak."[14] Gerhard Tappen wrote after the war of the prevalent belief in the OHL in early 1916, "the worth of the individual German soldier was so much greater than the enemy that numbers alone could not be decisive."[15]

The Intelligence Section of the OHL supported Falkenhayn's evaluation of the quality of French troops. Many French deserters spoke of the war-weariness of the French soldiers and particularly of the adverse effect on French morale of the failure of and the high casualties suffered during the offensives in September/October 1915.[16] Agent reports also spoke of a shortfall of junior officers in the front line.[17] Further, when the French began instituting a defense in depth and leaving their first trench line only lightly defended, German intelligence interpreted this to mean that the French command feared that their troops would break under the German *Trommelfeuer*.[18] Therefore, like Falkenhayn, the Intelligence Section saw the French army as a numerically strong force, but one with serious internal weaknesses.

The British, on the other hand, were seen to have an army with high morale – the lack of deserters attested to this – but for the most part with limited combat value. The Intelligence Section divided its assessment into three categories to correspond with the three parts of the British army in late 1915. The Germans believed that the pre-war army had been

12 Quoted in Wilhelm Solger, "Die Leitung des deutschen Westheeres im September und Oktober 1915 seit dem Beginn der Herbstschlacht in der Champagne und im Artois," unpublished manuscript in BA/MA, W10/51353, p. 1.

13 Theobald von Bethmann Hollweg, *Betrachtungen zum Weltkriege* (2 vols.) (Berlin: Reimar Hobbing, 1921), II, p. 42; Groener to Reichsarchiv, 5 March 1934, BA/MA, W10/51523; Afflerbach, *Falkenhayn*, p. 358.

14 Wild, "Kriegstagebuch," 11 December 1915.

15 Tappen to Reichsarchiv, 15 May 1931, N56/5.

16 "Beurteilung I," pp. 8–9. See also Nachrichten Offizier, AOK 6, "Nachrichten von der französischen Front im Abschnitt Angre-Ransart," 23 December 1915 in BA/MA, PH3/607, which paints a dismal picture of French morale.

17 "Agent 17," Report of 5 December 1915, in "Beurteilung I," p. 7. "Agent 17," in reality the Austrian Baron August Schluga, had begun working for German intelligence in 1866. From then until his death in 1916, he served the Germans well, obtaining details of the French deployment plan before the war and important intelligence during the war. See David Kahn, *Hitler's Spies* (London: Hodder & Stoughton, 1978), pp. 32–35. My thanks to James Beach for bringing this information to my attention.

18 Nachrichtenabteilung West, "Verteilung der französischen und englischen Infanterie und Maschinengewehre an der Kampffront," 26 January 1916, BA/MA, W10/51543.

largely destroyed, but that it had provided the necessary cadres to form the backbone of several new "regular" divisions. These divisions were seen as being roughly equivalent to German divisions. The Intelligence Section evaluated the Territorial divisions similarly. These two groups, however, made up less than half of the British divisions in France (14 $\frac{1}{2}$ of 36). The remainder was the so-called "Kitchener Divisions." The Germans evaluated the combat ability of these formations much lower than the rest of the army.[19] Their lack of experienced officers and combat experience meant that the Germans judged them, for the immediate future at least, incapable of effective offensive action. They concluded that, "the British army at the end of 1915 still makes an unfinished impression."[20]

Thus, of the two main enemy armies on the Western Front at the end of 1915, the French appeared the weaker to the Germans. Although the French army possessed sufficient reserves to last through normal operations in 1916, it was clearly at the peak of its strength.[21] The 1917 Class was called up in late 1915, to be ready for service at the front in mid-1916.[22] After this class was exhausted, the French would be forced to call up its younger classes earlier than expected. Further, evidence pointed to a French army with much diminished morale due to the length of the war and the failure of its own offensives the preceding year.

In addition, Falkenhayn also assumed that the French government and people did not have the necessary willpower to continue to accept the high level of casualties that occurred in any offensive action in *Stellungskrieg*. In common with many of his colleagues in the German army, the General Staff Chief believed that France was a nation in long-term decline, a decline made worse by a democratic political system that made the government beholden to public opinion. Already early in 1915, the General Staff Chief had spoken of the French nation as being weary of war and ripe for a peace offer. The failure of their major offensive in late 1915, upon which such great expectations had been lavished, could only diminish the already shaky morale of the French people. The great question at the beginning of 1916 was how many additional sacrifices would the people of France bear before demanding that their government bring an

19 The experience of fighting against the British in Artois reinforced this belief. The Germans believed that the Kitchener divisions had such a limited combat capability that "generals had to lead assaults personally." Falkenhayn lost a friend from China in this way. Bethmann to Jagow, 4 October 1915, AS5157, PRO, GFM 34/2587 (*Weltkrieg geh.*, Bd. 23).

20 AOK 4, "Die englische Armee," 19 October 1915, in "Beurteilung II," pp. 7–8. See also OHL, *Kurze Zusammenstellung über die französische, englische und belgische Armee* (3rd ed.) (Berlin: E. S. Mittler, 1915), pp. 53–62.

21 Indeed, the same could be said of the German army. Manpower shortages meant that Falkenhayn believed no further formations could be raised. Falkenhayn, *General Headquarters*, p. 226.

22 "Beurteilung I," p. 5; OHL, *Kurze Zusammenstellung*, pp. 24–25.

end to the war. These views would play a central role in Falkenhayn's strategy for 1916.

Falkenhayn's strategic plans

Falkenhayn faced a challenging strategic problem at the end of 1915. Although he assumed Russia would be incapable of offensive action for the foreseeable future, Russia had not been knocked from the war.[23] Germany still needed to maintain significant forces in the east to protect against any possible Russian action, however small.[24] Therefore, Falkenhayn could only count on a 25 or 26 division reserve in the west.[25] In France, he faced two enemies, who each possessed large reserves and who were each firmly ensconced behind well-constructed trenches. The General Staff Chief had to determine where and how to launch an attack with limited resources which would decide the war in 1916. Through December 1915 and January 1916, he developed his final ideas.

Although Falkenhayn believed Great Britain to be Germany's main enemy, Britain was the more difficult to defeat. Falkenhayn felt that they occupied a defensive position on the Continent which could not be assailed with the forces at Germany's disposal. (The British sector had one of the highest concentrations of troops anywhere on the front.) Further, he believed that even if Germany were to deal the British force on the Continent a powerful blow, this would not force Britain from the war. Such an offensive would leave Britain largely unharmed and would leave the army of its French ally wholly intact. Despite these difficulties, Falkenhayn felt that Germany's goal in 1916 should be to convince Britain that it could never defeat Germany. In order to accomplish this, he planned to strike Britain directly by unleashing unrestricted submarine warfare against British shipping.[26] However, far more important to the Chief of the General Staff, Britain would be hurt by knocking "England's best sword" out of its hand – France.[27]

23 In early January 1916, Falkenhayn reported to Bethmann that the Russian army was incapable of any "large-scale offensive" for the immediate future. Bethmann, diary entry for 7 January 1916, in Janßen, *Der Kanzler und der General*, p. 288.

24 The *Ostheer*, excluding the 11th Army in the Balkans, consisted of $47\frac{1}{2}$ divisions in February 1916. *Der Weltkrieg*, X, p. 427.

25 This number was deemed insufficient for a breakthrough even in early 1915 (see Chapter 7). This belief, however, was not shared by Falkenhayn's close advisor, Wild, who believed a reserve of twenty-four divisions was sufficient to launch a major offensive in the west. Wild, "Kriegstagebuch," 11 December 1915.

26 Space prevents a detailed discussion of the debate over the U-boat campaign. For a recent overview, see Afflerbach, *Falkenhayn*, pp. 376–404.

27 Falkenhayn, *General Headquarters*, pp. 212–217; Groener to Reichsarchiv, 5 March 1934, BA/MA, W10/51523. After the war, Falkenhayn published in his memoirs his plan for the Verdun offensive, which he had supposedly given to the Kaiser around Christmas

Therefore, in order to conclude the war in 1916, Falkenhayn returned to an idea first formed in November 1914 and attempted during the summer campaign in Russia – to force an end to the war by compelling one enemy into a separate peace.[28] Here again Falkenhayn faced a difficulty. In order for France to be forced into peace with Germany, its army would first have to be destroyed, or at least seriously weakened. Falkenhayn believed that a weakening of the French army would either compel the French public to demand an end to the sacrifices of their army or would bring back *Bewegungskrieg* to the Western Front and break the stalemate of the trenches. Although the OHL felt that the French had severe internal weaknesses, they still held two advantages – sizeable reserves and a strong position in the field.

The failure of the Entente offensives on the Western Front through the course of 1915 had demonstrated the difficulties of conducting an operationally successful breakthrough against an enemy with strong reserves. In late 1915, Falkenhayn clearly believed that the Germans would be unable to destroy the French army through conventional means.[29] Therefore, another method had to be found. This "new way" would combine lessons from the war to date and would incorporate some unique strategic and operational concepts. Indeed, a former member of his staff later wrote that he could "find no analogue" in military history for the General Staff Chief's singular approach.[30]

* * *

Falkenhayn had begun to turn his gaze westwards even before the conclusion of operations in the east in 1915. In mid-November, he gave to the 5th Army the task of planning several offensives, from which would ultimately spring the "attack in the area of the Meuse," or the battle of Verdun. His original concept was to carry out three separate limited offensives: the main undertaking, Operation "Schwarzwald," against

1915. The original of the "Christmas Memorandum" could not be located after the war, leading historians to conclude that the document published in Falkenhayn's memoirs was a post-war fabrication. (For the most recent discussion of this subject, see Afflerbach, *Falkenhayn*, pp. 543–545.) Given the questionable provenance of the Christmas Memorandum, I have not used it as the basis for this section of the study, but rather have gone back to contemporary documents to reconstruct Falkenhayn's planning process.

28 For German diplomatic moves toward France in 1916, see Fritz Fischer, *Germany's Aims in the First World War* (New York: W. W. Norton & Co., 1967), pp. 224–228; L. L. Farrar, Jr., "Peace Through Exhaustion: German Diplomatic Motivations for the Verdun Campaign," *Revue Internationale d'Histoire Militaire* 32 (1972–75), pp. 477–494.

29 Falkenhayn, *General Headquarters*, pp. 212–213; Groener to Reichsarchiv, 5 March 1934, BA/MA, W10/51523. Falkenhayn stressed repeatedly before Verdun the impossibility of a mass attack.

30 Groener to Reichsarchiv, 5 March 1934, BA/MA, W10/51523. See also Jehuda Wallach, *The Dogma of the Battle of Annihilation: The Theories of Clausewitz and Schlieffen and their Impact on the German Conduct of Two World Wars* (Westport, CT: Greenwood Press, 1986), p. 170.

Belfort in Upper Alsace; and two secondary operations, "Waldfest," against Verdun and "Kaiserstuhl," in the Vosges. Falkenhayn left the goals of these operations temporarily open.[31]

On 3 December, Falkenhayn apprised the Kaiser of the state of planning on these operations and sought his approval for their go ahead. At this audience, the first strands of Falkenhayn's "new method" began to emerge. Generaloberst Hans von Plessen recorded the meeting in his diary:

> General von Falkenhayn rolled out for His Majesty a serious picture of the situation with the conclusion that to carry the war to its end, an attack in the *west*, where *all* available strength has already been collected, must be conducted . . . it is to be then that the Entente will attack us in the west and thereby bleed themselves white [*sich dabei verblutet*].[32]

Although his ideas were not clearly defined in early December, Plessen's diary entry indicates that by this point Falkenhayn had contrived the notion that the French must be forced to attack German positions, thereby suffering high casualties. He intended that the attack on Belfort, supported by smaller attacks elsewhere along the front, would threaten the French in such a way as to cause them to respond immediately with a counterattack.[33] Contrary to post-war interpretation, this evidence demonstrates that, from its inception, the ultimate goal of these operations was the *Verblutung*, or bleeding to death, of the French army.[34] This idea was to become more clearly defined as the planning process continued.

Both Falkenhayn and Generalleutnant Constantin Schmidt von Knobelsdorf, the Chief of Staff of the 5th Army, soon began to have doubts as to the suitability of these plans, however. An operation against Belfort had its difficulties. First, it was far from the main areas of fighting and, hence, poorly serviced by rail lines. Second, Falkenhayn feared operations

[31] Wilhelm Solger, "Die OHL in der Führung der Westoperationen Ende 1915 bis Ende August 1916: I. Vom 3.XII.15–8.I.16. Die Entstehung des Operationsplanes," unpublished manuscript, BA/MA, W10/51318, pp. 2–12 (hereafter, Solger, "Entstehung").

[32] Plessen, "Tagebuch," 3 December 1915. Emphasis in original. This seems to be the first use of the word "verbluten" in Falkenhayn's strategic plans. See Solger, "Entstehung," p. 7; Afflerbach, *Falkenhayn*, p. 364.

[33] Falkenhayn's intentions in early December were repeated by the Kaiser in an interview with a Reichsarchiv researcher after the war. Alfred Niemann, "Bericht über den Vortrag, den S. M. der Kaiser am 25. Februar 1934 von mir entgegengenommen hat," BA/MA, W10/51523, pp. 1–2 (hereafter, Niemann, "Kaiser Vortrag"). See also Tappen, "Besprechung," p. 5.

[34] Wolfgang Foerster, "Falkenhayns Plan für 1916. Ein Beitrag zur Frage: Wie gelangt man aus dem Stellungskrieg zu entscheidungsuchender Operation?" *Militär-Wissenschaftliche Rundschau* 23 (1937), pp. 303–330; and Gerd Krumeich, "'Saigner la France'? Mythes et réalité de la stratégie allemande de la bataille de Verdun," *Guerres mondiales et conflits contemporains* Nr. 182 (April 1996), p. 25, both of whom claim that the concept only originated after the initial failure of the battle.

would be constricted by the proximity to the Swiss border.[35] Further, in the pre-war period, it had been agreed that in the case of war, the Italians would serve in Upper Alsace. In March 1914, the German and Italian General Staffs worked out a plan for the Italian forces to assault and take Belfort. Tappen believed that these plans must surely be in French hands by December 1915.[36] Knobelsdorf also raised objections to the secondary operation "Waldfest." He felt it lacked the forces necessary to threaten seriously the fortress of Verdun, which he believed should be the main result of the attack.[37] Most important, though, both men concluded that these operations would not result in the desired psychological effect, which was deemed necessary to cause the French to launch an immediate counteroffensive.

Accordingly, Falkenhayn began to reconsider his operation as it was currently planned. On 8 December, he had a long discussion with Tappen and Wild about the situation. Although no decision had been made, the General Staff Chief was clearly leaning toward scrapping the offensive against Belfort in favor of one against Verdun. An operation against Verdun had advantages. First, the area was well serviced by rail lines. Second, the fortress of Verdun sat in the center of a salient, which could be dominated by German guns. Wild recorded in his diary the advantages this would give: "During an attack from the north and the east, the [French] positions will soon be so diminished that not even a mouse can live in them."[38] Most importantly, Verdun was an object "for the retention of which the French General Staff would be compelled to throw in every man they have."[39] On the day after his discussion with Tappen and Wild, Falkenhayn ordered Knobelsdorf to Berlin for a discussion concerning the impending offensive. Falkenhayn asked him to come prepared to discuss turning "Waldfest" into a major operation.[40]

Knobelsdorf arrived in Berlin on 14 December with a plan to attack the French salient at Verdun and to take the fortress. The 5th Army envisioned an attack along the front from Four de Paris (southwest of

35 Erich von Luckwald to Bethmann, 17 February 1916 (copied from *Reichskanzlei. Weltkrieg 1914/18. 15.Allg. Milit.-und Marine Berichte aus dem Gr.H.Qu.* Bd. 1) BA/MA, W10/51543. Luckwald was the Foreign Office representative at the OHL.

36 Tappen, "Besprechung," p. 5.

37 Knobelsdorf to Falkenhayn (personal letter), 3 December 1915. Reprinted in Hermann Wendt, *Verdun 1916. Die Angriffe Falkenhayns im Maasgebiet mit Richtung auf Verdun als strategisches Problem* (Berlin: E. S. Mittler, 1931), p. 226.

38 Wild, "Kriegstagebuch," 11 December 1915. See also Tappen, "Kriegstagebuch," 8 December 1915.

39 Falkenhayn, *General Headquarters*, p. 217. Knobelsdorf recognized that by attacking Verdun, they would have to reckon with "at least half the French army." Knobelsdorf to Ziese-Beringer, 6 March 1933, printed in Hermann Ziese-Beringer, *Der einsame Feldherr: Die Wahrheit über Verdun* (2 vols.) (Berlin: Frundsberg-Verlag, 1934), II, pp. 200–201.

40 OHL to AOK 5, 9 December 1915, quoted in Solger, "Entstehung," pp. 15–17.

Varennes) to Ornes (i.e., an attack against the fortress from the north, northwest, and northeast along both banks of the Meuse). They hoped to put the 5th Army in a position to dominate the fortress of Verdun with heavy artillery, making it unusable by the French.[41] However, while Falkenhayn agreed in general with the goals of the 5th Army's plan, he believed it would require too much strength (23 divisions). Instead, he asked Knobelsdorf to develop a more limited plan of operations, one that focused on one axis of advance rather than three.[42] Thus, although the General Staff Chief believed that Knobelsdorf's initial plan required too much strength, on 15 December the decision was taken to scrap plans to attack Belfort and concentrate instead on an offensive against Verdun.[43] Falkenhayn promised Knobelsdorf five army corps from the OHL reserve for the operation and set the start date for the "beginning of February." However, against the advice of the 5th Army, he restricted the initial attack to the east bank of the Meuse only.[44]

Falkenhayn hoped that the 5th Army's attack on Verdun would either seize the fortress quickly or that the threat to the fortress would cause the French to send all their reserves to hold it.[45] In a meeting with the Chiefs of Staff of the *Westheer*, he outlined the likely Entente responses to the attack:

> (1) They [the French high command] believe Verdun to be so well defended that they leave it alone. Very good for us, therefore unlikely.
> (2) They send all available forces to the fortress . . .
> (3) French counteroffensive on another point [of the line]. Possibly same points as before, Artois, Champagne, Woevre, Upper Alsace. To be greeted with joy. OHL believes it sure that all such attacks would collapse with severe French casualties.
> (4) They attempt to hold Verdun with all available forces, while the English attempt an attack. Questionable whether it would succeed, especially as the English army is at the moment going through a great upheaval with the insertion of the Kitchener units, which are being mixed with the old units down to the battalion level.[46]

[41] This plan had been developed by the 5th Army in October. Marginal comment by Knobelsdorf to Solger, "Entstehung," p. 23.

[42] AOK 5, "Kriegstagebuch," 16 December 1915, BA/MA, W10/51318.

[43] The exact date on which the Kaiser was informed of the change of plans has never been clear. Based on the Kaiser's post-war testimony, the Reichsarchiv concluded that Falkenhayn had informed the Kaiser of his changing plans between 10 and 12 December, i.e., before Falkenhayn's meeting with Knobelsdorf. However, it is clear that the Kaiser was well informed about Falkenhayn's intentions, even if he never read a Christmas Memorandum. *Der Weltkrieg*, X, p. 25. See also Niemann, "Kaiser Vortrag," p. 2; Afflerbach, *Falkenhayn*, p. 365.

[44] AOK 5, "Kriegstagebuch," 16 December 1915, BA/MA, W10/51318.

[45] For Falkenhayn's intentions regarding the taking of Verdun, see below (pp. 194–197).

[46] AOK 7, "Kriegstagebuch," 11 February 1916, quoted in Wilhelm Solger, "Die OHL in der Führung der Westoperationen Ende 1915 bis Ende August 1916: II.

According to the post-war testimony of both Tappen and Kaiser Wilhelm II, Falkenhayn believed the fourth possibility to be the most likely: The attack would cause the French to send all their reserves and to strip units from their front line to support Verdun. Thus, by seizing or by threatening to seize such a vital point in the French line, the Germans could deal quickly with the entire French reserve, binding them in the Verdun salient where they would exhaust themselves in fruitless attacks against the German positions supported by powerful artillery, as had happened in the Champagne in September 1915.[47] As Tappen put it: "we were of the opinion that the enemy, who would already have suffered heavily from our attacks, would suffer extraordinarily high casualties from our powerful heavy artillery during his counterattacks."[48] In response to this situation, the British would be forced to launch an offensive designed to relieve the French before their army was ready; thereby, like the French, wearing themselves down.[49]

Indeed, the basic features of Falkenhayn's operational ideas had filtered their way through the army long before the final plans for the offensive had been determined. In early December 1915, Dutch intelligence passed on a document to British intelligence that outlined well Falkenhayn's thinking:

> The German General Staff is said to have delivered itself as follows regarding the present position of affairs on the WESTERN front: –
>
> In order to carry through successfully a really energetic break-through, we lack unfortunately the necessary numbers . . . Therefore our one and only way of forcing a decision is to adopt an enormous Artillery offensive and thus destroy by our tremendous fire all the enemy's hopes.[50]

Thus, the General Staff Chief hoped to reach an operationally favorable position without relying on a "mass attack." By attacking such a sensitive point in the French line, which had the added advantage of being dominated by German guns, Falkenhayn did not need to resort to employing the "mass tactics," which had proved so costly and so ineffective for the Entente. The operations of the war to date, especially the *Herbstschlacht*,

Vom 9.I.16–21.II.16. Die Vorbereitung des Angriffs auf Verdun und die Weitergestaltung der damit in Verbindung stehenden Operationsgedanken," unpublished manuscript in BA/MA, W10/51529, pp. 112–113 (hereafter, Solger, "Vorbereitung"). See also *Der Weltkrieg*, X, pp. 39–40.

47 Niemann, "Kaiser Vortrag," p. 3; Afflerbach, *Falkenhayn*, pp. 363–364.

48 Tappen, "Besprechung," p. 13.

49 Hermann von Kuhl to Reichsarchiv, 28 October 1932, BA/MA, W10/51318.

50 Intelligence Report, Rotterdam, 7 December 1915, Archives du Service Historique de l'Armée de Terre, Vincennes, 7 N 1018. My thanks to James Beach for a copy of this document.

had shown the devastating effect of German artillery. Therefore, Falkenhayn intended the heavy artillery to carry the burden in this battle. In effect, the enemy would "bleed himself white" by counterattacking into the German positions supported by heavy artillery. All the General Staff Chief needed to do was retain sufficient forces to reinforce any threatened point of the German front and to retain adequate reserves to carry out his own counteroffensive to mop up the remnants of the enemy armies once the Entente strength had been broken as a result of their offensive action.[51]

Falkenhayn had found his "new way." His strategy for winning the war in 1916 would consist of two phases. First, the operation at Verdun would result in the removal of the French, and hopefully the British, reserves. If the losses incurred during the first phase did not compel the French to come to the peace table, it would at least create the conditions necessary for the second phase. Once the Entente reserves had been worn down, the German army would fall on the now-weakened Entente front. This offensive would mop up the remnants of a severely weakened French army, forcing France from the war and ejecting the British army from the Continent.[52]

Several points were crucial to this plan's success. First, the Germans had to retain sufficient reserves to meet the expected Entente relief offensives. Second, they had to keep sufficient forces to launch a German counteroffensive once the Entente forces had worn themselves out in their relief offensives. This pressure influenced greatly Falkenhayn's plans for the conduct of the first phase of his strategy – Operation "Gericht." And finally, Falkenhayn's plan for 1916 relied upon the enemy doing exactly what Falkenhayn wanted.

Plans for the first phase

On 6 January, the 5th Army submitted its plan of attack to the OHL. It began: "The decision to take the fortress of Verdun in an expeditious manner rests on the proven ability of the heavy and heaviest artillery." In keeping with their instructions from the OHL, the 5th Army planned initially to attack only the French positions upon the east bank of the

[51] Tappen to Reichsarchiv, comments to RA Nr. 45, 18 October 1934, BA/MA, N56/5.

[52] In keeping with their ideas of *Vernichtungsstrategie*, the Reichsarchiv assumed that Falkenhayn intended the war's decision to come from this counterstroke. However, this second attack was meant to clear up a foe who had already defeated himself with his own attacks, rather than to be "decisive" itself. See *Der Weltkrieg*, X, pp. 671–672; Foerster, "Falkenhayns Plan," pp. 319–322. Cf. Afflerbach, *Falkenhayn*, p. 357; and Wendt, *Verdun*, pp. 43ff.

Meuse, stating, "whoever possesses the Côtes . . . on the east bank, as well as the positions upon those heights, is also in possession of the fortress." They envisioned reaching the line Froide Terre–Fort Souville–Fort Tavannes.[53] From these heights, they believed it would be possible to suppress the French positions on the west bank using artillery fire. The attack plan called for the initial assault to be carried out by three army corps, which would be joined by two additional corps as the attack developed.

Contrary to Falkenhayn's wishes, however, the plan also called for an attack on the west bank following on the heels of the initial assault on the east. The 5th Army claimed that only after the taking of the west bank would Verdun be completely neutralized. They planned for the VI Corps, reinforced by an additional corps, to advance "soon after the attack on the east bank has started." As a final goal for the offensives on both banks, the 5th Army envisioned flattening the Verdun salient, in effect, seizing the fortress.[54]

This attack along both banks of the Meuse was central to the 5th Army's plan to take the fortress of Verdun, or at least to take the heights dominating the fortress. Even before Knobelsdorf had left Berlin on 16 December, tensions between the desires of the 5th Army and Falkenhayn over this had developed. At their meeting, Knobelsdorf had spoken firmly for an attack along both banks. He feared that the French artillery on the heights of the west bank would be able to fire into the flank of the German attack as it progressed.[55] Similar fears were held by almost everyone else involved in planning the offensive.[56] In late January, Oberst Max Bauer, the heavy artillery specialist in the OHL, traveled to the 5th Army's front to check upon the attack preparations. He too returned to Mézières convinced that the attack on Verdun would only succeed if launched simultaneously on both banks and he tried to change Falkenhayn's mind on the matter.[57]

Falkenhayn, however, refused to consider a simultaneous attack along both banks.[58] First, he believed that Germany did not have the necessary

53 See also *Der Weltkrieg*, X, p. 121.

54 AOK 5, "Angriffsentwurf," Nr. 78, 4 January 1916, BA/MA, W10/51526; reprinted in Ziese-Beringer, *Feldherr*, II, pp. 197–200; Kronprinz Wilhelm, *Meine Erinnerungen aus Deutschlands Heldenkampf* (Berlin: E. S. Mittler, 1923), pp. 161–164.

55 AOK 5, "Kriegstagebuch," 16 December 1915, BA/MA, W10/51318.

56 Tappen to Reichsarchiv, 9 February 1934, BA/MA, N56/5; Wild, "Kriegstagebuch," 23 February 1916; Gerhard von Heymann (former Ia of the 5th Army) to Reichsarchiv, 28 August 1935, BA/MA, W10/51523; *Der Weltkrieg*, X, p. 27.

57 Max Bauer, *Der grosse Krieg in Feld und Heimat* (Tübingen: Osiander'sche Buchhandlung, 1921), p. 101; marginal comments by Knobelsdorf to Solger, "Entstehung," p. 24.

58 Despite Falkenhayn's clear refusal, Knobelsdorf began planning for an attack on the west bank immediately upon his return to Stenay. Untitled and unpublished manuscript on the attack on the west bank of the Meuse in BA/MA, W10/51526, p. 5 (hereafter, "Angriff auf dem Westufer").

Fig. 12 The commander of the 5th Army, the German Crown Prince Wilhelm

manpower to undertake a large-scale offensive. He feared that when the anticipated Entente relief offensive came, the OHL would not have sufficient reserves to hold the line.[59] When pressed to widen the Verdun offensive to the west bank as well, Falkenhayn expressed this fear to Tappen: "I am responsible. I do not want to come to the same dangerous situation as in the autumn [of 1915] during the battle in the Champagne. I will not allow that to happen again."[60] In addition, as we have seen, Falkenhayn had concluded from the experience of 1915 that a "mass attack" could not succeed under the conditions prevalent on the Western Front. To attack with too large a force would only repeat the same mistakes of the Entente.[61]

Despite these reservations, Falkenhayn approved the 5th Army's plan of 4 January, seemingly giving in to the 5th Army's desires. As Hermann

[59] OHL to AOK 5, Nr. 22662 op., 28 January 1916, printed in Wendt, *Verdun*, pp. 35–36. See also, Hermann Geyer to Reichsarchiv, 27 December 1934, BA/MA, Geyer Nachlass, N221/25.

[60] Tappen to Reichsarchiv, 9 February 1934, BA/MA, N56/5.

[61] In a meeting to discuss future offensives on 3 February, Falkenhayn told Conrad that "a limited number of troops, correctly employed, holds out the prospect of success." k.u.k. Oberst Kundmann, diary entry for 3 February 1916, quoted in Solger, "Vorbereitung," p. 86.

Wendt has noted, however, he reserved for himself the final word as to how the offensive would progress. Falkenhayn agreed to provide the 5th Army with the additional forces necessary to widen their assault to include the west bank – the X Reserve Corps for the attack on the west bank and the XXII Reserve Corps for an attack by *Armeeabteilung Strantz*. However, he only agreed to send them "in good time."[62] Shortly before the offensive was to begin, Falkenhayn informed the 5th Army that the two promised corps would remain in the OHL reserve until he saw fit to release them for further operations. The X Reserve Corps, wrote Falkenhayn, "has to remain in the sector of the 3rd Army in case of an enemy counterattack in the Champagne, which is by no means unlikely . . ."[63] The XXII Reserve Corps was also held in reserve for the time being, "in consideration of the general situation on the Western Front."[64]

The 5th Army's plan also implied that they envisioned a rapid capitulation of the fortress of Verdun. At first glance, this goal seems at odds with Falkenhayn's idea of "bleeding white" the French army and it seems that the 5th Army did not understand this idea fully.[65] After all, this *Verblutung* would presumably take considerable time and involve hard fighting. A rapid capitulation of the fortress would hardly bring this about. However, Falkenhayn's goals for the first phase of his strategy were quite subtle. Although he repeatedly stressed the capture of Verdun was not his aim, a fall of the fortress would not be unwelcome.[66] The General Staff Chief wanted to destroy the French reserves. He envisioned this happening through a successful German defense of a French counterattack. As we have seen, he was unsure if this counterattack would come at Verdun or elsewhere on the front.

Indeed, there is evidence to suggest that Falkenhayn believed this goal would be achieved quickly as long as the 5th Army reached a position from which its heavy artillery could dominate the French counterattacks. First, he planned to launch his counteroffensive against a greatly weakened Entente front "around the middle of February."[67] Hermann von Kuhl took this to mean that Falkenhayn believed that the French would be forced by the German conquest of Verdun to send all their available forces to retake the fortress and, thereby, the enemy forces elsewhere

62 Wendt, *Verdun*, p. 34; Wallach, *Dogma*, p. 175.

63 OHL to AOK 5, Nr. 22662 op., 28 January 1916, printed in Wendt, *Verdun*, pp. 35–36.

64 OHL to AOK 5, Nr. 22987 op., 4 February 1916, printed in ibid., p. 36. The XXII RK was in reserve behind the 6th Army's sector, an area where Falkenhayn felt an Entente relief offensive was likely to fall.

65 See especially, Wendt, *Verdun*, pp. 31–34.

66 Falkenhayn, *General Headquarters*, pp. 217–218; Freytag-Loringhoven, *Menschen*, p. 291; Tappen to Hermann Wendt, 10 July 1919, BA/MA, N56/4.

67 Hermann von Kuhl, "Kriegstagebuch," 11 January 1916, BA/MA, W10/50652.

on the Western Front would be considerably weakened.[68] Second, in a meeting with Conrad on 3 February, the German General Staff Chief expressed the belief that a decision would be reached shortly after the start of the offensive. According to the diary of an Austrian staff officer present at the meeting, Falkenhayn told Conrad: "The operation against France could bring a decision in 14 days."[69]

There is, however, no denying the evident tensions between Falkenhayn's vision of events and that of the 5th Army. Although Knobelsdorf's post-war statement that he would not have carried out the offensive had he known Falkenhayn's real desires is disingenuous,[70] the 5th Army was at least uncomfortable with the General Staff Chief's goal of "bleeding white the French army." Crown Prince Wilhelm later wrote:

> What disturbed me was the frequently expressed idea of the Chief of the General Staff of the Field Army that the point [of the offensive] was to bring about the "bleeding white" of France's army regardless of whether or not the fortress fell in the process.[71]

The goals of the 5th Army were different from those of Falkenhayn. They clearly did not accept completely Falkenhayn's new strategic and operational approaches. In line with the German army's pre-war operational approach, they believed the fortress could and should be taken, and aimed for this at all stages of the offensive. As we shall see, this difference of opinion would have important consequences as the battle wore on.

Plans for the second phase

The day Falkenhayn received the 5th Army's initial plan, he set in motion the planning for his strategy's second phase – a final counterattack

68 Kuhl to Reichsarchiv, 7 January 1934, BA/MA, W10/51523.

69 k.u.k. Oberst Kundmann, diary entry for 3 February 1916, quoted in Solger, "Vorbereitung," p. 87.

70 Alistair Horne, *The Price of Glory: Verdun 1916* (London: Penguin Books, 1993, originally published 1962), p. 40. After the war, Knobelsdorf attempted to distance himself from the failure of the Verdun undertaking by claiming that he was not fully informed about Falkenhayn's goals for the offensive. (See, for instance, Knobelsdorf to Ziese-Beringer, 6 March 1933, in Ziese-Beringer, *Feldherr*, II, p. 200 and Knobelsdorf to Reichsarchiv, 6 January 1934, BA/MA, W10/50705.) It is clear, however, that the 5th Army knew that Falkenhayn's goal was the "bleeding white" of the French army and, indeed, propagated it even if they did not agree completely with the policy. See Berthold von Deimling, *Aus der alten in die neue Zeit* (Berlin: Verlag Ullstein, 1930), p. 209, for Knobelsdorf's instructions to the XV Army Corps before the battle; and Heymann's assertion that Falkenhayn repeatedly expressed his concept of "wearing down" the French army before the battle. Heymann to Reichsarchiv, 28 August 1935, BA/MA W10/51523. This also disproves Wallach's claim that Falkenhayn did not reveal his true intentions to his subordinates. See Wallach, *Dogma*, p. 174.

71 Kronprinz Wilhelm, *Erinnerungen*, p. 160. Cf. Horne, *Price of Glory*, p. 38, for a different translation of this passage.

designed to mop up the remnants of the shattered Entente armies. On 6 January 1916, Falkenhayn ordered the Chief of Staff of the 6th Army, Generalleutnant Hermann von Kuhl, to Berlin for a meeting. The two men met in the Ministry of War building on 8 January.[72] According to Kuhl's diary, Falkenhayn posed to him the question: "Can we carry out a large-scale offensive in the area of the 6th Army, and what forces would be necessary for such an operation?" Kuhl had an answer ready: the 6th Army proposed to carry out an attack "in the general direction of Albert, with the left wing of the 6th Army and the right wing of the 2nd Army," with the goal of rolling up the flank of the British forces. Twelve army corps would be necessary to carry out the offensive.[73] Like every other offensive proposal requiring such forces, Falkenhayn refused Kuhl's plan, again declaring it would require more resources than Germany possessed. Instead, he asked Kuhl to return to Douai and prepare a plan which would involve an attack with eight divisions and around twenty heavy batteries. He told Kuhl to expect an enemy much weakened by the forthcoming offensive at Verdun and the Entente relief offensives that were sure to follow.[74] The General Staff Chief hoped that this offensive by the 6th Army would "restore life to the solidified front" and would bring *Bewegungskrieg* once again to the Western Front.[75] The 6th Army should be ready to begin this more limited offensive "around the middle of February."

On 27 January, the 6th Army's new proposal for an offensive arrived at Mézières. The memorandum began inauspiciously by questioning Falkenhayn's assumption that the Entente would attack the 6th Army suddenly. Kuhl noted that each previous Entente offensive had taken place only after careful, prolonged preparation. Further, Kuhl's report pointed out that the British were still in the process of building their army. Consequently, the 6th Army was of the opinion that a British offensive could only take place in the late spring at the earliest.[76]

72 Despite giving up his position as Minister of War in January 1915, Falkenhayn retained his residence at the Ministry of War until December 1916. See Kriegsministerium Unterkunfts-Dept. to Falkenhayn, 6 December 1916, Nr. 2597/11 16U1, Falkenhayn Nachlass (N2088), BA-Lichterfelde.

73 This offensive proposal shared many similarities with the 11th Army's proposal from March 1915. See Chapter 7.

74 Kuhl, "Kriegstagebuch," 11 January 1916. See also Kronprinz Rupprecht von Bayern, *Mein Kriegstagebuch* (ed. Eugen von Frauenholz) (3 vols.) (Berlin: E. S. Mittler, 1929), I (diary entry for 10 January 1916), p. 412. Before the war, Kuhl had served for a long time in the *Grosser Generalstab*, last serving as an *Oberquartiermeister*. See Hanns Möller-Witten, *Festschrift zum 100.Geburtstag des Generals der Infanterie a.D. Dr.Phil. Hermann von Kuhl* (Frankfurt: E. S. Mittler, 1956), pp. 7–18.

75 Kuhl to Reichsarchiv, 28 October 1932, BA/MA, W10/51318; *Weltkrieg*, X, p. 30.

76 At this point in the memorandum, Falkenhayn wrote in the margin: "The decision will not be easy for them. However, I believe they must make it."

Despite these reservations, the memorandum went on, as ordered, to outline a plan of attack using the eight divisions from the OHL reserve under the conditions assumed by Falkenhayn. Kuhl proposed a counterattack at the spot in the front where the enemy attack had come. He felt that this counteroffensive should come at either of two moments: immediately after the British attack had collapsed or after they had broken into the first German position. In either case, Kuhl felt the German attack must come before the enemy had time to make good his losses and strengthen his position. He believed that the enemy would be weakest at the point where he had launched his own attack. Given the difficulty of timing such a counteroffensive properly, he requested the promised forces from the OHL reserve be put under the 6th Army's command and that the 6th Army be given engineering units to construct the necessary artillery and jumping-off positions.

Kuhl felt that the limited forces promised by the OHL would allow for only limited goals. The immediate objectives of this counterattack should be to deal the enemy a "powerful blow," to win key territory which would better the overall German position, and to inflict thereby a heavy blow to the enemy's morale. At the very best, Kuhl hoped the Germans might be able to take complete possession of the Loretto Heights (Vimy Ridge) (to which Falkenhayn noted in the margin: "Fortes Fortuna adjuvat!"). Kuhl would project no goals further than this. Reflecting the overall skepticism of the 6th Army, he refused to be drawn into further speculation as to the objectives of such an operation.[77]

A week later, Falkenhayn responded to the 6th Army's equivocal memorandum. Despite the opinion of the 6th Army, Falkenhayn stuck by his original assumptions. He wrote: "Contrary to the opinion held there, I believe that an enemy offensive or a serious weakening of the enemy on the front north of the Somme is almost certain when the . . . advance of the 5th Army on Verdun succeeds." He continued to believe that the German attack at Verdun would force the Entente to attack whether they wanted to or not. However, Falkenhayn was not sure where this attack would come. He believed that the attack might occur in the Champagne instead. Accordingly, he refused to release the promised OHL reserves to the 6th Army until the Entente relief offensive actually began. These forces, Falkenhayn promised, could be in the line within three or four days of the attack.[78]

[77] AOK 6 to OHL, Ia Nr. 267g, 24 January 1916, BA/MA, W10/51520; *Der Weltkrieg*, X, pp. 30–32. This document is also reprinted in Wendt, *Verdun*, pp. 230–232.

[78] OHL to AOK 6, Nr. 22621 op. 3 February 1916, BA/MA, W10/51520. See also Rupprecht, *Kriegstagebuch*, I (diary entry for 3 February), pp. 422–423.

The 6th Army continued to be unsettled by Falkenhayn's assumptions and plans. On 3 February, Kuhl wrote in his diary:

> I do not believe in French and English attacks. We shall have to see who is right... I fear we will come to nothing with our army. The counterattack is a complicated thing; from the start one is dependent upon the enemy and can easily mis-time things.[79]

These personal doubts were expressed in a report to the OHL several days later. After analyzing the experiences of a demonstrative attack in late January, Kuhl concluded that the Entente forces were certainly not planning a major offensive in the immediate future and that they were convinced that a German attack would not fall in the area of the 6th Army. In this report, Kuhl again questioned Falkenhayn's belief that a sudden Entente attack must take place after the beginning of the German offensive at Verdun. He felt it was highly unlikely that the Entente would attack the 6th Army if the Verdun attack succeeded. More likely, the British would relieve the French 10th Army, thus freeing more French troops for use at Verdun. However, Kuhl doubted that the British would then attack: "Whether they [the British] will attack, is doubtful, since they are in the process of re-ordering their units (divisions) and at this time apparently not ready . . ."[80]

Thus, as the first phase of Falkenhayn's strategy for 1916 began in February, the General Staff Chief's assessment of the situation on the Western Front stood in opposition to that of the 6th Army. Despite Falkenhayn's assurances, Crown Prince Rupprecht and Kuhl could not believe that the Entente would attack their army at short notice. Further, they did not believe the eight divisions promised by Falkenhayn would be enough to produce any meaningful results. As with the 5th Army, this difference of opinion with the 6th Army remained unresolved.

***

Believing the Champagne to be another likely area for an Entente relief offensive and an area that offered good prospects for a German counteroffensive, Falkenhayn approached the 3rd Army while he was dealing with the 6th. On 1 February, the General Staff Chief telegraphed Vouziers, "I would be thankful for an evaluation of whether and where, as well as with what necessary forces, you could conduct a large-scale counterattack [*ein grösserer Gegenstoss*] from your front at least to the area of Vitry

[79] Kuhl, "Kriegstagebuch," 3 February 1916.

[80] AOK 6 to OHL, Nr. 276 g, 7 February 1916, BA/MA, W10/51520. A portion of this document is published in Wendt, *Verdun*, p. 233.

le François . . ."[81] As with his query to the 6th Army, Falkenhayn asked the 3rd Army to assume that the French forces before them would be considerably weakened.[82]

Several days later, the 3rd Army sent its plan for an offensive to the OHL. The 3rd Army believed that any offensive undertaking must meet two important conditions. First, the location chosen for the breakthrough must be tactically advantageous to the Germans. Second, the location must allow for an operational exploitation of the tactical breakthrough. After examining their front, the 3rd Army recommended an attack along the Prunay–Vaudesincourt line. This portion of the front offered good rearward communications and the thickly wooded area could hide the concentration of assault troops. Further, the area had good observation points for artillery spotters and had many protected areas from which the artillery could fire. The one drawback was the distance between the German and French lines here – 300 to 1,000 meters. This obstacle would have to be overcome by digging jump-off trenches forward to the French lines and by a gas attack to shield the assaulting infantry from observation.

The 3rd Army projected that the initial tactical breakthrough would require six divisions and considerable heavy artillery and had as its objective the Vesle. Once this objective had been reached, the 3rd Army planned to exploit the successful tactical breakthrough by two further attacks which would advance southwest and southeast and drive the French back across the Marne and back to Vitry le François. This plan, like the 6th Army's initial plan, called for the use of considerable forces. The 3rd Army asked for 14 divisions from the OHL reserve to add to its 5 divisions. Additionally, the plan called for the use of considerable amounts of heavy artillery – in total, 86 heavy howitzer batteries, 24 mortar batteries, and 19 heavy cannon batteries. Most of these units would have to come from the OHL reserve as well. The 3rd Army believed it would take at least two months to make the necessary preparations for the offensive.[83]

Falkenhayn gave his by now normal response to the 3rd Army plan. On 7 February, he wrote to the 3rd Army refusing their plan on the grounds that it required strength beyond Germany's means. Once again, Falkenhayn stressed his belief that "mass attacks" like that of the 3rd

[81] This point lay close to 50 km from the German front lines in January 1916.

[82] Quoted in Solger, "Vorbereitung," p. 75. See also Fritz von Loßberg, *Meine Tätigkeit im Weltkriege 1914–1918* (Berlin: E. S. Mittler, 1939), pp. 204–205.

[83] AOK 3 to OHL, Ia Nr. 675 g, 4 February 1916, printed in Wendt, *Verdun*, pp. 234–236. See also Loßberg, *Meine Tätigkeit*, pp. 204–205.

Army's plan could not succeed under the conditions current in January 1916. Instead, he requested they prepare another plan which would use five or six divisions in the first wave, followed by a second wave of three or two divisions, i.e., the 3rd Army could have the same eight divisions promised to the 6th Army. Falkenhayn further promised enough heavy artillery to have one battery for every 150 meters of front.[84]

Unfortunately, the 3rd Army's second plan seems not to have survived the years since 1916.[85] In his memoirs, Fritz von Loßberg wrote only: "Immediately, the 3rd Army submitted a new plan for an offensive under the conditions assumed by General Falkenhayn. No answer was forthcoming."[86] Einem's war diary gives little more detail: "With the forces to be made available to use, we can neither turf out the enemy standing to the east of our front nor can we take Mourmelon. At best, we might reach the heights on Baconnes, take these, and dig ourselves in there. That is all."[87] The tone of Einem's diary entry suggests that the 3rd Army, like the 6th Army, expected little from a German counteroffensive with such limited resources. Again like the 6th Army, the 3rd Army set only limited objectives in its revised plan. The staffs of the two armies clearly felt the war to date had shown the great size of forces and the amount of heavy artillery necessary to carry out a successful breakthrough.

The lack of response from Falkenhayn to the 3rd Army's revised plan is evidence that he increasingly came to view a German counteroffensive in the Champagne as not worthwhile. As we will see, as the Verdun battle dragged on, Falkenhayn increasingly came to count on a British relief offensive in the area of the 6th Army, despite the continued skepticism of the 6th Army. Consequently, he let his plans for a German counterattack in the Champagne fall by the wayside. The surviving documentation, however, shows that Falkenhayn and the 3rd Army had different views of the situation on the Western Front. Falkenhayn expected the French to be severely weakened immediately after the attack on Verdun and thus vulnerable to an attack with limited resources. The 3rd Army, on the other hand, did not believe that significant gains could be achieved with

84 OHL to AOK 3, No Akten Nr., 7 February 1916, W10/51520. Falkenhayn's response prompted Einem to question why Falkenhayn had not informed the 3rd Army of the force limitations in his initial query. Einem, "Kriegstagebuch," 7 February 1916.

85 This second plan is not even discussed by the Reichsarchiv in any of the surviving *Forschungsarbeiten* or in *Der Weltkrieg*, X.

86 Loßberg, *Meine Tätigkeit*, p. 205.

87 Einem, "Kriegstagebuch," 10 February 1916. From this entry it appears that Loßberg presented the 3rd Army's revised plan to Falkenhayn at the *Chefbesprechung* on 11 February.

the eight divisions promised by Falkenhayn. Once again, the General Staff Chief's assumptions bore almost no relation to those of his subordinates in the field.

Secrecy and diversionary attacks

In December 1915, Falkenhayn returned to an approach that had served him well in the campaign in the east in April – strategic surprise. At Gorlice, the German forces had been able to catch the Russians largely unawares and, hence, completely unprepared to meet the German assault. Falkenhayn hoped to repeat this success in the west in 1916, and consequently took elaborate measures to ensure the secrecy of the forthcoming German assault.

To help cover the preparations for the offensive at Verdun, Falkenhayn ordered the other armies of the *Westheer* to prepare local offensives, a repeat of the *Nebenangriffen* he had used so effectively in the spring to deceive the Entente before the Gorlice undertaking.[88] Accordingly, in the days before the Verdun offensive began, a number of "offensives with limited goals" took place across the Western Front. On 14 February, the 4th Army launched an attack against the "Grosse Bastion" on the Lys Canal southeast of Ypres.[89] The 6th Army renewed its assault on the Giesler Heights east of Souchez.[90] Einem's 3rd Army launched a number of minor attacks on 12 and 13 February to better their field positions, which had taken such a battering in the *Herbstschlacht*.[91]

While the 5th Army did not carry out any diversionary attacks before the offensive, the army carried out its own covering measures, believing firmly that "the prerequisite for success was surprise."[92] First, the 5th Army declared to its troops that a French offensive was expected in February. The preparations they carried out for the Verdun offensive were ostensibly to prepare for this supposed French attack.[93] Further, the 5th Army increased its anti-aircraft defenses with the goal of preventing French reconnaissance flights from making it further than the line Montfaucon–Consenvoye–Azanes.[94] In a further effort to hide the

[88] Falkenhayn, *General Headquarters*, p. 223; *Der Weltkrieg*, X, pp. 270–276. Indeed, Crown Prince Rupprecht even got the impression that Falkenhayn intended to "exhaust" the enemy with small offensives. Rupprecht, *Kriegstagebuch*, I (diary entry for 25 December 1915), p. 409.

[89] *Der Weltkrieg*, X, pp. 270–271.

[90] Rupprecht, *Kriegstagebuch*, I, pp. 429–432; *Kriegstagebuch*, III, pp. 79–82.

[91] Loßberg, *Meine Tätigkeit*, pp. 207–208.

[92] Kronprinz Wilhelm, *Erinnerungen*, p. 163.

[93] "Angriff auf dem Westufer," p. 13.

[94] AOK 5, Ia Nr. 20 geh., 29 December 1915, printed in ibid., p. 15.

attack preparations from the French, most of the building of depots, troop laagers, artillery positions, and jumping-off trenches took place under the cover of night.[95] Last, the attacking corps were only brought into the line just before the assault so that the French would not recognize the German build up.[96]

Falkenhayn also attempted to keep the plans for the Verdun offensive as closely guarded as possible. Accordingly, when Knobelsdorf returned to the 5th Army's headquarters on 16 December to prepare the plans for the new offensive, Falkenhayn impressed upon him the importance of secrecy. However, this time Falkenhayn took this idea even further than when preparing for the Gorlice offensive in April 1915.[97] In order to reduce the number of potential leaks, he insisted that access to the planning process for Operation "Gericht" be kept to the absolute minimum and that discussions about the undertaking not be put to paper, but only carried out personally.[98]

Falkenhayn was so carried away with the concept of secrecy that he tried to keep the decision on Verdun from Germany's other strategic leaders for as long as possible. He particularly attempted to keep the Chancellor out of the loop. In a meeting shortly after Falkenhayn had approved the 5th Army's attack plan, he told Bethmann that he remained "undecided" whether or not to undertake a "large-scale offensive" on the Western Front.[99] Falkenhayn's *Geheimhaltung* continued right up to the beginning of the attack. On the eve of the original start date of the offensive, he complained to Admiral Georg von Müller that somehow Bethmann had "got wind of our proposed 'Offensive on the Western Front.'"[100]

Indeed, the General Staff Chief was almost as reticent with his staff at the OHL. Falkenhayn did not inform them of the change from Belfort to Verdun until Christmas Day 1915, leaving them to work on preparations for the Belfort undertaking long after the decision had been made to scrap

95 Kronprinz Wilhelm, *Erinnerungen*, pp. 164–165.

96 Ludwig Gold, *Die Tragödie von Verdun 1916*: Vol. I: *Die deutsche Offensivschlacht* (*Schlachten des Weltkrieges* Bd. 13) (Berlin: Gerhard Stalling, 1928), p. 23.

97 Falkenhayn's efforts led Wild to comment, "Falkenhayn is masterful at contriving deceptive measures." Wild, "Kriegstagebuch," 2 February 1916.

98 *Der Weltkrieg*, X, p. 28; Kronprinz Wilhelm, *Erinnerungen*, p. 160.

99 Bethmann, diary entry for 7 January 1916, printed in Janßen, *Der Kanzler und der General*, p. 288. His Austro-Hungarian allies fared even worse. Falkenhayn deliberately misled the Austrian plenipotentiary at the OHL about German attack plans. Herwig, *First World War*, p. 186.

100 Müller, *Kaiser and His Court* (diary entry for 9 February 1916), p. 134. In fact, on 2 February, Luckwald had reported to Bethmann: "I have heard . . . from a well informed source, that at the moment only an attack against Verdun is to be awaited." Luckwald to Bethmann, 2 February 1916 (copied from *Reichskanzlei. Weltkrieg 15/1*), BA/MA, W10/51543.

it.[101] This, however, was part of his campaign of strategic deception. The preparations for Operation "Schwarzwald" were continued in an effort to deceive the French as to where the German offensive would come.[102] Barracks were constructed, a 38.5 cm cannon was left in place to shell Belfort occasionally, and Crown Prince Wilhelm paid the area a number of visits prior to the launching of the attack on Verdun.[103] The OHL even went so far as to evacuate portions of the population from Alsace in early December.[104]

This secrecy had two significant consequences. First, it made it extremely difficult for Falkenhayn's subordinates to understand properly the General Staff Chief's strategic and operational ideas. At no point did he plainly tell the 5th Army or the other armies of the *Westheer* exactly what was required of them. Falkenhayn merely gave their staffs specific situations from which they were required to submit operational plans. Given the radical nature of his strategic and operational approach at Verdun, perhaps Falkenhayn feared a repeat of the feud that took place in late 1914 and early 1915 when he openly suggested that the German army deviate from pre-war theory. Regardless of the reason, such reticence would come to hamper operations in 1916.

Falkenhayn's extreme secrecy had another consequence. It was to make a reconstruction of Falkenhayn's plans for Verdun extraordinarily difficult for historians. No one person knew all of the General Staff Chief's plans in late 1915 and early 1916, and his insistence that the 5th Army carry out its communications with him in person has left little documentary evidence. The only full exposition of Falkenhayn's intentions is his "Christmas Memorandum," reputedly delivered by the General Staff Chief to the Kaiser "around Christmas" 1915. This memorandum, in which Falkenhayn outlined his strategic plan for winning the war in 1916, was published by him in his memoirs in 1919.[105] However, its authenticity has been repeatedly called into question. When writing the official history, the researchers of the Reichsarchiv were unable to locate a copy of this document in any of the existing army files, nor did any of

101 Geyer to Ernst Kabisch, 8 January 1932, BA/MA, N221/25. Geyer and the rest of the OHL recognized that Falkenhayn did this to maintain the illusion that a German offensive was really going to take place in Upper Alsace.

102 Tappen to Reichsarchiv, 16 June 1932, BA/MA, N56/5.

103 Luckwald to Bethmann, 17 February 1916 (copied from *Reichskanzlei. Weltkrieg 15*/1), BA/MA, W10/51543; "Kriegstagebuch der Adjutantur S. K. H. des Kronprinz," 8 February 1916, BA/MA, W10/51519.

104 Ministère de la Guerre, *Les Armées Françaises dans la Grande Guerre*, Tome IV: *Verdun et la Somme*, Vol. 1: *Les Projects Offensifs pour 1916 et la Bataille de Verdun* (Paris: Imprimerie Nationale, 1926), p. 136. (My thanks to James Beach for the use of his translation.)

105 Falkenhayn, *General Headquarters*, pp. 209–218.

the others involved in the plan ever admit to reading it.[106] Most recently, Holger Afflerbach has revisited this issue in his biography of Falkenhayn. After examining the evidence surviving in the Kriegsgeschichtliches Forschungsanstalt files, he concluded that the "Christmas Memorandum" was in all likelihood written by Falkenhayn after the war. However, he also concluded that it, in fact, reflected many of Falkenhayn's ideas in early 1916.[107]

The confusion created by the lack of documentary evidence has allowed an unusual number of interpretations of Falkenhayn's intentions during the battle. His contemporary critics used the battle as further evidence that Falkenhayn was unfit for high command. They saw it as a demonstration of his inability to make the difficult decisions a true *Feldherr* must make. To them, the General Staff Chief's indecisiveness resulted in a strategy of "half-measures" that had no clear objective.[108] A number of historians have also questioned Falkenhayn's ultimate goals. Some believed that the "Christmas Memorandum," with its emphasis on "bleeding the French army white," was in fact created after the war by Falkenhayn as a justification for his failed strategy and that the aim of attrition was only raised after the 5th Army failed to take the fortress quickly.[109]

However, when viewed within context of Falkenhayn's experiences in the war to date, his strategy at Verdun becomes clearer. After the failure of his Ypres offensive in 1914, the General Staff Chief had borrowed from the pre-war ideas of Moltke the Elder and Hans Delbrück to form an alternative strategy for Germany. This alternative strategy aimed not at defeating Germany's enemies decisively in the field and dictating a peace on German terms, but rather at breaking apart the alliance and compelling at least one of the members of the Entente to the negotiating table. However, this strategic goal had eluded Falkenhayn up until 1916. Russia had proved unwilling to come to the bargaining table despite the punishment it had suffered during the summer of 1915. The General Staff Chief believed that Germany could find no further successes there, and thus turned his sights back to the Western Front. There, he hoped to be able to split the Western Allies and bring an end to the war. However, the challenge of the tactical situation had first to be overcome before any

106 *Der Weltkrieg*, X, p. 2. The Reichsarchiv even called in an army psychologist, Dr. Wohlfahrt, to analyse the document, who concluded that the memo was written after the war. BA/MA, W10/50703.

107 Afflerbach, *Falkenhayn*, pp. 543–545. See also Wilhelm Groener's similar opinion. Groener to Reichsarchiv, 5 March 1934, BA/MA, W10/50705. (Partially quoted in Afflerbach, p. 544.)

108 This view of Falkenhayn pervades *Der Weltkrieg*, but was expressed most forcefully by the director of the KGFA, Foerster, in his "Falkenhayns Plan."

109 This argument has most recently been advanced by Krumeich, "'Saigner la France'?," pp. 17–29.

solution to Germany's strategic problem could be found. To this end, Falkenhayn developed a unique operational approach to complement his strategic approach.

Unable to break through the fortified front lines and unable to deal with the Entente reserves behind those lines, the General Staff Chief proposed instead to force the enemy to attack strong German positions. In order to compel the enemy, in this case the French, to do this, a sensitive point on the front had to be threatened. Falkenhayn intended his attack on Verdun to so endanger the fortress that the French would be forced to launch a counteroffensive, which would be defeated with great loss by the German guns located on the dominating heights over the battlefield. He believed that the French would thereby be placed in a very precarious strategic situation and the British would also be forced to launch a hastily planned relief offensive. This, too, would be repulsed with great losses. If these actions did not compel the French to open peace negotiations, a German counteroffensive would then be launched to mop up the remnants of the shattered British and French armies and break apart the Western alliance once and for all.

Although Falkenhayn certainly came up with a unique approach for winning the war in 1916, in formulating this strategy he drew heavily on the experiences of 1915. The war to date in the west had shown the impossibility of achieving a meaningful breakthrough. However, attacks with limited objectives were generally successful in reaching their goals with minimal casualties to the attackers. Further, the war on both fronts had demonstrated the deadly effect of artillery. In the east, Mackensen's offensives used heavy artillery to great effect to inflict large numbers of casualties upon the Russians. In the west, it had proved its worth in defense, again inflicting high losses on the attackers. Moreover, fortresses had proved incapable of withstanding the effect of the heavy artillery employed by the Germans.

Falkenhayn intended to apply the war's operational lessons at Verdun. The 5th Army would make a lunge forward in what amounted to a large-scale attack with limited objectives to seize the heights on the right bank of the Meuse. From this position not only would the Germans threaten the fortress of Verdun, but their artillery would dominate the battlefield. When the French counterattacked to relieve the pressure on the fortress, they would be attacking into strong German defensive positions. Through these attacks, the French army would "bleed itself white."[110]

110 Michael Geyer has described the Battle of Verdun as "the complete disjuncture between strategy, battle design and tactics." "German Strategy in the Age of Machine Warfare," in Peter Paret, ed., *Makers of Modern Strategy* (Princeton: Princeton University Press, 1986), p. 536. However, it is clear that Falkenhayn conceived of his plan on all these levels.

This plan clearly depended upon the enemy doing exactly as Falkenhayn desired, something that could not be guaranteed. Additionally, its success rested upon the 5th Army doing as Falkenhayn wanted. As the next chapters will show, neither of these two requirements were filled completely.

9 Verdun: the execution

For most of the war until February 1916, the Verdun salient had been a quiet sector, with no large-scale actions from either side since Sarrail's defense of the fortress against orders in 1914. In fact, the forts that made up the fortress of Verdun had been stripped of most of their artillery pieces during the second half of 1915 to provide the artillery deficient French army with heavy guns. By 15 October, forty-three heavy batteries had been removed from the fortifications.[1] The French High Command (the *Grand Quartier Général*, or GQG) had also begun making plans to abandon the entire right bank of the Meuse and were busy reinforcing the positions on the left bank.[2] The sector's casualty rate was low. On the German side, the XVI Army Corps suffered the highest number of casualties in the 5th Army during January 1916; it reported 153 dead, 488 wounded, and 11 missing.[3]

As 1916 began, Falkenhayn's campaign of strategic deception was working admirably. The Entente powers were unclear where a German offensive might fall. Initially, both British and French intelligence held that the main German offensive effort for 1916 would take place in Russia.[4] Although there was a great deal of intelligence arriving about German attack preparations across the Western Front, this was at first seen merely as a diversionary effort. Only slowly did the Entente awake

[1] Georges Blond, *Verdun* (trans. Frances Frenaye) (London: White Lion Publisher, 1976; originally published 1961), p. 30.

[2] Ministère de la Guerre, *Les Armées Françaises dans la Grand Guerre*, Tome IV: *Verdun et la Somme*, 1: *Les projects offensifs pour 1916 et la Bataille de Verdun* (Paris: Imprimerie Nationale, 1934), pp. 117ff.; H. A. DeWeerd, "The Verdun Forts," *The Cavalry Journal* 41, 70 (1932), pp. 27–28.

[3] Untitled and unpublished manuscript in BA/MA, W10/51526, p. 4 (hereafter, "Angriff auf dem Westufer").

[4] James Beach, "Haig's Intelligence: GHQ's Perception of the Enemy, 1916–1918: Intelligence in 1916," unpublished manuscript, p. 9; Henri Philippe Pétain, *Verdun* (trans. Margaret MacVeagh) (London: Elkin Mathews & Marrot, 1930), p. 38. See AOK 6, Nachrichten Offizier, "Ausländische Pressestimmen zu den letzten deutschen Unternehmungen im Westen, in der Zeit vom 25. Januar – 11. Februar 1916," BA/MA, PH3/607.

to the growing German threat in the west. By the end of January, sufficient intelligence had arrived to predict a major German offensive there. Again, however, German countermeasures prevented predicting where this attack would fall. The consensus of opinion in GQG was that the German main effort would take place in the Champagne, with diversionary attacks falling perhaps in Flanders and at Verdun.[5]

As a consequence, the French made no serious effort to reinforce the *région fortifée de Verdun* before February. On 12 February, the initial start date of the German campaign, the salient was defended by four divisions and two Territorial brigades under the command of General Herr. Additionally, with the heavy artillery removed from Verdun's forts, Herr could only count on a limited amount of field artillery. The 5th Army only identified sixty-five batteries in the days before the offensive.[6]

The 5th Army's plans and preparations

Shortly after Falkenhayn's decision to attack Verdun, the III Army Corps (Lochow), the VII Reserve Corps (Zwehl), the XV Army Corps (Deimling), and the XVII Army Corps (Schenck) were assigned to the 5th Army to form the attack group for the coming offensive. Each of these units had extensive experience on the Western Front. The VII Reserve Corps had captured the French fortress of Maubeuge early in the war, and the III Corps had even pioneered the concept of "attacks with limited objectives" at Vailly and Soissons. Each was also well rested, as they had been removed from the front line for rest and extensive training before being sent to the 5th Army.[7] Each corps was also reinforced by a reserve of 2,400 experienced men and 2,000 newly trained recruits. In the interests of secrecy, these units were fed into the Verdun sector slowly. The VII Reserve Corps arrived first in late December and the remainder followed toward the end of January.[8]

The 5th Army staff had begun planning for their undertaking shortly after Knobelsdorf's return from his meeting with Falkenhayn in Berlin on 16 December. The first result of this was the attack plan delivered to the OHL on 6 January, which outlined the general concepts behind the offensive. After the General Staff Chief had approved this, the 5th

5 *Les Armées Françaises*, IV/1, pp. 134–143.

6 Reichsarchiv, *Der Weltkrieg*, Bd. X: *Die Operationen des Jahres 1916 bis zum Wechsel in der Obersten Heeresleitung* (Berlin: E. S. Mittler, 1936), p. 69.

7 Ludwig Gold, *Die Tragödie von Verdun 1916*, Teil I: *Die deutsche Offensivschlacht* (*Schlachten des Weltkrieges*, Bd. 13) (Berlin: Gerhard Stalling, 1928), pp. 18–22.

8 *Der Weltkrieg*, X, p. 61; Hans von Zwehl, *Maubeuge – Aisne – Verdun: Das VII. Reserve-Korps im Weltkriege von seinem Beginn bis Ende 1916* (Berlin: Karl Curtius, 1921), pp. 132–133.

Army began to work out the details of their attack. On 27 January, this process was completed and orders went out to the assault corps and to the artillery commanders of these corps. Like the orders of the III Corps at its attacks on Vailly and Soissons in 1914–15 and like the 11th Army's orders for the breakthrough at Gorlice, the 5th Army's attack orders to its subordinates went into considerable detail and marked a continuing trend of higher commands interfering in what, before the war, would have been considered the responsibility of the commanding generals.

The 5th Army divided its zone of attack into four sectors, three of which would make up the main assault. Sector A was assigned to the VII Reserve Corps, sector B to the XVIII Corps, and sector C to the III Corps. Artillery preparation was to begin on the morning of 12 February. At 5:00p.m., the infantry of sectors A-C, supported by flame-throwers and grenadiers, would advance in open firing lines [*mit lichten Schützenlinien*] against the French first positions.[9] Where possible, they were to take possession of these positions and then reconnoiter the French second positions for calling in artillery fire to support the next day's assault. The 5th Army emphasized that during the attack the artillery was to pay special attention to avoid hitting the advancing German infantry.[10]

This portion of the 5th Army's order reads very much like a large-scale "attack with limited objectives." Each army corps was set specific goals. Its attack was to be carefully prepared by artillery fire and its assaulting infantry was to be well supported by fire. Great emphasis was placed on keeping German casualties low. Indeed, this was in keeping with Falkenhayn's general conception for the offensive – the artillery was to bear the burden of the battle, while the role of the infantry was to seize key terrain and to keep the pressure on the French. He later wrote, "our object . . . was to inflict upon the enemy the utmost possible injury with the least possible expenditure of lives on our part . . ."[11]

The next paragraph of the 5th Army's order, however, proclaimed that an important feature of the assault was its relentless pressure, and seemed to indicate that the offensive's goal was to break through the French positions rather than to seize terrain from which the artillery could dominate the battlefield. The 5th Army wrote:

[9] The III Corps was further supported by the *Sturmabteilung Rohr*, the fledgling stormtroop formation. See Bruce I. Gudmundsson, *Stormtroop Tactics: Innovation in the German Army, 1914–1918* (New York: Praeger, 1989), pp. 55–75; and Hellmuth Gruss, *Aufbau und Verwendung der deutschen Sturmbataillone im Weltkrieg* (Berlin: Junker und Dunnhaupt Verlag, 1939), pp. 28–31.

[10] AOK 5, Ia Nr. 418g., "Befehl für die Angriffskorps," 27 January 1916, BA/MA, W10/51534; reprinted in Gold, *Verdun*, I, pp. 258–260.

[11] Erich von Falkenhayn, *General Headquarters and its Critical Decisions 1914–1916* (London: Hutchinson, 1919), p. 224.

With artillery fire, as in the infantry attack, the entire course of the battle for the fortress of Verdun *depends on the momentum of the assault never faltering*. Through this method, the French will find no opportunity to make a stand in new positions to their rear and to re-organize their resistance once it has been broken.[12]

This portion of the order clearly reflected the 5th Army's desire to capture the fortress quickly, as opposed to Falkenhayn's idea of taking dominating terrain, and shows the continuing difference of opinion between the General Staff Chief and the 5th Army over the campaign's goals. Understandably, this dual goal present in the 5th Army's attack order created some confusion with its subordinates. Despite their requests for clarification, however, the 5th Army let its original order stand and each corps was left to itself to determine the meaning.[13] This would lead to difficulties once the attack was launched.

The 5th Army's initial goals – the seizure of Meuse Heights along the line Froide Terre–Fort Souville–Fort Tavannes – was in agreement with Falkenhayn's concept of the offensive. From there, the Germans would be in safe defensive positions and would be able to repel easily any French attempts to retake the lost terrain. However, at the beginning of the campaign the 5th Army's final goals diverged widely from Falkenhayn's. The attack plans of the 27th extended the offensive to the Woevre Plain as well as the Meuse Heights. The XV Army Corps (sector D) was to drive the French from the Plain shortly after the beginning of the main offensive on the Heights.[14] While this was perhaps a logical extension of the initial attack on the Heights, the 5th Army's order for the VI Reserve Corps to attack the west bank shortly after the start of the offensive went much further.[15] These two orders demonstrate the army's desire to take the fortress quickly and to continue on until the Verdun salient was flattened, rather than fighting a defensive battle designed to "bleed white" the French army.[16]

Falkenhayn and the 5th Army, however, were in agreement about how to employ their artillery. In keeping with Falkenhayn's general conception of the battle, the 5th Army planned for the artillery to bear a heavy burden in the assault on the French positions. Accordingly, the army issued a special "Order for the Activities of the Artillery and Mortars."

12 AOK 5, "Befehl für die Angriffskorps," para. 3. Emphasis added.

13 *Der Weltkrieg*, X, pp. 67–68; Hermann Ziese-Beringer, *Der einsame Feldherr: Die Wahrheit über Verdun* (2 vols.) (Berlin: Frundsberg-Verlag, 1933), I, pp. 159–162.

14 AOK 5, "Befehl für die Angriffskorps," para. 3.

15 AOK 5, "Weitere Mitteilungen" to the "Befehl für die Angriffskorps."

16 Gerhard von Heymann (Ia of 5th Army) to Reichsarchiv, 28 August 1916, BA/MA, W10/51523. See also Hermann Wendt, *Verdun 1916: Die Angriffe Falkenhayns im Maasgebiet mit Richtung auf Verdun als strategisches Problem* (Berlin: E. S. Mittler, 1931), pp. 31ff.

Fig. 13 The demanding assault at Verdun called for the use of new technology, including flamethrowers

Like the 11th Army at Gorlice, the 5th Army centralized control over the artillery.[17] Although the 5th Army left the task of targeting to the *Generäle der Fußartillerie* (Generals of the Foot Artillery) of each attack corps, their orders detailed certain batteries to perform specific tasks at specified times. A portion of the artillery pieces were given over to preparatory fire on the French positions. Permanent fortifications were to be engaged by the "heaviest" howitzers and flanking fire was to be carried out by heavy cannon batteries, to which also fell the task of bombarding possible French supply routes and assembly points. Further, the French artillery was to be suppressed by the large-scale use of special batteries firing gas shells. The remainder of the artillery, including the field artillery of each assault corps, was given the task of silencing the enemy artillery, and was placed under the direction of the *General der Fußartillerie* of the individual attack corps.[18] The 5th Army reserved for

[17] Kronprinz Wilhelm, *Meine Erinnerungen aus Deutschlands Heldenkampf* (Berlin: E. S. Mittler, 1923), pp. 166–167.

[18] This centralization of the corps' artillery under one officer met resistance amongst the divisions. [Richard] von Berendt, "Mit der Artillerie durch den Weltkrieg," *Wissen und Wehr* (1924), p. 186.

itself the right to alter the attack corps' artillery dispositions and the duty of coordinating the flanking fire of each corps.

In keeping with the lessons learned in the war to date, particularly those of the eastern campaign in 1915, the 5th Army laid great stress on close infantry/artillery cooperation. Their orders specified that accuracy was extremely important to knock out enemy strongpoints and to avoid hitting the German infantry during its advance. Fire was to be well observed and, therefore, would begin slowly, only building up pace gradually; true *Trommelfeuer* would only begin an hour before the infantry assault. When the infantry attacked at 5:00p.m., the artillery would shift its fire to the second French line. Artillery observers were to accompany the infantry forward and the position of the advance was to be signaled by field telephone, flares, or colored balloons.[19] Thus, unlike the Entente approach at this point in the war, the 5th Army emphasized accuracy rather than weight of fire.

The 5th Army also stressed that once the attack began the artillery fire was to be continuous, writing: "*It is of the utmost importance that the enemy remains constantly under heavy fire across the entire field of battle.*"[20] Not even at night were the French to be allowed a respite. During darkness, the artillery of each sector was to maintain a "lively harassing fire" [*ein lebhaftes Beunruhigungsfeuer*], while the long-range artillery was to fire on possible French assembly points.

Special provision was made to maintain this high rate of fire throughout the offensive. Initially, each artillery piece and mortar was supplied with what the OHL determined as three days worth of munitions. In total the OHL reckoned on firing 2,000,000 rounds during the first six days and an equal number over the next twelve days.[21] To keep the pace of fire steady, thirty-three and a half munitions trains would arrive daily.[22] Fire at the pace and for the duration envisioned by Falkenhayn, however, would take its toll upon the German artillery pieces. Therefore, five repair shops were set up close to the front so that minor repairs could be effected in the field. New barrels and other spare parts were stocked at these workshops. As the battle wore on, artillery pieces were shipped back for more comprehensive

[19] AOK 5, Ia Nr. 388g., "Befehl für die Tätigkeit der Artillerie und Minenwerfer," 27 January 1916, BA/MA, W10/51534; Kronprinz Wilhelm, *Erinnerungen*, pp. 168–169; Zwehl, *Maubeuge – Aisne – Verdun*, pp. 139ff.

[20] Ibid., para.11. Emphasis in original.

[21] By way of contrast, the British fired 1,768,873 shells during the first eight days of the battle of the Somme. Martin Samuels, *Command or Control? Command, Training and Tactics in the British and German Armies, 1888–1918*(London: Frank Cass, 1995), p. 158.

[22] Wilhelm Groener, *Lebenserinnerungen* (ed. Friedrich Freiherr Hiller von Gaertringen) (Göttingen: Vandenhoeck & Ruprecht, 1957), p. 209 (diary entry for 11 February 1916); *Der Weltkrieg*, X, p. 62.

repairs to factories that were geared to repair and ship them back to the front quickly.[23]

The 5th Army also carefully planned for a redeployment of the artillery once the infantry had reached their goals. The field guns, the mobile heavy howitzers, and the 10 cm cannons were to move forward first under the covering fire of the mortars, the "heaviest" howitzers, and the heavy cannon. Once these batteries were in place and firing, the remaining mobile artillery would move forward. To expedite this process, great attention was to be paid by the advancing troops to finding and preparing possible artillery and observation areas.[24]

Given that the artillery was to bear the main burden of the battle for Verdun, the 5th Army deployed what was for the time a massive array. All told, 1,201 pieces, more than twice the number used at Gorlice, were assembled for the first day of the assault.[25] Although close to a third of this number were "light" field guns (7.7 cm) or "light" field howitzers (10.5 cm) of the field artillery, the remainder were the "heavy" and "heaviest" guns and howitzers of the foot artillery, which ranged in size from 15 cm to 42 cm.[26] Indeed, to assemble this collection, the OHL had been forced to strip the other armies of the *Westheer* of their mobile, modern artillery and replace them with older models or with captured Russian guns.[27] The assault was to be further supported by the fire of 202 mortars and 8 flame-thrower companies.[28]

Great hope was placed in this collection of artillery. The gunners of the 5th Army bragged that the effectiveness of their fire would allow the infantry to make a "*Parademarsch nach Verdun.*"[29] The rest of the German leadership set great store on the artillery deployment as well. Adolph Wild von Hohenborn, who as Minister of War was responsible for equipping the army, wrote proudly that the "artillery deployment at the point of

23 Werner Freiherr von Grünau to Bethmann, 29 March 1916 (copied from *Reichskanzlei. Kriegsakten 1*, Bd. 6), BA/MA, W10/51543.

24 AOK 5, "Befehl für die Tätigkeit der Artillerie und Minenwerfer," para. 12.

25 For an example of the artillery order of battle for the attacking corps, see that of the VII Reserve Corps in Zwehl, *Maubeuge – Aisne – Verdun*, pp. 140, 212–213.

26 By contrast, the French only used 680 heavy guns during their Champagne offensive in September, most of which were of an older design and a much smaller caliber than the German heavy guns at Verdun. Ministère de la Guerre, *Les Armées Françaises dans la Grande Guerre*, Tome III: *Les offensives de 1915 – L'Hiver de 1915–1916* (Paris: Imprimerie Nationale, 1923), p. 310.

27 Gerhard Tappen, "Meine Kriegserinnerungen," unpublished manuscript in BA/MA, W10/50661, p. 172; Ernst von Wrisberg, *Heer und Heimat 1914–1918* (Leipzig: K. F. Koehler, 1921), pp. 59–60.

28 *Der Weltkrieg*, X, pp. 61–63. Wendt, *Verdun*, pp. 46–47 gives slightly different numbers, as does Gold, *Verdun*, I, pp. 35–36.

29 Cordt von Brandis, *Der Sturmangriff: Kriegserfahrungen eines Frontoffiziers* (1917), p. 5. My thanks to Bruce Gudmundsson for a copy of this document.

attack is of . . . unheard of strength."[30] Hans von Plessen wrote in his diary: "The 'Fat Berthas' (42 cm) will help us to victory here just as they did at Liège, Namur, Maubeuge, Antwerp!"[31] Wilhelm Groener had expressed a similar opinion of the ability of German heavy artillery to destroy modern fortresses, writing that enemy fortresses "cracked like empty nuts" under German fire.[32]

Indeed, the Germans had cause to be confident in the effect of their artillery. As Plessen and Groener noted, throughout the war the heavy artillery had proved its worth against fortifications, not only in the west, but also in the east.[33] Moreover, Wild observed that the Verdun salient was one great "fire sack." Placed as it was at the center of a great salient, Verdun could be easily enfiladed by German guns. German batteries could remain dispersed, and hence harder to hit with counter-battery fire, but still concentrate their own fire.[34] Also, as one artillery expert has noted, the Germans enjoyed a number of other advantages over their enemy:

> The terminal effect of the German shells, most of which were larger and fired at higher angles, was superior to that of the French shells. The rate of fire of German pieces, most of which had been built in the decade prior to the battle, was greater than that of the generally older French pieces. And, most significantly, the German artillery greatly outnumbered the French artillery in the sector. This overwhelming superiority in artillery gave Falkenhayn every reason to assume that the 5th Army would be able to gain permanent fire superiority over the French artillery while having enough firepower left over to repel French counterattacks and repeatedly bombard French infantry positions.[35]

Falkenhayn's first phase

By 12 February, the 5th Army stood ready to launch its offensive. The attacking corps had taken up position in the front line and the artillery batteries were in place and provisioned. The weather, unfortunately,

30 Adolph Wild von Hohenborn, "Kriegstagebuch," 1 February 1916, BA/MA, Wild Nachlass, N44/2.

31 Hans von Plessen, "Tagebuch," 7 January 1916, BA/MA, W10/50656.

32 Groener, diary entry for 20 August 1915 in *Lebenserinnerungen*, p. 247; See also, Erich von Luckwald to Bethmann, 17 February 1916 (copied from *Reichskanzlei. Weltkrieg 1914/18. 15.Allg. Milit- und Marine-Berichte aus dem Gr.H.Qu* Bd. 1) BA/MA, W10/51543; Holger Afflerbach, *Falkenhayn: Politisches Denken und Handeln im Kaiserreich* (Munich: Oldenbourg, 1994), pp. 363–364.

33 On the development and employment of the massive German guns, see the mistitled Richard Schindler, *Eine 42cm Mörser-Batterie im Weltkrieg* (Breslau: Hans Hofmann, 1934).

34 Wild, "Kriegstagebuch," 11 December 1915.

35 Bruce I. Gudmundsson, *On Artillery* (Westport, CT: Praeger, 1993), pp. 58–59.

intervened to postpone their assault. The attack's reliance upon artillery meant that good weather was essential for observation, and when morning broke on the 12th, the 5th Army's observers were blinded by rain and snow. For the next ten days, they waited for the weather to break. The assault troops froze in their jumping-off positions or marched back and forth between the front lines and their billets, while the staffs waited impatiently in the rear.[36]

The delay was not merely frustrating, however. It had serious consequences for the outcome of the offensive. The massing of so many troops and artillery batteries at Verdun could not be kept secret for long. In the days between the initial start date and 21 February, the French had received more detailed intelligence concerning the German attack, which caused them to reassess their earlier assumptions. By 21 February, the French were well informed about the strength of the German deployment at Verdun. Although the German deception measures were generally successful in keeping the Entente guessing as to where *the* major German offensive might fall, they realized a large attack was coming at Verdun.[37] While the GQG's request on 18 February that the British relieve the French 10th Army was rejected, reinforcements were nonetheless sent to Verdun to meet the impending German attack.[38]

On 12 February, the French force in the Verdun salient had consisted of five divisions. By 21 February, the defensive force had been considerably strengthened. Three French corps were now crowded into the salient – one corps of two divisions on the west bank and two corps, each of three divisions, on the east bank. A further three divisions were held in reserve. The French artillery strength had also grown. By the start of the 5th Army's offensive, the French had 388 field guns and 244 heavy artillery pieces in the salient.[39] Thus, rather than meeting a weak, surprised enemy on 21 February, the three German attack corps met an opponent reinforced and forewarned.[40]

[36] Gold, *Verdun*, I, pp. 48–50. Some assault units had to remain in dugouts which had filled with freezing water by 21 February.

[37] Joffre feared a German offensive in the Champagne, especially after the 3rd Army's diversionary attack there in early February. *Les Armées Françaises*, IV/1, Annexe 171; Joseph Joffre, *The Memoirs of Marshal Joffre* (trans. T. Bentley Mott) (2 vols.) (London: Geoffrey Bles, 1932), II, pp. 440ff.

[38] Beach, "Haig's Intelligence," pp. 12ff.; Douglas Haig, *The Private Papers of Douglas Haig, 1914–1919* (ed. Robert Blake) (London: Eyre & Spottiswoode, 1952) (diary entry for 19 February 1916), pp. 130–131.

[39] *Der Weltkrieg*, X, pp. 104–106; Wendt, *Verdun*, pp. 60–65.

[40] See Helmuth Otto, "Die Schlacht um Verdun (Februar–Dezember 1916)," *Militärgeschichte* 5 (1986), pp. 410–411. German Werth, *Verdun. Die Schlacht und der Mythos* (Gladbach: Weltbild Verlag, 1989), pp. 62ff.

However, the knowledge of the coming attack did not spare the defenders the intensity and accuracy of the 5th Army's opening bombardment. From 8:00a.m. until 5:00p.m., the 1,400 German artillery pieces and mortars pounded the French positions. Shells from the heavy artillery rained down on the city of Verdun, destroying bridges and setting fire to the train station. Long-range artillery cut the rail line. By 9:00a.m., all communication with the French front line had been cut, and reinforcements could not penetrate the thick German bombardment.[41] The 5th Army's battle report indicated that the French defensive fire was "generally weak" and was "scattered about without a set plan."[42]

In late afternoon, patrols from the attacking German units began probing the French first line. In general, they were met by little or no French fire. By 5:00p.m., the infantry of all three attack corps was engaged with the enemy. In sector A, the VII Reserve Corps met little resistance and was able to clear most of the Bois d'Haumont, capturing the French first and second trench lines. Its infantry reported that the artillery had completely destroyed the enemy positions and had stunned or killed the French defenders.[43] In sectors B and C, however, the XVIII Corps and the III Corps met with stiffer resistance. The XVIII Corps found that the French positions in Bois des Caures had not been fully destroyed. Consequently, they were able to take only a small portion of the first French trench. The III Corps faced a similar situation in Herbebois. Only after taking heavy casualties had they been able to wrestle most of the forward trench from French hands. Wherever the French had placed their defenses in wooded areas, the German artillery had been unable to prepare the battlefield properly, and the attacking infantry encountered shaken but reasonably unharmed French defenders in undamaged positions.[44] Additionally, on many areas of the front, the French second trench had not been under German observation and had, therefore, been largely spared German preparatory fire.[45]

For the next day's assault, German observers moved forward to direct the artillery fire, and after several hours of bombardment, the infantry of the attack corps advanced again. The VII Reserve Corps once more had great success, seizing the village of Haumont and outflanking the French

41 *Les Armées Françaises*, IV/1, pp. 216–221; Alistair Horne, *The Price of Glory: Verdun 1916* (London: Penguin Books, 1993; originally published 1962), pp. 70–76; Ian Ousby, *The Road to Verdun: France, Nationalism and the First World War* (London: Jonathan Cape, 2002), pp. 64–75.

42 AOK 5, "Gefechtsberichte I," 21 February 1916.

43 Zwehl, *Maubeuge – Aisne – Verdun*, pp. 151–155.

44 Kronprinz Wilhelm, *Erinnerungen*, p. 174.

45 AOK 5, "Gefechtsberichte I," 21 February 1916; *Der Weltkrieg*, X, pp. 72–74.

position in Bois des Caures.[46] This enabled the XVIII Corps finally to take the French first and second positions there. The III Corps was able to advance through the French second position in the Bois de Ville. For the first time during the offensive, French artillery fire from behind the Côte de Marre on the west bank of the Meuse hindered the German advance. German counter-battery fire, including a gas attack, was unsuccessful in silencing these batteries.[47]

The offensive's third day, 23 February, proceeded similarly to the first two days. The corps attacked after several hours of artillery preparation and after hard fighting seized the next French defensive position. By the end of the day, the attack's right flank had reached the Meuse at Brabant. On the left flank, the III Corps cleared the rest of the French from Herbebois and, in the center, the XVIII Corps captured the remaining trenches of the French second line. Once again, fire from the French batteries on the river's west bank caused considerable casualties amongst the attacking troops.[48] By the day's end, however, the entire French first defensive position was in German hands. By nightfall, the 5th Army ordered the first artillery displacement to take place.[49]

For the next several days, the Germans repeated their performance, with a few notable successes, particularly the capture of Fort Douaumont on 25 February.[50] By 27 February, the attack corps had generally reached their initial objectives. However, progress was now much slower and was costing many more casualties. At this point, it was clear that the French had decided to hold the heights and the right bank of the Meuse. Increasingly, the 5th Army was met by powerful French counterattacks, supported by heavy artillery fire from the west bank.[51] The progress of the offensive was further hampered by the difficulty of moving the artillery forward through the crater-pitted no man's land.[52] The 5th Army also maintained that the offensive strength of its attack corps was temporarily spent.[53] On the 27th, the OHL was forced to admit that "the enemy has brought the offensive on the [Meuse] Heights temporarily to a halt," and the first phase of the operation at Verdun came to a close.[54]

46 Zwehl, *Maubeuge – Aisne – Verdun*, p. 154.
47 AOK 5, "Gefechtsberichte I," 22 February 1916; *Der Weltkrieg*, X, pp. 74–78; Tappen, "Kriegserinnerungen," p. 178.
48 Kronprinz Wilhelm, *Erinnerungen*, p. 175.
49 AOK 5, "Gefechtsberichte I," 23 February 1916; *Der Weltkrieg*, X, pp. 76–78.
50 On the unbelievable story of the fall of this important fort, see Horne, *Price of Glory*, pp. 105–124; Ousby, *Verdun*, pp. 84–93.
51 AOK 5, "Gefechtsberichte I," 27 February 1916.
52 Kronprinz Wilhelm, *Erinnerungen*, p. 179.
53 Ibid., p. 177; *Der Weltkrieg*, X, p. 84.
54 OHL, "Kriegstagebuch," 27 February 1916, quoted in *Der Weltkrieg*, X, p. 100; Falkenhayn, *General Headquarters*, pp. 233–234. Cf. Wendt, *Verdun*, pp. 93ff.

The measures taken by the OHL and the tactics employed by the 5th Army allowed the offensive to produce significant results in its first phase. Although by 21 February the French had come to expect a German offensive at Verdun, they did not believe this would be the main German undertaking. The reinforcement that had arrived by the start of the offensive was by no means sufficient to halt the initial German advance. Further, the 5th Army's use of heavy artillery had allowed them to blast their way through the French defensive positions with little difficulty. As a consequence, by 27 February, the 5th Army had captured 216 officers, 14,534 men, 45 artillery pieces, including 17 heavy pieces, and 54 machine-guns.[55] All told, the French had lost 24,000 men by 26 February.[56] Additionally, they had advanced 3 kilometers forward over a 10 km front. The cost to the 5th Army, though, was not inconsiderable – around 25,000.[57]

However, despite these notable successes, the 5th Army had been unable to reach their goal of capturing the Meuse heights. The capture of these dominating hills was essential to the objective of "bleeding white" the French army while minimizing German casualties. So long as the French held these positions, they would be able to direct accurate artillery fire down upon the German troops and inflict high casualties upon the attackers.

The French response

The German assault had severely shaken the French defenders. The 72nd and 51st Reserve Divisions of the XXX Corps were all but destroyed,[58] and on 24 February, the commander of the *région fortifiée de Verdun*, General Georges Herr, issued orders to begin the evacuation of the right bank. His decision was initially supported by Marshal Joseph Joffre who believed that Verdun was not essential for the defense of France and, therefore, not worth holding. However, Aristide Briand overruled the French commander in his decision. The French Prime Minister had hurried to Joffre's headquarters when he learned of the German attack. Fearing the political consequences of losing the fortress, he ordered Joffre to hold Verdun. After much debate, the decision was made that, with

55 AOK 5, "Gefechtsberichte I," 27 February 1916.

56 Wendt, *Verdun*, p. 243.

57 Ernst Kabisch, *Verdun: Wende des Weltkrieges* (Berlin: Vorhut-Verlag Otto Schlegel, 1935), p. 108.

58 The 51st Reserve Division had lost 62 percent of its officers and 61 percent of its men in only four days of fighting. Wendt, *Verdun*, p. 74.

reinforcement, the right bank could indeed be held, and Herr's evacuation order was countermanded.[59] Joffre's new order read: "The Meuse must be held on the right bank. There can be no question of any other course than that of checking the enemy, cost what it may, on that bank."[60] General Philippe Pétain's 2nd Army, the immediate French reserve, was dispatched to the fortress with the orders to hold at all costs.[61] Going further than Castelnau, Pétain's first order after taking command at Verdun had an offensive component. He ordered: "Beat off at all costs the attacks of the enemy, and *retake immediately any piece of land taken by him*."[62]

Upon arriving in Verdun, Pétain began bringing in reserves and reorganizing the sector for defense. The first reinforcements, units of the XX Army Corps, began arriving in Verdun during the night of 24/25 February and were immediately deployed. The units of the 2nd Army began arriving shortly thereafter. By the 26th, there were nine French corps either deployed in the Verdun sector or on their way there.[63] Pétain ordered new positions to be constructed behind the front lines and the forts to be rearmed. Crucially, the ability of the defenders to continue to resist was ensured by the creation of a supply line which ran along a secondary road from Bar-le-Duc – what would become known as the "Sacred Way." From 27 February to 6 March, over 190,000 troops and 23,000 tons of munitions were brought along this route in to Verdun.[64]

Most importantly, however, Pétain took a special interest in reorganizing the French artillery. First, he ordered that the artillery be used aggressively and offensively to give the French infantry the impression the Germans did not dominate the battlefield.[65] This order had another, perhaps more significant, effect. It hit the Germans when they were at their most vulnerable – during the attack. Crossing no man's land to assault the French positions, the German troops were highly vulnerable to the fire of the French 75s, the French army's most numerous artillery piece, and Pétain's order ensured they were used to the utmost effect. Moreover, Pétain centralized the command over the French batteries, and the heavy artillery was deployed behind the hills of the west bank to

[59] Jere Clemens King, *Generals and Politicians: Conflict Between France's High Command, Parliament, and Government, 1914–1918* (Los Angeles: University of California Press, 1951), pp. 97–100. Cf. Horne, *Price of Glory*, pp. 126–131; Ousby, *Verdun*, pp. 94–96.

[60] Quoted in Pétain, *Verdun*, p. 76.

[61] *Les Armées Françaises*, IV/1, pp. 295–296; F. W. Prüter, "Der 24. Februar 1916 von Verdun von französischer Seite gesehen," *Wissen und Wehr* (1933), pp. 1–17.

[62] Quoted in Richard Griffiths, *Marshal Pétain* (London: Constable, 1970), p. 23. Emphasis added.

[63] Wendt, *Verdun*, p. 87. [64] Pétain, *Verdun*, p. 111; Ousby, *Verdun*, pp. 98–99.

[65] *Les Armées Françaises*, IV/1, p. 322.

Fig. 14 Philippe Pétain (center), commander of the French forces at Verdun

enfilade the Germans on the right.[66] With their good observation positions on the heights of both banks, the French artillery was now able to do great damage to the German assault troops.

By resolving to hold the right bank of the Meuse regardless of casualties, the French had taken a decisive step. They created a symbol that could not be voluntarily surrendered without doing great damage to French morale. Across the board, French soldiers and politicians now stressed the importance of holding Verdun. The Minister of War, General Joseph Galliéni, announced on 2 March: "The enemy may go on with his efforts. But the French nation, serene and confident, feels sure that our army is confronting him with a barrier that cannot be overthrown."[67] The theme was picked up by others in the GQG and by the government. A steady stream of visitors called on Pétain's headquarters, including President Raymond Poincaré.[68] Falkenhayn had indeed found an object for which the GQG was "compelled to throw in every man they have." However, not only was Verdun, the "moral bulwark of France,"[69] to be held at any

66 Ibid., pp. 320f.; Pétain, *Verdun*, pp. 101–102; Stephen Ryan, *Pétain the Soldier* (London: Thomas Yoseloff, 1969), p. 90.
67 Quoted in Pétain, *Verdun*, p. 112.
68 Blond, *Verdun*, pp. 131–132.
69 Pétain, *Verdun*, p. 15.

price, but any lost terrain was to be retaken by counterattack. The French had fallen headlong into Falkenhayn's trap.

Attack on the west bank

The slowdown of the offensive brought renewed calls from the 5th Army for further troops and artillery. Prior to the offensive, Falkenhayn had believed that the French artillery on the west bank could be suppressed by German counter-battery fire. However, this failed to be the case, even after the 5th Army created a special artillery task force to accomplish this mission.[70] Fire coming from the French batteries on the west bank continued to cause severe casualties and hamper the progress of the offensive. On 24 and 26 February, the 5th Army requested additional forces to expand the assault to the west bank. The General Staff Chief refused, remarking to Tappen that "due to the rapid advance on the east bank, we do not need to give [the 5th Army] additional forces."[71] He believed that the heights on the east bank would be captured soon and that the 5th Army would then be able to take the west bank with the forces at its disposal. Further, expanding the attack at Verdun did not fit into Falkenhayn's overall strategy for 1916. He reported to the 5th Army: "The point is not only to strike the French army but to destroy it. That will certainly occur when the Germans attack at another point after the French have brought together powerful forces at Verdun."[72] Sufficient reserves needed to be maintained to carry out this second phase. The 5th Army was so concerned about the flanking fire from the west, however, that an abortive attack was made by the VI Reserve Corps to take the French positions by a *coup de main*.[73]

Clearly, until 27 February when the first standstill in the offensive took place, Falkenhayn was satisfied with its results. To this date, the 5th Army had achieved its initial goals and looked likely to be able to take the Meuse Heights without reinforcement. However, once it became clear that the French had determined to hold the right bank at all costs and that the 5th Army could not seize rapidly the crucial heights, the General Staff Chief began to have doubts about the attack. He later wrote of this time: "the question that had to be considered by the GHQ was whether to intimate that the continuance of the operation on the Meuse would be abandoned, and a new enterprise started on another front."[74] The 6th

70 *Der Weltkrieg*, X, p. 93. 71 Tappen, "Kriegstagebuch," 26 February.

72 Heymann to Reichsarchiv, quoted in *Der Weltkrieg*, X, p. 277.

73 AOK 5, "Gefechtsberichte I," 27 February 1916; "Angriff auf dem Westufer," pp. 36–39; *Der Weltkrieg*, X, pp. 206f.

74 Falkenhayn, *General Headquarters*, p. 235; Tappen, "Kriegserinnerungen," p. 178.

Army had already sent the OHL a memorandum on a breakthrough operation in its sector,[75] and in early March, Falkenhayn began to receive plans for an offensive from the other armies of the *Westheer*.[76]

Despite his doubts, Falkenhayn was convinced by Knobelsdorf on 29 February to release two additional divisions to expand the offensive to the west bank. Knobelsdorf assured the General Staff Chief that when the western Meuse Heights were taken, the offensive on the east bank could be resumed and the ultimate goal, the heights on the east bank, reached.[77] Additionally, Falkenhayn's goal of destroying the French reserves had not yet been reached by the end of February. Although the French had sent substantial reinforcements to Verdun, they still maintained a considerable reserve. The Intelligence Section of the OHL reported that the French had deployed fifteen to eighteen divisions to the Verdun sector by the end of February. This, however, still left them with six or nine divisions in immediate reserve plus the fifteen divisions which would be freed by the British relief of the 10th Army.[78] A resumption of the offensive would cause the French to send in additional reinforcement and to launch further counterattacks.[79] Falkenhayn and Knobelsdorf agreed that the VI Reserve Corps, strengthened by the X Reserve Corps, should seize the line south of Avocourt–Côte 304 (north of Esnes)–"Mort Homme"–Bois de Cumières–Côte 265,[80] from which they believed it would be possible to destroy the French artillery on the west bank and allow the attack on the east to proceed.[81]

The assault on the west bank was meant to progress much like the previous attacks on the east bank. The infantry assault would follow a powerful artillery bombardment designed to destroy the first French defensive positions and to neutralize the French artillery. To accomplish this, the organic artillery of General der Infanterie Heinrich von Gossler's two-corps strong assault group was reinforced by twenty-five heavy artillery batteries. As during the attack on the east bank, the group's artillery was centralized under the command of one officer. The group was to be further supported by fire from the German heavy batteries on the east bank

75 AOK 6, "Der Durchbruch," Nr. 41494, 26 February, BA/MA, W10/51520.

76 *Der Weltkrieg*, X, pp. 279–283. See Chapter 10 below.

77 The 11th Bavarian Division and the 22nd Reserve Division under the X Reserve Corps and twenty-one heavy batteries were transferred from the OHL reserve to the 5th Army. "Angriff auf dem Westufer," p. 46; AOK 5, "Gefechtsberichte I," 29 February 1916.

78 "Die Beurteilung der Kampfkraft der französischen Armee durch die deutsche OHL zwischen 1.1 und 29.8.16," BA/MA, W10/51521, pp. 26–30; *Der Weltkrieg*, X, p. 286.

79 Falkenhayn, *General Headquarters*, p. 237.

80 Two hills close together, Côte 285 and Côte 285.9, together made up the "Mort Homme." See Horne, *Price of Glory*, p. 156.

81 Luckwald to Bethmann, 15 March 1916 (copied from *Reichskanzlei. Weltkrieg 15/1*) BA/MA, W10/51543.

and by a crossing of the Meuse by a brigade of the VII Reserve Corps.[82] Given the limited artillery, Gossler determined to split his attack into two separate phases. The first, scheduled to begin on 6 March, would take the eastern portion of the attack's goals ("Mort Homme" and Côte 265), while the second would follow on 9 March and take Avocourt and Côte 304.[83]

At 08:00a.m. on 6 March, the artillery of Gossler's attack group began its preparatory fire, and at 11:50, the infantry began their assault. Once again the heavy artillery bombardment had done its task. Communications between the French front line and the rear were cut and the defenders were severely shaken.[84] Quickly the German assault troops overran the first French positions. However, the attack soon began to falter under heavy French fire and determined French resistance. The VII Reserve Corps' brigade became bogged down in fighting in Regnéville and was unable to support the assault on Côte 265.[85] Consequently, this attack also became stuck, and only after repeated, costly assaults was the hill taken at 6:00p.m.[86] Despite some successes, the right wing of the attack also failed to take its objective for the day, "Mort Homme."

Over the next week, Gossler's attack group tried to take "Mort Homme," but met with only slow progress. Despite powerful artillery preparation and good artillery support during the battle, the infantry was able to take its objectives only with great casualties and after repeated assaults. In several places German advances were thrown back by French counterattacks, and, as the battle went on, Gossler was forced to keep two-thirds of his force in reserve to meet these counterattacks.[87] The advance of the German infantry was further hampered by French artillery fire, which tore into their ranks while they formed for an assault as well as during the attack itself. Finally, on 14 March, the group was able to take the northern-most hilltop of "Mort Homme" and hold it against violent French counterattacks.[88] The summit, however, remained in French hands, and would do so until late May.[89]

[82] Gossler, Ia Nr. 380, 3 March 1916, BA/MA, W10/51526.
[83] Ibid., paragraphs 6–8; "Angriff auf dem Westufer," pp. 49–50.
[84] Horne, *Price of Glory*, p. 157.
[85] Despite Horne's assertion that the German attack went as planned on this day, the Reichsarchiv wrote that the "unity of the attack collapsed" when the brigade of the VII Reserve Corps became bogged down in Regnéville. Horne, *Price of Glory*, p. 157; "Angriff auf dem Westufer," p. 58.
[86] "Gefechtsberichte I," 6 March 1916.
[87] "Gefechtsberichte I," 8 March and 10 March 1916.
[88] *Der Weltkrieg*, X, pp. 212–213.
[89] For a recent overview of this costly offensive, see Markus Klauer, *Die Höhe Toter Mann während der Kämpfe um Verdun in den Jahren 1916/1917* (Velbert: Gesellschaft für Druck und Veredelung, 2001).

After more than a week of hard fighting, Gossler's group had finally reached the objectives of the first phase of his attack.[90] However, even this did not bring relief for the German troops on the east bank. French artillery fire from behind the Côte de Marre and Bois Bourrus still ranged over the German positions, causing severe casualties. The artillery brought up to Côte 265 by the Germans to combat the French artillery was itself taken under heavy, systematic fire.[91] It was clear to the German leadership that Côte 304, the objective of Gossler's second phase, would now have to be taken to ensure the safety of the German gains so far and to combat effectively the French artillery on the west bank.[92]

Gossler's attack group began the second phase of its offensive on 20 March. After another heavy barrage, which included a special bombardment of over 13,000 trench mortar rounds, the 11th Bavarian Division and the 11th Reserve Division attacked the French positions south of Malancourt and in the Bois d'Avocourt.[93] Once again, the German troops reached their initial goals with little difficulty. Rather than continue the attack immediately, Gossler's group paused to consolidate their new positions and to prepare another heavy barrage for the next day's assault. On 22 March, the two divisions advanced against the French positions on "Termite Hill," a key position on the way to the summit of Côte 304. They were met with a hail of artillery and machine-gun fire. The French also took the German assembly points and lines of communication under heavy artillery fire. The combination brought the German advance to an immediate halt.[94] Although some small gains were made during the day, the cost to the Germans was high, and the positions they reached remained under such heavy French fire that they were able to dig in only with great difficulty.[95]

By 30 March, Gossler's attack group had still not taken Côte 304, despite losing around 20,000 men.[96] On this day, the XXII Reserve Corps was brought in as reinforcement and General der Artillerie Max von Gallwitz was given command over the newly created *Angriffsgruppe West*. This reorganization and reinforcement, however, did little to improve the situation and Côte 304 was not to fall until May.

90 The three divisions of Gossler's attack group lost nearly 10,000 men between 6 and 20 March. *Der Weltkrieg*, X, p. 213.

91 Ibid.

92 AOK 5, "Gefechtsberichte für die Zeit vom 15.3.16–3.4.16," 18 March 1916, BA/MA, W10/51583 (hereafter, "Gefechtsberichte II").

93 *Der Weltkrieg*, X, p. 215.

94 Ludwig Gold, *Die Tragödie von Verdun 1916*, Teil III: *Toter Mann – Höhe 304* (*Schlachten des Weltkrieges*, Bd. 15) (Oldenburg: Gerhard Stalling, 1935), pp. 28–36.

95 "Gefechtsberichte II," 22 March 1916.

96 *Der Weltkrieg*, X, p. 221.

The attacks on the west bank in March show clearly how the conditions on the battlefield had changed since the offensive's beginning on 21 February. The Germans had lost the advantage of surprise and were now attacking a determined, well-supplied enemy in strong defensive positions. Although the German artillery was still superior to the French and could annihilate the French forward positions when need be, the attacking German infantry suffered severe casualties from French counter-fire aimed at both the assaulting infantry and at their rearward communications. Forward progress could only be achieved after intense preparation and was often repulsed by French counterattacks. When the Germans could hold the positions they had seized, the French artillery caused continued losses.

The attack on the west bank showed another important characteristic of the offensive. When a "key" position, such as "Mort Homme" or Fort Douaumont, was captured, often another terrain feature had to be taken to ensure its retention. Even if the attrition of the French army had not been the goal of the German leadership, this characteristic ensured that the battle would be almost continuous until a safe defensive position could be reached.[97]

Standstill and doubts

The attacks on the west bank had not achieved their goal of allowing the advance on the east bank to proceed, and by the end of March progress at Verdun had once more come to a standstill. Additionally, the offensive had cost the Germans dearly. From the offensive's start until the end of March, the Germans had suffered 81,607 casualties.[98] Falkenhayn again questioned how the campaign should be continued, fearing that the offensive might come to be another Ypres.[99] On 27 March, Wild recorded in his diary: "At Verdun it goes slowly – unfortunately! To Falkenhayn's earnest question whether the operation should be stopped, I answered no . . . *France* must be tapped of much more blood . . ."[100] The General Staff Chief's unease with the course of the operation caused another sharp exchange with the 5th Army, who wanted additional forces to continue the offensive.

[97] Afflerbach, *Falkenhayn*, p. 370.

[98] Wendt, *Verdun*, p. 243. Wendt used the now-lost OHL files to calculate German casualties through the battle.

[99] Afflerbach, *Falkenhayn*, p. 371.

[100] Wild, "Kriegstagebuch," 27 March 1916. Emphasis in original. See also Tappen, "Kriegserinnerungen," p. 179.

On 31 March, the 5th Army answered Falkenhayn's request for justification for further reinforcement.[101] The 5th Army clearly had a much more positive view of the situation at this stage than did the General Staff Chief. Their letter indicated that they believed the offensive had brought the French army to the brink of exhaustion, and that the French were no longer capable of large-scale offensives. This made them conclude that "the fate of the French army will be decided *at Verdun*," and that the "annihilation of the trained French reserve as well as the reserve of material and munitions should be completed with all possible speed." The 5th Army wanted to continue the attack on the east bank until it had reached at least the line Ouvrage de Thiaumont–Fleury–Fort Souville–Fort de Tavannes. On the west bank, they wanted to allow the "enemy reserves to destroy themselves over the course of time through violent counterattacks."[102] Clearly, the initially reluctant command of the 5th Army had accepted Falkenhayn's goal of "bleeding the French army white" completely.[103]

Despite the 5th Army's conversion to Falkenhayn's idea of attrition, the General Staff Chief did not agree with much of their letter. On 4 April, he wrote back to correct some of the 5th Army's misconceptions, advising them that they both underestimated French strength and overestimated German resources. He reckoned that the French still possessed considerable reserves.[104] As for German strength, he wrote: "The assumption that we are in the position to relieve the worn-out units with fresh, high-quality units at any time and that we are able to provide a continuous replacement of material and munitions is false." The resumption of the offensive on the east bank was impending. If this assault were unsuccessful, Falkenhayn requested that the 5th Army confer with the commanders of its units and advise the OHL whether a continuation of the offensive was worthwhile and, if so, to recommend how it should proceed. The General Staff Chief recognized clearly that if the offensive were broken off without taking the Meuse Heights, it would be considered a failure, but was willing to accept this price if the 5th Army believed the offensive had reached the end of its progress.[105]

The offensive of early April was not a success, and in the middle of the month, Knobelsdorf collected reports from the attacking corps over the

101 Falkenhayn to AOK 5, Nr. 5937 op., 30 March 1916, BA/MA, W10/51553.

102 AOK 5 to OHL, Nr. 848g., 31 March 1916, BA/MA, W10/51584.

103 In his memoirs, Crown Prince Wilhelm distanced himself from this position, writing that it was only Knobelsdorf who was now an adherent to the idea of the "Maasmühle." Kronprinz Wilhelm, *Erinnerungen*, pp. 186–189. See also Wendt, *Verdun*, pp. 119–120.

104 The General Staff Chief believed the French to possess up to thirteen divisions in reserve, in addition to fourteen British divisions. See his comments to AOK 5 Nr. 848.

105 Falkenhayn to AOK 5, Nr. 26159, 4 April 1916, BA/MA, W10/51584.

prospects of the offensive. The commanders of the 5th Army's corps all spoke for a continuation of the offensive. They were unanimous that they could not remain in their current locations for several reasons. First, and most importantly, the infantry in the front line were exposed to withering fire in their current positions. General der Infanterie Bruno von Mudra, who had commanded the *Angriffsgruppe Ost*, spoke for all the units when he wrote:

> The attacking infantry is exposed to continuous fire from heavy and field artillery, at times coming from their flanks, at times from their rear. The rearward communications, the rest positions, and even the reserves are similarly exposed to enemy fire of all calibers.
>
> Therefore, the infantry suffers heavy losses daily in the forward positions, and does not suffer any less in the lines of communication and in the rest positions. The bringing forward of supplies and necessary replacements requires an inordinate amount of time and effort.[106]

The construction of suitable defensive positions was difficult, as the infantry of the German attack corps stood exposed in land which had been swept clean by the German artillery fire and was now exposed to continuous French fire. Further advance was imperative to push the French from the high ground above the German positions and ensure the retention of the offensive's gains so far.[107]

A second reason given for the continuation of the offensive was psychological. General der Infanterie Berthold von Deimling, commander of the XV Army Corps, wrote: "Enduring passively the fire of the French heavy artillery and gas rounds, without being able to move forward themselves, places great demands on the moral strength of the infantry."[108] The commanders and staffs of the units involved in the offensive clearly felt that progress was needed to sustain the morale of their troops.

Knobelsdorf presented Falkenhayn with the reports of the attack corps on 20 April. As a further inducement, he told the General Staff Chief that, if the offensive did not go forward, it would have to go back. He did not believe they could stay in their current position, so a withdrawal to the offensive's start line would be necessary if they did not make further progress. Rejecting Mudra's approach of advances by individual divisions

106 Mudra to AOK 5, Nr. 480 pers., 21 April 1916, BA/MA, W10/51583. Mudra commanded the *Angriffsgruppe Ost* from 19 March to 15 April, when he was replaced by Lochow. *Der Weltkrieg*, X, p. 146.

107 VII RK to AOK 5, "Absichten des VII.RK," Ia 29/IV g., 18 April 1916; Angriffsgruppe Ost to AOK 5, Ia Nr. 350 geh., 18 April 1916, BA/MA, W10/51583.

108 Deimling to Falkenhayn, Ia. Nr. 285 geh., 19 April 1916, BA/MA, W10/51583. See also, Berthold von Deimling, *Aus der alten in die neue Zeit* (Berlin: Verlag Ullstein, 1930), pp. 208–211.

in "attacks with limited objectives," Knobelsdorf pressed for a resumption of the offensive on a large scale, i.e., a simultaneous attack by all the units in a given sector. In this way, he still hoped to make considerable progress and reach the line Ouvrage de Thiaumont–Fleury–Fort Souville–Fort de Tavannes rapidly.[109] In the end, Falkenhayn was swayed by the opinions of the 5th Army's staff and its corps commanders and decided to continue the offensive along the lines proposed by the 5th Army's chief.

From this decision on, there was no turning back on the offensive. By the end of April, twenty-one German divisions, most of the OHL reserve, were engaged in the Verdun sector, and additional units had been brought in from the Eastern Front.[110] At the offensive's beginning, the capture of Verdun had not been Falkenhayn's goal. From May, however, the expenditure of blood and the value placed on the fortress by the French nation meant that anything less than its capture would be considered a failure by Germans and enemies alike. Indeed, the Kaiser had announced on 1 April: "The decision of the War of 1870 took place in Paris. This war will end at Verdun."[111] What had been only the first phase of Falkenhayn's strategy in 1916, now came to be the decisive element. German prestige, as well as Falkenhayn's personal reputation, was now closely bound to the success or failure of the offensive.[112]

From the end of April, the offensive would suck in more and more German units and result in severe German casualties. Knobelsdorf's approach of large-scale, all-out assaults replaced Mudra's approach of attacks with limited objectives. Moreover, by April the nature of the battle had changed. German troops now attacked a strong enemy in solid defensive positions. Progress could only be made slowly and at great cost. This brought about a shift in where the attrition of the French army was to occur. While the original idea had been for the *Verblutung* of the French to come from their attacks against secure German defensive positions, after the initial successes in February the attrition was carried out instead by German attacks and French local counter-thrusts. Despite this shift in approach, Falkenhayn, who believed that German troops

109 AOK 5 to OHL, Ia Nr. 995 geh., 20 April 1916, BA/MA, W10/51583.

110 *Der Weltkrieg*, X, p. 298. Eight divisions were left in the OHL reserve, but all of the OHL's artillery reserve was engaged at Verdun.

111 Horne, *Price of Glory*, p. 165.

112 Already by the end of March, the army's leaders had begun questioning the wisdom of the offensive, and Kuhl had made the observation: "Now the whole thing has become a mighty trial at Verdun, a question of prestige." Kuhl, "Kriegstagebuch," 27 March 1916. See also, Rupprecht, *Kriegstagebuch*, I, p. 439 (diary entry for 20 March 1916); Einem to his wife, 25 March 1916, BA/MA, N324/52; Jehuda Wallach, *The Dogma of the Battle of Annihilation: The Theories of Clausewitz and Schlieffen and Their Impact on the German Conduct of Two World Wars* (Westport, CT: Greenwood Press, 1986), p. 173; Otto, "Verdun," p. 412.

attacked more effectively than French, still felt the gruesome task could be accomplished. Even though the German units were suffering horribly, the General Staff Chief maintained that the French were suffering more; "for two Germans put out of action five Frenchmen had to shed their blood."[113] This shift in the method of attrition focused attention on tactics.

Tactics

As we have seen, before the offensive had begun Falkenhayn had rejected the use of "mass tactics" to attempt a breakthrough on the Western Front. Instead, he chose to deploy a relatively small number of troops backed by a powerful artillery force. The artillery rather than the infantry was to be the main striking arm. Generally, the tactics employed by the attack corps in their initial assaults reflected this idea. The assaulting infantry "hugged" the artillery bombardment, advancing to within a short distance of the falling shells.[114] In this way, they were able to rush the French positions as soon as the artillery shifted their fire to more distant targets. To reduce further the time the advancing infantry was exposed to possible enemy defensive fire, patrols went forward and cleared and marked lanes of advance through the French wire.[115] Further, German long-range artillery was largely successful in isolating the foremost French positions from the rear, making reinforcement almost impossible. These tactics were successful at keeping the German casualties to a minimum while maximizing the enemy's losses.

However, already at the offensive's beginning, Knobelsdorf's concept of how the attack was to be conducted vied with Falkenhayn's tactical ideas. The 5th Army's attack order of 27 January had allowed the commanders of the attack corps to choose for themselves how they would conduct their battle. The order allowed for either a procedure along the lines of Falkenhayn's ideas or for an attack along the 5th Army's concept of a rapid assault carried out with all possible strength. Consequently, the General Staff Chief's principles were sometimes ignored by the attacking troops. For instance, already on the third day of the offensive, the 6th

113 Falkenhayn, *General Headquarters*, p. 237; General Schjerning made a similar observation to Grünau, saying that the French suffered two and a half to three casualties for every German. Grünau to Bethmann, 29 March 1916 (copied from *Reichskanzlei. Kriegsakten 1/6*) BA/MA, W10/51543.

114 See Brandis, *Sturmangriff*, p. 8; Gudmundsson, *On Artillery*, p. 60.

115 "Die deutsche Taktik bei Verdun," *Militär-Wochenblatt* 66–67 (1916), pp. 1610–1612. This unsigned article also ridicules French reports that Germans were using "infiltration tactics" at Verdun.

Division of the III Corps ordered its troops to attack and take the Herbebois "regardless of casualties." On the same day, the III Corps' other division, the 5th, sent its troops into the attack on Wavrille with its band playing "Prussia's Glory" and "Yorck's March."[116] The Reichsarchiv's work on the battle recalled the bloody assault by the Prussian Guards during the Franco-Prussian War by naming the attack by the 5th Division's neighbor on Wavrille a "St. Privat assault."[117] Increasingly, the units of the 5th Army followed Knobelsdorf's concept rather than Falkenhayn's, especially as new units were drafted in to continue the offensive.

Disturbed by the growing losses and the disregard for the original tactical ideas, Falkenhayn issued a memorandum to the units of the 5th Army in mid-March in an effort to convince them to employ tactics which limited German casualties as far as possible.[118] Drawing on the experience of the battle so far, the General Staff Chief advocated the increased use of "storm units," or *Stoßtruppe*, over the traditional attack waves used by many units. These *Stoßtruppe* were to be made up of one or two squads of select infantry with a combat engineering squad under the command of a company commander.[119] They were to be liberally armed with automatic weapons and hand grenades and, if needed, with trench mortars or flame throwers. Using terrain to mask their advance, these special units were to precede the main body of the attacking infantry and reduce enemy strongpoints that could not be neutralized by artillery fire, thus facilitating the advance of the main body.[120] In another departure from traditional practice, the main body of the infantry was to advance through the enemy positions, leaving strongpoints and pockets of resistance to be reduced by following troops.

Falkenhayn also had much to say about artillery. In general, he wrote, "the psychological effect of the heavy artillery is very great." However, while the field artillery worked very well with the infantry, the foot artillery did not do so well. He recommended better links between the two arms, advising that "mixed battle groups of heavy and field artillery under the direction of a single commander and, as far as possible, with common observers and communication with the infantry is more effective than the two operating on their own." The General Staff Chief also stressed

[116] Kabisch, *Verdun*, pp. 70–71.

[117] Gold, *Verdun*, I, pp. 111–114; Horne, *Price of Glory*, p. 96.

[118] Erich von Falkenhayn, "Einige Erfahrungen aus den Kämpfen im Maasgebiet," Nr. 27956 op., 15 March 1916, BA/MA, W10/51534.

[119] Falkenhayn cautioned against using combat engineers in infantry roles; they were specialist troops to be used for clearing obstacles, strongpoints, etc.

[120] For the impact of Verdun on the development of "stormtroop tactics" see Gudmundsson, *Stormtroop Tactics*, pp. 55–75; Gruss, *Aufbau und Verwendung*, pp. 28–35.

Fig. 15 The assault at Verdun would force the Germans to develop new tactics, including early stormtroop tactics

the importance of concentrating widely dispersed artillery batteries on specific targets. To facilitate this, he wrote that the artillery should be controlled by an officer in the corps headquarters, who was only to release special artillery battle groups to the divisions on a task-by-task basis.[121]

As the battle continued, Falkenhayn issued other memoranda along similar lines. In mid-April, he again returned to the concept of close infantry/artillery cooperation and advised that the infantry advance as close as possible behind the artillery bombardment:

> they press into the trenches of the enemy almost at the same time as the last impact of the covering [artillery] fire. If this results in losses from our own fire, these will be accepted as they cannot be compared with those suffered by attackers who would delay their assault.[122]

While the General Staff Chief acknowledged that this procedure was not new, he felt once again the evidence of the offensive to date had shown

[121] These methods presaged those that would be used by the Germans effectively in the March 1918 offensives. See David Zabecki, *Steel Wind: Colonel Georg Bruchmüller and the Birth of Modern Artillery* (Westport, CT: Praeger, 1994).

[122] Falkenhayn, "Entwurf," Nr. 26648 op., 14 April 1916, W10/50705.

that not all units had understood the concept completely, and that it was necessary to stress its importance to the units of the 5th Army.

Once again, however, Falkenhayn's efforts to reintroduce tactics that would keep German casualties to a minimum were undermined by Knobelsdorf, who rejected the step-by-step advance implicit in the General Staff Chief's tactics. Instead, as the battle continued, Knobelsdorf continually pushed his subordinates to maintain the momentum of any assault; in essence, to attack without regard for casualties. Commanders who disagreed with his view point, such as Mudra, were sacked.[123] This approach further exacerbated German casualties.

In another effort to keep German casualties to a minimum, Falkenhayn also tried to influence German defensive tactics. As the German front line was clearly visible to French observers, it could be taken under accurate artillery fire. Therefore, the General Staff Chief advised the front line formations to thin out their first line. Instead, they were to concentrate the main defense on the second line. There, the defensive position was to become more responsive to French attacks. Machine guns were to be set up with interlocking fields of fire. Each man was to know his position during an attack and was to have a specific zone of the battlefield to cover. From the second line, immediate counterattacks were to be launched to re-take the first line if it fell to the enemy. Falkenhayn also drew upon the German experience of French fire to outline the use of artillery in the defense. At the first signs of an attack, German artillery was to begin bombarding French trenches and assembly points. At the onset of an attack, the artillery was to cut off the attacking infantry from behind with a barrage [*Sperrfeuer*], which was to be prepared beforehand.[124] Falkenhayn hoped in this way to inflict the greatest possible number of casualties on the French during their frequent counterattacks.

However, the General Staff Chief's efforts to reduce casualties by better defensive tactics were largely unsuccessful. As with the German attacks, casualties largely came from artillery fire, rather than infantry action. The exposed position of the German defenders kept them vulnerable to French fire, which was able to range over the first and second lines as well as the lines of communication easily. The report of the Chief of Staff of the X Reserve Corps on 13 May is typical of the situation: "The troops lie day and night under the *Trommelfeuer* of the enemy artillery. The average daily loss of the three divisions is 230 men. The construction of deeper

123 Heymann to Ernst Kabisch, 28 August 1935, BA/MA, W10/51523; Wendt, *Verdun*, p. 127.

124 OHL to all AOKs, Nr. 27793 op., 12 May 1916, BA/MA, W10/51584.

firing and communications trenches . . . has been continually frustrated by enemy artillery fire."[125]

In the end, Falkenhayn's efforts to reduce German casualties did not produce great results. In part, this was caused by the 5th Army's insistence that each attack be pressed home with all possible vigor. More importantly, the 5th Army's poor tactical position compelled them to attack under unfavorable conditions. Until the French could be prized from the commanding position on the Meuse Heights, the 5th Army would be subject to the effects of heavy French artillery fire and would go on losing large numbers of casualties. Forced to continue its assaults and unwilling to institute tactics which would limit casualties, the 5th Army ultimately faced the same attrition as their French enemy.

Conclusion

At the offensive's beginning, Falkenhayn had hoped his operational attrition would result in France losing quite rapidly its will to resist. This, however, did not happen. The very symbol that compelled France to expend so much life also provided a rallying point for the French nation. Instead of rapid results, Falkenhayn had increasingly to rely upon the effects of a steady hemorrhaging of the French army brought about by a near continuous German offensive. This shift demanded considerably more troops than Falkenhayn had envisioned at the offensive's beginning, and by the end of April, most of the OHL reserve was engaged at Verdun, suffering severe casualties themselves in their effort to wear down the enemy.

Although German casualties were high, the OHL could take solace in their belief that French casualties were much higher. Falkenhayn maintained that they were suffering five dead or wounded for every two Germans. On 11 March, he told Karl Georg von Treutler, the Foreign Office representative in the OHL, that the French had already suffered 100,000 casualties, the equivalent of a "strong army,"[126] and that if they did not surrender Verdun soon they would easily suffer a further 100,000 through the effects of the German artillery.[127] By May, the General Staff Chief believed that France had lost 525,000 to Germany's 250,000,[128]

[125] X. RK to AOK 5, 13 May 1916, quoted in Wendt, *Verdun*, p. 148.
[126] Karl Georg von Treutler to Gottlieb von Jagow, AS 926, 11 March 1916, PRO, GFM 34/2589 (*Weltkrieg geh.*, Bd. 28).
[127] Treutler to Bethmann, AS 969, 15 March 1916, PRO, GFM 34/2589 (*Weltkrieg geh.* Bd. 28a).
[128] Tappen, "Besprechung," p. 8.

and by the end of the month, he believed the French army was down to as little as 300,000 reserves.[129]

Despite the fact that the Germans were doing considerable damage to the French army, the French were not experiencing the number of casualties assumed by Falkenhayn. The policy instituted by Pétain ensured that the French army was able to withstand the punishment. Pétain had realized quite early that the battle would consume large numbers of French troops and, on 9 March, he requested from Joffre a steady supply of reserves. Joffre, afraid of not having enough troops to take part in the planned Anglo-French offensive on the Somme, initially refused Pétain's request. However, Pétain claimed that Verdun could not be held without a continuous flow of replacements. Joffre gave in, and Pétain instituted his policy of rapid rotation of units through the battle. If a division took more than 50 percent casualties, it was removed from the front line for rest and re-fit.[130] In this way, the French were able to deal with the frightful level of casualties inflicted by the Germans without the morale of the army breaking.

By the end of April, Falkenhayn had been stalemated by the French. The 5th Army's failure to capture their initial goal, the vitally important heights, had left them in a tactically unfavorable position and had forced them to continue the offensive at a disadvantage. This failure caused the nature of how the French army was to be "bled white" to be shifted to a much more costly approach, i.e., through continued German attacks and the French counterattacks these prompted, rather than through French counterattacks into strong German defensive positions. Further, the steps taken by Pétain had ensured that the French army would be able to survive the battering given by the Germans at Verdun. As the spring turned into summer, it looked as though the battle would drag on until the army of one side or the other cracked from the strain.[131] However, the stalemate was to be broken by the very element which Falkenhayn had hoped would ultimately result in the collapse of the Entente – a British relief offensive.

[129] Fritz von Loßberg, *Meine Tätigkeit im Weltkriege 1914–1918* (Berlin: E. S. Mittler, 1939), pp. 211–212; see also Kuhl, "Kriegstagebuch," 26 May 1916. Wild, as well, believed that "without a doubt, the French losses at Verdun [were] considerably higher" than the German. See Treutler to Jagow, 30 June 1916, PRO, GFM 34/2590 (*Weltkrieg geh.*, Bd.30). On the difficulties both sides had in calculating casualties, see Afflerbach, *Falkenhayn*, pp. 371–372.

[130] Griffiths, *Pétain*, pp. 25–26.

[131] Despite the generally good morale of the French, their army was experiencing great strain. In May, Auguste Terrier wrote to Marshal Louis Lyautey: "I have found, in many of our military leaders, the idea that Verdun has devoured the best forces in the army, notably those which we wanted to use in the common offensive . . . " Quoted in Griffiths, *Pétain*, p. 25.

10 Verdun: the failure

As Chapter 8 has shown, Falkenhayn's strategy for 1916 was divided into two phases: first, the assault on Verdun, which was to bind the French reserves in the Verdun salient where they would be relentlessly ground down and hopefully result in a French government more amenable to a negotiated settlement; second, a German counteroffensive to mop up the French and British armies after they had been bled white by their own relief offensives. Together, these two phases were to break apart the western alliance and pave the way for peace. Although the course of the battle at Verdun caused the General Staff Chief to alter slowly his strategic plan, he never completely gave up hope that the second phase could still be carried out. However, when the necessary precursor to Falkenhayn's counteroffensive, the long-awaited Entente relief offensive, finally did come, it broke with a ferocity that was entirely unexpected and produced completely unanticipated results.

Continued plans for Falkenhayn's second phase

While the 5th Army was engaged in wearing down the French reserves, Falkenhayn waited anxiously for an Entente relief offensive to fall elsewhere. Shortly after the beginning of the Verdun offensive, when it seemed likely that the 5th Army would quickly reach its initial goals, he began asking the armies of the *Westheer* for their assessments of the situation before their fronts and for plans for offensives.[1] These began arriving in early March.[2]

Of the many plans, Falkenhayn paid the closest attention to the 6th Army, where, as we have seen in Chapter 8, he thought the Entente relief offensive would most likely take place. Already on 27 February, the

[1] Erich von Falkenhayn, *General Headquarters and its Critical Decisions, 1914–1916* (London: Hutchinson, 1919), p. 235; Gerhard Tappen, "Meine Kriegserinnerungen," unpublished manuscript in BA/MA, W10/50661, p. 178.

[2] For their details, see Reichsarchiv, *Der Weltkrieg*, Bd. X: *Die Operationen des Jahres 1916* (Berlin: E. S. Mittler, 1936), pp. 279–281.

General Staff Chief had requested an assessment of the situation and plans for an offensive from the 6th Army.[3] They had replied the next day with a report already prepared by Hermann von Kuhl entitled "Der Durchbruch."[4] In this, Kuhl cogently outlined the difficulties and requirements of a breakthrough operation. However, given that Falkenhayn had previously rejected such a tactically ambitious plan and had ordered the 6th Army to prepare for an offensive using only limited forces, it is not clear what Kuhl's intentions were in sending this curious report. With the offensive at Verdun still under way, there was even less of a possibility that Falkenhayn would release the twenty-four divisions and numerous heavy artillery batteries needed for the 6th Army's plan. Quite possibly, Kuhl wanted to make Falkenhayn aware of the different opinion still held by the 6th Army regarding the possibility of any serious results coming from a counterattack following an Entente relief offensive.[5]

In the meantime, the assault on the heights along the right bank of the Meuse had come to a standstill as the French poured in reserves to hold their position. As Chapter 8 has shown, the OHL was forced to acquiesce to the 5th Army's requests for additional troops to expand the offensive to the heights on the left bank in order to restart the stalled offensive. With this attack underway, Falkenhayn visited the 6th Army to assess the situation there for himself on 8 March.[6] At this meeting, the 6th Army's command once more expressed their long-held doubts that the Entente would undertake an ill-prepared relief offensive, and they attempted to impress upon Falkenhayn the forces they thought necessary to conduct an operation which would "bring mobility once again to the front." Crown Prince Rupprecht and his chief of staff stated their belief that the front before the 6th Army was too thickly occupied by the enemy to achieve a meaningful result with the eight divisions promised by the OHL. Indeed, the ground they covered was so familiar that Kuhl was unclear why the General Staff Chief had made the visit. Their talk resulted in no clear decisions for the future. Falkenhayn declared that the OHL did not have the number of divisions requested by the 6th Army. Further, he expressed

[3] Kronprinz Rupprecht von Bayern, *Mein Kriegstagebuch* (ed. Eugen von Frauenholz) (3 vols.) (Berlin: E. S. Mittler, 1929), vol. I, p. 432 (diary entry for 27 February).

[4] AOK 6, "Der Durchbruch," Nr. 41494, 26 February 1916, BA/MA, W10/51520; Hermann von Kuhl, "Kriegstagebuch," 28 February 1916, BA/MA, W10/50652.

[5] Both Rupprecht and Kuhl still felt that a hasty relief offensive was unlikely. See Rupprecht, *Kriegstagebuch*, I, pp. 431–432 (diary entry for 23 February 1916); and Kuhl, "Kriegstagebuch," 3 March 1916.

[6] Gerhard Tappen, "Kriegstagebuch," 8 and 9 March 1916, BA/MA, Tappen Nachlass, N56/1.

Fig. 16 Crown Prince Rupprecht Bavaria (fourth from left), commander of the 6th Army, and his Chief of Staff, Hermann von Kuhl (seventh from left) with their staff

once again his doubts about the efficacy of a large-scale breakthrough attempt. At its conclusion, Kuhl recognized clearly the strategic dilemma facing Falkenhayn. Germany could not gather sufficient forces to achieve a breakthrough without making the other fronts dangerously weak. He was forced to ask, "how should we . . . win the war?"[7]

However, even after Falkenhayn's discouraging visit to Douai, the 6th Army continued to plan for an offensive using the eight divisions promised by the OHL. On 16 March, they sent another proposal to Mézières. The goal of this proposed offensive was the capture of Arras. As the British had just taken over this sector of the front from the French 10th Army, the 6th Army believed that the time was right for an offensive – the British reserve was at its lowest and they did not know their new positions well. If the city could be taken, the 6th Army believed it would make a great psychological impact upon the Entente.[8]

[7] Kuhl, "Kriegstagebuch," 8 March 1916; Rupprecht, *Kriegstagebuch*, I, pp. 435–436 (diary entry for 8 March 1916).

[8] AOK 6, "Angriff bei Arras," Ia Nr. 282g., 16 March 1916, BA/MA, W10/50705; reprinted in Rupprecht, *Kriegstagebuch*, III, pp. 82–84.

The 6th Army wanted to launch a two-pronged attack north and south of the city. Due to artillery limitations, this attack would have to take place in two parts. First, they hoped to seize the heights at Ecurie to the Scarpe. After this position was taken, the heavy artillery would be shifted to support an attack south of the city. The army would need at least twenty additional heavy batteries and munitions for a five-day battle, as well as the eight divisions from the OHL reserve. They believed they could be ready to launch the offensive in two to three weeks.[9]

On 19 March, Kuhl was ordered to Mézières for a meeting with Falkenhayn. The General Staff Chief ordered Kuhl to make all preparations for the attack on Arras. However, Falkenhayn told Kuhl that the 6th Army's attack would be dependent on the course of the offensive against Verdun. If things went well there, Falkenhayn promised thirty additional heavy batteries to the 6th Army, which would allow for the two-pronged attack to take place simultaneously.[10] So once again, the decision was postponed.

By the end of March, even Falkenhayn was forced to admit that an Entente relief offensive was not likely to come quickly and that the overall situation on the front would not permit a great German success resulting from the employment of limited forces.[11] Further, the operation at Verdun was drawing in more and more of the OHL's reserves, reducing the forces available for a second undertaking. The prospects of the second phase of Falkenhayn's strategy occurring began to fade into the background as the *Verblutung* of the enemy reserves looked likely to take longer than anticipated. Although as Chapter 8 has shown Falkenhayn clearly had his doubts about the action at Verdun, it was increasingly difficult for him to break off the offensive, especially as there was no prospect of success anywhere else. With an Entente relief offensive unlikely and great numbers of troops tied up in Verdun, the idea of a second offensive transformed into a secondary offensive with limited goals.

Thus, in early April, Falkenhayn revived the 6th Army's Arras attack plan. On 4 April, he telegraphed the 6th Army, asking them whether or not they would be prepared to launch their offensive. In the meantime, however, the OHL reserve had been depleted by the Verdun offensive and Falkenhayn inquired whether the offensive could be conducted with

[9] See Kuhl, "Kriegstagebuch," 16 March 1916. Kuhl wrote that he did not believe the OHL would go for their plan.

[10] Kuhl, "Kriegstagebuch," 20 March 1916.

[11] Tappen, "Kriegserinnerungen," p. 179. Cf. Holger Afflerbach, *Falkenhayn: Politisches Denken und Handeln im Kaiserreich* (Munich: Oldenbourg, 1994), pp. 373f.

four rather than eight additional divisions. In their stead, the General Staff Chief proposed reinforcement through additional heavy artillery batteries.[12]

The 6th Army answered immediately. They did not feel that the number of additional divisions would be sufficient to capture Arras. They did believe that the four divisions plus the artillery reinforcement would enable them to capture Loos, although it would not have the same psychological result. The 6th Army stated that they would require at least three weeks to make the necessary preparations.[13] They had already issued the required orders for the preparation of the attack on Loos, when Falkenhayn's reply arrived on 10 April. To their surprise, the General Staff Chief ordered them to continue preparations for the attack on Arras.[14]

Accordingly, the 6th Army updated their plan for the seizure of Arras. The situation before the 6th Army had altered since they last planned for the attack. The British had had the time to strengthen their positions, rebuilding the poorly constructed French trenches in a way that made the attack much more difficult. Accordingly, although they believed eight additional divisions would suffice, the 6th Army raised their requirement for heavy artillery. Once again, they planned to take the city in two stages, launching first a northern and then a southern attack.[15]

However, once more, events at Verdun forced a postponement of the Arras attack, this time permanently. By the end of April, most of the OHL reserve was engaged at Verdun, including all of the OHL's modern heavy artillery.[16] Falkenhayn was forced to put aside any idea of a secondary attack, at least until the attritional battle had reached its conclusion.

Just as Falkenhayn had begun to give up the possibility of carrying out his strategy's second phase any time soon, the signs of an enemy relief offensive began to appear. In early April, the 2nd Army began reporting that the British before their front were making preparations for a large-scale attack; they were digging jumping-off trenches and were ranging their artillery.[17]

[12] Falkenhayn to AOK 6, OHL Nr.26234op., 6 April 1916, BA/MA, W10/51534; *Der Weltkrieg*, X, p. 294.

[13] AOK 6 to OHL, Ia Nr. 291, 6 April 1916, BA/MA, W10/51534; Rupprecht, *Kriegstagebuch*, I, pp. 443–445 (diary entry for 6 April 1916).

[14] Falkenhayn to AOK 6, BA/MA, W10/51534; Kuhl, "Kriegstagebuch," 11 April 1916.

[15] AOK 6, "Doppelangriff bei Arras," Ia Nr.301geh., 17 April 1916, BA/MA, W10/51520.

[16] At the end of April, the OHL reserve consisted of only eight divisions. *Der Weltkrieg*, X, p. 298.

[17] Ibid., p. 295.

The Entente relief offensives

The preparations observed by the 2nd Army were, in fact, the beginnings of the long-planned battle of the Somme. At a conference at Chantilly between 6 and 8 December 1915, the Entente leaders arrived at a common strategy for 1916. Like Falkenhayn, they had decided on a two-phased approach; first, to wear down the German reserves; second, powerful, coordinated attacks launched on the Western and Eastern Fronts to achieve victory. Time, however, was needed to build the British army to the necessary strength and to reorganize the Russian army, still smarting after a disastrous 1915. A second conference in mid-February 1916 between the French and the British had worked out the outlines of the western offensive. The two allies were to attack at the point of the juncture of their two armies, along the Somme River. The French were to contribute forty divisions and attack along a 40 km front, while twenty-five British divisions attacked along a 22 km front. The offensive was scheduled to begin on 1 July.[18]

However, the German offensive at Verdun had a great impact on the planned Anglo-French offensive. Immediately after the German attack, Marshal Joseph Joffre requested that Douglas Haig relieve the French 10th Army and launch a British relief attack as soon as possible.[19] While Haig agreed to relieve the 10th Army, he did not feel a British offensive would contribute much to taking the pressure off the French at Verdun. The British commander-in-chief wanted to marshal his forces for the main offensive later in the year.[20] As the Verdun offensive wore on and the French army suffered more and more casualties, the French contribution to the joint offensive diminished. By 1 May, the French army had lost over 130,000 men and had rotated 42 divisions through the "*Maasmühle*," or "Meuse mill." With such losses, they were forced to lower their commitment to the offensive to thirty rather than forty divisions. Later the same month, the French contribution fell to twenty-two divisions, and Joffre again asked Haig to move forward the offensive in the wake of the German seizure of Fort Vaux.[21] At a meeting on 26 May,

[18] James E. Edmonds, ed., *Military Operations: France and Belgium 1916*, vol. I: *Sir Douglas Haig's Command to the 1st July: Battle of the Somme* (London: Macmillan, 1932), pp. 1–35; William Philpott, *Anglo-French Relations and Strategy on the Western Front 1914–18* (London: Macmillan, 1996), pp. 112–128.

[19] Joseph Joffre, *The Memoirs of Marshal Joffre* (trans. T. Bentley Mott) (2 vols.) (London: Geoffrey Bles, 1932), II, pp. 465–466.

[20] Edmonds, *Military Operations 1916*, I, pp. 36–37; B. H. Liddell Hart, *The Real War 1914–1918* (London: Faber & Faber, 1930), pp. 247–248.

[21] Ministère de la Guerre, *Les Armées Françaises dans la Grande Guerre*, Tome IV: Vol. 2: *La Bataille de Verdun et les offensives des Alliés* (Paris: Imprimerie Nationale, 1933), pp. 171–188.

Joffre expressed the strain felt by the French army when he declared to Haig that "the French army would cease to exist," if the Anglo-French offensive were not carried out by 1 July at the latest.[22]

The Germans were well aware of the declining French commitment to the joint offensive, and Falkenhayn saw this as a sign that the *Verblutung* of the French army was succeeding. However, it is clear that the OHL also overestimated the effects of Verdun and underestimated the enemy. Already in March, incoming reports spoke of the reduced number of French divisions taking part in the impending offensive. Karl Georg von Treutler reported, somewhat prematurely, from the OHL that "it is barely conceivable that the French can take their place in the great spring offensive."[23] Over the next few months, Falkenhayn continued this train of thought. In April, Werner Freiherr von Grünau was able to report that, although the French might have enough reserves to carry out an offensive, they did not have the heavy artillery needed to bring significant results.[24] In May, Falkenhayn insisted that the attack on Verdun had reduced the planned Entente offensive substantially, as the French were no longer in any position to take part with any great numbers of troops.[25]

With the attention of the OHL focused totally on the Western Front, it was the Russians who surprised everyone (including themselves) by achieving unexpected success with their offensive in June. On the evening of 5 June, Falkenhayn began receiving disturbing messages from the Austro-Hungarian AOK. The first arrived from Conrad, who informed Falkenhayn that "the attack of the entire Russian Southwest Front [had begun] on 4 June." Consequently, the Austrian General Staff Chief requested that Falkenhayn reinforce the southern Eastern Front from the forces of OberOst, as had been agreed on 23 May.[26] Falkenhayn,

22 Douglas Haig, *The Private Papers of Douglas Haig, 1914–1919* (ed. Robert Blake) (London: Eyre & Spottiswoode, 1952), pp. 144–145 (diary entry for 26 May 1916); A. H. Farrar-Hockley, *The Somme* (London: Pan Books, 1966; first published, 1964), p. 70; cf. *Les Armées Françaises* IV/2, p. 175.

23 Karl Georg von Treutler to Theobald von Bethmann Hollweg, 17 March 1916 (copied from *Kriegführung Nr.15/ 1*) BA/MA, W10/51543.

24 Werner Freiherr von Grünau to Bethmann, 17 April 1916 (copied from *Reichskanzlei. Weltkrieg 1914/18. 15. Allg.Milit,- und Marine-Berichte aus dem Gr.H. Qu.* Bd. 1) BA/MA, W10/51543.

25 Erich von Luckwald to Bethmann, 12 May 1916 (copied from *Reichskanzlei, Weltkrieg 15/1*) BA/MA, W10/51543. See also Falkenhayn's comments at the *Chefbesprechung* of 26 May. Kuhl, "Kriegstagebuch," 26 May; Fritz von Loßberg, *Meine Tätigkeit im Weltkrieg 1914–1918* (Berlin: E. S. Mittler, 1939), pp. 221–222.

26 Conrad to Falkenhayn, AOK Op. Nr. 25770, 5 June 1916, BA/MA, W10/51519. The Central Powers had been aware of the impending Russian offensive, but expected it, like the earlier Russian offensive at Lake Narotch, to come to nothing. See Falkenhayn, *General Headquarters*, p. 241; *Der Weltkrieg*, X, pp. 437–439; Afflerbach, *Falkenhayn*, pp. 411–412.

intent on not being drawn away from the Western Front and skeptical as ever of the Austrians, declined this shifting of reserves, insisting that the Russian forces facing OberOst were far superior and, therefore, none could be spared.[27] Conrad's messages were followed shortly after by two from Generalleutnant August von Cramon, the German liaison officer in the AOK. Cramon's messages carried the first reports of the collapse of the Austro-Hungarian 4th Army, and a further personal request for German reinforcement.[28]

Although Falkenhayn was reluctant to be distracted by the Eastern Front, the situation was rapidly deteriorating there. On 5 June, the four Russian armies of General Alexei Brusilov's Southwest Front launched what was intended to be a secondary attack for a relief offensive for Italy. However, they achieved a completely unexpected success, as the Russian 8th Army broke through the three defensive positions and practically annihilated the Austro-Hungarian 4th Army. On the first day alone, the Austro-Hungarian X Corps lost 80 percent of its effectives and the Corps Szurmay to its south was almost as badly treated. By the offensive's second day, Russian troops had penetrated the Austrian reserve position and had advanced around 20 km to the 4th Army's headquarters at Lutsk. All along the Austro-Hungarian/Russian front, the Russian attackers achieved notable successes, if not as sweeping as those of the 8th Army. By 12 June, the Russians could report that they had taken large numbers of prisoners. The four Russian armies that had taken part in Brusilov's offensive had captured close to 193,000 officers and men. With casualties, the Austro-Hungarian army on the Eastern Front had lost over half of their strength.[29]

However, the scale and the nature of the defeat was slow in filtering through the Central Powers' chain of command. Falkenhayn had responded negatively to Cramon's personal plea for assistance on 5 June,

27 Falkenhayn to Conrad, OHL Nr. 28852 op., 5 June 1916, BA/MA, W10/51519; Falkenhayn, *General Headquarters*, pp. 244–245. Falkenhayn claimed that there were 1200 Russian battalions along OberOst's front as opposed to 232 battalions along *Heeresgruppe Prinz Leopold*'s front. He was, in fact, correct. Two-thirds of the Russian army, 1400 battalions, were still deployed against the German sector of the front. See Holger Herwig, *The First World War: Germany and Austria-Hungary, 1914–1918* (London: Arnold, 1997), p. 208.

28 Wilhelm Solger, "Die Oberste Heeresleitung in der Führung der Westoperationen Ende 1915 bis Ende August 1916: VII. Vom 5.Juni–30.Juni 1916. Vom Eintreffen der Nachrichten über den Erfolg der Brussilow-Offensive bis zum Vorabend der Sommeschlacht (30.Juni)," unpublished manuscript in BA/MA, W10/51592, p. 365 (hereafter, Solger, "Führung der Westoperationen").

29 Bundesministerium für Landesverteidigung, *Oesterreich-Ungarns Letzter Krieg*, Bd. IV: *Das Kriegsjahr 1916* (Vienna: Verlag der Militärwissenschaftlichen Mitteilungen, 1933), pp. 375–403; Norman Stone, *The Eastern Front, 1914–1917* (London: Hodder and Stoughton, 1975), p. 254; Herwig, *First World War*, pp. 208–217.

repeating his assertion that OberOst was in no position to send reinforcements. He added: "Also in the west, where I daily await an English attack, reserves are not available." He suggested that the Austro-Hungarians give up their Italian offensive to find the necessary reinforcement.[30] Over the next several days, however, the true picture of the defeat became clear. The German General Staff Chief was forced on 7 June to relinquish part of his western reserve (one corps) to help restore the position in the east, and after meeting Conrad on 8 June decided a further two divisions would be necessary to stabilize the front.[31]

Despite the scale of the defeat in the east, perhaps not fully recognized in far-away Mézières, the OHL was clearly optimistic about the prospects for ultimate victory.[32] On 9 June, Adolf Wild von Hohenborn recorded the opportunity the Brusilov offensive offered the Central Powers:

> The Russian advance must become a victory for us. Corps Bernhardi and the X Army Corps are not enough. I advised that we send also the 11th Bavarian Division, the 3rd Guard Division, and another two corps. It must be a rapid, energetic strike that demonstrates to the Russians that the time for them to be thinking about offensives is over and that makes the world and Rumania aware that Russia has to remain in her trenches. In the meantime, [the operation at] Verdun, where the situation recently has developed very well, will continue, while the knowledge of the transports [of our troops] from the west will hopefully tempt the English to attack at last. If all goes well, we could also conduct a good operation in the west some time in August.[33]

Clearly, the offensive was seen by some in the OHL as an opportunity to settle the score with Russia once and for all. The day after Wild recorded the above opinion in his diary, he outlined how he would accomplish this: The German attack group would "slice off" Brusilov's salient, destroying the Russian force therein.[34] Falkenhayn was again faced with the question of whether to send troops for a potentially decisive counteroffensive in the east or to retain forces to meet the impending Entente offensive in the west.

[30] Falkenhayn to Cramon, 5 June 1916, quoted in Solger, "Führung der Westoperationen," p. 365. On 15 May, Conrad's long-desired offensive against Italy on the Asiago Plateau had begun, involving fourteen divisions, including six removed from the Eastern Front. See *Oesterreich-Ungarns Letzter Krieg*, IV, pp. 253–349; Herwig, *First World War*, pp. 204–207.

[31] *Der Weltkrieg*, X, p. 457. A further five divisions were dispatched from OberOst.

[32] For the OHL's attitude toward the Russian offensive, see Afflerbach, *Falkenhayn*, pp. 415ff.

[33] Adolf Wild von Hohenborn, "Kriegstagebuch," 9 June 1916, BA/MA, Wild Nachlass, N44/2.

[34] Wild, "Kriegstagebuch," 10 June 1916.

However, Falkenhayn appears never to have taken Wild's idea of a powerful eastern counteroffensive seriously.[35] His eyes continued to be set firmly on the Western Front, and he rejected sending more forces than were absolutely necessary to the east. On 24 June, he informed OberOst that he still expected that the war's decision would fall in France.[36] The General Staff Chief was supported in this belief by Gerhard Tappen, who on 21 June had drawn up an assessment of Germany's strategic situation. His report began with the assumption that the war could only be settled in the west. He continued, "a decision in the west cannot be achieved when the English are met purely defensively. When the English attack and storm [*Angriff und Ansturm*] is broken, they must be driven back."[37]

Indeed, through June, the intentions of the Western Allies had become clearer. On 14 June, the Intelligence Section of the OHL reported that twenty to twenty-two British divisions were preparing to attack the 2nd Army north of the Somme. An additional, diversionary attack was expected west or southwest of Lens.[38] Several days later, they reported that the French role in the offensive would not merely be limited to a diversionary attack, but would include a major effort south of the Somme. For this attack, the French had 19 divisions in reserve (although only 6 "white" and 2 "colored" divisions of these had not been through Verdun), but almost no heavy artillery.[39]

Both Wild's diary entry and Tappen's assessment demonstrate that the OHL had not given up their idea of a counterattack following the successful defense of an Entente offensive. The increasing signs of the impending Somme offensive had, in fact, given new hope to this phase of Falkenhayn's strategy. The General Staff Chief, however, was running up against the same problem that he had faced since he had taken over directing Germany's strategy – a lack of reserves. As the Entente preparatory bombardment began on 24 June, the Intelligence Section gave their final assessment of the Western allies' dispositions before the assault. They believed that the offensive would fall primarily against the 2nd Army on a front between Monchy au Bois in the north and the Avre in the south. In total, they believed that the British and French had deployed thirty-nine to forty-one divisions, together with a large force of artillery.[40] Facing this

35 Falkenhayn, *General Headquarters*, pp. 247ff.
36 Falkenhayn to OberOst, 24 June 1916, quoted in *Der Weltkrieg*, X, p. 320.
37 Gerhard Tappen, "Beurteilung der Lage am 21.6.1916," printed in Solger, "Führung der Westoperationen," pp. 383–384.
38 Nachrichtenabteilung West, "Vortrags-Notizen, England," 14 June 1916, BA/MA, W10/51592.
39 Solger, "Führung der Westoperationen," pp. 377–378.
40 Nachrichtenabteilung West, "Vortrags-Notizen," 24 June 1916, BA/MA, W10/51592.

enemy concentration were the thirteen divisions of *Generaloberst* Fritz von Below's 2nd Army.

To marshal the necessary forces for the defense against the Entente attack and for any subsequent counterattack, Tappen had written in his assessment of 21 June that the German involvement in the east should be limited to only the smallest possible force and reserves should be gathered for the task. Indeed, Falkenhayn had begun doing just that. Already on 9 June, he had telegraphed Conrad to report that no further forces could be sent to the east as the situation in the west "is so serious that all the available reserves must be sent to the threatened front."[41] This was reinforced by Falkenhayn on 24 June, when he telegraphed OberOst that no additional troops would be forthcoming from the west.[42] The General Staff Chief began looking for forces from other areas of the Western Front, including Verdun. On 24 June, he sent the following message to the 5th Army:

> The general situation makes it very desirable that the *Heeresgruppe* limit seriously the use of men, material, and munitions. The opinion is requested as to how this can be carried out after Pw. Thiaumont, Fleury, and a certain area of the foreground to Fort Vaux are taken.[43]

Further, Falkenhayn began stripping other armies of units to add to the OHL reserve. The 3rd Army was forced to give up a division and the 7th Army created a division out of battalions removed from its units.[44] However, even with the measures taken, the Germans could only gather twelve divisions as a reserve force, four of which were placed at the disposal of the 2nd Army by the end of June.[45]

With hindsight, it is clear that the Germans were facing one of the most trying phases of the war in late June 1916. At the time, however, the strategic situation seemed fairly promising to the OHL.[46] The Germans had never taken the Russian offensive seriously, and, indeed,

41 Falkenhayn to Conrad, OHL Nr. 28981 op., 9 June 1916, BA/MA, W10/51529.

42 Falkenhayn to OberOst, 24 June 1916, quoted in *Der Weltkrieg*, X, pp. 320–321. Although Wild wrote that "Falkenhayn vacillates back and forth over a campaign in the east" (Wild, "Kriegstagebuch," 26 June 1916), it is obvious from his messages to OberOst and AOK that he never intended to launch a large-scale offensive there.

43 Falkenhayn to AOK 5, Nr. 29769 op., 24 June 1916, printed in *Der Weltkrieg*, X, p. 195.

44 *Der Weltkrieg*, X, p. 348.

45 Ibid., pp. 319f. The Reichsarchiv lists only seven divisions remaining in the OHL reserve after reinforcement of the 2nd Army. They appear to have overlooked the 123rd Infantry Division, which was deployed behind the 4th Army. (See "Die Front gegen Frankreich: Stand am 1.Juli 1916 morgens," Map 4, *Der Weltkrieg*, X.)

46 For Falkenhayn's optimism, see Georg von Müller, *The Kaiser and His Court: The First World War Diaries of Admiral Georg von Müller* (ed. Walter Görlitz) (London: MacDonald, 1961), diary entry for 20 June 1916, p. 174; Afflerbach, *Falkenhayn*, p. 416.

it had apparently been contained by mid-June.[47] Further, the Verdun offensive had achieved good results with the attack on Fleury on 22/23 June.[48] Although the French were taking part in the Somme offensive, the Verdun offensive had seemingly reduced their contribution to a token force. Therefore, the brunt of the offensive would fall to the inexperienced British, whom, as Chapter 9 has shown, the Germans had rated poorly at the beginning of the year. Nothing had happened between January and June to change their assessment of the tactical worth of the "Kitchener divisions."

To meet this attack, Falkenhayn had reinforced the 2nd Army with four divisions and a good deal of artillery from the OHL reserve. The long and obvious Entente preparatory period allowed the Germans to know almost exactly where the attack would fall. Below's army had ample time to reinforce their field positions. The defensive lessons drawn from the *Herbstschlacht* had been circulated throughout the *Westheer*, and the 2nd Army had constructed the layered defensive system indicated by that experience.[49] Although it was clear that the Entente had considerably superior forces arrayed against the 2nd Army, the situation was far better for the Germans than it had been before any previous Entente offensive. The General Staff Chief could expect that the 2nd Army would be able to withstand the attack from an inexperienced enemy without great difficulty.

Falkenhayn's optimism and his continued desire for a German counteroffensive dictated his deployment of the *Westheer* before the Somme offensive. It was clear by the middle of June where the Anglo-French assault would fall. On 15 June, the General Staff Chief had informed the 6th Army's Chief of Staff that the "main attack would fall against the 2nd Army, with a secondary attack at Lens."[50] Despite this knowledge and the knowledge of the enemy forces arrayed against the 2nd Army, Falkenhayn reinforced this army with only four divisions, maintaining

47 In the event, the Russian advance was stopped more by Russian logistical difficulties and timidity than by the efforts of the Central Powers. Stone, *Eastern Front*, pp. 255ff. This point seems to have been recognized by the OHL as well. Wild wrote, "the Russians themselves appear to be so astonished by their easy result that they do not know what they should do next." Wild, "Kriegstagebuch," 10 June 1916.

48 Using the new "Green Cross" gas shells, the Germans had managed to take the fortified village of Fleury on the east bank of the Meuse with relatively little difficulty. *Der Weltkrieg*, X, pp. 186–194; Bruce Gudmundsson, "Counter-Battery Fire: The Case of Fleury," *Tactical Notebook* March 1992.

49 For an example of the changes implemented after the *Herbstschlacht*, see AOK 2, "Experience Gained From the September Offensives on the Fronts of the Sixth and Third Armies," Ia Nr. 290 geh., 5 November 1915, British Army Translation, Stationary Service Series (SS) 454. (My thanks to Dr. Martin Samuels for a copy of this document.)

50 Kuhl, "Kriegstagebuch," 15 June 1916.

eight in the OHL reserve. Further, the 6th Army was not reduced at all to provide reserves for the 2nd Army. Holding a shorter front than Below's army, the 6th Army still consisted of seventeen and a half divisions and large amounts of heavy artillery on the eve of the Somme battle. Additionally, the OHL maintained three divisions from its reserve behind the 6th Army's front.[51]

In retrospect, given the outcome of the battle of the Somme, this deployment seems ludicrous. Indeed, to explain this strange deployment, the Reichsarchiv stated after the war that Falkenhayn had misinterpreted where the enemy offensive would take place, writing that he believed the 6th Army would also be attacked.[52] However, there can be only one explanation for leaving such a substantial force deployed away from where the Entente offensive was to fall – Falkenhayn intended to launch his counteroffensive with Crown Prince Rupprecht's army once the British had exhausted themselves in fruitless attacks on the 2nd Army.

Throughout the year, Falkenhayn had favored the offensive plans of the 6th Army for use as his counterattack. Now that the British attack was finally coming, the conditions seemed right to implement these plans. Although the 6th Army's original plan for a counteroffensive had recommended attacking at the point of the unsuccessful Entente attack, it had also explored the possibility of attacking another, weakly held portion of the front.[53] Falkenhayn could assume that the British would attack on the Somme with their best divisions, leaving the remainder of their front occupied by second-rate and inexperienced formations, thus presenting the 6th Army with an opportunity to counterattack the British at a point of the front held by less-effective units.[54] With the British reserves destroyed during their offensive and the French army depleted by the continuing action at Verdun, the General Staff Chief could expect any local breakthrough achieved by the 6th Army to turn into a strategic success.

After the war, Tappen maintained that throughout the summer the OHL had kept a number of their "best" divisions available for this counteroffensive.[55] He described how he, Falkenhayn, and Wild had continually discussed how to employ these formations most effectively.[56]

[51] Solger, "Führung der Westoperationen," p. 397.
[52] *Der Weltkrieg*, X, pp. 317–318. See also Afflerbach, *Falkenhayn*, p. 419.
[53] AOK 6 to OHL, Ia Nr. 267g., 24 January 1916, BA/MA, W10/51520. See Chapter 8.
[54] See Tappen, "Kriegserinnerungen," p. 189.
[55] Tappen to Reichsarchiv, 21 October 1932, BA/MA, N56/5; Tappen, "Kriegserinnerungen," pp. 189–190.
[56] Tappen, "Besprechung mit dem Generalleutnant a.D. Tappen im Reichsarchiv am 6.IX.1932," N56/5, p. 2 (hereafter, Tappen, "Besprechung"); Tappen, "Kriegserinnerungen," p. 197.

Now, as the Somme offensive was about to begin, a number of these divisions were deployed with, or in the area of, the 6th Army, ready to launch a counteroffensive once the British had exhausted themselves in their attacks to the south.[57]

Intriguingly, however, the General Staff Chief had not yet made definite plans for the employment of the reinforced 6th Army by the beginning of the Somme. This can, in part, be explained by Falkenhayn's secrecy. After the war, Tappen remembered how the two men would often outline different plans for the employment of these reserves on a blackboard at the OHL. To keep them secret, however, the blackboard would be wiped clean once the two had finished their conversation.[58] The fact that plans had already been drawn up by the 6th Army for a counteroffensive would also have contributed to Falkenhayn's reluctance to be drawn any further into details. All that was needed was for these plans to be updated. The offensive at Gorlice had shown how quickly a large-scale operation could be organized and launched.

Thus, as the Somme offensive began, the General Staff Chief had set the scene for the decision in the west. The 2nd Army had been reinforced enough that he believed them capable of holding their own in the coming battle. The offensive at Verdun had been scaled back somewhat, but the 5th Army was to keep up the pressure on the French to continue to bleed the French army there.[59] Finally, forces for the counterstroke had been mustered and their deployment had even begun. All that was needed was for the British finally to begin their long-expected offensive.

The failure of Falkenhayn's strategy

On 24 June, the Entente preparatory bombardment began, marking the start of what was to be the greatest test of the *Westheer* since the war's

[57] The seventeen and a half divisions of the 6th Army included the Guard Reserve Corps, the II Bavarian Corps, IV Army Corps, and the IX Reserve Corps, all rated as "first class" formations by the Entente. Further, the OHL reserve behind the 6th Army included another "first class" unit, the 3rd Guard Division. For the deployment on 1 July 1916, see *Der Weltkrieg*, X, p. 319. For this rating of the German units see, US War Office, *Histories of the 251 Divisions of the German Army which Participated in the War* (London: Naval and Military Press, 1989; originally published 1920). This work is a compilation of the Entente intelligence assessments of the German divisions.

[58] Tappen, "Besprechung," p. 2.

[59] On 27 June, the 5th Army had responded to Falkenhayn's call for a restriction of the Verdun offensive by stating that they would carry on with the resources of the 5th Army alone. AOK 5 to OHL, Ia Nr. 1657g., 27 June 1916, printed in Hermann Wendt, *Verdun 1916: Die Angriffe Falkenhayns im Maasgebiet mit Richtung auf Verdun als strategisches Problem* (Berlin: E. S. Mittler, 1931), p. 170.

beginning. For the next eight days, the Entente artillery pounded the German positions. In the British sector alone, the 1,896 artillery pieces and trench mortars of the British 4th Army fired more than 1,732,800 rounds.[60] The British guns were joined by 1,400 French artillery pieces. This opening bombardment signaled that the forthcoming battle was to be, above all, one of material and one that the Germans would have great difficulty countering.[61] Facing the Entente artillery concentration of almost 3,300 artillery pieces were only the 2nd Army's 598 light and 246 heavy guns.[62]

Indeed, the strength of the offensive surprised the OHL considerably. Although the infantry assaults of the initial days had been largely thrown back with great loss to the attackers, the 2nd Army had suffered under the weight of the Entente bombardment, and their early reports spoke of the effectiveness of the enemy fire. Most worryingly, the 2nd Army reported the loss of numerous artillery batteries, crucial elements of the defensive system, to the overwhelming enemy fire.[63] Additionally, the OHL's insistence that any Entente gain be retaken through an immediate counterthrust drained German units further. Soon, the German defenders were suffering far higher casualties than they had even at the height of the assaults on Verdun. During the offensive's first ten days alone, the 2nd Army had lost 40,187, as compared to the 25, 989 men lost during the first ten days of the Verdun battle.[64]

Moreover, even as the Somme offensive was beginning, the Russians scored renewed successes in their offensive against the Austrian front. During June, a complete reorganization of the Eastern Front had taken place. German units from OberOst and the divisions from the OHL reserve had been placed into Austro-Hungarian formations in an effort to increase their combat capability. The local counterattacks launched by these units, however, did little to stabilize the situation. Once the Russian logistics had caught up with Brusilov's rapid initial advance, the Russians were ready to go again. They continued to punish the Central Powers' forces through late June and early July.[65] To make matters worse, the Russians extended their offensive to the OberOst's sector of the front when General Evert's Western Front attacked on 2 July at Baranovitchi.[66]

60 Edmonds, *Military Operations 1916*, I, pp. 300–301; *Weltkrieg*, X, p. 340.
61 See Hew Strachan, "The Battle of the Somme and British Strategy," *Journal of Strategic Studies* 21, 1 (1998), pp. 79–95.
62 *Der Weltkrieg*, X, Anlage 1, "Deutsche und feindliche Artillerie bei Verdun und an der Somme."
63 *Der Weltkrieg*, X, p. 352.
64 Wendt, *Verdun*, p. 176.
65 *Oesterreich-Ungarns Letzter Krieg*, IV, pp. 547–623; *Der Weltkrieg*, X, pp. 469–481.
66 Stone, *Eastern Front*, pp. 259–263; *Der Weltkrieg*, X, pp. 499–503.

Given the seemingly precarious situation in the east, calls began for OberOst to take over command of the entire Eastern Front.[67]

By early July, the situation was seen as extremely serious by much of the army's leadership,[68] and on 8 July, Falkenhayn was forced to justify his strategy in an audience with the Kaiser. As this is one of the few contemporary documents showing the General Staff Chief's intentions, it is worth quoting at length. He began by outlining the strategic views with which he had begun the year:

> Up to this point, our entire strategy has been directed by the following simple ideas:
>
> In the east, due to conditions within Russia, it appeared to be enough to maintain, in its entirety, that which was won in the previous year.
>
> In the west, we were determined to bring France to her senses by means of a good bleeding [*durch Blutabzapfung*]. This should have forced the English into an offensive, which we hoped would bring them heavy losses but no important gains and which would later bring the opportunity for us to launch a counter-offensive.
>
> In this way, we expected our three main enemies to have lost their appetite for continuing the war so profoundly by winter that a victorious peace would have to develop in some form.

Falkenhayn regretted, however, that the collapse of the Austrians in the east had made this plan much more difficult, if not impossible, to carry out. He rejected the building of a powerful attack group in the east, as was advocated by Wild and others, on the grounds that he did not believe it would reach any real decision. Instead, he wanted to reinforce the Austrians with individual units and re-establish the front there through small-scale counterattacks. The east would have to hold out with its own resources because "at the moment, we are engaged in the decisive battle in the west." It was in France, not Russia, that the war would be won or lost. Falkenhayn believed that, in large part due to his attritional battle at Verdun, the offensive on the Somme represented the last throw of the dice on the part of the Western Allies. If Germany could hold out on the Somme, then France would be forced to sue for peace, as "in consideration of their manpower, France [could not] endure another winter campaign."[69]

67 See Wild, "Kriegstagebuch," 24 June 1916; Plessen, "Tagebuch," 17 and 25 June 1916. This proposal was energetically rejected by the Kaiser.

68 Plessen wrote in his diary, "the overall situation is critical." Plessen, "Tagebuch," 6 July. Similarly, Moriz von Lyncker, the head of the Kaiser's Military Cabinet, wrote to his wife that Germany was facing a "critical time." Lyncker to his wife, 7 July 1916, BA/MA, W10/50676. Cf. Rupprecht, *Kriegstagebuch*, I, pp. 498ff. Falkenhayn himself felt the strain acutely. See Wild, "Kriegstagebuch," 15 July 1916.

69 Erich von Falkenhayn, "Vortrag bei Sr. Majestät am 8. Juli 1916," BA/MA, W10/51584; printed in Wendt, *Verdun*, pp. 174–176. Cf. Afflerbach, *Falkenhayn*, pp. 420–421.

Fig. 17 German soldiers advancing across the wasteland around Verdun were vulnerable to French artillery fire causing the severe attrition of the German army as well as the French

By the end of the first week of July, Falkenhayn's strategy was rapidly unraveling. His audience with the Kaiser indicates that by the end of the first week of the battle of the Somme, Falkenhayn had given up his idea of a counterstroke to a failed Entente offensive. The Germans just did not have the troops necessary for such an undertaking. The four divisions that the OHL had been forced to send east in early June had depleted their reserve from which any counterthrust in the west would develop,[70] and the intensity of the battle of the Somme to date had shown just how much effort would be needed to defend against the Entente assault. By 2 July, Falkenhayn had been forced to send the 2nd Army seven divisions. By 9 July he had sent the 2nd Army an additional seven divisions. These units came from Falkenhayn's precious OHL reserve and from the powerful 6th Army.[71] Falkenhayn's presentation to the Kaiser indicated that the

[70] Falkenhayn and Tappen later blamed the sending of these divisions to the east for the end of the plans for a western counteroffensive. Falkenhayn, *General Headquarters*, p. 262; Tappen to Reichsarchiv, 15 May 1931, BA/MA, N56/5.

[71] *Der Weltkrieg*, X, Anlage 3: "Verzeichnis der vom 1.Juli bis Ende August auf dem Kampffelde eingesetzten Generalkommandos und Divisionen, ihre Ablösungen, Verschiebungen und Verluste."

General Staff Chief now believed the war would be won in the west by a successful defense on the Somme, rather than by any German offensive action. He now felt that a successful defense would convince the French that they could not defeat the Germans and that there was no longer any alternative but a negotiated peace.

As the summer wore on and the attacks on the Somme increased in their intensity, the situation deteriorated even further. Losses were so high that, in mid-July, Falkenhayn instituted a major reorganization of the *Westheer* designed to free solid units for employment on the Somme. The 6th Army lost most of its best units and the remainder of the OHL reserve was allocated to the 2nd Army. By the end of August, the OHL reserve had been reduced to one division, the Guard Ersatz Division. So many formations were deployed on the Somme that Falkenhayn had split the 2nd Army into two army groups to manage the battle more effectively. Further, the *Westheer*, including the 5th Army, was forced to give up portions of its heavy artillery, thus restricting their offensive capability.[72]

The severe crisis caused by the Entente attacks on both fronts also had a major impact on the 5th Army's offensive at Verdun. While, in consideration of the forthcoming Entente attack, Falkenhayn had ordered the 5th Army to limit their attacks, he agreed to their proposal to make one last effort to take Fort Souville. This was the last major French work remaining on the east bank, and its possession would have meant that the 5th Army had finally reached their territorial goals from the offensive's beginning. With the Meuse Heights on the east bank finally in their hands, the 5th Army would then have been in a strong defensive position and would have been able to dominate Verdun and its environs with their artillery. Further, Falkenhayn had believed that the continuation of the offensive would continue to wear down the French reserves even as the Somme progressed. When the attack on Fort Souville failed on 12 July, the General Staff Chief ordered the 5th Army to go "strictly on the defensive."[73] The 5th Army was permitted to undertake local attacks to better their tactical position, but no further large-scale assaults were to take place. Falkenhayn hoped that this would give the French the impression that the offensive was still under way, and, hence, would keep large numbers of troops in the Verdun salient.[74] Thus, by the middle of July,

[72] On 12 July, Falkenhayn informed the Kaiser that 150 of the 5th Army's modern heavy artillery pieces would be transferred to the Somme front. Plessen recognized that this meant the Verdun operation would be severely restricted. Plessen, "Tagebuch," 12 July 1916.

[73] *Der Weltkrieg*, X, pp. 199ff.

[74] Falkenhayn, *General Headquarters*, p. 268.

Falkenhayn was not only forced to give up his counteroffensive, he was forced to scale back considerably his battle of attrition.[75]

Falkenhayn's strategy for 1916 had faltered on a number of levels. Although he had correctly chosen a point for which the French would thrown in every available man, the General Staff Chief, not for the first time, had underestimated his enemy. The will of the French army, government, and people was far stronger than had been anticipated. The war had already demanded great sacrifices of the French nation and this meant that Falkenhayn's goal of a negotiated peace would be unlikely. The will to continue the war to a victorious end at all costs allowed the belligerents to absorb tremendous casualties. Although the French army was clearly suffering badly by the summer of 1916, it was able to maintain its morale and even contribute forces to the Somme offensive, thanks to the rotation system instituted by Pétain. Moreover, despite the pressure imposed on the French army, it was never close enough to collapse to force the British to launch an ill-prepared relief offensive. The enemy had clearly not reacted as Falkenhayn had anticipated.[76]

Falkenhayn had also overestimated the German army's ability to inflict casualties upon their enemy. Although the Germans caused more casualties than they themselves took, the ratio was not the five Frenchmen killed to two Germans assumed by the OHL. In part, this was due to the tactical methods employed by the 5th Army. As their initial goals were more far-reaching than Falkenhayn's (i.e., the capture of the fortress), they pushed their units to attack regardless of casualties. Even after they had accepted the General Staff Chief's goal of "bleeding white" the French army, they still applied costly tactics. Falkenhayn had been unable to impose his concept of "attritional" operations, with their emphasis on limited objectives, on the army, who continued for the most part to employ tactics more appropriate to *Bewegungskrieg* and *Vernichtungsstrategie*.

Further, the failure to seize the vital Meuse Heights made Falkenhayn's approach all the more difficult. If this terrain feature had been taken early in the battle, the Germans would have been in a reasonably secure defensive position. From there, the powerful German artillery would have been able to inflict a disproportionate number of casualties on the

[75] Although combat still took place at Verdun, the offensive had largely been ended by this point. It did not drag on in the same manner as before as is often asserted. Horne, *Price of Glory*, pp. 277ff.; Afflerbach, *Falkenhayn*, pp. 418–419.

[76] Hermann Ziese-Beringer's argument that the Verdun offensive caused the French army mutinies in 1917 clearly overstates the importance of Verdun in this event. The unsuccessful Nivelle offensives were the primary reason. See *Der einsame Feldherr: Die Wahrheit über Verdun* (2 vols.) (Berlin: Frundsberg-Verlag, 1934). Cf. Wolfgang Foerster, "Falkenhayn – der einsame Feldherr?" *Deutsche Wehr* 38, 3 (1934), pp. 41–43.

counterattacking French, as the defensive battles of 1915 had shown. The failure to take the Heights had a profound effect on the battle. The 5th Army was compelled to carry out a number of further offensives purely to better the army's poor tactical position. At this point, the nature of how the French army was to be ground down also shifted. No longer would the attrition come solely from French counterattacks as had been initially envisioned, now the attrition was also to come from German attacks and local French counterattacks. This shift made it clear that the task of "bleeding white" the French army would not be as easy as the General Staff Chief had anticipated at the battle's outset.

This prolongation of the battle had two important consequences. First, it became extremely difficult to give up the offensive now without at least capturing Verdun. German prestige was now just as closely bound to the fate of the fortress as was that of the French. Second, it made an Entente relief offensive all the more important. By the middle of April, it was clear that the Verdun offensive would not lead to a rapid French capitulation. Therefore, to defeat an Entente relief offensive and to launch a counterattack increasingly looked like the only way out of the stalemate. Thus, Falkenhayn looked forward with anticipation to the Entente offensive on the Somme. This, however, was to be the final nail in the coffin of Falkenhayn's *Ermattungsstrategie*. The collapse of the Austro-Hungarian front and unexpected ferocity of the Anglo-French attack quickly ended any ideas of a victorious German counterattack. The German army was stretched merely to hold its positions on both fronts.

Falkenhayn's fall and the German abandonment of *Ermattungsstrategie*

By August, it was clear to all that Falkenhayn's strategy for 1916 was in tatters. The offensive at Verdun, which was designed to wear down the French army and lead the French government to negotiate peace, had reached a costly stalemate. Although the French army was certainly bled white by its decision to hold on to the fortress at all costs, it was still able to participate in the Somme offensive, and there were no signs that the French government was close to suing for peace. Moreover, the Verdun offensive had cost the German army dearly as well as the French. The most reliable account of the battle's casualties comes from Hermann Wendt's study of Verdun. According to this work, from the offensive's start on 21 February until its end on 31 August, the 5th Army had suffered 281,333 casualties, while the French had suffered around 315,000.[77]

[77] Wendt, *Verdun*, pp. 243–244; *Der Weltkrieg*, X, p. 405.

To make matters worse, the British relief offensive, so long awaited by Falkenhayn, was wearing out the German army far more effectively than German action at Verdun wore down the French. On top of the crisis on the Western Front, the Russians, whom Falkenhayn had thought incapable of effective offensive action, were scoring major successes against a nearly exhausted Austro-Hungarian army. Falkenhayn's attempt to apply *Ermattungsstrategie* had failed miserably. His attempt to wear down the enemy's reserves had, in fact, led to the near exhaustion of the German army. Instead of peace, Falkenhayn's best efforts had led to the darkest hour of the war for Germany.

The General Staff Chief began to show the strain. By all accounts, the experience of 1916 caused not only the attrition of the French and German armies, but of Falkenhayn as well. He is described as being in broken health by the end of summer 1916.[78] On 28 August, Wilhelm Groener described him to Oberst Ulrich Freiherr von Marschall, one of Falkenhayn's staunchest supporters in the Military Cabinet: "The youthful general of 1914 has become an old man as a result of the failure at Verdun. Not only the extraordinary responsibility [of the post] but also the exhausting feud with Ludendorff has badly affected his nerves."[79] Worse, however, the General Staff Chief began to lose control over the German army itself.

The obvious failure of Falkenhayn's strategy for 1916 had undermined his already weak support within the army. As the situation deteriorated over the summer, the calls for a restriction of his authority, or even for his dismissal, became more vocal. Since June, many, including Falkenhayn's friend Wild, had been advocating that Falkenhayn's nemesis, Hindenburg, take over command of the entire Eastern Front.[80] By August, the situation had become so threatening that even Falkenhayn's staunchest supporters, the Kaiser's Military Cabinet, had turned against him. Since the Ypres offensive in 1914, Falkenhayn had faced mistrust from his subordinates in the army, not least because of his clear rejection of the army's traditional ideas about warfare. What little confidence in him that existed before the battle of Verdun was lost as it became clear that Falkenhayn's new strategic and operational approach had failed. Just as Falkenhayn had come to power rapidly in the midst of the command crisis following the defeat at the Marne, so he lost power rapidly in the crisis of 1916. With no support within the army or the government, the Kaiser was forced, against his better judgment, to replace him with Hindenburg, with Ludendorff

[78] See Afflerbach, *Falkenhayn*, pp. 531ff.
[79] Groener, *Lebenserinnerungen* (diary entry for 28 August 1916), p. 316.
[80] Wild, "Kriegstagebuch," 24 July 1916. See also, Plessen, "Tagebuch," 2 July 1916.

as his "First Quartermaster General."[81] On 29 August, the "duo" took over the direction of Germany's strategic effort, and on 2 September, the new strategic leadership ended once and for all the offensive at Verdun.[82]

With Falkenhayn's dismissal came the end of the German dalliance with *Ermattungsstrategie*. The new leaders refocused German efforts. Instead of a strategy designed to split the Entente and to lead to a negotiated peace on moderate terms with at least one of Germany's enemies, Hindenburg and Ludendorff returned to the traditional German strategic goal of a dictated peace with large-scale annexations, much to the delight of Falkenhayn's enemies in the army. This victor's peace was to be brought about in the time-honored manner. The Third OHL rejected Falkenhayn's operational approach of wearing down the enemy and went back to the methods dictated by pre-war theory. Hindenburg and Ludendorff came to power promising to crush Germany's enemies by means of great "decisive" battles. Königgrätz and Sedan were once again the models by which German strategy would be guided. The final results of this shift back to *Vernichtungsstrategie* are, of course, well known.[83]

81 Karl-Heinz Janßen, *Der Kanzler und der General: Die Führungskrise um Bethmann Hollweg und Falkenhayn 1914–1916* (Göttingen: Musterschmidt-Verlag, 1967), pp. 238–252; Afflerbach, *Falkenhayn*, pp. 424–450; and, Afflerbach, "Wilhelm II as Supreme Warlord in the First World War," *War in History* 5, 4 (1998), pp. 440–446.

82 Wendt, *Verdun*, p. 187.

83 On the strategic goals of the Third OHL, see Gerhard Ritter, *The Sword and the Sceptre: The Problem of Militarism in Germany*, Vol. III: *The Reign of German Militarism and the Disaster of 1918* (trans. Heinz Norden) (Coral Gables, FL: University of Miami Press, 1973); Martin Kitchen, *The Silent Dictatorship: The Politics of the German High Command under Hindenburg and Ludendorff, 1916–1918* (London: Croom Helm, 1976). Their operational ideas have not been well examined. For an introduction, see Martin Kitchen, *The German Offensives of 1918* (London: Tempus, 2001).

Conclusion

Since its outbreak, the battle of Verdun has been spoken of in superlatives. During the war and in its immediate aftermath, the French and Germans generally found something positive to say about the experience. Obviously, this was easier for the French, who could claim some sort of victory in the battle. Thus, Marshal Philippe Pétain declared, it was at Verdun, "the moral bulwark" of France, that the German advance on France was stopped.[1] At the time, the battle was seen by the French as "the great test, a purely French affair, since there was only three or four colonial battalions in it and no British. Verdun, fought with unequal material strength, was almost a victory of the race."[2] However, on the German side also the battle was spoken of in glorious terms. Paul von Hindenburg, for example, described Verdun as "a beacon light of German valor."[3]

In the years after the war, however, the battle came to be seen no longer as a "heroic" struggle, but rather as a symbol of the tragic waste of World War I. One historian even described it as "the most senseless episode in a war not distinguished for sense anywhere."[4] During the battle's course, 259 of France's 330 infantry battalions and 48 German divisions were rotated through the roughly 10 mile by 10 mile "Meuse Mill," as the area was called by the Germans.[5] In this killing zone, the French army suffered some 315,000 and the German army some 281,000 casualties.[6] It

[1] Henri Philippe Pétain, *Verdun* (trans. Margaret MacVeagh) (London: Elkin Mathews & Marrot, 1930), p. 15.

[2] Marc Ferro, *The Great War, 1914–1918* (London: Routledge, 1995; first published, 1969), p. 77.

[3] Paul von Hindenburg, quoted in Holger Herwig, *The First World War: Germany and Austria-Hungary 1914–1918* (London: Arnold, 1997), p. 184.

[4] A. J. P. Taylor, *The First World War: An Illustrated History* (New York: Perigee Books, 1980; first published, 1963), p. 123.

[5] Ferro, *Great War*, p. 77; AOK 5, "Bezeichnung der Kämpfe seit 21.2.1916," Ia Nr. 3953, 25 October 1916, BA/MA, W10/51534.

[6] Hermann Wendt, *Verdun 1916: Die Angriffe Falkenhayns im Maasgebiet mit Richtung auf Verdun als strategisches Problem* (Berlin: E. S. Mittler, 1931), pp. 243–244; Reichsarchiv, *Der Weltkrieg*, Bd. X: *Die Operationen des Jahres 1916* (Berlin: E. S. Mittler, 1936), p. 405.

Fig. 18 The remains of one of the forests around Verdun after months of intense shelling by both sides

has also been estimated that during the extended battle close to 12 million artillery rounds were fired.[7] From this great battle of material, the French and German armies, if not nations, emerged radically altered. As epitomized by the post-war writings of Ernst Jünger, the German soldier had become a new type of soldier, one who was practically fused with technology and who operated as a true fighting "machine." Humanity had been removed from the battlefield.[8] The French victims were spoken of as "the lost children of 1916."[9] As one historian has noted, "for sheer horror no battle surpasses Verdun."[10]

This view that the battle of Verdun was a futile undertaking, in which large numbers of French and German soldiers lost their lives for no real reason or gain, is reinforced by German soldiers commenting on

7 Information Division, US Army Garrison, Verdun, "Battlefields of Verdun 1914–1918," September 1962, p. 13.

8 For example, see Ernst Jünger, *The Storm of Steel* (London: Chatto & Windus, 1929). Although Jünger was writing about the experience on the Somme, the shift that took place in the soldiers' images of themselves began at Verdun. See Bernd Hüppauf, "Langemarck, Verdun and the Myth of a *New Man* in Germany after the First World War," *War and Society* 6, 2 (1988), pp. 70–103.

9 Ferro, *Great War*, p. 76.

10 Cyril Falls, *The First World War* (London: Longmans, 1960), p. 156.

Falkenhayn's strategy. Despite the fact that the Kaiserreich succumbed in the end to the *Ermattungsstrategie* of its enemies, German soldiers rejected Falkenhayn's strategy of attrition both during and after the war. Most German officers had never accepted the eclipse of traditional German *Vernichtungsstrategie*. The successes of Hindenburg and Ludendorff in the east suggested to them that this strategy could still work, even under the vastly altered strategic conditions of World War I. They conveniently overlooked the fact that Russia was not, in the end, defeated in a great, decisive battle as Hindenburg and Ludendorff desired, but rather was brought down by internal unrest caused by the strain of a long and indecisive war.[11] Indeed, even when Hindenburg and Ludendorff attempted to apply their ideas to the west, the result was dismal failure. Despite great tactical success in the spring 1918 offensives, the Germans could not bring an end to the war.[12]

In the interwar period, the Reichsarchiv and a group of like-minded writers together formed what could be labeled as the "Schlieffen School."[13] These writers, all former officers, were intent on preventing another indecisive war like World War I. Accordingly, they looked back to the ideas supposedly advanced by Schlieffen to illustrate how the war should have been fought. Rather than acknowledge the false assumptions upon which the *Vernichtungsstrategie* practiced by Hindenburg and Ludendorff was based, the Schlieffen School looked to other German commanders to explain the reasons for Germany's defeat. In doing so, they blamed the shortcomings of particular commanders for Germany's problems during the war. Thus, the Schlieffen Plan failed not because of its faults but because Moltke the Younger had not fully understood Schlieffen's concept. Falkenhayn and his strategy were treated similarly.

The Reichsarchiv painted Falkenhayn as an irresolute commander, who, like his predecessor Moltke the Younger, had not understood the principles taught by Schlieffen.[14] Indeed, in keeping with their rejection of

[11] Norman Stone, *The Eastern Front, 1914–1917* (London: Hodder and Stoughton, 1975), pp. 282ff.

[12] Martin Kitchen, *The German Offensives of 1918* (London: Tempus, 2001).

[13] See Jehuda Wallach, *The Dogma of the Battle of Annihilation: The Theories of Clausewitz and Schlieffen and their impact on the German Conduct of Two World Wars* (Westport, CT: Greenwood Press, 1986), pp. 209–228; Annika Mombauer, "Helmuth von Moltke and the German General Staff: Military and Political Decision-Making in Imperial Germany, 1906–1916" (University of Sussex, D.Phil. Thesis, 1997), pp. 250ff.

[14] This idea, raised during the war, became a common refrain after the war. See Hans von Haeften, quoted in Ekkehart P. Guth, "Der Gegensatz zwischen dem Oberbefehlshaber Ost und dem Chef des Generalstabes des Feldheeres 1914/15: Die Rolle des Majors v. Haeften im Spannungsfeld zwischen Hindenburg, Ludendorff und Falkenhayn," *Militärgeschichtliche Mitteilungen* 1 (1984), p. 90. For post-war usage, see Wolfgang Foerster, *Graf Schlieffen und der Weltkrieg* (Berlin: E. S. Mittler, 1925), p. 86.

the fact that *Vernichtungsstrategie* had ceased to be a viable strategy during the war, post-war German writers sought to deny that Falkenhayn had even pursued a strategy of attrition. Instead, according to this interpretation, Falkenhayn made the choices that he did merely because he lacked the strength of will to decide upon a single course of action which would risk everything on a powerful, war-winning blow.[15] Wilhelm Groener's words are representative of these writers:

> Whoever had the opportunity to observe General v. F[alkenhayn] at work as General Staff Chief was forced to lament that the otherwise so intelligent man never found a great operational idea with far-reaching goals and never set all available strength against such a goal, but rather always stuck, as it were, to the insignificant [operations].[16]

The Reichsarchiv even went so far as to commission a psychological profile of the former General Staff Chief to support their interpretation. Based on "photographs and handwriting," the Reichsarchiv's psychologists concluded that Falkenhayn was "no real man of will" (*kein eigentlicher Willensmensch*).[17] Thus, to the Reichsarchiv and others of this school, Falkenhayn's supposed failings as a commander, rather than the strategy he followed, contributed to Germany's defeat.[18]

To the writers of this school, the campaign at Verdun was the ultimate example of Falkenhayn's indecisiveness. Rather than set all of Germany's reserves against the fortress, capture it, and effect a rupture in the French defensive system, Falkenhayn had attacked this strongpoint with only eight divisions. Further, he starved the 5th Army of reserves during the crucial early stages of the operations, holding fresh divisions to defend against a phantom Entente relief offensive. To make matters worse, Falkenhayn fed reinforcements to the 5th Army piecemeal, which served to continue the operation, but which were not enough to bring a decision. In their analysis of the battle of Verdun, the writers of the German official

15 For example, see *Der Weltkrieg*, X, pp. 661ff.; Max Bauer, *Der grosse Krieg in Feld und Heimat* (Tübingen: Osiander'sche Buchhandlung, 1921); Wilhelm Solger, "Falkenhayn," in Friedrich von Cochenhausen, ed., *Heerführer des Weltkrieges* (Berlin: E. S. Mittler, 1939), pp. 72–101; Wilhelm Groener, "Protokoll über die 890. Sitzung der Mittwochsgesellschaft von 1864," 11 January 1933, USNA, M-137, Roll 13.

16 Wilhelm Groener, "Die Strategie Falkenhayns," Vortrag in der Mittwochsgesellschaft, 29 May 1935, USNA, M-137, Roll 13.

17 See the synopsis of the unpublished report of Prof. Dr. Lersch, Dr. Rudert, and Dr. Wohlfahrt in BA/MA, W10/50709.

18 This interpretation has had great strength within historiography. For examples, see B. H. Liddell Hart, *Reputations* (London: John Murray, 1928), p. 78. Liddell Hart titled his essay on Falkenhayn, "Erich von Falkenhayn: The Extravagance of Prudence" (in fact, Liddell Hart seems to have drawn heavily on Max Bauer's *Der grosse Krieg in Feld und Heimat*). Also Alistair Horne, *The Price of Glory: Verdun 1916* (New York: Penguin, 1993; published 1962), *passim*.

history argued that the General Staff Chief had not, in fact, intended to "bleed the French army white" at the outbreak of the operation.[19] Instead, they maintained that this goal came about only after the failure of his initial plan of forcing the French to strip their front of reserves. The authors of the official history insisted that only in late March and early April did Falkenhayn arrive at the formulation he later adumbrated in his post-war writings. They concluded that he switched his goals to the bleeding white of the French army merely because he did not have the force of will to decide either to continue the Verdun offensive with sufficient forces or to break off the battle and try elsewhere.[20]

However, in order to understand Falkenhayn properly, the strategy he attempted at Verdun, indeed his strategy from the time he came to occupy the position of Chief of the General Staff in 1914, has to be looked at in a wider context. It must be seen in the light not just of the challenges of the war, but also in the light of the response of German military intellectuals to the changing nature of war at the end of the nineteenth and beginning of the twentieth centuries. The rise of *Volkskrieg* and the significance of the institution of whole "nations in arms" across Europe was not lost on all German strategic commentators before 1914. The strategy followed by Falkenhayn during the war had its antecedents in the alternative ideas of warfare developed by perceptive German military thinkers in the wake of the Franco-German War.

The ability of the French republican government to raise and equip new armies after the complete defeat of the Imperial armies in 1870 indicated to astute observers that the age of *Volkskrieg* had returned. As during the Revolutionary/Napoleonic Wars, the states of Europe began tapping deeply into the resources of their nation after the defeat of France in 1871 in order to ensure the safety of their borders. However, several aspects had changed between 1815 and 1870. Now, central governments were better organized and, hence, better able to exploit the resources of their respective nations. Moreover, the size of populations had grown considerably, allowing a manifold increase in the size of armies. Most importantly, industrialization had occurred throughout the Continent, and its fruits were harnessed by the growing armies of Europe.

19 *Der Weltkrieg*, X, pp. 671–672.

20 Ibid., pp. 671–674. This argument was reinforced with the semi-official account written by one of the Reichsarchiv's key writers. See Wolfgang Foerster, "Falkenhayns Plan für 1916. Ein Beitrag zur Frage: Wie gelangt man aus dem Stellungskriege zu entscheidungsuchender Operation?" *Militär-Wissenschaftliche Rundschau* (1937), pp. 304–330. While Falkenhayn's most recent biographer, Holger Afflerbach, recognizes that Falkenhayn's aim from the start of the offensive was the *Verblutung* of the French, he sidesteps the question of Falkenhayn's supposed changing of aims as the battle progressed. See Afflerbach, *Falkenhayn*, pp. 373ff.

To some pre-war observers, this trend, combined with the progress of the *Volkskrieg* of 1870–71, offered a serious challenge to prevailing strategic wisdom. Indeed, the architect of the stunning German victories in the Wars of Unification, Helmuth von Moltke the Elder, recognized clearly the dangers this shift in warfare posed for Germany. Facing enemies who had created "nations in arms," Germany could no longer count on being able to defeat its enemies' armies totally. Consequently, Moltke doubted he would be able to repeat the events of the Wars of Unification, where Germany had been able to dictate terms to a beaten foe. This fear led him to institute changes in Germany's war plans. No longer did he assume that the army alone could produce a victory; Germany's diplomats would play a crucial role in securing a negotiated peace. Thus, the father of *Vernichtungsstrategie* himself saw its limitations and how its utility had diminished in the age of *Volkskrieg.*

At the same time that Moltke and others within the army were questioning the efficacy of a strategy of annihilation, Hans Delbrück was challenging it from his position as a civilian military commentator. He developed an alternative to the army's *Vernichtungsstrategie* – *Ermattungsstrategie*, or a strategy of attrition. Although this theory was historically based, it was clearly intended to be applicable to the contemporary situation, where it looked increasingly unlikely that a war could be won quickly and decisively. Delbrück, like Moltke the Elder, envisioned a strategy that closely linked civilian political goals with achievable military ones. The result would not be a campaign with the great "decisive" battles favored by the many in the army, but rather a war that resulted in a negotiated peace after great exertion by both sides.

The events of late summer 1914 proved Moltke the Elder and Hans Delbrück right. The failure of Germany's war plan at the battle of the Marne also represented the failure of the concept *Vernichtungsstrategie*, at least under the conditions prevailing during World War I. The new General Staff Chief, Erich von Falkenhayn, understood that Germany just did not have the resources to defeat its enemies in a rapid, decisive campaign demanded by the pre-war theory. Instead, he embraced the ideas of Moltke and Delbrück and adopted *Ermattungsstrategie* as his new course. Under Falkenhayn's leadership, Germany attempted to end the war not with a peace dictated by Germany, but rather through a negotiated peace, albeit on terms favorable to Germany.

Falkenhayn, however, faced the problem of implementing this strategy. As Hans Delbrück noted after the war, Falkenhayn had embraced *Ermattungsstrategie* in 1914, but "was not schooled in its methods."[21] In finding

21 Hans Delbrück, "Falkenhayn und Ludendorff," *Preußische Jahrbücher* 180 (1920), p. 277.

an operational approach to match his new strategy, he ran up against the two major, mutually supporting difficulties of World War I. First, on the strategic level, the war permitted governments to exploit even further the manpower and industrial resources of their nations. Thus, they were able to maintain huge armies in the field, spread across the Continent of Europe. Losses could be made good by the large populations, and when manpower became scarce, unexploited areas of society, such as female labor, could be tapped into. The armies of World War I could not simply be swept away, as they had been in the past. On the tactical level, the killing power of these industrial mass armies meant that even tactical successes eluded World War I generals. Thus, they first had to find a solution to the tactical deadlock before any strategic solution could be found. In other words, Falkenhayn needed to develop a brand new operational method to complement his *Ermattungsstrategie.*

However, before Falkenhayn could begin developing his new ideas, their very legitimacy was challenged by an officer corps unwilling to accept that the war had shown their traditional doctrinal concepts to be outdated. The bitter feud that engulfed the army in late 1914 and early 1915 nearly unseated Falkenhayn from his position as General Staff Chief. While in the end he retained control over Germany's war effort, the dispute demonstrated the depth of hostility toward him and his ideas. Although an ambitious man, Falkenhayn had always been reserved in his personal relations. The feud caused him to withdraw even further. Moreover, as his enemies also remained in key positions, the battle showed that he had to tread very carefully in openly advocating new strategic and operational ideas that challenged accepted wisdom within the army.

Throughout 1915, he attempted different solutions to Germany's military situation. Ever believing that the war would be decided in France, he initially planned to execute a breakthrough of the Western Front, which would force the Western Allies apart and hopefully lead to peace negotiations. However, the desperate situation of Germany's ally forced Falkenhayn to turn his attentions eastward in spring 1915. Once involved in the east, he sought, with no success, to force Russia into a separate peace. In the meantime, the *Westheer* stood firm against powerful Entente offensives.

Although no decision was reached during 1915, there was much to be learned from operations during the year. One of the most important lessons Falkenhayn took from the experience was that the Chancellor, Theobald von Bethmann Hollweg, could not be relied upon to provide diplomatic support for his strategic goal of forcing one of Germany's enemies into a separate peace. Despite the serious difficulties of such an undertaking, the General Staff Chief concluded that a purely military means would have to be found to compel one of Germany's enemies to the peace table. However, the experiences of 1915 held out some hope that he might be able to find an operational complement to his strategy. While the campaign in Russia had suggested that a breakthrough might be possible given the proper tools, the fighting on the Western Front suggested otherwise. Upon further examination, contrary to the beliefs of OberOst and many historians since, the combat in the east showed that, in fact, strategic breakthroughs had not occurred.[22] Instead, the tactical German breakthroughs resulted in the Russian army withdrawing and re-establishing a defensive line further to the rear. However, the tactical methods employed on the Eastern Front in 1915 had caused the severe attrition of the Russian army, particularly when it was forced to fight for a politically significant object. At the same time, the experience of defending the Western Front against powerful Entente attacks had shown forcefully the power of German artillery when situated in strong defensive positions. From these rather contradictory experiences, Falkenhayn fashioned an new operational approach designed to support his *Ermattungsstrategie*.

By late 1915, the General Staff Chief was convinced that the war would have to be concluded by the end of 1916 or else the Central Powers would have exhausted their resources. A way had to be found to accelerate the process of wearing down the will and resources of the Entente to force at least one enemy to the peace table. Operations in Russia and in France suggested an approach that was to develop into the application of attrition to the battlefield at Verdun, and from these operations Falkenhayn developed his unique strategy for winning the war. His approach attempted to deal simultaneously with the two great difficulties of World War I. The General Staff Chief accepted that a breakthrough was impossible due to the defensive power of modern weapons. Therefore, he attempted to utilize this power to his own ends. By threatening a politically significant object, Falkenhayn intended to force the French to "bleed themselves white" in counterattacks to a successful German attack with limited objectives, and thereby deal with the French reserves and in the process hopefully break the weak will of the French people. Simultaneously, the strength of France's key ally – Great Britain – was to be drained away by a similar method. Falkenhayn assumed that the British would be forced to launch an ill-prepared offensive to relieve the pressure on the French, which would wear down the strength of their army. A German counteroffensive would then sweep the remnants of the broken French and British

22 Herbert Rosinski, for instance, argued that "a mobile form of strategy" was still able to be carried out in the east throughout the war. Herbert Rosinski, *The German Army* (Washington, DC: The Infantry Journal, 1940), pp. 91–92.

armies from the field and bring a negotiated peace, at least with France. The strategic problem of Entente manpower reserves was to be solved on the tactical level using the very weapons which had created the tactical deadlock.

Falkenhayn had, indeed, chosen his target well. The French were more than willing to sacrifice their soldiers to retain the fortress of Verdun. However, his plan broke down in its execution. Although to accomplish the gruesome task of killing off French manpower he had accumulated a vast park of heavy artillery, the 5th Army was unable to reach the positions on the Meuse Heights necessary to accomplish their mission safely. Thus, the battle degenerated into a slogging match, where the German army, despite the beliefs of the OHL, was worn down almost as greatly as the French. The General Staff Chief had both underestimated the strength of French willpower and overestimated the killing ability of the German army. Falkenhayn was unable to inflict enough casualties upon the French to force them to sue for peace. To make matters worse, the 5th Army, never fully committed to Falkenhayn's concept of slowly hemorrhaging the French army, attacked with abandon in an effort to seize ground. In the process, the German army suffered almost as horribly as the French. At the same time, the British resisted all pressure for a premature relief offensive, and the second strand of Falkenhayn's strategy unraveled. When the British offensive finally came in July, it was far more ferocious than anyone in the OHL had predicted, and this put the final nail in the coffin of Falkenhayn's strategy and his tenure as Chief of the General Staff.

However, Falkenhayn's strategy of attrition contained within it an even greater flaw than the problems with its execution. Although the General Staff Chief's strategic goal was a moderate peace with at least one of the Entente, he failed to recognize that any peace on German terms was politically unacceptable to Germany's enemies. In this matter, Bethmann Hollweg saw much more clearly. In going to war in 1914, France, Russia, and Great Britain had wagered too much to conclude the war with a negotiated peace. In order to fight the modern, industrial war that was World War I, each nation needed to mobilize vast resources and demand great sacrifices of its people. Thus, a peace that returned to the status quo ante bellum, or worse, that gave Germany even the tokens of a victory, would result in the fall of any Entente government. However, no Entente government ever came close to concluding such a peace. To do so not only would have been political suicide, but would have marked the end of their nation as a Great Power, and no European nation was willing to admit such a thing without the entire resources of the nation being exhausted. In such a case, the victor could dictate whatever peace he liked, as Germany found in 1918. Thus, the expense of the war, both in material and in emotional terms, precluded World War I being ended through a peace of understanding and made Falkenhayn's strategic goal of a separate peace on moderate terms with at least one of Germany's enemies completely unrealistic.

Entente leaders, on the other hand, were much better placed to conduct a strategy of attrition. With their greater reserves of manpower and their vast industrial and economic power, the Entente could afford the costs of wearing down the German army.[23] Faced with the same tactical stalemate as Falkenhayn, the military leaders of the Entente embraced Falkenhayn's operational goals, if not all his methods. However, safe in the knowledge that they could win a long fight, Entente leaders remained committed to a peace dictated on their terms.[24] As the war dragged on and the sacrifices grew, so did the political goals of the Entente, so that by the time the German army had been worn down to the extent that it could no longer defend itself in 1918,[25] the Entente goals were the complete dismemberment of the political systems of the Central Powers. Through attrition on the battlefield, the Entente armies reached the goal of the traditional operational approach advocated by most German soldiers – a peace dictated to a prostrate enemy.

23 See Gerd Hardach, *The First World War 1914–1918* (London: Allen Lane, 1977).

24 France, in particular, was dedicated to a "total victory," see John F. V. Keiger, "Poincaré, Clemenceau, and the Quest for Total Victory," in Roger Chickering and Stig Förster, eds., *Great War, Total War: Combat and Mobilization on the Western Front, 1914–1918* (Cambridge: Cambridge University Press, 2000), pp. 247–263, but Britain too remained wedded to peace on its terms, see David French, "The Strategy of Unlimited Warfare? Kitchener, Robertson, and Haig," in *ibid.*, pp. 281–295.

25 On the collapse of the German army in 1918, see Wilhelm Deist, "The Military Collapse of the German Empire: The Reality Behind the Stab-in-the-Back Myth" (trans. E. J. Feuchtwanger), *War in History* 3, 2 (1996), pp. 186–207.

Bibliography

UNPUBLISHED DOCUMENTS

BUNDESARCHIV/MILITÄRARCHIV, FREIBURG

Nachlässe

Below, Otto von (N87)
Beseler, Hans von (N30)
Cramon, August von (N266)
Einem, Karl von (N324)
Dommes, Wilhelm von (N512)
Foerster, Wolfgang (N121)
Geyer, Hermann (N221)
Groener, Wilhelm (N46)
Haeften, Hans von (N35)
Hahnke, Wilhelm von (N36)
Hindenburg, Paul von (N429)
Hoffmann, Max (N37)
Kluck, Alexander von (N550)
Mackensen, August von (N39)
Mertz von Quirnheim, Hermann Ritter (N242)
Moltke, Helmuth von (N78)
Pentz, Hans Henning von (N128)
Seeckt, Hans von (N247)
Tappen, Gerhard (N56)
Wandel, Franz von (N564)
Wild von Hohenborn, Adolf (N44)
Winterfeldt, Detof von (N299)

Preussisches Heer 3 (Grosser Generalstab)

PH3/256 "Aufmarsch und operative Absichten der Franzosen in einem zukünftigen deutsch-französischen Kriege"
PH3/443 "Mobilmachungsplan für das deutsche Heer zum 1. April 1914"
PH3/528 "Denkschriften über England, das englische Expeditionskorps, Belgien und Italien sowie Anlagen zu den Denkschriften"
PH3/529 "Denkschrift über die Kriegsrüstungen Deutschland, Österreich-Ungarn und der feindlichen Staaten"
PH3/530 "Denkschriften über Oesterreich-Ungarn und Frankreich, 1913–1914"

PH3/533 "Nachrichten über feindliche Armeen Jan–Apr 1915"
PH3/542 "N.O. 2 Eingegangene Meldungen 1.12.14–31.3.15"
PH3/548 "Nachrichten über den Gegner an den Nachrichtenoffizier beim AOK 2 (März-Dez. 1916)"
PH3/607 "Meldungen und Berichte über den Gegner von NO des 2., 4, und 6 AOK, Okt 15–Aug 16"
PH3/6546. Abteilung, Grosser Generalstab, "Berichte über fremde Armeen, 1907–1911"
PH3/657 "Mitteilungen über russische Taktik" and "Die wichtigsten Veränderungen im Heerwesen Russlands im Jahre 1913"
PH3/663 "Grosse Generalstabsreisen 1905 und 1906"

Reichsheer 61 (Kriegsgeschichtliches Forschungsanstalt Akten)
W10/50123 – "Clausewitz Auffassungen zum 'Totalen Krieg' und 'Absoluten Krieg'"
W10/50155 – "Das Bruchmüllerische Angriffsverfahren"
W10/50157 – "Taktischer und Operativer Durchbruch"
W10/50158 – "Grundsätze für die Führung in der Abwehrschlacht im Stellungskriege"
W10/50160 – "Die Artillerie und die Durchbruchsangriffen in der Abwehrschlacht im 1.WK"
W10/50182 – "Die Entwicklung des operativen Angriffsgedankens in Frankreich von Frankfurter Frieden bis zum Weltkrieg"
W10/50203 – "Kriegsgeschichtliche Beispiele für Volkskrieg vom nordamer Unabhängigkeitskrieg 1775 bis zum bel. Franktireur Krieg 1914"
W10/50205 – "Statistiche Unterlagen über Truppenstarken, Munition und Ausgaben im deut. Heer vor Kriegsausbruch"
W10/50211 – "Die Entwicklung des Verhältnisses zwischen GenSt und KM"
W10/50220 – "Der Schlieffenplan"
W10/50221 – "Entwürfe zu Schlieffens Operationspläne gegen Russland"
W10/50222 – "Materialsammlung zur 'Darstellung der operativen Verhandlungen des Grafen Schlieffen mit Österreich-Ungarn'"
W10/50223 – "Der Kriegsplan für den Zweifronten Krieg"
W10/50267 – "Welche Nachrichten besass der deut. GGS über Mobilmachung und Aufmarsch des franz. Heeres in den Jahren 1885–1914"
W10/50276 – "Die militärpolitische Lage Deutschlands"
W10/50294 – "Spionage und Agenten, 1915–17"
W10/50355 – "Das russische Heer 1914"
W10/50358 – Excerpts from the Auswärtiges Amt Files Relating to Italy 1915
W10/50472 – "Kriegsrohstoffabteilung im Kriegsministerium"
W10/50629 – Aufzeichnungen des Generalmajors van den Bergh
W10/50634 – Tagebuch Einem (6.9.14–12.11.18)
W10/50635 – Tagebuch Falkenhayn (26.7–4.8.1914)
W10/50636 – General a.D. Franke, "Erinnerungen 1913–1916"
W10/50652 – Persönliches KTB des Generals der Inf. a.D. von Kuhl (Nov 15–Nov 18)

W10/50656 – Tagebuch Plessen (Oct 14–23 Dec 17)
W10/50661 – Tagebuch Tappen and Kriegserinnerungen
W10/50671 – "Gefechtsberichte und KTB des Oberkommando der Heeresgruppe Deut. Kronprinz (21.2.16–3.16)"
W10/50676 – Comments to "Der Krieg im Westen 1914"
W10/50683 – Falkenhayn/Conrad Memoranda, May 1915
W10/50689 – Telegram Exchange about Gorlice, Apr–May 1915
W10/50696 – Telegram Exchange Between Hgr Mackensen and OHL, Summer/Fall 1915
W10/50704 – "Die Führung Falkenhayns"
W10/50705 – Verdun Planning and Planning 1916
W10/50707 – Planning in West 1915
W10/50708 – "Protokoll des stellvertretenden Chef d. Adm.St. (1.1.16)"
W10/50709 – Materialsammlung for Band X
W10/50712 – "Losbrechen der Sommeschlacht bis zum Rücktritt Falkenhayns (1.Juli–28.Aug)"
W10/50728 – Nachlass Mackensen
W10/50730 – Correspondence Between Moltke and Ludendorff, 1912
W10/50731 – Analysis of Austria-Hungary in Pre-War Period
W10/50744 – Misc. Materialsammlungen und Forschungsarbeiten, 1914–1918
W10/50755 – Training Documents, 1914–1918
W10/50756 – "Organization und Gang der Ausbildung der Offiziere und Mannschaften . . . 1914–1918"
W10/50872 – Gas Attack at Ypres, 1915
W10/50897 – "Äusserungen des Generals von Moltke über die Möglichkeit einer schnellen Feldzugsentscheidung im Westen"
W10/51063 – Documents Relating to the Hentsch Mission and Falkenhayn's Promotion
W10/51151 – "Die Umstellung vom Bewegungs- zum Stellungskrieg"
W10/51158 – "OHL – Die Entscheidung vom 4.Nov.1914"
W10/51159 – "Die OHL im Westen 2–28 Nov 1915"
W10/51160 – "Die OHL im Westen"
W10/51170 – Comments to Bände V and VI
W10/51176 – Comments to Bände V and VI
W10/51177 – Comments to Bände V and VI
W10/51305 – Correspondence Relating to Band VII
W10/51306 – Political Position Before Italy's Entry
W10/51309 – "Der Kriegseintritt Italiens und der Mehrfrontkrieg"
W10/51310 – Files from the Austwärtiges Amt, 1915
W10/51312 – "Die Leitung des deut. Westheeres im Mai, Juni, Juli 1915"
W10/51313 – "Transportbewegungen vom Ost–zum Westkriegschauplatz Sep/Oct 15"
W10/51314 – "Herbstschlacht 1915"
W10/51318 – "3.XII.15–8.I.16: Die Entstehung des Operationsplanes"
W10/51322 – "Seekrieg 1915"
W10/51329 – "1.Durchbruchsversuche Feb 14–Apr 16"

W10/51345 – "Die Westfront August bis Dezember 1915"
W10/51346 – "Die Westfront August bis Dez 1915"
W10/51347 – "Herbstschlacht 1915"
W10/51350 – "Artois 22 Sep.–Oct. 1915 (Luftstreitkräfte)"
W10/51352 – "OHL und 25. and 26. Sep 15"
W10/51353 – "Leitung des Westheeres in Herbschlacht"
W10/51356 – "Winterschlacht 1915"
W10/51358 – "3.Armee in Herbstschlacht"
W10/51369 – Drafts for the Campaign in East Fall/Winter 1915
W10/51373 – "Beurteilung der Feindliche Lage (Ost) Jan–Mar 1915"
W10/51380 – "Die Urheberschaft am Entschluss" (Gorlice)
W10/51388 – "OHL, Ost-Operationen 18.5–10.1915"
W10/51393 – Austrian Forschungsarbeit about Gorlice
W10/51408 – Comments to Band VIII
W10/51441 – Comments to Band VII
W10/51445 – Comments to Band VII (East)
W10/51448 – Comments to Band VIII
W10/51449 – Comments to Band VII
W10/51489 – Materialsammlung for 1915–1916
W10/51490 – Correspondence Relating to Band X
W10/51519 – "Kriegführung in Westen: Abschriften und Auszüge aus Akten und Tagebüchern betr. 1916"
W10/51520 – "Tageweise Aktenauszüge betr. die Leitung des Westheeres (Jan–Aug 16)"
W10/51521 – "Beurteilung der Fran., Eng., und Bel. Armeen 1915–16"
W10/51523 – "Die OHL und die Kämpfe um Verdun" and "Falkenhayn in Rückblick"
W10/51526 – "Lage bei der 5.Armee im Abschnitt westlich der Maas bei Beginn der Angriffsvorbereitungen (Dez–Jan 16)"
W10/51528 – Comments and Materialsammlung on Verdun
W10/51529 – "Die Vorbereitung des Angriffs auf Verdun und die Weitergestaltung der damit in Verbindung stehenden Operationsgedanken."
W10/51534 – OHL Files Relating to Verdun
W10/51535 – Drafts of Band X
W10/51543 – Materialsammlung for Verdun 1916
W10/51544 – "Westfront bis zum Sommer 1916"
W10/51553 – AOK 5 Files Relating to Verdun, 1916
W10/51583 – "HgKP Gefechtsberichte 15.3.16–3.4.16"
W10/51584 – Matterialsammlung for Verdun (Mar–Apr 16)
W10/51592 – "Die OHL in der Führung der Westoperationen Ende 1915 bis Ende August 1916: VII: Vom 5.Juni–30.Juni 1916"
W10/51611 – Sommeschlacht 1916 (Teil 2)
W10/51614 – Sommeschlacht

BUNDESARCHIV/ABTEILUNG REICH UND DDR, BERLIN-LICHTERFELDE

Erich von Falkenhayn Nachlass (N2088)

STAATSBIBLIOTHEK ZU BERLIN-PREUSSISCHER KULTURBESITZ-HANDSCHRIFTENABTEILUNG

Hans Delbrück Nachlass

PUBLIC RECORD OFFICE, KEW

Personal Papers

Friedrich Graf von Pourtalès (GFM 25/3)
Gottlieb von Jagow (GFM 25/14)

War Office Papers

WO106	Directorate of Operations Files
WO157	Directorate of Military Intelligence Files

German Foreign Ministry Archive

GFM 6/141	Russland 93/17
GFM 10/89	Russland 72 geh.
GFM 10/289	Russland 131/5 sec.
GFM 11/68	Deutschland 121/secreta
GFM 14/21	Belgien 60 geh.
GFM 14/22	Belgien 60 geh.
GFM 14/90	Deutschland 121/31 geh.
GFM 20/3	Belgien 51
GFM 21/26	Deutschland 121/Gen.
GFM 21/27	Deutschland 121/8
GFM 21/41	Deutschland 121/26
GFM 21/42	Deutschland 121/26
GFM 21/319	Deutschland 121/14
GFM 21/412	Deutschland 121/7
GFM 21/413	Deutschland 121/7
GFM 34/2580	Geheime Berichte aus GHQ
GFM 34/2584	Weltkrieg geh. (Apr.–June 1915)
GFM 34/2585	Weltkrieg geh. (June–Aug. 1915)
GFM 34/2586	Weltkrieg geh. (Aug.–Sept. 1915)
GFM 34/2587	Weltkrieg geh. (Sept.–Nov. 1915)
GFM 34/2587	Weltkrieg geh. (Nov.–Dec. 1915)
GFM 34/2588	Weltkrieg geh. (Jan.–Mar. 1916)
GFM 34/2589	Weltkrieg geh. (Mar.–May 1916)
GFM 34/2590	Weltkrieg geh. (June–July 1916)
GFM 34/2591	Weltkrieg geh. (July–Oct. 1916)

US NATIONAL ARCHIVES RECORD GROUP 242 (CAPTURED GERMAN RECORDS)

Personal Papers

Groener, Wilhelm. Microfilm Publication M-137
Ludendorff, Erich. Microfilm Publication T-84

Mertz von Quirnheim, Hermann. Microfilm Publication M-958
Schlieffen, Alfred Graf von. Microfilm Publication M-961
Seeckt, Hans von. Microfilm Publication M-132

Others

Akten des königlichen Militär-Kabinett Abteilung I. (Mobilmachung 1914) Microfilm Publication M-962

PUBLISHED PRIMARY SOURCES (BRITISH ARMY CENTRAL DISTRIBUTION SERVICE/ARMY PRINTING AND STATIONARY SERVICE SERIES)

CDS 303: "Experiences Gained in the Winter Battle in Champagne from the Point of View of the Organization of the Enemy's Lines of Defence and the Means of Combatting an Attempt To Pierce Our Line," German 3rd Army Headquarters, 14 April 1915

CDS 304: "Proposals for the Technical Methods To Be Adopted in an Attempt To Break Through a Strongly Fortified Position, Based on the Knowledge Acquired from the Errors which Appear To Have Been Committed by the French during the Winter Campaign in Champagne," German 3rd Army Headquarters, 14 April 1915

SS 405: "Notes on German Artillery Emplacements, 1915"

SS 454: "Experience Gained from the September Offensives on the Fronts of the Sixth and Third Armies," German 2nd Army Headquarters, 5 November 1915

SS 471: "Essential Principles for the Defence of Positions as Laid Down in Instructions Issued by GHQ," German 2nd Army, 1 August 1915

PUBLISHED PRIMARY SOURCES (OFFICIAL HISTORIES AND STUDIES)

Armee-Oberkommando 3. *The Champagne-Herbstschlacht.* Munich: Albert Langen, 1916.

Bayerisches Kriegsarchiv. *Die Bayern im Großen Kriege 1914–1918: Auf Grund der amtlichen Kriegsakten dargestellt* (2nd ed.). Munich: Verlag des Bayerischen Kriegsarchivs, 1923.

Beumelburg, Werner. *Loretto.* (*Schlachten des Weltkrieges*, Band 17) Berlin: Gerhard Stalling, 1927.

Bundesministerium für Landesverteidigung. *Österreich-Ungarns Letzter Krieg* (7 vols.). Vienna: Verlag der Militärwissenschaftlichen Mitteilungen, 1934–38.

Doerstling, ed. *Kriegsgeschichte des Königlich Preußischen Infanterie-Regiments Graf Tauentzien v. Wittenberg (3.Brandenb.) Nr. 20.* Zeulenroda: Bernhard Sporn, 1933.

Edmonds, James E., ed. *Military Operations: France and Belgium 1916*, Vol. I: *Sir Douglas Haig's Command to the 1st July: Battle of the Somme*. London: Macmillan, 1932.

Flex, Walter. *Die russische Frühjahrsoffensive 1916* (*Der grosse Krieg in Einzeldarstellungen* Heft 31). Oldenburg: Gerhard Stalling, 1919.

Friedeburg, Friedrich von. *Karpathen- und Dniester-Schlacht 1915 (Schlachten des Weltkrieges* Band 9). Berlin: Gerhard Stalling, 1924.

Gold, Ludwig. *Die Tragödie von Verdun 1916 (Schlachten des Weltkrieges* Bände 13–15). Berlin: Gerhard Stalling, 1928.

Großer Generalstab, Kriegsgeschichtliche Abteilung. *Der deutsch-französische Krieg 1870–71* (8 vols.). Berlin: E. S. Mittler, 1874–1881.

Die Kriege Friedrichs des Grossen: Der Erste Theil: Der Erste Schlesische Krieg, 1740–1742 (2 vols.). Berlin: E. S. Mittler, 1892–93.

Studien zur Kriegsgeschichte und Taktik III: *Der Schlachterfolg.* Berlin: E. S. Mittler, 1903.

Studien zur Kriegsgeschichte und Taktik V: *Der 18 August 1870.* Berlin: E. S. Mittler, 1906.

Hüttmann, Adolf and Friedrich Wilhelm Krüger. *Das Infanterie-Regiment von Lützow (1.Rhein.) Nr. 25 im Weltkriege 1914–1918.* Berlin: Wilhelm Kolk, 1929.

Kalm, Oskar Tile von. *Gorlice* (*Schlachten des Weltkrieges* Band 30). Berlin: Gerhard Stalling, 1930.

Kirchbach, Arndt von. *Kämpfe in der Champagne* (*Winter 1914–Herbst 1915*) (*Der grosse Krieg in Einzeldarstellungen* Heft 11). Oldenburg: Gerhard Stalling, 1919.

Meyer, Gustav. *Der Durchbruch am Narew* (*Juli-August 1915*) (*Der grosse Krieg in Einzeldarstellungen* Heft 27/28). Oldenburg: Gerhard Stalling, 1919.

Ministère de la Guerre. *Les Armées Françaises dans la Grande Guerre* (10 vols.). Paris: Imprimerie Nationale, 1922–1939.

Pehlmann. *Die Kämpfe der Bug-Armee* (*Der grosse Krieg in Einzeldarstellungen* Heft 26). Oldenburg: Gerhard Stalling, 1918.

Philipp, Albrecht. *Die Ursachen des Deutschen Zusammenbruchs im Jahre 1918* (*Vierte Reihe im Werk des Untersuchungsausschusses*), Bd. III. Berlin: Deutsche Verlagsgesellschaft für Politik, 1925.

Reichsarchiv. *Der Weltkrieg 1914–1918: Die militärischen Operationen zu Lande* (14 vols.). Berlin: E. S. Mittler, 1925–56.

Trach, Leonhard Graf von Rothkirch Freiherr von. *Gorlice-Tarnow (Der grosse Krieg in Einzeldarstellungen* Heft 21). Oldenburg: Gerhard Stalling, 1918.

PUBLISHED PRIMARY SOURCES (OTHERS)

Anon. "Erinnerungen an Galizien 1915," *Wissen und Wehr* (1922) 163–178.

Bauer, Max. *Der grosse Krieg im Feld und Heimat.* Tübingen: Osiander'sche Buchhandlung, 1921.

Berendt, [Richard]. "Mit der Artillerie durch den Weltkrieg," *Wissen und Wehr* (1924) 36–47, 185–197.

Berghahn, Volker R. and Wilhelm Deist. *Rüstung im Zeichen der wilhelminischen Weltpolitik: Grundlegende Dokumente, 1890–1914.* Düsseldorf: Droste, 1988.

Bernhardi, Friedrich von. *Delbrück, Friedrich der Grosse und Clausewitz. Streiflichter auf die Lehren des Professor Dr. Delbrück über Strategie.* Berlin: E. S. Mittler, 1892.

Germany and the Next War. London: Edward Arnold, 1912.

How Germany Makes War. London: Hodder & Stoughton, 1914.

Denkwürdigkeiten aus meinem Leben. Berlin: E. S. Mittler, 1927.

Bethmann Hollweg, Theobald von. *Betrachtungen zum Weltkriege* (2 vols.). Berlin: Reimer Hobbing, 1919–21.

Bloch, Jean. *The Future of War.* New York: Garland Publishing, 1971.

Brandis, Cordt von. *Der Sturmangriff: Kriegserfahrungen eines Frontoffiziers.* No publisher, 1917.

Bronsart von Schellendorf, Paul von. *Geheimes Kriegstagebuch, 1870–1871.* Ed. Peter Rassow. Bonn: Athenäum, 1954.

Caemmerer, Rudolf von. *Die Befreiungskriege 1813/15. Ein strategische Überblick.* Berlin: E. S. Mittler, 1901.

Die Entwicklung der strategischen Wissenschaft im 19. Jahrhundert. Berlin: Wilhelm Baensch, 1904.

The Development of Strategical Science During the 19th Century. London: Hugh Rees, 1905.

Cardinal von Widdern, Georg. *Deutsch-französischer Krieg 1870–1871: Der Krieg an den rückwärtigen Verbindungen der deutschen Heere* (6 vols.). Berlin: R. Eisenschmidt, 1893–99.

Claer, Eberhard von. "Meine Tätigkeit als Chef des Ingenieur- und Pionierkorps und General-Inspekteur der Festungen sowie als General vom Chef des Ingenieur- und Pionierkorps im Großen Hauptquartier," *Vierteljahreshefte für Pioniere* (Nov. 1937) 199–206.

Clausewitz, Carl von. *Vom Kriege.* Leipzig: Insel-Verlag, 1937.

On War. Trans. and ed. Michael Howard and Peter Paret. Princeton, NJ: Princeton University Press, 1976.

Historical and Political Writings. Ed. and trans. Peter Paret and David Moran. Princeton, NJ: Princeton University Press, 1992.

"Über das Fortschreiten und den Stillstand den kriegerischen Begebenheiten." Ed. Hans Delbrück. *Zeitschrift für preußische Geschichte und Landeskunde* 15 (May–June 1878) 233–264.

Conrad von Hötzendorf, Franz Graf. *Aus meiner Dienstzeit 1906–1918* (5 vols.). Vienna: Rikola Verlag, 1925.

Private Aufzeichnungen: Erste Veröffentlichen aus den Papieren des k.u.k. Generalstabs-Chef. Ed. Kurt Peball. Vienna: Amalthea, 1977.

Cramon, August von. *Unser österreichisch-ungarischer Bundesgenosse im Weltkriege.* Berlin: E. S. Mittler, 1920.

Daniloff, Jurij. *Rußland im Weltkriege 1914–1915.* Trans. Rudolph Freiherr von Campenhausen. Jena: Frommannsche Buchhandlung, 1925.

Deimling, Berthold von. *Aus der alten in die neue Zeit.* Berlin: Verlag Ullstein, 1930.

Deist, Wilhelm, ed. *Militär und Innenpolitik im Weltkrieg 1914–1918* (2 vols.). Düsseldorf: Droste, 1970.

Delbrück, Hans. *Krieg und Politik 1914–16.* Berlin: Georg Stilke, 1918.

Weltgeschichte. Vorlesungen, gehalten an der Universität Berlin 1896–1920. Vol. 5: *Neuzeit von 1852 bis 1888.* Berlin: Otto Stollberg, 1928.

History of the Art of War: The Modern Era. Trans. Walter J. Renfroe, Jr. Westport, CT: Greenwood Press, 1985.

Delbrück's Modern Military History. Trans. and ed. Arden Bucholz. Lincoln: University of Nebraska Press, 1997.

"Clausewitz," *Zeitschrift für preußische Geschichte und Landeskunde* 15 (March–April 1878) 217–231.

"Duplik," *Zeitschrift für preußische Geschichte und Landeskunde* 16 (May–June 1879) 305–314.

Review of *Militärische Testament Friedrichs des Grossen* in *Zeitschrift für preußische Geschichte und Landeskunde* 16 (Jan.–Feb. 1879) 27–32.

"Wiederabdruck der Duplik aus dem Mai–Juniheft," *Zeitschrift für preußische Geschichte und Landeskunde* 16 (July–Aug. 1879) 408–422.

"Friedrich der Grosse als Feldherr," *Zeitschrift für preußische Geschichte und Landeskunde* 18 (Nov.–Dec. 1881) 541–573.

"Die methodische Kriegführung Friedrichs des Grossen," *Preußische Jahrbücher* 54 (1884) 195–212.

"Die Strategie des Perikles erläutert durch die Strategie Friedrichs des Grossen," *Preußische Jahrbücher* 64 (1889) 258–305, 450–486, 503–528.

"Zukunftskrieg und Zukunftsfriede," *Preußische Jahrbücher* 96 (1899) 203–229.

"Ein Nachwort zu Kosers Aufsatz über Friedrich des Grossen Kriegführung," *Historische Zeitschrift* 93 (1904) 66–70.

"Zur Kriegführung Friedrichs des Grossen: Ein zweites Nachwort," *Historische Zeitschrift* 93 (1904) 449–456.

Review of *General von Schlichting und sein Lebenswerk* in *Preußische Jahrbücher* 151 (1913) 342–347.

"Falkenhayn und Ludendorff," *Preußische Jahrbücher* 180 (1920) 249–281.

"Die strategische Grundfrage des Weltkrieges," *Preußische Jahrbücher* 183 (1921), pp. 289–308.

Einem, Karl von. *Erinnerungen eines Soldaten 1853–1933.* Leipzig: v. Hase & Koehler, 1933.

Ein Armeeführer erlebt den Weltkrieg, Persönliche Aufzeichnungen. Ed. Junius Alter. Leipzig: v. Hase & Koehler, 1938.

Falkenhausen, Ludwig Freiherr von. *Flankenbewegung und Massenheer.* Berlin: E. S. Mittler, 1911.

Falkenhayn, Erich von. *General Headquarters and its Critical Decisions 1914–1916.* London: Hutchinson, 1919.

Die oberste Heeresleitung, 1914–1916, in ihren wichtigsten Entschliessungen. Berlin: E. S. Mittler, 1920.

Foch, Ferdinand. *The Memoirs of Marshal Foch* (2 vols.). Trans. T. Bently Mott. London: William Heinemann, 1931.

François, Hermann von. *Gorlice 1915: Der Karpathendurchbruch und die Befreiung von Galizien.* Leipzig: K. F. Koehler, 1922.

Freytag-Loringhoven, Hugo Freiherr von. *Deductions From the Great War.* London: Constable & Co., 1918.

Heerführung im Weltkriege: Vergleichende Studien (2 vols.). Berlin: E. S. Mittler, 1920.

Feldherrngröße: Vom Denken und Handeln hervorragender Heerführer. Berlin: E. S. Mittler, 1922.

Menschen und Dinge, wie ich sie in meinem Leben sah. Berlin: E. S. Mittler, 1923.

"Friedensarbeit und Kriegslehren," *Beiheft zum Militär-Wochenblatt* (1899).

"Die Offensive mit beschränktem Ziel," *Vierteljahrshefte für Truppenführung und Heereskunde* 8 (1911) 250–257.

Gallwitz, Max von. *Meine Führertätigkeit im Weltkrieg 1914–16.* Berlin: E. S. Mittler, 1929.

"Zur Nordost-Offensive im Sommer 1915," *Militär-Wochenblatt* 28 (1936) 1219–1222.

German General Staff. *Ypres, 1914.* Nashville: The Battery Press, 1994.

Goltz, Colmar Freiherr von der. *Leon Gambetta und seine Armeen.* Berlin: F. Schneider, 1877.

Das Volk in Waffen: Ein Buch über Heerwesen und Kriegführung unserer Zeit. Berlin: R. von Decker, 1883.

Von Roßbach bis Jena und Auerstedt. Berlin: E. S. Mittler, 1906.

The Nation in Arms. London: Hugh Rees, 1906.

Jena bis Pr. Eylau. Berlin: E. S. Mittler, 1907.

The Conduct of War. London: Kegan Paul, Trench, Truebner & Co., 1908.

Jena to Eylau. London: Kegan Paul, Trench, Treubner & Co., 1913.

Denkwürdigkeiten. Berlin: E. S. Mittler, 1929.

"Antikritik," *Zeitschrift für preußische Geschichte und Landeskunde* 16 (May–June 1879) 292–304.

"Entgegnung auf die Duplik des Herrn Delbruck in May–Juniheft," *Zeitschrift für preußische Geschichte und Landeskunde* 16 (July–Aug. 1879) 391–407.

Groener, Wilhelm. *Lebenserinnerungen: Jugend, Generalstab, Weltkrieg.* Ed. Friedrich Freiherr Hiller von Gaertringen. Göttingen: Vandenhoeck & Ruprecht, 1957.

Haig, Douglas. *The Private Papers of Douglas Haig, 1914–1919.* Ed. Robert Blake. London: Eyre & Spottiswoode, 1952.

Hindenburg, Paul von. *Out of My Life.* London: Cassel & Co., 1920.

Aus meinem Leben. Leipzig: S. Hirzel, 1934.

Hintze, Otto. "Friedrich der Grosse nach dem Siebenjährigen Kriege und das Politische Testament von 1768," *Forschungen zur Brandenburgischen und Preußischen Geschichte* 32 (1920) 1–56.

Hoenig, Fritz. *Zwei Brigaden.* Berlin: E. S. Mittler, 1882.

24 Stunden Moltkescher Strategie entwickelt und erläutert an den Schlachten von Gravelotte und St. Privat. Berlin: E. S. Mittler, 1891.

Der Volkskrieg an der Loire im Herbst 1870 (6 vols.). Berlin: E. S. Mittler, 1893–99.

Meine Ehrenhandlung mit dem Oberst und Flügeladjutant von Schwarzkoppen und dem Oberst und Abteilungschef im Generalstabe von Bernhardi. Berlin: No publisher, 1902.

"Two Brigades," trans. Paul Romer. *Journal of the Military Services Institute* 12 (1891) 601–608, 828–841, 1088–1093, 1284–1295.

"Die ein- und zweipolige Strategie," *Deutsche Heeres-Zeitung* 70, Nr. 18 and 19 (1892).

Hoffmann, Max. *Die Aufzeichnungen des Generalmajors Max Hoffmann*. Ed. Karl-Friedrich Nowak. Berlin: E. S. Mittler, 1929.

War Diaries and Other Papers (2 vols.). Trans. Eric Sutton. London: Martin Secker, 1929.

Hölze, Erwin, ed. *Quellen zur Entstehung des Ersten Weltkrieges: Internationale Dokumente, 1901–1914*. Darmstadt: Wissenschaftliche Buchgesellschaft, 1978.

Jähns, Max. *Geschichte der Kriegswissenschaft*, Vol. III: *Das XVII. Jahrhundert seit dem Auftreten Friedrichs des Grossen*. Munich: Oldenbourg, 1891.

"Über den Wandel der strategischen Anschauungen Friedrichs des Grossen," *Allgemeine Zeitung*, 23 February 1892, pp. 4–7.

Joffre, Joseph. *The Memoirs of Marshal Joffre* (2 vols.). Trans. T. Bentley Mott. London: Geoffrey Bles, 1932.

Keim, August. "Kriegslehre und Kriegsführung," *Beiheft zum Militär-Wochenblatt* (1889).

Kluck, Alexander von. *The March on Paris and the Battle of the Marne 1914*. London: Edward Arnold, 1920.

Wanderjahre – Kriege – Gestalten. Berlin: R. Eisenschmidt, 1929.

Koser, Reinhold. "Die preußiche Kriegsführung im Siebenjährigen Kriege," *Historische Zeitschrift* 92 (1903) 239–273.

"Zur Geschichte des preußischen Feldzugsplanes vom Frühjahr 1757," *Historische Zeitschrift* 93 (1904) 71–76.

"Zustaz," *Historische Zeitschrift* 93 (1904) 456–458.

Kriegsministerium. *Exerzir-Reglement für die Infanterie*. Berlin: E. S. Mittler, 1888.

Exerzier-Reglement für die Infanterie. Berlin: E. S. Mittler, 1906.

Felddienst-Ordnung. E. S. Mittler, 1908.

Kuhl, Hermann von. *Der Marnefeldzug 1914*. Berlin: E. S. Mittler, 1921.

Der deutsche Generalstab in Vorbereitung und Durchführung des Weltkrieges. Berlin: E. S. Mittler, 1920.

Loßberg, Fritz von. *Meine Tätigkeit im Weltkrieg 1914–1918*. Berlin: E. S. Mittler, 1939.

Ludendorff, Erich. *Meine Kriegserinnerungen 1914–1918*. Berlin: E. S. Mittler, 1919.

Kriegführung und Politik. Berlin: E. S. Mittler, 1922.

Mein militärischer Werdegang. Munich: Ludendorff, 1933.

Mackensen, August von. *Briefe und Aufzeichnungen*. Ed. Wolfgang Foerster. Leipzig: Bibliographische Institut, 1938.

Moltke, Helmuth Graf von. *Gesammelte Schriften und Denkwürdigkeiten*. (8 vols.) Berlin: E. S. Mittler, 1891–92.

Militärische Werke, Vol. I: *Militärische Korrespondenz*. Berlin: E. S. Mittler, 1897.

The Franco-German War of 1870–1871. Trans. Archibald Forbes. London: Harper & Brothers, 1907.

Graf Moltke: Die Aufmarschpläne 1871–1890. Ed. Ferdinand von Schmerfeld. Berlin: E. S. Mittler, 1929.

Vom Kabinettskrieg zum Volkskrieg: Eine Werksauswahl. Ed. Stig Förster. Berlin: Bouvier, 1992.

Moltke, Helmuth von. *Erinnerungen, Briefe, Dokumente, 1877–1916.* Ed. Eliza von Moltke. Stuttgart: Der Kommende Tag A. G., 1922.

Moser, Otto von. *Feldzugsaufzeichnungen 1914–1918 als Brigade-, Divisionskommandeur und als kommandierender General.* 3rd ed. Stuttgart: Chr. Belser A. G. Verlagsbuchhandlung, 1928.

Müller, Georg von. *The Kaiser and His Court: The First World War Diaries of Admiral Georg von Müller.* Ed. Walter Görlitz. Trans. Mervyn Savill. London: MacDonald, 1961.

Nicolai, Walter. *Geheime Mächte. Internationale Spionage und ihre Bekämpfung im Weltkrieg und Heute.* Leipzig: K. F. Koehler, 1923.

Pétain, Henri Philippe. *Verdun.* Trans. Margaret MacVeagh. London: Elkin Mathews & Marrot, 1930.

Riezler, Kurt. *Tagebücher, Aufsätze, Dokumente.* Ed. Karl Dietrich Erdmann. Göttingen: Vandenhoeck & Ruprecht, 1972.

Roloff, Gustav. "Eine vermeintliche neue Auffassung der Strategie Friedrichs des Grossen," *Beilage zur Allgemeine Zeitung* Nr. 16 (1892).

Roon, Albrecht Graf von. *Denkwürdigkeiten aus dem Leben des General-Feldmarschalls Kriegministers Grafen von Roon.* (3 vols.) Berlin: E. S. Mittler, 1892.

Rupprecht von Bayern, Kronprinz. *Mein Kriegstagebuch.* (3 vols.) Ed. Eugen von Frauenholz. Berlin: E. S. Mittler, 1929.

Schlichting, Sigismund von. *Taktische und strategische Grundsätze der Gegenwart.* (3 vols.) Berlin: E. S. Mittler, 1898–99.

Moltkes Vermächtniss. Munich: Verlag der Allgemeine Zeitung, 1901.

"Über das Infanteriegefecht," *Beihefte zum Militär-Wochenblatt* (1879).

Schlieffen, Alfred von. *Gesammelte Schriften.* (2 vols.) Berlin: E. S. Mittler, 1913.

Cannae. Berlin: E. S. Mittler, 1925.

Dienstschriften: Bd. I: *Die taktisch-strategischen Aufgaben.* Berlin: E. S. Mittler, 1937.

Dienstschriften: Bd. II: *Generalstabsreisen – Ost – aus den Jahren 1891–1905.* Berlin: E. S. Mittler, 1938.

Briefe. Ed. Eberhard Kessel. Göttingen: Vandenhoeck & Ruprecht, 1958.

Seeckt, Hans von. *Aus meinem Leben 1866–1917.* Ed. Friedrich von Rabenau. Leipzig: Hase & Koehler, 1938.

Stürgkh, Josef. *Im deutschen Grossen Hauptquartier.* Leipzig: Paul List, 1927.

Tappen, Gerhard. *Bis zur Marne.* Oldenburg: Stalling, 1920.

Waldersee, Alfred Graf von. *Denkwürdigkeiten des General-Feldmarschalls Alfred Graf von Waldersee.* (3 vols.) Ed. Heinrich Otto Meisner. Stuttgart: Deutsche Verlags-Anstalt, 1923.

Wild von Hohenborn, Adolf. *Briefe und Tagebuchaufzeichnungen des preussischen Generals als Kriegsminister und Truppenführer im Ersten Weltkrieg.* Ed. Helmut Reichold (Schriften des Bundesarchivs 34). Boppard: Harald Boldt, 1986.

Wilhelm, Kronprinz. *Meine Erinnerungen aus Deutschlands Heldenkampf.* Berlin: E. S. Mittler, 1923.

Wrisberg, Ernst von. *Heer und Heimat 1914–1918.* Leipzig: K. F. Koehler, 1921.

Yorck von Wartenburg, Maximilian Graf. *Napoleon als Feldherr.* (2 vols.) Berlin: E. S. Mittler, 1885.

Kurze Übersicht der Feldzüge Alexanders des Grossen. Berlin: E. S. Mittler, 1897.

Zechlin, Egmont. "Ludendorff im Jahre 1915. Unveröffentlichte Briefe," *Historische Zeitschrift* 211 (1970) 316–353.

Zwehl, Hans von. *Maubeuge – Aisne – Verdun: Das VII. Reserve-Korps im Weltkriege von seinem Beginn bis Ende 1916.* Berlin: Karl Curtius, 1921.

SECONDARY SOURCES

Afflerbach, Holger. *Falkenhayn: Politisches Denken und Handlen im Kaiserreich.* Munich: Oldenbourg, 1994.

"Wilhelm II as Supreme Warlord in the First World War," *War in History* 5, 4 (1998) 427–449.

Albertini, A. *General Falkenhayn: Die Beziehungen zwischen den Generalstabschefs des Dreibundes.* Berlin: E. S. Mittler, 1924.

Asprey, Robert B. *The German High Command at War: Hindenburg and Ludendorff Conduct World War I.* New York: William Morrow and Company, 1991.

Auwers, –. "Einige Betrachtungen zu General Groeners 'Testament des Grafen Schlieffen'," *Wissen und Wehr* (1927) 146–172.

Baer, C. H., ed. *Der Völkerkrieg*, Bd. 6. Stuttgart: Julius Hoffmann, 1915.

Balck, William. *Entwickelung der Taktik im Weltkriege.* Berlin: R. Eisenschmidt, 1922.

"Über den Infanterieangriff," *Militär-Wochenblatt* 29 (1919) 561–564.

Bald, Detlef, ed. *Militärische Verantwortung in Staat und Gesellschaft: 175 Jahre Generalstabsausbildung in Deutschland.* Koblenz: Bernard & Graefe, 1986.

Beach, James. "Haig's Intelligence: GHQ's Perception of the Enemy, 1916–1918," unpublished manuscript, October 1998.

Beck, Ludwig. *Studien.* Stuttgart: K. F. Koehler, 1955.

Berendt, Richard von. "Mit der Artillerie durch den Weltkrieg," *Wissen und Wehr* (1924) 26–47 and 185–197.

"Einfluss der Festungen auf die Operation," *Wissen und Wehr* (1925) 263–269.

Bergh, Max van den. *Das Deutsche Heer vor dem Weltkriege: Eine Darstellung und Würdigung.* Berlin: Sanssouci Verlag, 1934.

Bischoff, Kurt. *Im Trommelfeuer: Die Herbstschlacht in der Champagne 1915.* Leipzig: Verlag Buchhandlung Gebrüder Fändrich, 1939.

Blond, Georges. *Verdun.* Trans. Frances Frenaye. London: White Lion Publishers Ltd., 1976 [1961].

Boetticher, Friedrich von. *Schlieffen.* Göttingen: Musterschmidt Verlag, 1957.

Bond, Brian. *War and Society in Europe, 1870–1970.* London: Fontana Paperback, 1984.

The Pursuit of Victory: From Napoleon to Saddam Hussein. Oxford: Oxford University Press, 1996.

Borgert, Heinz-Ludger. "Grundzüge der Landkriegführung von Schlieffen bis Guderian," *Handbuch zur deutschen Militärgeschichte 1648–1939*, Vol. IX. Munich: Bernard & Graefe, 1979.

Bothmer, Count A. "The Campaign on the Loire in the Autumn of 1870 (review of *Der Volkskrieg an der Loire im Herbst 1870*)," *United Services Magazine* (US) NS, 7 (1893) 1032–1044.

Brose, Eric Dorn. *The Kaiser's Army: The Politics of Military Technology in Germany during the Machine Age, 1870–1918*. Oxford: Oxford University Press, 2001.

Brückner, –. "Der Durchbruchsangriff vor dem Weltkriege in Anwendung und Theorie," *Militär-Wissenschaftliche Rundschau* 3 (1938) 586–601.

Buchfinck, Ernst. *Feldmarschall Graf von Haeseler*. Berlin: E. S. Mittler, 1929.

"Feldmarschall Graf von Haeseler," *Wissen und Wehr* (1936) 1–9.

"Haeseler, wie er wirklich war," *Wissen und Wehr* (1936) 785–793.

Buchheit, Gert. *Vernichtungs- oder Ermattungsstrategie. Vom strategischen Charakter der Kriege*. Berlin: Paul Neff, 1942.

Bucholz, Arden. *Hans Delbrück and the German Military Establishment: War Images in Conflict*. Iowa City: University of Iowa Press, 1985.

Moltke, Schlieffen and Prussian War Planning. Providence, RI: Berg, 1991.

Buhle, P. "Bewegungskrieg und Stellungskrieg," *Militär-Wochenblatt* 24 (1933) 781–782.

Burchardt, Lothar. *Friedenswirtschaft und Kriegsvorsorge: Deutschlands wirtschaftliche Rüstungsbestrebungen vor 1914*. Boppard am Rhein: Harald Boldt, 1968.

Campbell, Frederick. "The Bavarian Army, 1870–1918: The Constitutional and Structural Relations with the Prussian Military Establishment." Ph.D. Dissertation, Ohio State University, 1972.

Cecil, Lamar. *Wilhelm II. Prince and Emperor, 1859–1900*. Chapel Hill, NC: University of North Carolina Press, 1989.

Wilhelm II. Emperor and Exile. Chapel Hill, NC: University of North Carolina Press, 1996.

Chickering, Roger. *Imperial Germany and the Great War, 1914–1918*. Cambridge: Cambridge University Press, 1998.

Chickering, Roger and Stig Förster, eds. *Great War, Total War: Combat and Mobilization on the Western Front, 1914–1918*. Cambridge: Cambridge University Press, 2000.

Clark, Alan. *The Donkeys*. London: Hutchinson, 1961.

Cochenhausen, Friedrich von, ed. *Von Scharnhorst zu Schlieffen, 1806–1906: Hundert Jahre preußisch-deutscher Generalstab*. Berlin: E. S. Mittler, 1933.

Coetzee, Marilyn Shevin. *The German Army League: Popular Nationalism in Wilhelmine Germany*. Oxford: Oxford University Press, 1990.

Collins, D. N. "The Franco-Russian Alliance and Russian Railways, 1891–1914," *The Historical Journal* 16, 4 (1973) 777–788.

Craig, Gordon. *The Politics of the Prussian Army*. New York: Oxford University Press, 1956.

"Delbrück: The Military Historian," in Peter Paret, ed., *Makers of Modern Strategy from Machiavelli to the Nuclear Age*. Princeton: Princeton University Press, 1986.

Creveld, Martin van. *Supplying War: Logistics from Wallenstein to Patton*. Cambridge: Cambridge University Press, 1977.

Cron, Hermann. *Die Organisation des deutschen Heeres*. Berlin: E. S. Mittler, 1931.

Daniels, Emil and Paul Rühlmann, eds. *Am Webstuhl der Zeit: Eine Erinnerungsgabe Hans Delbrück dem Achtzigjährigen von Freunden und Schülern dargebracht.* Berlin: Reimar Hobbing, 1928.

Deist, Wilhelm, ed. *The German Military in the Age of Modern War*. Providence, RI: Berg, 1985.

Militär, Staat und Gesellschaft: Studien zur preußisch-deutschen Militärgeschichte. Munich: Oldenbourg, 1991.

"The Military Collapse of the German Empire: The Reality Behind the Stab-in-the-Back Myth." Trans. E. J. Feuchtwanger. *War in History* 3, 2 (1996) 186–207.

Demeter, Karl. *The German Officer Corps in Society and State 1650–1945*. London: Weidenfeld and Nicolson, 1965.

DeWeerd, H. A., "The Verdun Forts," *The Cavalry Journal* 41, 70 (1932) 27–28.

Doerr, Hans. "Der 'Grosse Chef,'" *Wehrkunde* 6 (1957) 542–550.

Dollinger, Hans, ed. *Der Erste Weltkrieg*. Munich: Kurt Desch, 1965.

Düffler, Jost and Karl Holl, eds. *Bereit zum Krieg: Kriegsmentalität im wilhelminischen Deutschland, 1890–1914*. Göttingen: Vandenhoeck & Ruprecht, 1986.

Echevarria, Antulio J. *After Clausewitz: German Military Thinkers Before the Great War*. Lawrence: University Press of Kansas, 2000.

"Neo-Clausewitzianism: Freytag-Loringhoven and the Militarization of Clausewitz in German Military Literature Before the First World War." Ph.D. Thesis. Princeton University, 1994.

"On the Brink of the Abyss: The Warrior Identity and German Military Thought before the Great War," *War and Society* 13, 2 (1995) 23–40.

"Borrowing from the Master: Uses of Clausewitz in German Military Literature before the Great War," *War in History* 3, 3 (1996) 274–292.

"A Crisis in Warfighting: German Tactical Discussions in the Late Nineteenth Century." *Militärgeschichtliche Mitteilungen* 55, 1 (1996) 51–68.

"General Staff Historian Hugo Freiherr von Freytag-Loringhoven and the Dialectics of German Military Thought," *Journal of Military History* 60 (July 1996) 471–494.

Falls, Cyril. *The First World War*. London: Longmans, 1960.

Farrar, L. L. *The Short War Illusion: German Policy, Strategy and Domestic Affairs, August–December 1914*. Santa Barbara, CA: ABC-Clio, 1973.

Divide and Conquer: German Efforts to Conclude a Separate Peace, 1914–1918. New York: Columbia University Press, 1978.

"The Short War Illusion: The Syndrome of German Strategy, August-December, 1914," *Militärgeschichtliche Mitteilungen* 2 (1972) 39–52.

"Peace Through Exhaustion: German Diplomatic Motivation for the Verdun Campaign," *Revue Internationale d'Histoire Militare* 32 (1972–75) 477–494.

Farrar-Hockely, A. H. *The Somme*. London: Pan Books, 1966; originally published 1964.

Ferguson, Niall. *The Pity of War*. London: Allen Lane, 1998.

Ferro, Marc. *The Great War, 1914–1918*. London: Routledge, 1995.

Fiedler, Siegfried. *Kriegswesen und Kriegführung im Zeitalter der Millionenheere.* Bonn: Bernard & Graefe, 1993.

Fischer, F. *Germany's Aims in the First World War.* New York: W. W. Norton & Co., 1967.

Foerster, Roland G., ed. *Generalfeldmarschall von Moltke: Bedeutung und Wirkung.* Munich: Oldenbourg, 1991.

Die Wehrpflicht: Entstehung, Erscheinungsformen und politisch-militärische Wirkung. Munich: Oldenbourg, 1994.

Foerster, Wolfgang. *Graf Schlieffen und der Weltkrieg.* Berlin: E. S. Mittler, 1921.

Aus der Gedankenwerkstatt des Deutschen Generalstabes. Berlin: E. S. Mittler, 1931.

"Falkenhayns Plan für 1916. Ein Beitrag zur Frage: Wie gelangt man aus dem Stellungskrieg zu Entscheid ungsuchender Operation?," *Militär-Wissenschaftliche Rundschau* 2, 3 (1937) 304–330.

"Falkenhayn – der einsame Feldherr?," *Deutsche Wehr* 38, 3 (1934) 41–43.

"Einige Bemerkungen zu Gerhard Ritters Buch 'Der Schlieffenplan'," *Wehr-Wissenschaftliche Rundschau* (1957) 37–44.

Foley, Robert T. "Schlieffen's Last Kriegsspiel," *War Studies Journal* 3, 2 (1998) 117–133 and 4, 1 (1999) 97–115.

"East or West? Erich von Falkenhayn and German Strategy 1914–1915," in Matthew Hughes and Matthew Seligmann, eds. *Leadership in Conflict 1914–1918.* London: Leo Cooper, 2000.

"From *Volkskrieg* to *Vernichtungskrieg*: German Military Thought, 1871–1933," in Beatrice Heuser and Anja Hartmann, eds., *War, Peace and World Orders.* London: Routledge, 2001.

"Institutionalised Innovation: The German Army and the Changing Nature of War," *RUSI Journal* 147, 2 (2002) 84–90.

"The Origins of the Schlieffen Plan," *War in History* 10, 2 (2003) 253–263.

"More than He Appeared: Hermann von Kuhl and the German General Staff," in David Zabecki, ed., *Chiefs of Staff.* Annapolis: Naval Institute, 2005.

Foley, Robert T., ed. *Alfred von Schlieffen's Military Writings.* London: Frank Cass, 2002.

Förster, Stig. *Der Doppelte Militarismus: Die Deutsche Heeresrüstungspolitik zwischen Status-Quo-Sicherung und Aggression, 1890–1913.* Stuttgart: Franz Steiner, 1985.

"Facing People's War: Moltke the Elder and German Military Options After 1871," *Journal of Strategic Studies* 10, 2 (1987) 209–230.

"Der deutsche Generalstab und die Illusion des kurzen Krieges, 1871–1914. Metakritik eines Mythos," *Militärgeschichtliche Mitteilungen* 54 (1995) 61–95.

Förster, Stig and Jörg Nagler, eds. *Great War, Total War: Combat and Mobilization on the Western Front, 1914–1918.* Cambridge: Cambridge University Press, 2000.

On the Road to Total War: The American Civil War and the German Wars of Unification, 1861–1871. New York: Cambridge University Press, 1997.

Förster, Stig, Manfred Boemeke, and Roger Chickering, eds. *Anticipating Total War: The German and American Experiences, 1871–1914.* Cambridge: Cambridge University Press, 1999.

Frantz, Gunther. *Russlands Eintritt in den Weltkrieg: Der Ausbau der russischen Wehrmacht und ihr Einsatz bei Kriegsausbruch.* Berlin: Deutsche Verlagsgesellschaft für Politik und Geschichte, 1924.

"Die Entwicklung des Offensivgedankens im russischen Operationsplan," *Wissen und Wehr* (1924) 373–392.

"Russlands Westaufmarsch seit 1880," *Wissen und Wehr* (1930) 235–255.

"Betrachtungen zum Ostfeldzug 1915," *Deutsche Wehr* 19/20 (May 1934).

French, David. "The Meaning of Attrition," *English Historical Review* 103 (1988) 385–405.

Frevert, Ute, ed. *Militär und Gesellschaft im 19. und 20. Jahrhundert.* Stuttgart: Klett-Cotta, 1997.

Fuller, William C. *Strategy and Power in Russia 1600–1914.* New York: The Free Press, 1992.

Gersdorff, Ursula von. "Bibliographie des Militärgeschichtlichen Forschungsamtes 1956–1965," *Wehr-Wissenschaftliche Rundschau* 15, 3 (1965) 720–729.

Geyer, Hermann. "Lehren für den Kampf um Festungen aus den Ereignissen des Weltkrieges auf dem westlichen Kriegsschauplatz," *Wissen und Wehr* (1925) 441–512.

Geyer, Michael. *Deutsche Rüstungspolitik, 1860–1980.* Frankfurt: Suhrkamp, 1984.

Gilbert, Felix. "From Clausewitz to Delbrück to Hintze: Achievements and Failures of Military History," *Journal of Strategic Studies* 3, 3 (1980) 11–20.

Goerlitz, Walter. *History of the German General Staff 1657–1945.* Trans. Brian Battershaw. New York: Praeger, 1957.

Golovin, N. N. *The Russian Army in World War I.* New Haven: Yale University Press, 1931.

Grabau, Albert. *Das Festungsproblem in Deutschland und seine Auswirkung auf die strategische Lage von 1870–1914.* Berlin: Junker und Dünnhaupt, 1935.

"Great European War: Week by Week," *The Sphere*, 21 November 1914.

Groener, Wilhelm. *Das Testament des Grafen Schlieffen: Operative Studien über den Weltkrieg.* Berlin: E. S. Mittler, 1927.

Der Feldherr wider Willen: Operative Studien über den Weltkrieg. Berlin: E. S. Mittler, 1931.

"Das Testament des Grafen Schlieffen," *Wissen und Wehr* (1925) 193–217.

Grün, –. "Die schwere Artillerie der Division," *Wissen und Wehr* (1925) 621–629.

Gruss, Hellmuth. *Aufbau und Verwendung der deutschen Sturmbataillone im Weltkrieg.* Berlin: Junker und Dunnhaupt, 1939.

Gudmundsson, Bruce. *Stormtroop Tactics: Innovation in the German Army, 1914–1918.* New York: Praeger, 1989.

On Artillery. Westport, CT: Praeger, 1993.

"Trench Mortars," *Tactical Notebook* (March 1992).

Gudmundsson, Bruce and John English. *On Infantry.* Revised ed. London: Praeger, 1994.

Guth, Ekkehart. "Der Gegensatz zwischen dem Oberbefehlshaber Ost und dem Chef des Generalstabes des Feldheeres 1914/15: Die Rolle des Majors von

Haeften im Spannungsfeld zwischen Hindenburg, Ludendorff und Falkenhayn," *Militärgeschichtliche Mitteilungen* 1 (1984) 75–111.

Haeussler, Helmut. *General Wilhelm Groener and the Imperial German Army*. Madison: State Historical Society of Wisconsin, 1962.

Hale, Lonsdale. *The 'People's War' in France 1870–1871*. London: Hugh Rees, 1904.

Hallé, Guy le. *Le système Séré de Rivières ou le témoignage des Pierres*. Louvier: Ysec, 2001.

Herre, Paul. *Kronprinz Wilhelm: Seine Rolle in der Deutschen Politik*. Munich: C. H. Beck, 1954.

Herwig, Holger. *The First World War: Germany and Austria-Hungary, 1914–1918*. London: Arnold, 1997.

"From Tirpitz Plan to Schlieffen Plan: Some Observations on German Military Planning," *Journal of Strategic Studies* 9 (1986) 53–63.

"Clio Deceived: Patriotic Self-Censorship in Germany After the Great War," *International Security* 12, 2 (1987) 262–301.

"Germany and the 'Short-War' Illusion: Toward a New Interpretation?" *Journal of Military History* 66 (July 2002) 681–694.

Höbett, Lothar. "Schlieffen, Beck, Potiorek und das Ende der gemeinsamen deutsch-österreichisch-ungarischen Aufmarschpläne im Osten," *Militärgeschichtliche Mitteilungen* 12 (1984) 7–30.

Hoffmann, Joachim. "Wandlungen im Kriegsbild der preussischen Armee zur Zeit der nationalen Einigungskriege," *Militärgeschichtliche Mitteilungen* 1 (1968) 5–33.

"Die Kriegslehren des Generals von Schlichting," *Militärgeschichtliche Mitteilungen* 1 (1969) 5–35.

"Der Militärschriftsteller Fritz Hoenig," *Militärgeschichtliche Mitteilungen* 1 (1970) 5–25.

Hoffmeister, E. "Von Moltke zu Falkenhayn," *Wissen und Wehr* (1938) 513–536.

Holmes, Terence M. "The Reluctant March on Paris: A Reply to Terence Zuber's 'The Schlieffen Plan Reconsidered,'" *War in History* 8, 2 (2001) 208–232.

"The Real Thing: A Reply to Terence Zuber's 'Terence Holmes Reinvents the Schlieffen Plan,'" *War in History* 9, 1 (2002) 111–120.

Hölzle, Erwin. "Das Experiment des Friedens im Ersten Weltkrieg 1914–1917," *Geschichte in Wissenschaft und Unterricht* 8 (1962) 465–522.

Horne, Alister. *The Price of Glory: Verdun 1916*. New York: Penguin Books, 1993.

Hossbach, Friedrich. *Die Entwicklung des Oberbefehls über das Heer in Brandenburg, Preußen und im Deutschen Reich von 1655–1945*. Würzburg: Holzner, 1957.

Howard, Michael. *The Franco-Prussian War*. London: Rupert Hart-Davis, 1961.

"Men Against Fire: Expectations of War in 1914," *International Security* 9, 1 (1984) 41–57.

Hughes, Daniel J. *Moltke on the Art of War: Selected Writings*. Novato, CA: Presidio Press, 1993.

"Schlichting, Schlieffen, and the Prussian Theory of War in 1914," *Journal of Military History* 59 (April 1995) 257–278.

Huntington, Samuel P. *The Soldier and the State*. London: Harvard University Press, 1994 [1957].

Hüppauf, Bernd. "Langemarck, Verdun and the Myth of a New Man in Germany after the First World War," *War and Society* 6, 2 (1988) 70–103.

Janßen, Karl-Heinz. *Der Kanzler und der General. Die Führungskrise um Bethmann Hollweg und Falkenhayn, 1914–1916*. Göttingen: Musterschmidt, 1967.

"Der Wechsel in der Obersten Heeresleitung 1916," *Vierteljahrshefte für Zeitgeschichte* 7 (1959) 337–373.

Jany, Curt. *Geschichte der Königlich Preußischen Armee*. Bd. IV: *Die Koniglich Preußische Armee und das Deutsche Reichsheer 1807 bis 1914* (Berlin: Karl Siegismund, 1933).

Jarausch, Konrad. *The Enigmatic Chancellor: Bethmann Hollweg and the Hubris of Imperial Germany*. London: Yale University Press, 1973.

Kabisch, Ernst. *Verdun: Wende des Weltkrieges*. Berlin: Vorhut-Verlag Otto Schlegel, 1935.

"Vom missverstandenen Schlieffen," *Militär-Wochenblatt* 44 (1934) 1503–1505.

"Einiges Neue zum Handstreich auf Lüttich 1914," *Militär-Wochenblatt* 45 (1936) 2045–2050.

Kahn, David. *Hitler's Spies*. London: Hodder & Stoughton, 1978.

Kanter, Sanford. "Exposing the Myth of the Franco-Prussian War," *War and Society* 4, 1 (1986) 13–30.

Kaulbach, Eberhard. "Schlieffen zur Frage der Bedeutung und Wirkung seiner Arbeit," *Wehr-Wissenschaftliche Rundschau* 13 (1963) 137–149.

Kennan, George F. *The Fateful Alliance: France, Russia and the Coming of the First World War*. Manchester: Manchester University Press, 1984.

Kennedy, Paul. *The War Plans of the Great Powers, 1880–1914*. London: Allen & Unwin, 1979.

Kennedy, Paul, ed. *Grand Strategies in War and Peace*. New Haven, CT: Yale University Press, 1991.

Kessel, Eberhard. *Moltke*. Stuttgart: K. F. Koehler, 1957.

"Die doppelte Art des Krieges," *Wehr-Wissenschaftliche Rundschau* 4, 7 (1954) 298–310.

Kielmannsegg, Peter Graf von. *Deutschland und der Erste Weltkrieg*. Frankfurt: Akademische Verlagsgesellschaft Athenaion, 1968.

Kiliani, Emanuel von. "Die Operationslehre des Grafen Schlieffen und ihre deutschen Gegner," *Wehrkunde* 10 (1961).

King, Jere Clemens. *Generals and Politicians: Conflict Between France's High Command, Parliament and Government, 1914–1918*. Los Angeles: University of California Press, 1951.

Kitchen, Martin. "The Traditions of German Strategic Thought," *International History Review* 1, 2 (1979) 163–190.

Klauer, Markus. *Die Höhe Toter Mann während der Kämpfe um Verdun in den Jahren 1916/1917*. Velbert: Gesellschaft für Druck und Veredelung, 2001.

Kloster, Walter. *Der deutsche Generalstab und der Präventivkriegs-Gedanke*. Stuttgart: Kohlhammer, 1932.

Knox, Alfred. *With the Russian Army, 1914–1917* (2 vols.). London: Hutchinson, 1921.

Kolb, Eberhard. "Der schwierige Weg zum Frieden. Das Problem der Kriegsbeendigung 1870/71," *Historische Zeitschrift* 241 (1985) 51–79.

Krafft von Dellmensingen, Konrad. *Der Durchbruch: Studie an Hand der Vorgänge des Weltkrieges 1914–1918.* Hamburg: Hanseatische Verlagsanstalt, 1937.

Kraft, Heinz. *Staatsräson and Kriegsführung in kaiserlichen Deutschland 1914–1916: Der Gegensatz zwischen dem Generalstabschef von Falkenhayn und dem Oberbefehlshaber Ost im Rahmen des Bündniskrieges der Mittelmächte.* Frankfurt: Musterschmidt Verlag, 1980.

"Das Problem Falkenhayn. Eine Würdigung der Kriegführung des Generalstabschefs," *Welt als Geschichte* 1, 2 (1962) 49–78.

Krumeich, Gerd. "'Saigner la France'? Mythes et réalité de la stratégie allemande de la bataille de Verdun," *Guerres mondiales et conflits contemporains* 182 (1996) 17–29.

Kuhl, Herman von. *Der Weltkrieg 1914–1918* (2 vols.) Berlin: W. Kolk, 1929.

"Graf Schlieffen und der Weltkrieg," *Wissen und Wehr* (1923) 1–8.

Laffin, John. *British Butchers and Bunglers of World War I.* Gloucester: Alan Sutton, 1988.

Lahme, Rainer. *Deutsche Aussenpolitik, 1880–1894. Von Gleichgewichtspolitik Bismarcks zur Allianzstrategie Caprivis.* Göttingen: Vandenhoeck & Ruprecht, 1990.

Lange, Sven. *Hans Delbrück und der 'Strategiestreit': Kriegführung und Kriegsgeschichte in der Kontroverse 1879–1914.* Freiburg: Rombach, 1995.

Lefebvre, Jacques-Henri. *Die Hölle von Verdun: Nach den Berichten von Frontkämpfern.* Trans. Veronika Fischer. Verdun: Mémorial de Verdun, 1997.

Lehmann, Gustav. *Die Mobilmachung von 1870/71.* Berlin: E. S. Mittler, 1905.

Lehmann, Konrad. "Ermattungsstrategie – oder nicht?" *Historische Zeitschrift* 151 (1935) 48–86.

Liddell Hart, B. H. *Reputations: Ten Years After.* London: John Murray, 1928.

The Real War 1914–1918. London: Faber and Faber, 1930.

Strategy. London: Faber and Faber, 1967.

Liebmann, –. "Die deutschen Gefechtsvorschriften von 1914 in der Feuerprobe des Krieges," *Militär-Wissenschaftliche Rundschau* 2 (1937) 456–487.

Liss, Ulrich. "Graf Schlieffen's letztes Kriegsspiel," *Wehr-Wissenschaftliche Rundschau* 15, 3 (1965) 162–166.

Löbel, Uwe. "Neue Forschungsmöglichkeiten zur preussisch-deutschen Heeresgeschichte: Zur Rückgabe von Akten des Potsdamer Heeresarchiv durch die Sowjetunion," *Militärgeschichtliche Mitteilungen* 51 (1992) 143–149.

Luvaas, Jay. "European Military Thought and Doctrine, 1870–1914," in Michael Howard, ed. *The Theory and Practice of War.* London: Cassel & Co., 1965.

Malkasian, Carter. *A History of Modern Wars of Attrition.* Westport, CT: Praeger, 2002.

Mantey, Friedrich von. "Betrachtungen über den Ansatz zur Verfolgung nach den Grenzschlachten und über die Schlacht bei St. Quentin im August 1914," *Wissen und Wehr* (1927) 535–567.

"Graf Schlieffen und der jüngere Moltke," *Militär-Wochenblatt* 10 (1935) 395–398.

"Schlieffen-Plan von 1905, Moltke-Pläne 1908 bis 1914 und Schlieffen-Plan 1912," *Militär-Wochenblatt* 16 (1935) 651–654.

"In welchem Masse vermögen Verkehrsmittel den Ansatz und Verlauf militärische Operationen zu beeinflussen?" *Wissen und Wehr* (1939) 37–51.

Maurer, John H. *The Outbreak of the First World War: Strategic Planning, Crisis Making, and Deterrence Failure*. London: Praeger, 1995.

Meisner, Heinrich Otto. *Der Kriegsminister 1814–1914*. Berlin: Hermann Reinshagen, 1940.

Militärattachés und Militärbevollmächtigte in Preussen und im Deutschen Reich. Berlin: Rütten & Loening, 1957.

Menning, Bruce. *Bayonets Before Bullets: The Imperial Russian Army, 1861–1914.* Bloomington: Indiana University Press, 1992.

Messerschmidt, Manfred. *Militär und Politik in der Bismarckzeit und im Wilhelminischen Deutschland.* Darmstadt: Wissenschaftliche Buchgesellschaft, 1975.

Mette, Siegfried. *Vom Geist deutscher Feldherren: Genie und Technik 1800–1918.* Zurich: Scientia, 1938.

Miller, Forrest A. *Dmitrii Miliutin and the Reform Era in Russia*. Charlotte, NC: Vanderbilt University Press, 1968.

Möller-Witten, Hanns. *Festschrift zum 100. Geburtstag des Generals der Infanterie a.D. Dr. Phil. Hermann von Kuhl.* Frankfurt: E. S. Mittler, 1956.

"General der Infanterie v. Kuhl zum 95. Geburtstag," *Wehr-Wissenschaftliche Rundschau* 6, 7 (1951) 77–78.

Mombauer, Annika. *Helmuth von Moltke and the Origins of the First World War.* Cambridge: Cambridge University Press, 2001.

"Helmuth von Moltke and the German General Staff: Military and Political Decision-Making in Imperial Germany, 1906–1916." D.Phil. Thesis, University of Sussex, 1997.

"A Reluctant Military Leader? Helmuth von Moltke and the July Crisis of 1914," *War in History* 6, 4 (1999) 417–446.

"Helmuth von Moltke: A General in Crisis?," in Matthew Hughes and Matthew Seligmann, eds. *Leadership in Conflict 1914–1918*. London: Leo Cooper, 2000.

Mommsen, Wolfgang. *Grossmachtstellung und Weltpolitik: Die Aussenpolitik des Deutschen Reiches, 1870–1914*. Frankfurt: Ullstein, 1993.

Moritz, Albrecht. *Das Problem des Präventivkrieges in deutschen Politik während der ersten Marakkokrise*. Frankfurt: Ullstein, 1974.

Moser, Otto von. *Kurzer strategischer Überblick über den Weltkrieg 1914–1918.* Berlin: E. S. Mittler, 1923.

Mosier, John. *The Myth of the Great War: A New Military History of World War One*. London: Profile Books, 2001.

Müller-Loebnitz, Wilhelm. *Die Führung im Marne-Feldzug 1914*. Berlin: E. S. Mittler, 1939.

Murawski, Erich. "Die amtliche deutsche Kriegsgeschichtsschreibung über den Ersten Weltkrieg," *Wehr-Wissenschaftliche Rundschau* 9 (1959) 513–531, 584–598.

Nehring, Walter K. "General der Kavallerie Friedrich von Bernhardi – Soldat und Militärwissenschaftler," in Dermont Bradley and Ulrich Marwedel, eds.

Militärgeschichte, Militärwissenschaft und Konfliktsforschung: Eine Festschrift für Werner Hahlweg. Osnabrück: Biblio, 1977.

Offer, Avner. *The First World War: An Agrarian Interpretation*. Oxford: Clarendon, 1989.

Ortenburg, Georg. *Waffen und Waffengebrauch im Zeitalter der Millionenheere*. Bonn: Bernard & Graefe, 1992.

Ostertag, Heiger. *Bildung, Ausbildung und Erziehung des Offizierkorps im deutschen Kaiserreich: Eliteideal, Anspruch und Wirklichkeit*. Frankfurt: Peter Lang, 1990.

"Bibliotheksbestände und literarische Interessen – Indikatoren für das Bildungsniveau im Offizierkorps im Kaiserreich 1871 bis 1918?" *Militärgeschichtliche Mitteilungen* 1 (1990) 57–71.

Otto, Helmuth. *Der preussisch-deutsche Generalstab unter der Leitung des Generals von Schlieffen 1891–1905*. East Berlin: Deutscher Militärverlag, 1966.

"Die Schlacht um Verdun," *Militärgeschichte* 5 (1982) 408–415.

"Der Bestand Kriegsgeschichtliche Forschungsanstalt des Heeres im Bundesarchiv, Militärisches Zwischenarchiv Potsdam," *Militärgeschichtliche Mitteilungen* 51 (1992) 429–441.

Ousby, Ian. *The Road to Verdun: France, Nationalism and the First World War*. London: Jonathan Cape, 2002.

Paret, Peter. "Hans Delbrück on Military Critics and Military Historians," *Military Affairs* (Fall 1966) 148–152.

Paret, Peter. ed. *Makers of Modern Strategy from Machiavelli to the Nuclear Age*. Princeton: Princeton University Press, 1986.

Pedroncini, Guy. "La bataille de Verdun. Regards sur sa conduite par les Français," *Guerres mondiales et conflits contemporains* 182 (April 1996) 7–15.

Péricard, Jacques. *Verdun 1916: Histoire des combats qui se sont livrés en 1916 sur les deux rives de la Meuse*. Paris: Nouvelle Libraire de France, 1997.

Pertev, Demirhan. *Generalfeldmarschall Colmar Freiherr von der Goltz*. Göttingen: Göttinger, 1960.

Philpott, William. *Anglo-French Relations and Strategy on the Western Front 1914–18*. Cambridge: Macmillan, 1996.

Porch, Douglas. *The March to the Marne: The French Army, 1871–1914*. Cambridge: Cambridge University Press, 1981.

"The Marne and After: A Reappraisal of French Strategy in the First World War," *Journal of Military History* 53 (1989) 363–385.

Preisdorff, Kurt von, *et al. Soldatisches Führertum*. Hamburg: Hanseatische Verlagsanstalt, 1936–42.

Prior, Robin and Trevor Wilson. *Passchendaele: The Untold Story*. London: Yale University Press, 1996.

Prüter, F. W. "Der 24. Februar 1916 vor Verdun von französischer Seite gesehen," *Wissen und Wehr* (1923) 1–17.

Rahne, Hermann. "Die militärische Mobilmachungsplanung und -technik in Preußen und im deutschen Reich (Mitte des 19. Jahrhunderts bis zur Auslösung des zweiten Weltkrieges)." Ph.D. Thesis, Karl-Marx-Universität, Leipzig 1972.

Raulff, Heiner. *Zwischen Machtpolitik und Imperialismus: Die deutsche Frankreichpolitik 1904–05*. Düsseldorf: Droste, 1976.

Regele, Oskar. *Feldmarschall Conrad: Auftrag und Erfüllung 1906–1918*. Vienna: Herlod, 1955.

Ritter, Gerhard. *Der Schlieffenplan: Kritik eines Mythos*. Munich: R. Oldenbourg, 1956.

The Schlieffen Plan: Critique of a Myth. London: Oswald Wolff, 1958.

The Sword and the Scepter: The Problem of Militarism in Germany (4 vols.) Trans. Heinz Norden. Coral Gables, FL: University of Miami Press, 1969.

Röhl, John C. G. *The Kaiser and His Court: Wilhelm II and the Government of Germany*. Cambridge: Cambridge University Press, 1994.

Rosinski, Herbert. *The German Army*. Ed. Gordon Craig. New York: Praeger, 1966.

Rüdt von Collenberg, Ludwig. "Die staatsrechtliche Stellung des preussischen Kriegsministers von 1867 bis 1914," *Wissen und Wehr* (1927) 293–312.

"Die Oberste Heeresleitung und der Oberbefehlshaber Ost im Sommerfeldzug 1915," *Wissen und Wehr* (1932) 281–296.

Rutherford, Ward. *The Tsar's War 1914–1917: The Story of the Imperial Russian Army in the First World War*. Cambridge: Ian Faulkner Publishing, 1992.

Ryan, Stephen. *Pétain the Soldier*. London: Thomas Yoseloff, 1969.

Samuels, Martin. *Doctrine and Dogma: German and British Infantry Tactics in the First World War*. New York: Greenwood Press, 1992.

Command or Control? Command, Training and Tactics in the British and German Armies, 1888–1918. London: Frank Cass, 1995.

"Directive Command and the German General Staff," *War in History* 2, 1 (1995) 22–42.

Sarter, Adolph. *Die deutschen Eisenbahnen im Kriege*. Stuttgart: Deutsche Verlags-Anstalt, 1930.

Schäfer, Theobald von. "Das Kriegsjahr 1915 im Osten und die Frage des einheitlichen Oberbefehls," *Wissen und Wehr* (1932) 65–73.

Scheibe, Friedrich Carl. "Marne und Gorlice: Zur Kriegsdeutung Hans Delbrücks," *Militärgeschichtliche Mitteilungen* 53 (1994) 355–376.

Schleier, Hans. "Treitschke, Delbrück und die 'Preussische Jahrbücher' in den 80er Jahren des 19.Jahrhunderts," *Jahrbuch für Geschichte* 1 (1967) 134–179.

Schmidt-Bückeburg, Rudolf. *Das Militärkabinett der preussischen Könige und deutschen Kaiser: Seine geschichtliche Entwicklung und staatsrechtliche Stellung, 1787–1918*. Berlin: E. S. Mittler, 1933.

Schneider, Paul. *Die Organisation des Heeres*. Berlin: E. S. Mittler, 1931.

Schulte, Bernd F. *Die deutsche Armee, 1900–1914*. Düsseldorf: Droste, 1977.

"Neue Dokumente zu Kriegsausbruch und Kriegsverlauf 1914," *Militärgeschichtliche Mitteilungen* 1 (1979) 123–185.

Schwarzmüller, Theo. *Zwischen Kaiser und "Führer": Generalfeldmarschall August von Mackensen*. Paderborn: Ferdinand Schöningh, 1996.

Schwertfeger, Bernhard. *Die grossen Erzieher des deutschen Heeres: Aus der Geschichte der Kriegsakademie*. Potsdam: Akademische Verlagsgesellschaft Athenaion, 1936.

Seeckt, Hans von. *Gedenken eines Soldaten*. Berlin: E. S. Mittler, 1929.

Seeßelberg, Friedrich, *et al. Der Stellungskrieg 1914–1918*. Berlin: E. S. Mittler, 1926.

Senger und Etterlin, Ferdinand von. "Cannae, Schlieffen und die Abwehr," *Wehr-Wissenschaftliche Rundschau* 13 (1963) 26–43.

Showalter, Dennis E. *German Military History, 1648–1982: A Critical Bibliography*. New York: Garland Publishing, 1984.

Tannenberg: Clash of Empires. Hamden, CT: Archon Books, 1991.

Wars of Frederick the Great. New York: Longmans, 1996.

"The Retaming of Bellona: Prussia and the Institutionalization of the Napoleonic Legacy, 1815–1876," *Military Affairs* (April 1980) 57–63.

"The Eastern Front and German Military Planning, 1871–1914 – Some Observations," *East European Quarterly* 15, 2 (June 1981) 163–180.

"Army and Society in Imperial Germany: The Pains of Modernization," *Journal of Contemporary History* 18 (1983) 583–618.

"Goltz and Bernhardi: The Institutionalization of Originality in the Imperial German Army," *Defense Analysis* 3, 4 (1987) 305–318.

"Army, State, and Society in Germany, 1871–1914: An Interpretation," in Jack P. Dukes and Joachim Remak, eds. *Another Germany*. London: Westview Press, 1988.

"German Grand Strategy: A Contradiction in Terms?," *Militärgeschichtliche Mitteilungen* 2 (1990) 65–102.

"The Political Soldiers of Imperial Germany: Myths and Realities," *German Studies Review* 16 (1994) 59–77.

"From Deterrence to Doomsday Machine: The German War of War, 1890–1914," *Journal of Military History* 64 (July 2000) 679–710.

Snyder, Jack. *The Ideology of the Offensive: Military Decision Making and the Disasters of 1914*. London: Cornell University Press, 1984.

Solger, Wilhelm. "Falkenhayn," in Friedrich von Cochenhausen, ed. *Heerführer des Weltkrieges*. Berlin: E. S. Mittler, 1939.

Staabs, Hermann von. *Aufmarsch nach zwei Fronten auf Grund der Operationspläne von 1871–1914*. Berlin: E. S. Mittler, 1925.

Stadelmann, Rudolf. *Moltke und der Staat*. Krefeld: Scherpe-Verlag, 1950.

"Die Friedensversuche im ersten Jahre des Weltkrieges," *Historische Zeitschrift* 156 (1937) 485–545.

Stevenson, David. *Armaments and the Coming of War: Europe, 1904–1914*. Oxford: Clarendon, 1996.

Stone, James. "The War Scare of 1875 Revisited," *Militärgeschichtliche Mitteilungen* 53 (1994) 304–326.

Stone, Norman. *The Eastern Front, 1914–1917*. London: Hodder and Stoughton, 1975.

Strachan, Hew. *European Armies and the Conduct of War*. London: George Allen & Unwin, 1983.

The First World War. London: The Historical Association, 1997.

The First World War. Vol. I: *To Arms*. Oxford University Press, 2001.

"Germany in the First World War: The Problem of Strategy," *German History* 12, 2 (1994) 237–249.

"The Battle of the Somme and British Strategy," *Journal of Strategic Studies* 21, 1 (1998) 79–95.

Strachan, Hew. ed. *The Oxford Illustrated History of the First World War*. Oxford: Oxford University Press, 1998.

Stuhlmann, Friedrich. "Artillerieaufstellung und Munitionsverbrauch im Kriege 1914–1918," *Wehr und Waffen* (1932) 163–169, 207–221.

Sweet, Paul R. "Leaders and Policies: Germany in the Winter of 1914–1915," *Journal of Central European Affairs* 16, 3 (Oct. 1956).

Taylor, A. J. P. *The First World War: An Illustrated History*. New York: Perigee Books, 1980; first published 1963.

Teske, Hermann. *Colmar Freiherr von der Goltz. Ein Kämpfer für den militärischen Fortschritt*. Göttingen: Musterschmidt, 1957.

Thimme, Annelise. *Hans Delbrück als Kritiker der Wilhelminischen Epoche*. Düsseldorf: Droste Verlag, 1955.

Tunstall, Graydon A. *Planning for War Against Russia and Serbia: Austro-Hungarian and German Military Strategies, 1871–1914*. New York: Columbia University Press, 1993.

Uhle-Wettler, Franz. *Erich Ludendorff in seiner Zeit*. Berg: Kurt Vowinckel-Verlag, 1995.

Ullrich, Volker. "Entscheidung im Osten oder Sicherung der Dardenellen: Das Ringen um den Serbien Feldzug 1915," *Militärgeschichtliche Mitteilungen* 2 (1982) 45–63.

Unruh, Karl. *Langemarck: Legende und Wirklichkeit*. Koblenz: Bernard & Graefe, 1986.

Van Evera, Stephen. "The Cult of the Offensive and the Origins of the First World War," *International Security* 9, 1 (1984) 58–107.

Vogt, Adolf. *Oberst Max Bauer. Generalstabsoffizier im Zwielicht 1869–1929*. Osnabruck: Biblio, 1974.

Wallach, Jehuda L. *Das Dogma der Vernichtungsschlacht: Die Lehren von Clausewitz und Schlieffen und ihre Wirkungen in zwei Weltkriegen*. Frankfurt: Bernard und Graefe, 1967.

The Dogma of the Battle of Annihilation: The Theories of Clausewitz and Schlieffen and their Impact on the German Conduct of Two World Wars. Westport, CT: Greenwood Press, 1986.

Wegener, Wolfgang. *The Naval Strategy of the World War*. Trans. Holger H. Herwig. Annapolis: Naval Institute Press, 1989.

Wehler, Hans-Ulrich. *Krisenherde des Kaiserreichs 1871–1918*. Göttingen: Musterschmidt, 1973.

"Absoluter und Totaler Krieg von Clausewitz zu Ludendorff," *Politische Vierteljahresschrift* 10 (Sept. 1969) 220–248.

Wendt, Hermann. *Verdun 1916: Die Angriffe Falkenhayns im Maasgebiet mit Richtung auf Verdun als strategisches Problem*. Berlin: E. S. Mittler, 1931.

Werth, German. *Verdun: Die Schlacht und der Mythos*. Bergisch Gladbach: Weltbild, 1979.

Wetzell, Georg. *Von Falkenhayn zu Hindenburg-Ludendorff: Der Wechsel in der deutschen Oberste-Heeresleitung im Herbst 1916 und der rumänische Feldzug*. Berlin: E. S. Mittler, 1921.

Wienskowski, Hellmuth von. *Falkenhayn*. Berlin: K. Siegismund, 1937.

Wolf, Horst. *Der Nachlass Hans Delbrück*. Berlin: Deutsche Staatsbibliothek, 1980.

Wöllwarth, –. "Die Ursachen des Stellungskrieges," *Deutsche Wehr* 18 (3 May 1934) 270–271.

Wynne, G. C. *If Germany Attacks: The Battle in Depth in the West*. London: Faber & Faber, 1939.

Ziekursch, Johannes. "Ludendorffs Kriegserinnerungen. Ein Vortrag," *Historische Zeitschrift* 121 (1920) 441–465.

Ziese-Beringer, Hermann. *Der einsame Feldherr: Die Wahrheit über Verdun* (2 vols.). Berlin: Frundsberg, 1934.

Zoellner, Eugen Ritter von. "Schlieffens Vermächtnis," *Militär-Wissenschaftliche Rundschau*. Sonderheft, 1938.

Zuber, Terence. "The Schlieffen Plan Reconsidered," *War in History* 6, 3 (1999) 262–305.

"Terence Holmes Reinvents the Schlieffen Plan," *War in History* 8, 4 (1999) 262–305.

Zwehl, Hans von. *Erich von Falkenhayn: Eine biographische Studie*. Berlin: E. S. Mittler, 1926.

"Der General v. Falkenhayn als Chef des Generalstabes des Feldheeres," *Monatshefte für Politik und Wehrmacht* (1920) 113–126.

Zweig, Arnold. *Education Before Verdun*. Trans. Eric Sutton. New York: Viking Press, 1936.

Index